Also by Christopher Hill

THE EXPERIENCE OF DEFEAT

MILTON AND THE ENGLISH REVOLUTION

THE WORLD TURNED UPSIDE DOWN

ANTICHRIST IN SEVENTEENTH-CENTURY ENGLAND

GOD'S ENGLISHMAN: OLIVER CROMWELL AND
THE ENGLISH REVOLUTION

REFORMATION TO INDUSTRIAL REVOLUTION

INTELLECTUAL ORIGINS OF THE ENGLISH REVOLUTION

SOCIETY AND PURITANISM
IN PRE-REVOLUTIONARY ENGLAND

THE CENTURY OF REVOLUTION

PURITANISM AND REVOLUTION

ECONOMIC PROBLEMS OF THE CHURCH

THE GOOD OLD CAUSE (EDITED WITH E. DELL)

LENIN AND THE RUSSIAN REVOLUTION

THE ENGLISH REVOLUTION, 1640

A TINKER AND A POOR MAN

Christopher Hill

A TINKER AND A POOR MAN

*John Bunyan
and His Church,
1628–1688*

W.W. NORTON AND COMPANY
NEW YORK • LONDON

Library of Congress Cataloging-in-Publication Data
Hill, Christopher.
    A tinker and a poor man.
    Also published under title: A turbulent, seditious,
and factious people.
    Includes bibliographic references and index.
    1. Bunyan, John, 1628–1688. 2. Authors, English—
Early modern, 1500–1700—Biography.   3. Puritans—
England—Clergy—Biography.   4. Christian literature,
English—History and criticism.   5. Dissenters,
Religious—England—History—17th century.   6. England—
Church history—17th century.   I. Title.
PR3331.H55   1988b   828'.407[B]   88-45350

Printed in the United States of America

ISBN 0-393-30662-3

W.W. Norton & Company, Inc., 500 Fifth Avenue, New York, N.Y. 10110
W.W. Norton & Company Ltd., 37 Great Russell Street, London WC1B 3NU

1 2 3 4 5 6 7 8 9 10

FOR BRIDGET
BELOVED COMRADE AND FELLOW PILGRIM

CONTENTS

PREFACE

I have incurred many debts in writing this book. My long-standing interest in Bunyan was rekindled by an invitation to give a lecture in Bedford in 1978, as part of the town's celebration of the tercentenary of the publication of *The Pilgrim's Progress*. But the book derives more directly from the Sir D. Owen Evans Memorial Lectures which I was invited to give in Aberystwyth in 1985. I am extremely grateful to Principal and Mrs Owen for their gracious hospitality on this occasion. The present volume also incorporates the Miriam Leranbaum Memorial Lecture delivered at the State University of New York, Binghamton, in 1985. Thanks are due to Professor and Mrs Norman Burns for generous hospitality there. I subsequently had many lively discussions about Bunyan in England, the United States, Australia, and New Zealand, from which I learnt a great deal. The visit to Australia was made possible by an invitation extended to my wife and myself to spend a term at the University of Adelaide in 1987. It is difficult to express the gratitude which we feel for the warmth, stimulus, and leisure for writing which we enjoyed there.

My object in this book has been to set Bunyan against the history of his own turbulent times, which formed him and which he influenced; and to rescue him from those who see him as the anatomist of a timeless 'human condition'. I am very conscious of standing on the shoulders of giants. There are the great Bunyan editors—George Offor, H. G. Tibbutt, G. Parsloe, F. M. Harrison, and G. B. Harrison (whom I had the privilege of meeting in New Zealand in 1987). There is the never-to-be-forgotten biographer John Brown, Hale White (Mark Rutherford), and the polymath genius Jack Lindsay; W. York Tindall and Henri Talon. More recently Joyce Godber, Roger Sharrock, R. L. Greaves, James Turner, and Graham Midgley have illuminated Bunyan's career and writings. As always seems to happen, I found myself following many trails which L. B. Wright had blazed. The *Biographical Dictionary of British Radicals in the Seventeenth-Century*, edited by R. L. Greaves and R. Zaller, proved invaluable. David Zaret's *The Heavenly Contract* was most useful. I am deeply indebted to Rudolf G. Wagner and Valentine Boss whose work stimulated my interest in Bunyan's international impact.

I did not read Richard Ashcraft's seminal *Revolutionary Politics and Locke's Two Treatises of Government* until my book was nearly finished. I found it stimulating in several respects. Ashcraft demonstrates that Locke's biographers have ignored evidence for his involvement in radical politics because they could not conceive of a philosopher indulging in anything so practical as politics or anything so naughty as radical politics. Bunyan was not engaged in conspiracy as Locke was, but his piety did not preclude radicalism. Ashcraft provides new and convincing evidence that many of Bunyan's dissenting colleagues and friends were actually involved in revolutionary conspiracy. He confirms R. L. Greaves's *Deliver Us From Evil: The Radical Underground in Britain, 1660–1663* (Oxford UP, 1986). Both books will help us to a better understanding of the society in which Bunyan lived, and so of Bunyan himself and of his writings. Professor Greaves and Roger Lane removed some howlers by reading the proofs.

Ian Gentles, J. Sears McGee, Aileen Ross, and Judy Sproxton all generously permitted me to read work in advance of publication. I also owe thanks for help and kindness to Bernard Capp, Geoff Eley, Robert Evans, Kenneth Haley, Anne Laurence, Roger Lonsdale, Isabel Rivers, Roger Sharrock, Michael Tolley, and Austin Woolrych. I cannot find words to express my gratitude to Bob Owens, who not only put his own research at my disposal but read the whole of this book at a penultimate stage. He saved me from many errors, forced me to rethink some slovenly passages, and made helpful positive suggestions. The book would have been in much worse shape without his seasonable counsel. Kim Scott Walwyn, Frances Whistler, and John Waś at the Oxford University Press were invariably understanding and supportive; Elisabeth Sifton at Knopf was, as always, indefatigable in correcting my errors and making helpful suggestions. My daughter Dinah nobly retyped the whole thing from a very messy typescript. The book is dedicated to Bridget, who was a mine of extensive and peculiar information about Baptists, marriage, women, self-denial, and many other relevant matters. She suffered and shared Bunyan for many years, providing constant stimulus, encouragement, and sympathy. She even read the proofs.

C.H.

ABBREVIATIONS

The following abbreviations have been used for Bunyan's writings:

MW	Miscellaneous Works (Oxford UP).
Offor	*The Works of John Bunyan*, ed. G. Offor (3 vols., 1860).
GA	*Grace Abounding to the Chief of Sinners*, ed. R. Sharrock (Oxford UP, 1962).
Mr. B.	*The Life and Death of Mr. Badman*, in Offor, iii.
Poems	*The Poems*, ed. Graham Midgley (MW vi (1980)).
HW	*The Holy War*, ed. R. Sharrock and J. F. Forrest (Oxford UP, 1980).
PP	*The Pilgrim's Progress from this world to that which is to come*, ed. J. B. Wharey and R. Sharrock (Oxford UP, 1967).
Genesis	*An Exposition on the Ten First Chapters of Genesis, and Part of the Eleventh* (posthumous), in Offor, ii.

Other abbreviations used in the notes:

Brown	John Brown, *John Bunyan (1628–1688): His Life, Times and Work*, rev. F. M. Harrison (1928).
Bayly	Lewis Bayly, *The Practice of Piety* (date of first publication uncertain: before 1613). I have used the 55th edn. (1723).
CSPD	*Calendar of State Papers Domestic*
Dent	Arthur Dent, *The Plaine Mans Path-way to Heaven* (Amsterdam, 1601).
DNB	*Dictionary of National Biography*
EcHR	*Economic History Review*
MCPW	John Milton, *Complete Prose Works*, ed. D. M. Wolfe (Yale UP, 1953–82).
MER	C. Hill, *Milton and the English Revolution* (1978).
Newey	Vincent Newey (ed.), *The Pilgrim's Progress: Critical and Historical Views* (Liverpool UP, 1980).
OED	*Oxford English Dictionary*
PBHRS	Publications of the Bedfordshire Historical Record Society.
P. and P.	*Past and Present*
Sharrock	R. Sharrock, *John Bunyan* (1968).

Sharrock, *Casebook*	R. Sharrock (ed.), *The Pilgrim's Progress: A Casebook* (1976).
Talon	H. Talon, *John Bunyan: The Man and His Works* (English trans., 1951).
Tibbutt, *Minutes*	*The Minutes of the First Independent Church (now Bunyan Meeting) at Bedford, 1656–1766*, ed. H. G. Tibbutt (PBHRS; 1976).
Tindall	W. Y. Tindall, *John Bunyan, Mechanick Preacher* (New York, 1934).
TRHS	*Transactions of the Royal Historical Society*
UP	University Press
VCH	*Victoria County History*
WTUD	C. Hill, *The World Turned Upside Down* (Penguin edn.).

BUNYAN'S WRITINGS

SOME DATES

1603–25	James I, King of England
1618–48	Thirty Years War
1625–49	Charles I, King of England
1628	*June*: Petition of Right
	Aug.: Assassination of Buckingham
	Nov.: John Bunyan born
1629–40	Personal rule of Charles I, without Parliaments
1634–9	Ship Money
1637	Trials of Prynne, Burton, Bastwick, and Lilburne
1637–8	Ship Money Case: trial of John Hampden
1639–40	'Bishops' War' with Scotland
1640	*Apr.–May*: The Short Parliament
	Nov.: The Long Parliament
1641	*Nov.*: Revolt in Ireland
1642–5	Civil War
1643	*Sept.*: Solemn League and Covenant with Scotland
1644	*Nov.*: Milton's *Areopagitica*; Bunyan joins Parliamentary army at Newport Pagnell
1645	*Apr.*: Self-Denying Ordinance; Formation of New Model Army
	June: Parliamentary victory at Battle of Naseby
1646	*Feb.*: Abolition of feudal tenures and Court of Wards
	Oct.: Abolition of episcopacy
1647	*Apr.*: Mutiny in Army; Election of Agitators
	June: Cornet Joyce seizes the King on the authority of the Agitators
	July: Bunyan demobilized
	Aug.: Army occupies London
	Oct.–Nov.: Putney Debates
1648	Second Civil War
1648	*Dec.*: Pride's Purge
1649	*Jan.*: Trial and execution of Charles I
	Mar.–May: Republic established; Abolition of House of Lords
	Bunyan's first marriage
	May: Defeat of Army mutiny at Burford; Suppression of Levellers
1650	Suppression of Diggers
	Compulsory attendance at parish church abolished

1671	Milton publishes *Paradise Regained* and *Samson Agonistes*
1672	*Jan.*: Bunyan appointed pastor to the Bedford congregation
	Mar.: Bunyan released from prison; Charles II's Second Declaration of Indulgence; Bedford congregation licensed as 'Congregational'; Marvell publishes (anonymously) *The Rehearsal Transpros'd*
1673	Parliament forces withdrawal of Declaration of Indulgence Test Act. James Duke of York declares himself a Roman Catholic
1676–7	*Dec.–June*: Bunyan's second imprisonment
1678	The Popish Plot
1679	*Jan.*: Cavalier Parliament dissolved
1679–81	Three Parliaments in rapid succession; Bills passed to exclude James Duke of York from the succession
1679	Expiry of the Licensing Act
1681–5	Charles II rules without Parliament, in defiance of the Triennial Act
1683	Rye House Plot; purges of corporations
1685	Death of Charles II; James II succeeds
	May–June: Argyll's rebellion in Scotland defeated
	June–July: Monmouth's rebellion; defeated at Battle of Sedgmoor
	Oct.: Revocation of Edict of Nantes in France; Huguenot emigration
	Dec.: Bunyan conveys his property to his wife
1687	*Apr.*: James II's First Declaration of Indulgence
1687–8	Further purges of corporations
1688	*Apr.*: Second Declaration of Indulgence
	June: Trial and acquittal of Seven Bishops for protesting against the Declaration of Indulgence
	Aug.: Death of Bunyan
	Nov.: William of Orange lands in England
	Dec.: James II flees to France; William and Mary declared King and Queen
1689	Toleration Act
1689–92	Bunyan's posthumous works published

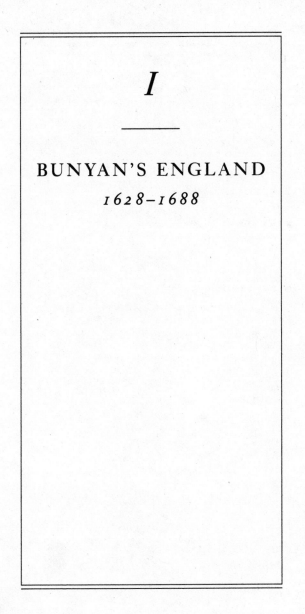

I

BUNYAN'S ENGLAND

1628–1688

1. *The English Revolution*

I am privy enough to mine own means and do freely confess that
in this work I have received much light from others: and therefore
do not as a judge give sentence upon other men's works, but as
one that would furnish the same feast, bring in my dish among
them ... to further that which is already happily begun, and to
provoke others of greater gifts to come after with their great
lights and lanterns in their hands.   ARTHUR DENT[1]

Subtle conjectures at the aims and inward cogitations of such as
fall under their pen ... is ... none of the least virtues in a
historian, where conjecture is thoroughly grounded, not forced
to serve the purpose of the writer in advancing his style or
manifesting his subtlety in conjecturing. But these conjectures
cannot often be certain, unless withal so evident, that the nar-
ration itself may be sufficient to suggest the same also to the
reader.   THOMAS HOBBES[2]

TO the making of books on Bunyan there is no end: a new one
calls for justification. Mine is an attempt to put Bunyan back
into the revolutionary age in which he lived. Biographers have
tended to emphasize either Bunyan the religious figure or Bunyan
the great writer. He was indeed both, but that is not the whole
story. I was brought up by parents who urged me to read *The
Pilgrim's Progress* as an improving book. Naturally, I left it on the
shelf. But in my first year at the university, 1931, I heard Bernard
Shaw deliver a savage attack on the National Government, in the
course of which, as a throwaway thought, he remarked that Bunyan
was England's greatest prose writer. At the time I was outraged by
the Shavian paradox: one never knew how seriously to take him.
But when I came to read Bunyan I saw Shaw's point. On another
occasion Shaw said of *The Pilgrim's Progress* 'the whole allegory is a
consistent attack on morality and respectability, without a word
that one can remember against vice and crime.' Shaw had his own
heightened and telling way of putting things, and I would not want
to underwrite that remark. But Shaw was insisting that Bunyan was
not the conventionally pious 'man of God' that both his admirers

---

[1] *The Ruine of Rome* (1603), Epistle to the Reader, sig. A 3v.
[2] Trans. of Thucydides's *History of the Peloponnesian War*, in *English Works*, ed. W. S.
Molesworth, 11 vols. (1839–45), viii. p. viii.

and his detractors often took him for. "A turbulent, seditious, and factious people," Bunyan's own summary of how he and his church were regarded by many respectables in 1662, comes close to Shaw's view.[3] Seventeenth-century Puritans were very different from twentieth-century nonconformists: Bunyan was a man of his age, who lived through and learnt from the most turbulent, seditious, and factious sixty years of recorded English history.

In this introductory section I have not attempted to give a balanced account of this crucial and controversial period. I have attempted rather to portray aspects of its history which were likely to come home to a tinker of Elstow, to a Parliamentarian soldier, to a nonconformist citizen of Bedford. Accordingly I have tried where possible to cite examples from Bedfordshire and its neighbourhood, to quote Bedfordshire men and women. And to let Bunyan speak for himself as much as possible, thus saving myself from having to eulogize his prose.

We do not know the exact date of Bunyan's birth, but he was baptized on 30 November 1628, two days after John Felton, the assassin of the Duke of Buckingham, had been hanged. This was one of the few successful political assassinations in English history, and seems to have been very popular. As late as 1645 a London lady was asking, 'Is there never a Felton yet living?' Her target seems to have been the 'stuttering fool', Charles I.[4] Felton, son of a Bedfordshire man, claimed to have been motivated by the charge of treason which the House of Commons had brought against Buckingham, the favourite of King Charles I. A few months earlier in 1628 Charles had reluctantly accepted the Petition of Right, the first successful attempt by Parliament to limit royal power. But he jibbed at allowing the Petition to be printed. People outside the charmed circle of politics must not know anything about the mysteries of state which only their social superiors were supposed to understand.

Bunyan died on 31 August 1688, two months before the Glorious Revolution, in which William the Liberator came over from the Netherlands to save protestantism in England, and Charles I's second son, James II, fled into exile. Bunyan's life thus

[3] Shaw, *Man and Superman* (1907), Epistle Dedicatory; *PP*, 5, 'The Author's Apology for his Book.' Bunyan is here being ironical at the expense of his 'man of God'. See pp. 108, 132–3 below.

[4] *Middlesex County Records*, ed. J. C. Jeaffreson (1888), iii. 93; cf. ibid. 108–a man condemned to hard labour in March 1629 for threatening to 'Felton' an adversary.

spans the crisis of the seventeenth century, which transformed England from a country in which the King aspired to rule by his prerogative power independent of a representative Parliament, and in which the Church of England enjoyed a monopoly of religious worship as well as a considerable share in political power, to a country in which Parliament controlled both the central government and the church, and in which dissent received some limited toleration.

When Bunyan was less than a year old, the personal rule of Charles I (1629–40) began. During this period he summoned no Parliament, and used control of the judges to subordinate law to the royal will. Since taxes could not be voted in the traditional way, Charles arbitrarily demanded payment of a levy known as Ship Money. In 1637 John Hampden and others opposed Ship Money in the courts, but the judges (by a narrow majority) declared it lawful, a decision which could have made the crown financially independent of Parliament. Meanwhile Archbishop Laud was introducing unaccustomed ceremonies into the worship of the Church, which many protestants suspected foreboded a return to catholicism. Laud was a leading member of Charles's government which enforced these ceremonies. In 1637 the lawyer William Prynne, the Revd Henry Burton, and Dr John Bastwick were mutilated, heavily fined, and imprisoned for life for publishing criticisms of the government and the church. Laud was also attempting an increase of tithe payments to the clergy, which would have enhanced their status at the expense of propertied Englishmen. A papal agent was received at Whitehall – the first for eighty years.

Charles's financial straits forced him to abandon any effective foreign policy, at a time when many of his subjects thought England ought to intervene on the protestant side in the Thirty Years War, or at least to assist French Huguenots against Louis XIII's persecution. Far from that, the last protestant stronghold in France, La Rochelle, surrendered in the month before Bunyan was born, despite feeble English attempts to relieve it. In the sixteen-thirties the Earl of Strafford was building up an army in Ireland which was alleged to be papist and which could be used to reinforce absolute monarchy in England. Strafford showed a disregard for legal and property rights which frightened those who believed that similar methods might be introduced into England.

Opponents of Ship Money, and London tithe-payers, were saved by the outbreak of war between England and Scotland in 1639. Scots had been outraged by an attempt to increase the authority of bishops in their country, and by the imposition of a version of the English Prayer Book modified in a Catholic direction. In 1638 the National Covenant was signed all over Scotland, and an army was raised. Charles had no money to pay his reluctant troops who — rather than fighting the Scots — preferred rabbling their (allegedly) papist officers and throwing down enclosures and the rails round altars which Laud had introduced into churches. The government effectively collapsed.

Charles was forced to call a Parliament — the Short Parliament of April 1640 — but it made demands that the King refused to accept. The Scottish army advanced into England virtually unopposed and occupied Newcastle, the source of London's coal. So far from rallying to the government, merchants refused to lend money. Order could no longer be preserved in the capital. Another Parliament had to be called in November 1640 — the Long Parliament. In its first year this Parliament dismantled the royal bureaucracy, and declared unparliamentary taxation illegal. Prynne, Burton, and Bastwick returned in triumph to London. Strafford was executed, Laud imprisoned (executed 1646): other ministers fled abroad. An act was passed to ensure that Parliament could not be dissolved without its own consent, thus for the first time making it a permanent part of the constitution. Popular riots and pressure on King and Parliament in London, riots against enclosure and against papists all over the country, suggested the possibility of a total breakdown. Ireland took advantage of the confusion to rise against English rule in November 1641: who was to command the army to suppress this revolt? Many who had hitherto supported Parliament feared that social subordination was in danger of being undermined. This 'party of order' began to think royal rule the lesser evil; and this enabled Charles to gather an army to fight the civil war.

Parliament in its turn raised an army. After two years of indecisive fighting Oliver Cromwell and others forced through the Self-Denying Ordinance which deprived peers and MPs of their commands. It was then possible to create a more professional force — the New Model Army 'wherein there is not one lord'. This army was based on Oliver Cromwell's principles of religious toleration and the career open to the talents, which had made his troops the most effective fighting force in the country.[5] Meanwhile censorship had broken down, and there was an unprecedented outpouring of newspapers and pamphlets on all sorts of subjects, from political democracy to communism, from the authenticity and authority of the Bible to free love. Church courts collapsed: men and women were free to organize themselves in con-gregations, away from supervision by parson and squire. Wide sections of the population – those whom Charles had not wanted to read the Petition of Right – took part in politics and in these discussions. Nothing like it had happened in England before.

Bunyan was at his most impressionable age when all this was going on. He no doubt heard about the controversies over Ship Money. Bedfordshire was one of the counties in which opposition to the tax seems to have been widespread. By 1638 Ship Money receipts were less there than almost anywhere in England. Oliver St John, of an old Bedfordshire family, led the defence in Hampden's case. When Charles tried to recruit an army to oppose the Scottish invaders in 1640, the county was 'so restive that we shall not get nearly our number of men from them', the Earl of Northampton reported in June.[6]

There had long been political opposition in the county. Faced in 1626 with a demand for payment of a forced loan not authorized by Parliament, a group of taxpayers met—unprecedentedly – to discuss it. 'The opinion of every hundred' was 'not to give to his majesty in this way, but in a Parliamentary way'. Since the demand was 'not grounded upon good precedent, . . . they feared future danger' if they acceded. 'The general opinion was that in a Parliamentary way every man would be willing to contribute to his ability': Parliamentary taxation 'was most equal and most indifferent'.[7] There are few surviving examples of such

[5] [W. Walwyn], *A Pearle in a Dounghill* (1646), in *Freedom in Arms: A Selection of Leveller Writings*, ed. A. L. Morton (1975), 83. For the New Model Army see Appendix; B. S. Manning, *The English People and the English Revolution* (1976), *passim.*

[6] Joyce Godber, *History of Bedfordshire, 1066–1888* (Bedfordshire County Council, 1969), 246, 269; *The Story of Bedford: An Outline History* (Luton, 1978), 66; *VCH Bedfordshire*, i. 41–2.

[7] P. D. Gilmore, 'The Papers of Richard Taylor of Clapham (c. 1579–1641)', PBHRS 25 (1947), 106–8. Taylor opposed Laud's religious policies—though he was to be a royalist in the civil war. See now Ann Hughes, *Politics, Society and Civil War in Warwickshire, 1620–1660*, (Cambridge UP, 1987), 51.

constitutional awareness and political sophistication and courage at so early a date. But knowledge of this meeting has survived by accident, so it may not be as exceptional as it appears. Men would not advertise such get-togethers.

It prepares us, nevertheless, for the fact that when civil war came there were few royalists in Bedfordshire. It was one of only three English counties where in the Long Parliament all the members, for county and borough alike, were supporters of Parliament. In Bedfordshire, Clarendon said, the King had not 'any visible party, nor one fixed quarter'.[8] Oliver St John became one of the leaders of the Commons.

Bunyan was 14 in 1642. At the age of 16 he joined or was conscripted into the Parliamentary army, in which he served for nearly three years, though he seems to have seen little military action. He was posted to the garrison of Newport Pagnell, just across the border in Buckinghamshire, where he remained until the war was over. Newport Pagnell was a centre of radical debate concerning church and state during and after the civil war. In the months before Bunyan was demobilized Charles I had surrendered, the rank and file of the New Model Army had insisted on having a say in the determination of events in England, and Cornet Joyce had been despatched by the elected representatives of the rank and file ('Agitators') to take the King out of the control of Parliament's Commissioners. The Army had begun its intervention in politics, a process which led ultimately to the trial and execution of Charles as a traitor to the people of England, to the proclamation of the republic, and abolition of the House of Lords. Again these were happenings unheard of in England hitherto, or indeed in Europe.

Historians to this day are not agreed about the causes of the civil war, still less about the Revolution which followed it. Nor were contemporaries. Among views which Bunyan would certainly have heard were political explanations—the King had ruled tyrannically, without consulting Parliament, which represented the people. (But did it represent the people? Only about one in ten adult males had the vote, as royalists and Levellers pointed out. This

---

[8] Brown, 14–15, 38–9, 41, 124–5; A. Fletcher, *The Outbreak of the English Civil War* (1981), ch. 6, *passim*; D. and S. Lysons, *Magna Britannia* for Bedfordshire (1978), 7–8 (1st pub. 1806); the Earl of Clarendon, *The History of the Rebellion* (Oxford UP, 1888), ii. 502 (cf. 369).

dispute led to wide discussions on the nature of the state and of political obligation, on the rights of Englishmen, and the rights of man. Bunyan must have heard such discussions, perhaps participated in them.) Another widely held view was that the war had been necessary to frustrate an international plot to restore catholicism to England, a plot in which Charles I, his French papist Queen, Henrietta Maria, Archbishop Laud, and many of the aristocracy and gentry were alleged to be involved.[9] But God frustrated this plot, protected his England, and raised the New Model Army to rout the King and the 'papists and delinquents' who supported him. The Parliament's party, by contrast, was composed of 'an honest, sober, grave people, that groaned under oppressions, thirsted after grace, the reformed party of the nation.'[10]

Some of these people who thirsted after grace believed that the war was a prelude to the millennium. The best contemporary scholarly opinion held that the prophecies in Daniel and Revelation foretold startling events in the 1650s: for Milton and many others Christ was 'shortly expected king' whose reign, significantly, would put an end to all earthly tyrannies. In the 1650s Bunyan shared the belief that the last days were at hand; and though after 1660 he realized that attempts to predict a date had been mistaken, he never abandoned his basic conviction.[11]

James Harrington in 1656 said that the war had been fought about property. In the century before 1640, Harrington and many others believed, property (and especially landed property) had passed from King and aristocracy to those whom Harrington called 'the people' – those with sufficient money to buy land and make themselves gentlemen, if they were not gentlemen already. Bunyan is unlikely to have read Harrington; but in the army he could have heard earlier and simpler class analyses. In 1647, for instance, Lawrence Clarkson, then a Leveller, later a Ranter, demanded, 'Who are the oppressors but the nobility and gentry;

[9] See the important book by Caroline Hibbard, *Charles I and the Popish Plot* (North Carolina UP, 1983), *passim*.

[10] Major-General Lambert, speaking in a debate in Parliament on the causes of the civil war, 9 Feb. 1659, *Diary of Thomas Burton*, ed. J. T. Rutt (1828), iii. 187. I cite these views not as necessarily true, but as widely held opinions which Bunyan was likely to have heard.

[11] *MCPW*, i. 616. See pp. 151–3 below.

and who are oppressed – if not the yeoman, the farmer, the tradesman and the like?' Two years later Gerrard Winstanley the Digger asked, 'Do not all strive to enjoy the land? The gentry strive for land, the clergy strive for land, the common people strive for land . . . I affirm it was made for all; and true religion is to let everyone enjoy it.'[12]

For a country boy to be plunged into the middle of discussions like this, on subjects which could never before have been openly talked about by ordinary people, must have been an overwhelming experience. In the 1640s censorship and age-old ecclesiastical controls had broken down. Any group of men and/or women who so wished could get together and elect a chairman – often a so-called 'mechanic preacher', a man who worked with his hands six days a week. Under him they conducted discussions which might stray very far from what we regard as 'religious' in the narrow sense of the word, into economics, morals, and politics. They had escaped from the control of their betters. In this world of radical speculation Bunyan mixed with way-out groups, like the Ranters: he tells us so. I shall return to this later.

It did not last. The New Model Army was at first the agency of radical politics. It purged conservatives ('Presbyterians') from the House of Commons in December 1648, brought Charles I to public trial and execution (a unique, traumatic historical event), abolished the House of Lords, proclaimed a republic. Of eleven judges of Charles I whom Parliament exempted from pardon after the restoration, two were Bedfordshire men.[13] But the officers of this Army were gentlemen, or had profited from the war sufficiently to become gentlemen. Gradually they lost their radical enthusiasms. Simultaneously the Army forfeited what popularity it had enjoyed with the radicals. It exacted unprecedented sums in taxation for no very obvious purpose except to maintain itself in power: the expected reforms did not come. There followed a series of attempts at 'settlement' – the Commonwealth of 1649, Bare-bone's Parliament in 1653, the Protectorate of Oliver Cromwell (1653–8), and his son Richard (1658–9). Ultimately a coalition of

---

[12] [Clarkson], *A general charge or impeachment of high treason in the name of Justice-Equity against the communalty* (1647), 10–14; Winstanley, *A New-year's Gift for the Parliament and Army* (1650), in *The Law of Freedom and Other Writings* (Cambridge UP, 1983), 185.
[13] Brown, 127.

former Parliamentarians and former royalists, with strong support from the City of London and from a section of the Army, restored Charles I's son as Charles II.

The restoration was a compromise from which the gentry emerged victorious. A pamphlet of 1660 on the rule of the gentry makes this clear. In addition to their local power, 'this sort of people have by influence and in effect the command of this nation; ... they sit at the helm in the supreme councils; they command in chief at sea and land; they impose and collect taxes.' Sheriffs, JPs, and judges are all gentlemen, 'by the influence of which powers they so order all elections to Parliament ... that ... the commonalty in their votes are managed by them as the horse by his rider.'[14] The restoration was a devastating defeat for the hopes of 'mechanic preachers' like the tinker John Bunyan. Dissenters were henceforth excluded from local and national politics.

The years after 1660 saw an uneasy balance. Many gentlemen longed to exact vengeance for the ignominy which they had suffered during the revolutionary decades. Pressure for persecution of nonconformists came from the House of Commons rather than from the King or even the bishops (also restored in 1660). But dissenters had become too numerous during the freedom of the Revolution for it now to be possible to suppress them altogether, as bishops and government had hoped to do before 1640.

The gentry, much as they disliked lower-class dissenters, had no wish to restore the independent power of bishops as it had existed before the civil war. The executive arm of the church, the High Commission, was not restored. (If ever Satan 'set up a shop on earth to practise his trade in, it was our High Commission Court', Bunyan's friend John Owen had said in 1644.) Without the High Commission ecclesiastical censures lost their bite. Charles II's government was always nervous lest too severe religious persecution should lead to social unrest; and both Charles and his brother James wished to establish liberty of worship for Roman Catholic dissenters as well as for protestants. As time went on, the

---

[14] [Anon.], *A Discourse for a King and Parliament* (1660), 1–2. The interesting thing about this pamphlet is that, as its title suggests, it was not written by a radical. Sir Roger L'Estrange reprinted passages from it in *The State and Interest of the Nation With respect to His Royal Highness the Duke of York* (1680), 4–5. He may be the original author. See R. Ashcraft, *Revolutionary Politics and Locke's Two Treatises of Government* (Princeton UP, 1986), 239–42.

nonconformist interest prospered, especially in London, and became an important source of loans for government.[15] So the restored establishment was not monolithic.

I shall be looking later at the politics of the reigns of Charles II (1660–85) and James II (1685–8). Charles first played off nonconformists against Tory–Anglicans, possibly in the hope of thereby winning toleration for Roman Catholics. In 1670 he promised Louis XIV of France that he would declare himself a catholic. He was indeed reconciled to the church of Rome on his deathbed, but we may doubt whether he intended his promise to Louis as anything but a means of extorting money.

In 1678–81 there was a prolonged crisis. The 'Popish Plot' to murder the King and establish Roman Catholicism in England, which Titus Oates alleged, was mostly a fraud, pursued by the Earl of Shaftesbury and the Whigs for their own political purposes. But behind it lay the fact that James was a dedicated papist, who lacked Charles's saving laziness and cynicism. There was every reason to suppose that if and when he succeeded he might really try to carry out the policy which his brother had professed. So attempts were made to exclude him from the succession and substitute Charles's illegitimate son the Duke of Monmouth. Charles skilfully outmanœuvred the exclusionist Whigs, who badly overplayed their hand by encouraging London mobs. ('Remember '41' the Tories cried.) Nor were hereditary landowners pleased by the idea of the heir to the throne being a bastard. In the last four years of his reign, in alliance with the Tory gentry and the Church of England, the wily Charles was able to break the Act of 1664 which called for Parliaments every three years. Lord William Russell, MP for Bedford 1679–81, became a Whig martyr when he was executed in 1683 for alleged complicity in the alleged Rye House Plot.

Charles was busy remodelling the charters of town corporations (which returned most MPs) so as to have a docile Parliament if he ever had to call one. He looked like making himself independent, though it is doubtful whether such a position was tenable in the long run. But his death at the early age of 55 exposed the obstinate incompetence of his brother James. An ill-prepared and ill-organized invasion by the Duke of Monmouth in 1685 was

---

[15] Owen, *Works* (1850–3), xiii. 28; Gary S. de Krey, *A Fractured Society: The Politics of London in the First Age of Party, 1688–1715* (Oxford UP, 1985), Pt. III, ch. 3B–4.

defeated, and a docile Parliament made James financially secure. But he abandoned the Tory–Anglican alliance which had served his brother so well, employed Catholics in his government and – even more alarmingly – in the army and navy. Most foolishly of all he undid his brother's purges of corporations, turning out loyal Tories and Tory JPs and substituting old Cromwellians and dissenters, including men associated with Bunyan's Bedford congregation. It looked like social revolution to the extruded gentry. In the summer of 1688 a group of Whigs, Tories, and bishops invited James's son-in-law William of Orange to come over and save English protestantism. 'The protestant wind' blew him over in November, two months after Bunyan's death.

The settlement of 1688–9 secured the supremacy of Parliament, and the Toleration Act of 1689 gave limited religious freedom but not political rights to dissenters. Parliament had replaced the King as effective controller of the church in 1660. The alliance of bishops and gentry in Parliament, of parsons and squires in the villages, defeated Charles II's indulgence policy. The first opposition to James came in 1687 from the Seven Bishops, who refused to order his Declaration of Indulgence to be read from the pulpit: their acquittal after being charged with seditious libel was greeted with popular enthusiasm. Until 1688 Parliament had been struggling with the crown for control of the judiciary; after the Glorious Revolution that battle too was won. The struggle for control of the corporations which elected MPs was finally lost by James. The war on two fronts – against popery and absolutism on the one hand, and against radical democracy on the other – was finally won. The smoothness of the bloodless revolution of 1688 gave no chance for lower-class insubordination. The course was set for England's development until the nineteenth century.

Dissenters did not win the liberty and equality for which they had hoped: but they were rescued from the intermittent persecution of the preceding three decades. We must never forget the atmosphere of fear and semi-legality in which dissenters lived and in which Bunyan wrote his greatest works. He spent nearly one-third of his adult life in prison; and he made no compromises with the establishment in church and state. If we consider him only as a great literary classic, or as a religious thinker, we are in danger of forgetting the context in which he wrote. The Latitudinarian Edward Fowler, future Bishop, saw Bunyan as a 'firebrand' and 'malicious schismatic', 'a downright Ranter', who should not be tolerated.[16] We must ask, how far Bunyan was free to say what he thought? In what he published before 1660 we may assume that he came nearest to liberty of expression. There was also a period of relative freedom from censorship between 1678 and 1682. In the dozen treatises which he left unpublished at his death we may suppose that he said more of what he believed, though in works which he had prepared for publication he may have been anxious to avoid upsetting the censor. At other periods the censorship was strict, if irregularly enforced. It should be directed, said Sir Roger L'Estrange, against 'the great masters of the popular style'.[17] Throughout this book I have noted the date of any of Bunyan's works cited. If we are to recover his uncensored thought, questions of dating are relevant.

Always Bunyan was aware that many of the positions he adopted were unacceptable to ruling persons in church and state. We smile condescendingly when we read Professor Smith's sneers at Bunyan's ignorance of syllogisms, or other parsons deploring his presumption in publishing at all. But this is the worst kind of hindsight. Posterity has accepted that Bunyan is a great writer; his contemporary critics did not know that this was going to happen. They knew that he was a tinker, and they attributed most of what they regarded as the horrors of the revolutionary decades to the religious toleration which had allowed artisans to preach, and to the freedom of the press which had allowed them to publish. They also knew that Bunyan had been given a long prison sentence for refusing to obey the law, and that he continued to break what Parliament regarded as the law as soon as he was released.

We must therefore be alert to the devices of allegory, use of Biblical myths, parable, metaphor, and irony which Bunyan regularly employed. His main themes are simple, clear, and straightforwardly expressed: but their application contains a wealth of overt and covert allusions, some of which I have tried to bring out. There are risks in trying to read between the lines. But there was a chasm between Bunyan's thinking and that of the JPs who sent him to jail; between him and the Latitudinarian clergy, the more liberal wing of the Church of England.

[16] See pp. 132–3 below.
[17] See pp. 362–3 below.

I am not suggesting that Bunyan's interests were primarily political; far from it. For him the first priority was to be able to worship and preach according to what he believed to be God's will. But many in authority in his society, especially among the gentry, thought religious dissent was in itself seditious. The issue of religious toleration became politicized when Charles II and James II linked toleration for protestant dissenters with toleration for Catholics. There were widely held and not groundless suspicions that James at least aspired to make himself absolute. Religious toleration under such auspices inevitably became a political issue, as John Milton and Andrew Marvell clearly saw. Whether Bunyan saw it equally clearly is uncertain; but the mere fact of being a protestant dissenter forced political decisions on him.

2. The Rich, the Poor, and the Middling Sort

> The third, fourth and fifth decades of the seventeenth century
> witnessed extreme hardship in England, and were probably
> among the most terrible years through which the country has ever
> passed; . . . many experienced extreme poverty, living desperately
> from one meagre harvest to the next.   PETER BOWDEN[1]

THE two generations before Bunyan's birth had been a para-
doxical period in which England as a whole was getting richer
but the poor were getting poorer. The combined effects of plunder
of the church at the Reformation and the growth of population, of
world trade and piracy, produced what Bowden called 'the great
divide'—'a massive redistribution of income in favour of the
landed class . . . as much at the expense of the agricultural wage-
earner and consumer as of the tenant farmer.' Real wages halved in
the sixteenth century, and continued to drop in the first three
decades of the seventeenth century. As a document of 1591 put it,
economic changes 'made of yeomen and artificers gentlemen, and
of gentlemen knights, and so forth upward; and of the poorest sort
stark beggars.'[2]

The divide affected especially the middling sort—yeomen, artisans, merchants. Those who were fortunately placed on trade
routes to London or a port, the skilful and the lucky, could prosper
by production for the market; those less well placed, less skilful, or
just unfortunate, might become so poor that they had to sell part of
their holding. The Bunyans were one such family. Those who had
to sell all would join the growing army of landless labourers or
vagabonds—a fate which the Bunyans managed to avoid. Poverty
was nothing new. But the division within the peasantry, setting
village élites against a class of permanent poor, was resented
because it was novel. Education became the key to a chance of
social betterment. The children of the very poor could not get the
necessary education because their labour was essential to the
economic survival of their families.

---

[1] 'Agricultural Prices, Farm Profits and Rents', in J. Thirsk (ed.) *The Agrarian History
of England and Wales*, iv, 1500–1600 (Cambridge UP, 1967), 620–1.
[2] Ibid. 695; R. H. Tawney, *The Agrarian Problem of the Sixteenth Century* (1912), 383.

Some were becoming increasingly conscious of scarcity in the midst of potential growth. This had not been so apparently crucial an issue in earlier centuries. Gentlemen and aristocrats always had abundance: peasants and wage labourers had no other perspective than continuing poverty tempered by dreams of the Land of Cokayne. But sixteenth-century economic developments opened up the possibility of escaping from the scarcity trap. Francis Bacon for the first time envisaged mankind controlling its own destiny as it advanced towards abundance. For some yeomen and artisans the prospects were immediate. By hard work, careful management, disciplined labour, avoidance of luxury and waste, they might hope to escape from poverty—and by employing the labour of their fellows.

Others were less fortunate. Small men were likely to lose their lands on enclosure. It has been estimated that one-quarter of the land of England was enclosed in the seventeenth century.[3] Even if it was by 'agreement', this normally meant the agreement of the well-to-do in a village. If a poor copyholder was allocated a plot of land, he was unlikely to be able to afford to hedge it, or to buy equipment to farm it. Capital was necessary for a man to profit by the new opportunities. In Blunham, Bedfordshire, the Earl of Kent enclosed by agreement with 'the most part of the better sort' of the inhabitants. Some sixty of those excluded from the agreement, including women, threw down the enclosure. Ultimately in James I's reign agreement was reached with a slightly more representative group of forty villagers—still not a majority, and only five of them were labourers. Those still excluded met in the church to swear mutual support in destroying the enclosure. The men of Pulloxhill, Bedfordshire, subscribed to a common fund to defend endangered common rights. There were riots against enclosures in 1618 which recalled those by 'the levellers of Northamptonshire', who had rebelled in 1607.[4]

John Winthrop, giving reasons for emigration to New England in the first year of Bunyan's life, spoke of 'many spending as much

---

[3] J. R. Wordie, 'The Chronology of England's Enclosure, 1500–1914', *EcHR*, 2nd Ser. 36 (1983), 494–5, 502–3.
[4] Joyce Godber, 'Some Documents Relating to Riots', PBHRS 49 (1970), 148–52; S. Peyton, 'Ecclesiastical Troubles in Dunstable c. 1616', ibid. 11 (1927), 110; *VCH Bedfordshire*, ii. 96. John Donne was rector of Blunham (normally non-resident) from 1622 until his death in 1631.

labour and cost to recover or keep sometimes an acre or two of land [which] would procure them many hundred as good or better in another country.' In England it was 'almost impossible for a good and upright man to maintain his charge and live comfortably'. Those who failed to keep up with their fellows, he said, were treated with scorn and contempt, or lapsed into intemperance or riot.[5] The reasons which Winthrop (and many others) gave for emigration were economic as well as religious; the two were closely connected.

The poor suffered many disadvantages. There were still bondmen in Cranfield in 1577 – the Bedfordshire manor from which Lord Treasurer Lionel Cranfield took his title in 1621. Under an act of 1563 the poor could be put to forced labour if they were unemployed. Anyone who *threatened* to leave his parish could be punished as a vagabond. Landlords often demanded their tenants' labour for building or other purposes; 'if any man refuse', retaliation will take the form of either 'raising him in the subsidy, or . . . doubling his charge for the wars'. That remark, from a sermon printed in 1615,[6] reveals the dual power of the gentry: they were JPs as well as landlords, and they assessed and collected taxes. In consequence they had pretty complete control over the lower orders. Forty-five years and one revolution later not much had changed in this respect. In 1660 the anonymous author of *A Discourse for a King and Parliament* observed that:

England is governed by the influence of a sort of people that live plentifully and at ease upon their rents, extracted from the toil of their tenants and servants, . . . each of whom within his own estate acts the prince; he is purely absolute; his servants and labourers are in the nature of his vassals; his tenants indeed are free, but in the nature of subjects. . . . By gentry I intend not only such as are so in blood . . . [but those who are rich enough to] take to themselves the degree and name of gentleman.[7]

The poor were rightless in many ways. 'No goods: to be whipped' was a frequent instruction after a trial. A man who was

---

[5] Winthrop, *Reasons to Be Considered . . . for the Intended Plantation in New England*, Proceedings of the Massachusetts Historical Soc., 8 (1864-5), 420-5.

[6] S. Peyton, 'An Elizabethan Inquiry Concerning Bondmen', PBHRS 9 (1925), 70-4; [D. and S.] Lysons, *Magna Britannia* for Bedfordshire (1978), 72; Charles Richardson, quoted in H. C. White, *Social Criticism in Popular Religious Literature in the Sixteenth Century* (New York, 1944), 236.

[7] Op. cit. 1-2. Cf. pp. 219-21, 279-80 below.

too poor to be worth fining could pay only with his blood, which had to cover his back before the flogging stopped. The poor were liable to be conscripted into the armed forces in time of war, an appalling fate to befall a man whose dependants would suffer during his absence and get little or no compensation if he were killed or wounded. Parishes were 'willing to give their moneys' to get their dependent poor press-ganged.[8] After any uprising, Francis Bacon said, 'rascal people . . . were to be cut off every man', whilst their socially superior leaders were let off much more lightly. When a felony was suspected, Francis Osborne, a Bedford-shire man, tells us, the houses of the poor were searched first. It was proverbial that big thieves prospered whilst little thieves were hanged. The saintly Bishop Lancelot Andrewes announced that he prayed for all, 'even down to the sordid craftsmen, even to the beggars'.[9] Theologians and philosophers debated seriously whether it was permissible to steal in order to save oneself from starvation, as John Donne and Thomas Hobbes thought, or whether it was a poor man's Christian duty to watch his family die quietly, as Richard Baxter held. In the starvation years of the 1590s and 1620s this was not an academic question. Wage-labourers and paupers were estimated at half the population: 'neither contem-porary nor modern economists can explain how they lived', said David Ogg.[10]

Not all the poor were so quietly Christian as Baxter would have wished. There are frequent references to 'the discontent of the common people against the gentry'.[11] Their 'bitter and distrustful attitude' was taken for granted. Many of the lower orders were 'apt beforehand unto tumults, seditions and broils', wrote the judicious

---

[8] Joan R. Kent, *The English Village Constable, 1580–1642: A Social and Administrative Study* (Oxford UP, 1986), 277; cf. 182–3. Freedom from conscription was one of five absolute liberties which the Leveller draft constitution of 1647, the Agreement of the People, would not allow even its sovereign Parliament to infringe; another was liberty of conscience.

[9] Bacon, quoted in V. G. Kiernan, *State and Society in Europe, 1550–1650* (Oxford, 1980), 115; cf. 145; F. Osborne, *Works* (11th edn., 1722), *Essays*, 35; Andrewes, *XCVI Sermons* (2nd. edn., 1631), 45.

[10] Donne, *Essays in Divinity*, ed. E. M. Simpson (Oxford UP, 1952), 68; Hobbes, *Leviathan* (Penguin edn.), 346; Baxter, *Chapters from a Christian Directory* (1925), 69–71; D. Ogg, *England in the Reign of Charles II* (Oxford UP, 1934), i. 85.

[11] *Journal of Sir Roger Wilbraham* (1607), ed. H. S. Scott, *Camden Miscellany* 10 (1902), 96. For inequality of rich and poor before the law see my *Society and Puritanism in Pre-Revolutionary England* (Penguin edn.), 373–4.

Hooker; 'apt to turn every pretence and colour of grievance into uproar and seditious mutiny' they said in Newcastle upon Tyne in 1633. From the 1640s the lower classes were freer to express their feelings; the new excise, a purchase tax falling heavily on articles of popular consumption, gave them an additional grievance. 'I hope within this year to see never a gentleman in England', cried a sectary in Northamptonshire in July 1643. 'It will never be a good world, while knights and gentlemen make us laws', Richard Baxter had often heard men say.[12]

The protestant doctrine of predestination was particularly appropriate to this environment. All individuals were at the mercy of the blind forces of the weather, the harvest, plague, war and the market, none of which they could understand or control. Yet success might give some merchants, yeomen, and artisans a sense of freedom from destiny which may have been illusory but was no less real for them. 'The Lord was with Joseph, and he was a lucky fellow', R. H. Tawney quoted a marginal note in the Geneva Bible as saying.[13] The struggle against scarcity was a struggle for the freedom of the individual and his family, freedom from falling into the bottomless pit of poverty from which there was no escape. This struggle for economic freedom must have seemed more real for the middling sort than the struggle for political liberties which figures more largely in the history books. Freedom meant the possibility of throwing off the burden on one's back, and travelling hopefully; but the only true abundance was to be found across the river of death.

Such a transitional society posed ethical problems which the preachers were called upon to solve. Economic behaviour, the work ethic, labour discipline, usury, enclosure — all became crucial issues, especially for the middling sort, parish élites, to whom Puritanism particularly appealed. The work ethic offered a way out of the poverty trap. Yet dangers at once loom. Robert Crowley depicted a landowner oppressing his tenants and defending himself by saying:

---

[12] John Barclay, *Icon Animarum* (1614), Englished by T. M[ay] (1631), 104-8; R. Hooker, *Of The Laws of Ecclesiastical Polity* (Everyman edn.), ii. 5-6; R. Welford, *History of Newcastle and Gateshead* (1884-7), iii. 315-16; [B. Ryves], *Angliae Ruina* (1647), 96; Baxter, *A Holy Commonwealth* (1659), 231.

[13] R. H. Tawney, *Religion and the Rise of Capitalism* (Penguin edn.), 179.

That with his own he might
Always do as he list.

Grasping characters make the identical point in the dialogues of William Perkins, Arthur Dent, Lewis Bayly,[14] and in Bunyan's *The Life and Death of Mr. Badman*. Not surprisingly Crowley saw the yeoman as standing in special need of godly advice against oppressing the poor on the one hand, and failing to labour hard enough in his calling on the other. Two generations later Thomas Taylor grappled with the problem: 'If any man provide not for his family, he is worse than an infidel, I *Tim.* 5.8.' But this may lead to compromise with Mammon, to covetousness.[15] A narrow line divides the protestant ethic from the unacceptable face of capitalism, a line which historians find almost as difficult to draw as contemporary theologians did.

'If the capitalist spirit consist of a relentless drive to accumulate wealth and a willingness to take risks in the pursuit of higher profits', a recent historian writes:

then these [Puritan] preachers did everything within their power to stifle it. . . . In early Stuart England an ethic of unbridled acquisitiveness would have brought ruin to most of those foolish enough to adopt it. The vast majority of the preachers' auditors could hope, at best, for a modest prosperity and the chance to pass along a suitable inheritance to the next generation. These were the aspirations that the preachers encouraged and assisted their followers to achieve. . . . The ethic of godliness, by harmonizing the requirements of economic survival and eternal salvation, may well have saved many of the middling sort from ruinous self-indulgence.[16]

This captures the paradox of the protestant and Puritan ethic. Its object was to encourage free enterprise, individualism, and so open doors; but also to protect the community and especially its poor. Many years ago I quoted Perkins asking by what standards we are to assess economic behaviour. Not, he replied, by the affection of covetous men, but by 'the common judgment and practice of the

[14] I frequently quote Dent and Bayly, because we know that Bunyan read them at an early and impressionable age.
[15] *Select Works of Robert Crowley*, ed. J. M. Cowper, Early English Text Soc. (1872), 46–7, 63–70; cf. 112–16, 156–7; Perkins, *Works* (1616–18), iii. 466, 471; Taylor, *The Principles of Christian Practice* (1653), 34 (published posthumously: Taylor died in 1633).
[16] W. Hunt, *The Puritan Moment: The Coming of Revolution in an English County* (Harvard UP, 1983), 127–8.

most godly, frugal and wise men with whom we live'. That, I commented, was to allow bourgeois society to set its own standards.[17]

I was placing Perkins in a long-term perspective of economic thought. It is right to emphasize that he also had a traditional anxiety to protect the poor and the community.[18] But when we come to consider Bunyan's economic thought, or that of Baxter and other later seventeenth-century casuists, we shall see that by then the doors have been opened wide. Bunyan, without wanting to quench individualism — far from it — is anxious now, perhaps too late, to emphasize community, charity, the rights of the poor. Bunyan knew, and came to know better the longer he lived, what was actually happening, how the rise of capitalism was disrupting the small producer world which he wanted to moralize, how even the godly succumbed to the values of the market. His Mr. Badman represents this face of capitalism.

Edward Dering, in his reading on Hebrews 1, delivered at St Paul's in 1572, emphasized the liberating consequences of the doctrine of justification by faith.

If I know myself by faith made a member of Christ, and his right is mine in the creatures of the world, and in his name and to his glory I use them, whatsoever God hath given me in the days of my pilgrimage, the profit is mine; I may use it to my necessity; and the pleasure is mine; I may use it to my delight

—silken garments, all sorts of meats, hunting and hawking—provided one lives within one's income. 'I allow not them which will needs wear cloth and are not able to buy cloth.' Dering was a gentleman by birth, and concerned here to reject the standards of medieval asceticism: the religious duty to save was a later accretion as Puritanism adapted itself to an increasingly capitalist society. So Bunyan was to write, 'some in our days ask, "who . . . have a right to the creatures, if not Christians, if not professors, if not church members?"' And this leads to pride and luxury, to 'daubing themselves with the lust-provoking fashions of the times, . . .

---

[17] Perkins, *Works*, ii. 790, quoted in my *Puritanism and Revolution* (Penguin edn.), 226.

[18] Eamon Duffy, 'The Godly and the Multitude in Stuart England', *The Seventeenth Century*, i (1986), 31–55.

naked breasts, frizzled fore-tops, wanton gestures, in gorgeous apparel.'[19]

Usury dates from pre-capitalist societies. From the sixteenth century onwards sophisticated thinkers—whether Popes or Calvin—accepted that lending money for profit is essential to the workings of a commercial society. The poor had to borrow money to tide them over the period between seed-time and harvest. The problem was to devise a formula which allowed businessmen in the big cities to keep the economy going, whilst giving some protection to those who had no reserves to fall back on in time of need. Bunyan's upbringing made him (like Baxter) distrust middlemen and place his main emphasis on the needs of the small consumer. Those who taught in the big cities—Calvin, Perkins, Ames—saw things differently.

So congregations of the godly middling sort attached especial importance to the economic behaviour of their members. The London artisan Nehemiah Wallington was upset when his apprentice was caught out passing off inferior wood as maple. His outraged customer bit deep when she said, 'You have lived under a faithful minister for a long time', and so for him 'to lie and cozen' was 'to bring a slander on religion'. Wallington sadly agreed: it would open the mouths of the wicked. On another occasion Wallington refrained—after some hesitation and with considerable reluctance—from passing a bad shilling, on the ground that it would be 'to God's dishonour, for it will cause men to say, "This is your religion! Men, see how he hath cozened and deceived me!"' When James Cole of Whitechapel in 1634 ran away from his creditors to take refuge among the godly in East Anglia and the Midlands, he found himself under great pressure from the reproaches of his own godly community: 'Above all, how have you given the enemy cause to rejoice and triumph, and the name of God, your good God, to be dishonoured by the wicked!'[20]

What is interesting here is that well before 1640 a godly community was imposing standards of economic behaviour on its members within the framework of the parish. The godly had

[19] Dering, quoted in J. O. W. Haweis, *Sketches of the Reformation and Elizabethan Age Taken from the Contemporary Pulpit* (1844), 265; *The Barren Fig-tree* (1673), MW v. 19–20.
[20] P. S. Seaver, *Wallington's World: A Puritan Artisan in Seventeenth-Century London* (1985), 96–7, 132, 141.

standards which were consciously higher than those of the craftsmen around them, and they must not let down these standards or
the community which accepted them.[21]

Such problems of economic conduct were becoming acute just
when the abolition of the confessional, penance, absolution, and
indulgences left laymen deprived of traditional forms of ecclesiastical guidance and consolation. But men and women still looked to
the ministry for advice. This accounts for the development of a
protestant casuistry which is very largely a guide to economic and
social conduct. From Perkins through Ames to Baxter there is a
steady stream of casuistry, to which Arthur Dent, Lewis Bayly, and
Richard Bernard contributed, and in which from the 1640s lay
mechanic preachers began to join. George Fox from the very
beginning of his preaching career was denouncing the deceitful-
ness of salesmen. He called on tradesmen to ask no more than a just
price, and to 'keep to Yea and Nay'.[22]

Bunyan played his part in this casuistry, as we shall see. He
discusses at length the duties of heads of households. 'A man that
governs his family well hath one qualification belonging to a pastor
or deacon in the house of God.' Servants should be given 'the same
bread of God as the master's children'. 'Thy work in thy place and
station, as thou art a servant, is as really God's ordinance, and as
acceptable to him, in its kind, as is preaching.'[23]

The work ethic could call in question the propriety of living on
rents. Perkins thought that 'such as live in no calling, but spend
their time in eating, drinking, sleeping and sporting' were guilty of
disobedience and rebellion against God. Those strong words were
not seriously followed up until the revolutionary decades. But then
sectaries in Chelmsford were only pursuing Perkins's logic when
(it is said) they argued that 'the nobility and gentry should . . . work
for their own maintenance; and if they will not work, they ought
not to eat.' Idle gentlemen, declared the anonymous *More Light
Shining in Buckinghamshire* in 1649, are vagabonds and ought to be
put into a house of correction and made to work. Gerrard

---

[21]   Ibid. 147, 173.

[22]   *The Short Journal and Itinerary Journals of George Fox*, ed. N. Penney (Cambridge
UP, 1925), 17, 21; Fox, '*A Cry for Repentance*' (1656), in *Gospel-Truth Demonstrated in a
Collection of Books* (1706), 76.

[23]   *Christian Behaviour* (1663), MW iii. 22–43. Cf. George Herbert, 'A servant with
this clause / Makes drudgery divine'.

Winstanley extended this to something like a labour theory of value: the rich live upon the labour of the poor, all landlords are thieves.[24] Once such sentiments had been freely expressed and discussed, they were not easily forgotten.

Some of the edge was taken off social antagonisms by the economic upturn which occurred in the second half of the seventeenth century. During Bunyan's lifetime the sixteenth-century population explosion and inflation both slowed down, and the problem of feeding England's vastly increased numbers was solved by an agricultural revolution. Vagabondage had ceased to be a serious problem by 1679, when we first hear of Bedford's house of correction.[25] Industrial monopolies had been abolished by the Long Parliament. But the main advantages of the new relative prosperity went to merchants and to landlords, now freer than before to evict copyholders and cottagers, and helped by the corn bounty on exports for which the gentry in the House of Commons had voted. Bunyan, as we shall see, had not much love for the gentry.

He had no love at all for the state church. Here he had much Bedfordshire history behind him. Before 1640 there had been Puritanism in the county, or at least disaffection with the national church. The great millenarian Puritan, Thomas Brightman, was vicar of Harnes, six and a half miles from Bedford, until his death in 1607. His major works had to be published abroad, and were available in England only after 1640. But then rhymed versions of his 'prophecies' were many times reprinted as Parliamentarian propaganda. Thomas Adams, 'the prose Shakespeare of Puritan theologians', whose works Bunyan may have read, was briefly vicar of Willington, four miles from Bedford. Many Bedfordshire parsons were in trouble for failing to wear the surplice. There were Brownist sectaries in Stadham and Cranfield in 1617. Dunstable had a Puritan tradition which went back to the Lollards. It may have owed its freedom to the fact that it was the only market town in Bedfordshire which had no lord or squire resident in the neighbourhood. In 1616 some of its inhabitants baptized a sheep in the parish church. Dunstable was the largest Ship Money

[24] Perkins, *Works*, iii. 63–4, 512–13; cf. i. 756; *Angliae Ruina*, 26–7; *The Works of Gerrard Winstanley*, ed. G. H. Sabine (Cornell UP, 1941), 633, 511–12; cf. 258, 580–1.
[25] Godber, *The Story of Bedford: An Outline History* (Luton, 1978), 55.

defaulter in the county in relation to its population.[26] There was a
communist Digger colony there in the early 1650s.

Ecclesiastical courts dealt with many men and women who
disregarded the laws of the church, including those for Sabbath
observance. Even watching football on Sunday was punished.
Preaching was discouraged. 'Gadding to sermons' outside one's
own parish appears to have been particularly prevalent. Laud
reported that Bedfordshire was the 'most tainted of any part
of the diocese' of Lincoln, and the Deputy-Recorder of Bedford
complained in 1634 that if 'godly men ... were thus troubled
for going to hear a sermon when their minister at home did
not preach, it would breed a scab in the kingdom.'[27] So local
grievances became national grievances. In Elizabeth's reign
religious refugees from France and the Netherlands had been
welcomed in the county, to its great economic advantage; in
Charles's reign two Bedfordshire ministers emigrated to New
England.

There was opposition to Archbishop Laud's demand that the
altar be railed off. In 1640 the vicar of St Paul's, Bedford, was cited
before the High Commission for not insisting on communicants
coming up to the altar to receive the sacrament. He was supported
by leading parishioners, including three who were later to be
founder-members of the congregation which Bunyan joined.
Eighty or ninety inhabitants of Bedford, including the mayor,
petitioned Archbishop Laud in 1640 (before the Long Parliament
met) against Giles Thorne, the Laudian Rector of St Mary's and St
Cuthbert's. Thorne, who had been a maintainer of the Book of
Sports, was arrested and imprisoned in 1642 and spent five years in
prison. John Pocklington, Rector of Yelden, fourteen miles from
Bedford, author of the notorious *Sunday No Sabbath*, had his
book burnt by order of Parliament in 1640. He was accused of

[26] J. Frank, *Hobbled Pegasus: A Descriptive Bibliography of Minor English Poetry,
1641–1660* (New Mexico UP, 1968), 49, 69, 92; Godber, *History of Bedfordshire,
1066–1888* (Bedford County Council, 1969), 193, 228–9, 265, 269; ead., *The Story of
Bedford*, 61. For Adams see *DNB*.

[27] D. and S. Lysons, *Magna Britannia* for Bedfordshire (1978), 93; Peyton, 'Ecclesi-
astical Troubles', 111–24; W. R. Prest, *The Rise of the Barristers: A Social History of the
English Bar, 1590–1640* (Oxford UP, 1986), 231, 394. The Deputy-Recorder was
Richard Taylor, a local gentleman who had been MP for Bedford in 1621, 1624, 1625,
and 1628, but lost his seat in 1640, apparently on account of his royalism (Godber, *The
Story of Bedford*, 65). Cf. Brown, 3, 7–8, 93–4, and p. 7 above.

maintaining 'divers wicked, popish and antichristian points, to the great danger and damage of this church and state'.[28]

The Presbyterian church established in the 1640s attempted, unsuccessfully, to impose parochial discipline on a national scale. After its failure, those who wished to join disciplined congregations were free to do so; compulsory church attendance broke down, and was formally abolished between 1650 and 1657. The traditional idea of a national church of which all English men and women were members was challenged. But if there was no state church there could be no trained and authorized interpreters of the Scripture in each parish, no control over the sermons preached or the subjects discussed: in modern terms no government power over the media. Such a situation caused the greatest alarm to the respectable classes: no elected Parliament in the mid-seventeenth century would vote for religious toleration. But this dangerous liberty ended in 1660 with the restoration of King and bishops; preaching tinkers with undesirable views were silenced.

[28] Brown, 5–13, 43, 68, 71; Lysons, *Magna Britannia*, 156; Godber, *The Story of Bedford*, 70–1, 74. [Anon.], *The Petition or Articles exhibited in Parliament against John Pocklington* (1641).

3. *Popular Literature*

Here are no far-fetched phrases to puzzle and amaze people, . . .
but an even and common language spoken usually and understood of everybody.
GERVASE MARKHAM[1]

LITERARY historians of the past generation have been putting Elizabethan and seventeenth-century literature into
quite a new perspective. They have rediscovered the popular
tradition in prose and verse. The reformation and the invention of
printing combined to produce a wider literate public, and a
demand for popular literature whose publication and circulation at
least were new. Fifteenth-century Lollards had propagandized
verbally and through manuscripts. Popular protestant propaganda
in print started in Henry VIII's reign with William Tyndale,
Simon Fish, and Henry Brinkelow. It flourished in the unprecedented freedom of the early years of Edward VI's reign. John
Bale, Hugh Latimer, Robert Crowley and Thomas Lever all wrote
for a popular as well as a cultivated audience. Latimer used homely
anecdotes and proverbs in his sermons at court, refusing to
separate popular from courtly prose. Bale, in addition to writing
protestant plays, made use of prose dialogue, sometimes written
with a plebeian scurrility. Editions were cheap, notably of
Crowley's writings; tracts were illustrated with woodcuts. Emblems were developed as a popular *protestant* literary form, quite
distinct from the intricate Counter-Reformation emblems which
appealed to intellectuals.[2]

Great literary figures of the past—Langland, Chaucer—were
annexed for the Lollard pre-protestant tradition, largely on the
basis of false attributions. Piers Plowman became a radical spokesman for opposition to enclosures and the nobility's misappropri-

---

[1] *Hobsons Horse-load of Letters* (1617), sigs. I. 2–I. 2v (1st pub. 1613), quoted in
L. B. Wright, *Middle-Class Culture in Elizabethan England* (N. Carolina UP, 1935),
142.

[2] J. N. King, *English Reformation Literature: The Tudor Origins of the Protestant
Tradition* (Princeton UP, 1982), 66–76, 93–4, 152–3, 327, 462–4. What follows draws
heavily on this pioneering book. See also Barbara Lewalski, *Protestant Poetics and the
Seventeenth-Century Religious Lyric* (Princeton UP, 1979), *passim*, and A. Sinfield,
Literature in Protestant England, 1560–1660 (1983), *passim*; Newey, 229. For emblems
see pp. 266–70 below.

ation of monastic lands. The thought of Bale and Crowley was millenarian and focused on social reform. Crowley compiled the first metrical psalter in English, in the metre which Sternhold and Hopkins were soon to popularize. His poems influenced both the techniques and the content of popular protestant poetry, down to the Bay Psalm Book of 1640 and Wigglesworth's *The Day of Doom* (1662). Crowley was sensitive to social injustice, opposing especially the sin of sloth, the rentier's sin. His masterpiece, *Philargyrie of Great Bretayne* (1551), was an allegory about a protestant aristocrat who used a Bible to rake gold coins into a sack.[3]

The popular tradition was welded together by Foxe's great *Book of Martyrs*, incorporating Gower and Chaucer, establishing a new type of Christian heroism which was not knightly or priestly, not upper class, nor even specifically male. The defenders of God's cause were mostly simple lay men and women from the artisan and yeoman class. And Foxe did all this in a popular idiomatic style, rich in detail of the everyday lives of ordinary people. His book was used as official propaganda by Queen Elizabeth; but it also became a bestseller, universally known by its popular title, not as *Acts and Monuments*. Bunyan acquired a copy to read when he was in Bedford jail.

So the popular literary tradition established itself. Translations of the psalms were sung by artisans, spinsters, and apprentices to popular ballad tunes. Tyndale had wanted the (symbolic) plough-man to whistle his psalms at the plough. Myles Coverdale's hymn-book, published in 1539, was burnt by order of Henry VIII. But Henry promoted Thomas Sternhold, translator of metrical psalms. From the reign of Edward VI onwards there were in-numerable versions of the psalms in English verse. In the 1560s William Kethe — the largest single contributor to the Geneva translation of the Bible — wrote 'A Ballet declaring the fal of the Whore of Babylon, intytuled "Tye thy Mane, Tomboye"'. Setting hymns and psalms to popular ballad tunes was continued in the seventeenth and eighteenth centuries by Muggletonians and followers of the millenarian John Mason.[4]

---

[3] H. C. White, *Social Criticism, in Popular Religious Literature in the Sixteenth Century* (New York, 1944), 1–40; King, *Reformation Literature, passim*; D. Norbrook, *Poetry and Politics in the English Renaissance* (1984), 42–3, 293.

[4] King, *Reformation Literature*, 178, 214, 218–20, 323–4, 334, 340–50, 356, 367. For Mason see my *Puritanism and Revolution* (Penguin edn.), 319.

The standard version came to be what Milton's nephew was to call 'Tom Sternhold's wretched pricksong for the people'. The Sternhold and Hopkins translation (1559–62) has not had a good press with literary historians. But it is difficult to overestimate its contribution to popular culture during the century after its publication, and hence its historical influence. No English song-book can have enjoyed equal popularity. Congregational singing was early introduced into New England. The New Model Army sang metrical psalms as it went into battle. So did a great crowd which spent a cold night in the Mendip Hills in August 1642, waiting to drive the royalist forces from Wells. The Sternhold and Hopkins version, which consecrated the quatrain as the standard for popular verse, ran to at least 288 editions before 1640; Bunyan quoted it in *Grace Abounding* and *The Pilgrim's Progress*. Edward Prys's *Book of Psalms* in Welsh, in popular metres for congregational singing, also enjoyed enormous popularity from its first publication in 1621.[5]

Most of the Marian martyrs whom Foxe celebrated would almost certainly have been regarded as heretics by Elizabeth (who indeed gave Foxe no promotion in her church). They had played their part in creating the protestant myth of God's humble Englishmen. The popular literature of the reign of Edward VI was equally expendable. The homely satire of a poet like Luke Shepherd 'took much at court' in Edward's reign, as well as with London readers. Christopher Tye in 1553 dedicated to Edward VI his arrangement of the Acts of the Apostles, to sing and play upon the lute.[6] But at Elizabeth's court the influence of preachers and commonwealthsmen was replaced by the taste of renaissance courtiers. The gulf between the native tradition of the gospellers and the courtly art of Sir Philip Sidney, William Webbe, and George Puttenham did not open up till the 1580s. But then it was decisive.

That great pioneering social historian L. B. Wright drew attention in the 1930s to the Elizabethan attack on popular poetry.

[5] M. R. Watts, *The Dissenters from the Reformation to the French Revolution* (Oxford UP, 1978), 308–9; L. Lupton, *History of the Geneva Bible* (n.d., 1973?), v. 70; R. Barclay, *The Inner Life of the Religious Societies of the Commonwealth* (1876), 451–8; P. Burke, *Popular Culture in Early Modern Europe* (1973), 320; Manning, *The English People and the English Revolution* (1976), 244; G. H. Jenkins, *Literature, Religion and Society in Wales, 1660–1730* (Wales UP, 1978), 148.

[6] King, *Reformation Literature*, 252–70; Diana Poulton, *John Dowland* (2nd. edn., 1982), 185–6.

'After the manner of academic critics in whatever age, they set themselves up as the keepers of the true literary heritage, and fought earnestly to protect their birthright from the rascal many.' Webbe in *A Discourse of English Poetrie* (1586) denounced 'the uncountable rabble of rhyming ballet-makers, . . . most busy to stuff every stall full of gross devices and unlearned pamphlets; . . . an alehouse song of five or six score verses, hobbling upon some tune of northern jig or Robin Hood', in ballad metre. That witnesses, among other things, to the popularity of the traditional poetry.[7] Puttenham's literary criticism was likewise socially oriented. Popular literature dealt with 'base and low matters' in 'a mean style' — 'the doings of the common artificer, serving man, yeoman, groom, husbandman, day labourer, sailor, shepherd, swineherd and such like.' Nor was it much better when literature moved up to the middling sort. These were still 'mean matters . . . that concern mean men', such as 'lawyers, gentlemen, and merchants, good householders and honest citizens'. Poetry should be written in the usual speech of the court, of London and 'sixty miles around', not of 'poor, rustical or uncivil people; neither shall [the poet] follow the speech of a craftsman or carter'.[8]

Puttenham advocated complicated Italian stanzas, naturally enough; he favoured poems shaped like a lozenge, a triangle, a pyramid, a pillar, or a sphere. He rejected *Piers Plowman*, Gower, Lydgate, and Chaucer, and 'any speech beyond the river of Trent', and objected to Skelton as 'but a rude and railing rhymer, . . . pleasing only the popular ear', whilst the radical tradition perceived Skelton as a proto-protestant and defender of native art against Italianate fashions. Puttenham looked back to Wyatt and Surrey, who had begun to polish the 'rude and homely manner of vulgar [= vernacular] poesy' into the 'sweet and stately measures and style of the Italian poesy'. Puttenham attacked the romances, *Bevis of Southampton*, *Guy of Warwick*, etc., because 'they were made purposely for the recreation of the common people'. Thomas Nashe was equally contemptuous of the 'few ragged rhymes . . . shuffled or slubbered up' by 'some stitcher, weaver . . . or fiddler'.[9]

[7] Wright, *Middle-Class Culture*, 91–5.

[8] George Puttenham, *The Art of English Poesie* (1589), in Gregory Smith, *Elizabethan Critical Essays* (Oxford UP, 1904), ii. 97–100, 150, 154, 158–9; A. Low, *The Georgic Revolution* (Princeton UP, 1985), 118.

[9] Gregory Smith, 62–5, 87, 96–101; cf. 156, 164–6; King, *Reformation Literature*, 255–6.

Until recently literary critics have tended to accept uncritically this view of the popular tradition. But it was not unchallenged in the sixteenth and seventeenth centuries. In 1578 Barnabe Rich in his *Allarme to England* defended the right of the unlearned to literary expression. Samuel Daniel too in his *Defence of Rhyme* (1603) was more tolerant of 'the general sort for whom we write'.[10]

Sidney sought for a middle way between the culture of ordinary people and the classical culture of the universities and the court; just as in religion he sought a middle way between sectaries and Counter-Reformation papists: the 1580s saw the beginnings of a Jesuit invasion. Catholics were depicted as unpatriotic peers and gentlemen on the one hand, the ignorant rabble on the other. Essex rioters in 1591 thought it would never be well until they were liberated by a Spanish invasion.[11] Spenser disliked the Many-Headed Monster—whether radical sectaries, egalitarian communists, or papists.

Sidney and Spenser were trying to establish a Calvinist literary consensus parallel to the Calvinist political and religious consensus, an Anglican insular patriotism which should be part of the protestant international. (Sidney was a great friend of the French protestant Duplessis-Mornay, and the Spenserian John Sylvester translated Du Bartas, the Huguenot poet.) This middle way in literature corresponds to the middle way of Archbishops Grindal and Abbott in the church, to which late seventeenth century nonconformists looked back as the true Church of England. Sidney had some regrets about rejecting the popular ballad tradition: he admitted rather shamefacedly to being moved by Chevy Chase. But his preference was for something more courtly. Just as in religion he rejected the Lollard tradition which passed through Anabaptism and Familism into the seventeenth-century sects, so he rejected the popular literary tradition which had been revivified in Edward VI's reign. Surrey during his last imprisonment (1547) had translated psalms into poulter's measure: but for their translation Sidney and his sister, the Countess of Pembroke, discarded the quatrains which Sternhold and Hopkins had made almost obligatory, and adopted sophisticated stanza forms.[12]

---

[10] King, *Reformation Literature*, 11–17; Rich, op. cit. sig. ˣ3v; Wright, *Middle-Class Culture*, 92–5.   [11] Hunt, *The Puritan Moment* (Harvard UP, 1983), 61.

[12] Sidney, *An Apology for Poetry*, in Gregory Smith, i. 178, 203; King, *Reformation Literature*, 210–11, 233.

Spenser did not share Sidney's distaste for the native literary tradition, and was rebuked by him for it. Spenser's 'framing of his style to an old rustic language' in *The Shepheardes Calendar*, said Sidney, 'I dare not allow'. Spenser looked back to Skelton, to the millenarian social reformers Bale and Crowley, and further back to a protestant Langland and Chaucer. Ralegh's 'Walsingham' too followed the popular ballad tradition, as well as emphasizing the theme of pilgrimage.[13]

The Spenserian succession of poets — Browne, Drayton, Sylvester — under James I looked to the young Prince Henry for patronage, and after his death they became increasingly alienated from the royal court.[14] This marked the beginnings of a new cultural divide, a crack in the Calvinist consensus. Historians of the drama see from this time a new questioning of divine right and a discussion of the limitations which the law lays on monarchs. The end of the great age of drama coincided with Shakespeare's retirement from the stage. The Authorized Version of 1611 was the last literary achievement of the Elizabethan consensus. Fulke Greville's *Life of Sidney* (believed to have been written 1610–12) represented a final despairing attempt to hold the consensus together.[15] L. B. Wright as usual went straight to the point about this great divide in English literature: 'The ridicule that formal critics lavished upon popular writers increased rather than diminished in the seventeenth century as the differentiation in literary taste as well as in social structure became more clearly marked.'[16]

Protestant propagandist prose had, in Cranmer's words, to be 'so plain, that the least child . . . in the town may understand thee.' The way to write well, Roger Ascham said in 1545, was 'to speak as the common people do, to think as wise men do.' Nicholas Udall attacked the high style: 'special regard [should] be had to the rude and unlettered people.' Latimer practised as well as preached this. There was ideological resistance to what were regarded as alien affectations in style. Ulpian Fulwell in 1575 said he could not 'interlace my phrases with Italian terms nor powder my style with French, English or inkhorn rhetoric . . . to feed the dainty ears of

[13] Gregory Smith, i. 196; King, *Reformation Literature*, 18, 342, 346, 431, 446–8.
[14] Norbrook, *Poetry and Politics*, 223.
[15] Cf. my *Writing and Revolution in Seventeenth Century England* (Brighton, 1985), 13–14, 41. I have argued the case at greater length in my *Intellectual Origins of the English Revolution* (Oxford UP, 1965), 7–13.   [16] Wright, *Middle-Class Culture*, 95.

delicate yonkers. And as I cannot, so if I could I would not.'[17] It was a defiance that Bunyan was often to echo. Insistence on plain native English became a Puritan commonplace.

Under Elizabeth popular prose reached its peak with the witty and fiercely satirical pamphlets of Martin Marprelate, writing in the Edwardian tradition, and claiming kinship with Piers Plowman. He defended himself against the charge of writing frivolously on serious subjects, as Bunyan was to do in his introductory poem to *The Pilgrim's Progress*. 'Jesting is lawful by circumstances, even in the greatest matters.' Marprelate brought Puritanism into the market-place: 'the very women and shop-keepers' discussed his pamphlets, an Italian visitor said. By the Marprelate tracts, Bishop Bancroft complained, 'the interest of the people in kingdoms is greatly advanced'.[18] Divisions in Elizabethan society were thus reflected in and influenced by developments in literature. The underground Marprelate press was suppressed. A sporadic radical and satirical trend continued in the witty writings of Thomas Scott and John Bastwick: but the former were produced in exile and smuggled into England: the latter led to Bastwick's ears being slit, to a stiff fine, and life imprisonment until the Long Parliament released him. Others refrained from publishing until the press was set free. John Everard's sermons, which in style help to bridge the gap between Marprelate and Richard Overton, were published only in the freedom from censorship established after he died in 1641.

Something of the Edwardian tradition survived in Puritan writers who aimed at a popular audience – Perkins, Dent, Bayly, Bernard. These men deliberately chose a plain and simple style, which differentiated them from court and university wits. The preacher must conceal his learning and human wisdom, Perkins advised. Perkins and John Preston made frequent use of dialogue, in prose and verse, to give their writings immediacy and punch,[19] and also perhaps to avoid committing themselves to risky views and so falling foul of the censor. Spenser, Ralegh, Roger Williams,

---

[17] King, *Reformation Literature*, 139–42; Wright, *Middle-Class Culture*, 329.

[18] Norbrook, *Poetry and Politics*, 63; my *Writing and Revolution*, 77, 92; Marprelate, *Hay any worke for Cooper* (1589), 4. I cite from the Scolar Press reprint (Leeds, 1967).

[19] Perkins, *Works*, ii. 470–3; cf. a ballad cited by Midgley in his Introduction to *Poems*, p. xxxii. The ob-sol style of the Puritan preachers moved towards dialogue: Perkins, Dent, and Preston often used it.

Samuel Hartlib, and James Harrington may all have used dialogue for this reason. Sidney found allegory useful as a defence against censorship. Even Puttenham observed that eclogues, 'under the veil of homely persons, and in rude speeches, . . . insinuate and glance at greater matters' which 'it might be unsafe to mention'. Spenserian poets – Browne, the Fletchers, Wither, and Milton – made the same use of allegory.[20]

Wright drew attention to the importance of cheap chap-books which 'provided the populace with a literature of escape'. His intuition has been confirmed by the researches of Margaret Spufford. From Bunyan's youth, if not earlier, expanding literacy built up a new market which an explosion of chap-books, from the revolutionary decades onwards, tried to meet.[21] Popular prose, whether on the stage, from the pulpit, or in chap-books, was English *as spoken*, not the literary compositions of a Hooker, a Donne, or a Milton. Popular prose reproduced what men and women said in the market-place. Interregnum broadsides and pamphlets were read aloud to illiterate audiences in alehouses and in the army.

The contrast between plain and ornate prose is usually considered in relation to sermon styles: the Puritan simple mode against the High Anglican court and academic mode of Bishop Andrewes and Dean Donne. But there were other types of plain prose. The navigators whom Hakluyt reprinted did not know whether they were writing Senecan or Ciceronian prose; informal letter-writers wrote as they spoke. Thomas Deloney in 1598 echoed early protestant propagandists when he promised 'a quiet and plain discourse', not 'curiously penned with picked words or chosen phrases', such as courtiers and scholars affect.[22] In comedies the lower classes and fools were given plain prose. Drama managed to incorporate popular prose, thanks perhaps to its dependence on gate takings. There was no Puttenham of the drama as it shook off its popular origins.

Puttenham thought that the best prose should incorporate that of the court and the City of London. But the City proved an

---

[20] Gregory Smith, ii. 40; my *Writing and Revolution*, 54–5.
[21] Wright, *Middle-Class Culture*, 376; M. Spufford, *Small Books and Pleasant Histories: Popular Fiction and its Readership in Seventeenth-Century England* (1981), ch. 4.
[22] Deloney, *The Gentle Craft*, Pt. II (1598), 174 (repr. 1639); cf. Gervase Markham, epigraph to this chapter.

unreliable ally for the monarchy. Between 1640 and 1660 there was no court, and prose flourished. Sprat after the restoration made the concession of advocating artisans' prose. Prose writing became less of a formal art. Dryden tried to bring back the court as arbiter of polite conversational tone, but by then utilitarian, scientific prose had established itself. London speech had conquered regional dialects as the London market had conquered England. After 1660 the ornate prose style was as dead as Laudian ceremonial in the church. Antiquarians can still find examples of either in remote country parishes, and there was an attempted revival under Charles II. But it was no longer a living tradition.

As England moved into civil war both sides had to appeal to a wide (and new) public opinion; to do this effectively styles had to be unadorned, direct, and homely. A writer like Richard Overton, who had things to say which were previously unpublishable, picked up the illegal radical tradition. He wrote at least six influential tracts over the names of Martin Marpriest, Martin Marprelate Junior, Martin Claw-Clergy, and was probably responsible for the republication of many of the Marprelate tracts in 1641. Overton specialized in dialogue, as did another Leveller, William Walwyn. Both wrote extremely wittily in an irreverent style that could appeal at all levels. Even a royalist pamphleteer like John Berkenhead adopted the new popular style. The closing of the theatres in 1642 forced a number of writers for the popular stage (of whom Overton was probably one) to turn to journalism, and this reinforced the use of racy and disrespectful dialogue.[23]

Charles I was no less horrified than Bishop Bancroft had been fifty years earlier at the publication of tracts on the mysteries of state, a subject which both believed should be concealed from the vulgar. When in November 1641 the House of Commons printed the Grand Remonstrance, a statement of its case against the King, Charles exclaimed, 'We are many times amazed to consider by what eyes these things are seen, and by what ears they are heard.' For the first time in English history ordinary people could read

[23] Marie Gimelfarb-Brack, Liberté, Égalité, Fraternité, Justice! La Vie et l'œuvre de Richard Overton, Niveleur (Berne, 1979), Pt. III; P. W. Thomas, Sir John Berkenhead, 1617–1679: A Royalist Career in Politics and Polemics (Oxford UP, 1969); Margot Heinemann, Puritanism and Theatre: Thomas Middleton and Opposition Drama under the Early Stuarts (Cambridge UP, 1980), ch. 13; Martin Butler, Theatre and Crisis, 1632–1642 (Cambridge UP, 1984), ch. 8.

about the government of their country: scurrilous verses about Archbishop Laud were accompanied by irreverent caricatures. The King's nephew, Prince Rupert, Duke of Cumberland, was referred to in print as Prince Robber, Duke of Plunderland.[24] There was insatiable curiosity for such novel material. But the demand for reading matter was not merely for news and propaganda, or religious controversy: it was also for entertainment. The sale of popular chap-books rocketed during the revolutionary decades. Many dealt with religious matters: but they also specialized in romances, versions of traditional stories adapted for popular consumption, with giants, knights errant and fair ladies, duels and enchantments; with ballads, chap-books almost certainly provided, apart from the Bible, the main reading for the middling sort and for those of the lower classes who were literate — as they did for Bunyan before his conversion. This was the public by which Bunyan's allegories were devoured.

The Revolution brought a revival of printed popular verse as well as of prose. Broadside ballads proliferated: newsbooks had verse headings. Verse was occasionally used in prose pamphlets by Winstanley, Coppe, Edward Burrough, and Roger Crab. The Digger poet Robert Coster published *A Mite Cast into the Common Treasury*, and there were unpublished Ranter poems. Ranters sang blasphemous songs to the well-known tunes of metrical psalms.[25] But after 1660 popular verse, like popular prose, came to be regarded as *socially* inferior. Sternhold and Hopkins were a bad joke in polite circles.

Linguistic Anglo-Saxonism played its part in stylistic controversies. There was opposition to the importation of foreign words, and Spenser deliberately used archaisms. Richard Verstegan boasted that the Normans 'could not conquer the English language as they did the land'. Sir Edward Coke, in a work which Charles I would not allow to be published, said, 'We would derive from the Conqueror as little as we could.' John Hare and others

---

[24] J. Nalson, *An Impartial Collection of the Great Affairs of State* (1682), ii. 747–8; my *Writing and Revolution*, 86.

[25] Coster's poems are reprinted in *The Works of Gerrard Winstanley*, ed. G. H. Sabine (Cornell UP, 1941), 655–61; Anne Laurence, 'Two Ranter Poems', *Review of English Studies*, NS 31 (1980), 56–9; [Anon.], *Strange Newes From the Old-Bayly* (1651), 2–3. For Burrough see his 'To the Reader', in George Fox's *The Great Mistery of the Great Whore Unfolded* (1659), sig. (d. 2); and for Crab my *Puritanism and Revolution* (Penguin edn.), 309–10.

demanded that the laws should be in English, and that the language should be purged of gallicisms.[26]

The new popular prose came of age in the 1640s and 1650s with Overton, Walwyn, John Warr, and Winstanley, with the Ranters Abiezer Coppe and Lawrence Clarkson, with the anonymous *Light Shining in Buckinghamshire* pamphlets (1648–9) and *Tyranipocrit Discovered* (1649), and with early Quakers. Winstanley specialized in vivid and unexpected epigrams: 'These men make themselves ministers as a man teaches birds to speak'; 'these great ones are too stately houses for Christ to dwell in; he takes up his abode in a manger.'[27] He and George Fox perfected what we may call 'rural prose', permeated with images drawn from the sights, sounds, smells, and activities of the countryside. Something of this re-appears in Bunyan. But he was not uninfluenced by the harder urban wit of Overton and Walwyn, Coppe and Clarkson. The vitality of the 'bad' characters in *Grace Abounding*, *The Pilgrim's Progress*, *The Holy War*, and especially *Mr. Badman*, owes something to Leveller and Ranter writings. In the years without censorship a new reading public had been created among the middling and meaner sort; after 1660 it could no more be suppressed than could dissent. Bunyan met its demands because he was heir to all these rich traditions of popular prose and poetry.

In this book I usually quote Bunyan's own words rather than summarizing them. Familiarity with his style contributes to our understanding of his personality. Bunyan had to choose his words with care, and we should read them with appreciation of the problems he had to face. Teasing his meaning out of layers of irony, Biblical allusion, and metaphor is a dangerous game, and one object of quoting Bunyan lavishly is to involve the reader in my interpretations rather than impose them on him or her. Bunyan's meaning will elude us if we attribute to him the simple assumptions of Victorian piety. Bunyan was not a simple man, and he lived in a difficult age.

[26] Verstegan, *Restitution of Decayed Intelligence* (1605), 222; Coke, *II Institutes* (1642), 745; *III Institutes* (1644), Proeme, sig. B 2v (the last three parts of the *Institutes* were published by order of the House of Commons); Hare, *St. Edward's Ghost, or Anti-Normanism* (1647), 13–22. See my 'The Norman Yoke', *Puritanism and Revolution*, ch. 3.

[27] See Winstanley, *The Law of Freedom and Other Writings* (Cambridge UP, 1983), 59–66.

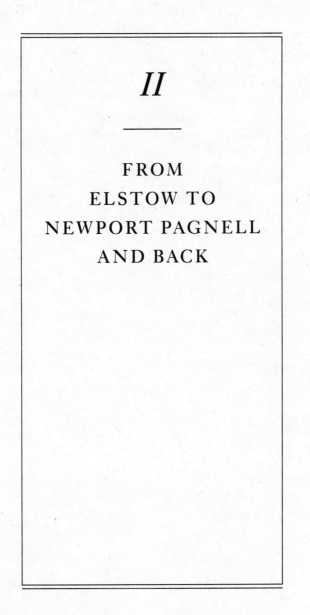

II

FROM
ELSTOW TO
NEWPORT PAGNELL
AND BACK

4. The Bunyans

My father's house being of that rank that is meanest and most
despised of all the families in the land.   BUNYAN[1]

BUNYANS had lived in and around Elstow, just south of
Bedford on the London road, since at least the twelfth century.
Early forms of the name suggest a French origin. It is ironical that
John Bunyan, whose prose is often praised for its Anglo-Saxon
purity, may descend from ancestors who came over with the
Conqueror. Perhaps they were employees of the wealthy nunnery
of Elstow, founded soon after the Conquest.[2]

But the family into which John Bunyan was born was no
different from any other smallholding family. His ancestors were
selling bits and pieces of land in the reigns of Henry VIII and
Elizabeth, until most of it had gone. Thomas Bunyan, John's great-
great-grandfather, was described as a 'victualler, common brewer
of beer' in 1542; he and his wife were many times fined for
infringing the assizes of beer and of bread. Under Mary I Thomas
Bunyan, with other Elstow villagers, was summoned before the
Privy Council for some unspecified offence: perhaps he was
already a protestant? John's grandfather, also Thomas, described
himself as a 'brazier' and 'petty chapman'. He was in trouble with
the ecclesiastical officials in 1617 for calling the churchwardens
liars. He sold more land, bringing the family holding down to nine
acres. When he died in 1641 he seems to have had little to leave
except his cottage; he bequeathed 6d to John. But at least he made a
will, as the very poor did not, and he made a gentleman his
executor. He signed with a mark.[3]

Bunyan's own father, also called Thomas, lived from 1603 to
1676. He was so poor that his one-hearthed house was exempt

[1] *GA*, 5.
[2] *VCH Bedfordshire*, iii. 279.
[3] F. A. Page-Turner, *Ancient Bedfordshire Deeds*, ii, *Deeds Relating to Elstow*, PBHRS
4 (1917), 237–42; Brown, 22–4, 27–9; S. R. Wigram, *Chronicles of the Abbey of Elstow*
(1885), 159; F. G. Emmison, *Bedfordshire Parish Records* (typescript in Bodleian
Library), i, *passim*; Joyce Godber, *John Bunyan of Bedfordshire* (Bedfordshire County
Council, 1972), 2.

from the hearth tax in 1673–4.[4] Bunyan's male ancestors were long-lived. Women's life-expectancy was much less. Bunyan's grandfather had four wives, his father three, Bunyan himself two. At least four of his grandfather's children died in infancy, as did Bunyan's brother Charles. John Bunyan's mother, an Elstow girl, was his father's second wife. Their son was always inclined to make the most of his lowly origins, and he may have exaggerated in the passage quoted as epigraph to this chapter. But his was clearly a humble background. Bunyan's father also made a will, which he too signed with a mark, presumably because he could not write. But his parents sent John 'to school to learn both to read and write'. He succeeded 'according to the rate of other poor men's children'. He later jeered at 'boys that go to the Latin school' and 'learn till they have learned the grounds of their grammar, and then they go home and forget all.'[5]

Bunyan's father does not seem to have been a Puritan. John was impressed when his first wife told him what a godly man her father was, how strict and holy his life. Whereas, Bunyan hints, his own father did not 'learn me to speak without this wicked way of swearing'. In 1663, when his father was still alive, he reflected 'how happy a thing it would be, if God should use a child to beget his father to the faith.' Bunyan himself claims to have had in his youth few equals for 'cursing, swearing, lying and blaspheming'. The fact that he had nightmares about hell when he was nine or ten years old may have been due to the eloquence of the Vicar of Elstow. Christopher Hall, who succeeded as Vicar in 1639, does not seem to have been a convinced Puritan: he continued to use the traditional vestments after 1640. The fact that he christened his son Oliver may signify approval of Cromwell, or it may be evidence of the adaptability which enabled Hall to retain his living through all vicissitudes until at least 1664.[6]

Until the reformation the village of Elstow had been dominated by its well-endowed nunnery, whose last occupants were buried in Bedford in 1557 and 1558. By Bunyan's time a manor-house had been built in the village, from the material of the convent, by

---

[4] Brown, 33, 293. Twenty-five of Elstow's sixty-one houses had only one hearth, eighteen had two, eight had three, and the remaining ten from four to seventeen each (ibid. 33).

[5] GA, 5; *Israel's Hope Encouraged* (posthumous), Offor, i. 618; Brown, 293.

[6] GA, 8; Brown, 43, 56–7.

Thomas Hillersden. His early death left his son a minor during the civil war. So Bunyan lacked first-hand contact with the sort of 'little gentlemen' whose 'pets' he was to deride later. Elstow also had its own fair, which lasted for three days in May and brought customers from far away. Vanity Fair in *The Pilgrim's Progress* suggests that it made a considerable impression on the young John. And brewing was a sufficiently important occupation in the village for Elstow brewers to petition in 1638 for freedom from recently imposed restrictions. In return they offered to pay 20*s* apiece.[7] This was a good instance of niggling (and expensive) interference with local economic life which helps to explain why in 1640 the government had no reserves of popular support to fall back on.

Before 1640 Bedfordshire was a relatively isolated agricultural county, and Elstow was still an open-field strip-cultivated village. Bedford had a population of around 2,000. It was to become important as the centre of a system of water communications which supplied the county with coal, salt, iron, wine, corn, and other consumer goods. On the day Bunyan was baptized in 1628 the Bedford Council went eagerly on record in favour of a scheme for making the river Ouse navigable to the sea. But it was not till the year of his death that the project was finally completed, to the town's great economic advantage.[8] Lace was the town's principal manufacture, introduced by Huguenot refugees in Elizabeth's reign.

Bedford was a sleepy country town, cut off by the bad roads which upset even the indefatigable Celia Fiennes when she rode them at the end of the century. From 1637 there was a weekly carrier, who took the century's best-known letters from Dorothy Osborne to her future husband Sir William Temple. Not until 1678 was there a London to Bedford post, running three times a week. But in 1642 Bedford's slumbers were sharply interrupted by the civil war, the marching and garrisoning of armies. There were skirmishes on the bridge in 1643 and in August 1645, two months after Oliver Cromwell had passed through with 600 horse and

[7] Brown, 18; D. and S. Lysons, *Magna Britannia* for Bedfordshire (1978), 52; *VCH Bedfordshire*, iii. 279–81; Godber, *John Bunyan*, 2.

[8] Godber, *The Story of Bedford: An Outline History* (Luton, 1978), 64–5, 70, 79–81, 84; ead., *History of Bedfordshire, 1066–1888* (Bedfordshire County Council, 1969), 259.

dragoons, which he stabled in St John's church.[9] Regular contact with London, and the general mobility of the revolutionary decades, must have transformed the area's consciousness of a wider world. This too was part of Bunyan's youthful experience.

[9] *VCH Bedfordshire*, iii. 4; Lysons, *Magna Britannia*, 51; Brown, 3; Godber, *History of Bedfordshire*, 257, 249, 262; ead., *The Story of Bedford*, 67; C. Morris (ed.), *The Journeys of Celia Fiennes* (1947), 332, 339–40.

5. In the Army

Being now in the Army, where wickedness abounded.

ANON[1]

. . . The strange wild faith of its plebeian rout,
Who sooner will believe what soldiers preach
Than what ev'n angels or apostles teach.

JOSEPH BEAUMONT[2]

i. Newport Pagnell

BUNYAN joined the Parliamentary army not later than November 1644. Whether he was conscripted or volunteered, his willingness to go may have been affected by his father's hasty remarriage, shortly after the death of John Bunyan's mother in June 1644. This marriage was not recorded in the parish register, and we do not know its exact date. The pious John Brown gives both August 1644 and March 1644 (1645 new style). Since a son was born in May 1645, August may have seemed the latest possible date to him. Remarriage was taken for granted in the seventeenth century, but whether the son was conceived in wedlock or not, the speed with which his father forgot John's mother may not have pleased the adolescent boy. There are other signs, in addition to Bunyan's silence about his father, that they may not have seen eye to eye. The short-lived son born in May 1645 was christened Charles: surely a provocative gesture of loyalty when John was in arms against King Charles?[3]

Bunyan was posted to Colonel Richard Cokayne's company in Newport Pagnell. Newport was on the frontier of Parliament's Eastern Association, and had changed hands between royalists and Parliamentarians more than once during the first two years of war. Bedfordshire contributed more than any other county in the Eastern Association to the maintenance of Newport's garrison, and provided most of its conscript troops. Cokayne was himself a Bedfordshire man; a member of his family was later to be a

---

[1] *An Account of the Life and Actions of John Bunyan* (1692).

[2] *Psyche: Or Loves Mystery* (1648), in *Complete Poems*, ed. A. B. Grosart (1880), ii. 67.

[3] Brown, 36, and pedigree opposite p. 20.

religious associate of Bunyan's. But by 1644 the fighting had moved away from the Midlands, and it is doubtful whether Bunyan saw much military action. His only wartime anecdotes are second-hand—'I heard once a story from a soldier . . .'; 'When I was a soldier . . . one of the company desired to go in my room' and was killed. But in *The Holy War*, published thirty-five years later, he took obvious pleasure in describing military exercises and manœuvres. In the posthumous *House of the Forest of Lebanon* he even depicts the Trinity in military formation.[4] He does not seem to have disliked the army as such.

The Parliamentary victory at Naseby in June 1645 virtually ended the war; but more than two years elapsed before Bunyan was demobilized. In August 1646 Parliament ordered the defence works at Newport Pagnell to be slighted (i.e. dismantled), and the garrison employed in Ireland. Bunyan appears to have volunteered for service in Ireland, possibly out of hostility to papist Irish rebels, possibly out of sheer boredom, possibly because it seemed to offer the only prospect of getting any of his arrears of pay. Some said that officers made men drunk before recruiting them.[5] Bunyan got as far as Chester, but then plans were changed, and his regiment was ordered to be demobilized on 21 July 1647. He came back to Elstow.

Bunyan at 19 was a very different young man from the one who might have grown up in a country village in peacetime. The Parliamentary army—like British armies in 1918–19 and 1945–6 —was rapidly radicalized in a period when there was little to do but talk. In nearby London there was in these years an unprecedented ferment of radical discussion. In 1644 Milton in *Areopagitica* hailed 'all this free writing and free speaking' that had taken place since Parliament had 'enfranchised, enlarged and lifted up our apprehensions degrees above themselves'. So long as men could remember, ordinary people had been totally excluded from politics; they existed only to be ruled, as an Elizabethan secretary of state had insisted.[6] But the urgent needs of recruitment propa-

---

[4] H. Roundell, 'The Garrison of Newport Pagnell During the Civil War', *Records of Bucks.*, ii. (1870), 211; Brown, 49; *The Jerusalem Sinner Saved* (posthumous), MW xi. 34; *GA*, 8; Offor, iii. 520.

[5] Brown, 47–8; C. H. Firth and G. Davies, *Regimental History of Cromwell's Army* (Oxford UP, 1940), i. 350–1.

[6] *MCPW*, ii. 559; Sir T. Smith, *The Commonwealth of England*, ed. I. Alston (1906), Bk. I, ch. 24.

ganda, and the deliberate encouragement of free discussion by commanders like Oliver Cromwell, plus the fluid political situation as the war came to an end, released an avalanche of political speculation.

By 1645 the Self-Denying Ordinance had excluded peers and most MPs from the military commands which they traditionally expected, and the New Model Army had won the war for Parliament. In London, Lilburne, Walwyn, and Overton, leaders of the future Leveller party, were agitating for a republic, a wide extension of the Parliamentary franchise, and extensive social and legal reforms. In April 1647 it was said that in the Army 'Lilburne's books are quoted . . . as statute law.' Two months before Bunyan left the army, the New Model mutinied; at the beginning of June representatives of the rank and file seized the King in defiance of Parliament and ignoring their own higher command. At a solemn rendezvous on 14 July 1647 the power of the lower ranks was confirmed by the setting up of an Army Council in which representatives of junior officers and privates sat side by side with the commanding generals. On 29 July the Army marched on London to take effective control.[7] At the end of October, in the famous Putney Debates, the Army Council discussed just how democratic the future constitution of England should be. Bunyan must have been apprised of these unprecedented happenings.

Coming events cast their shadows over Newport Pagnell, where the rank and file had their own reason for being restless. As early as January 1643 the garrison—like other units of the Parliamentary army—was in dire financial straits. Pay for officers and men was fourteen weeks in arrear, and nothing was coming in. Men pawned their clothes to buy food. In some units there was only one pair of breeches between two men; when one man was wearing them the other had perforce to stay in bed. In such circumstances officers had little control.[8] Unpaid soldiers were deserting *en masse*, taking their horses and arms with them; some of those who remained refused to fight and terrorized the countryside. In December 1644

---

[7] S. R. Gardiner, *History of the Great Civil War* (1893), iii. 237; J. Lindsay, *John Bunyan: Maker of Myths* (1937), 25; *VCH Bedfordshire*, ii. 51–3; A. Woolrych, *Soldiers and Statesmen: The General Council of the Army and its Debates, 1647–1648* (Oxford UP, 1987), 63. I use a capital A for Army only when referring to the New Model Army.
[8] *The Letter-Books 1644–1645 of Sir Samuel Luke*, ed. H. G. Tibbutt (1963), 122, 602; cf. 616.

deserters were threatened with hanging; next month Parliament passed a special ordinance proclaiming martial law in Newport Pagnell and Aylesbury. This did not prevent more than half the men pressed in 1645 from deserting.[9] In April of that year soldiers on the verge of mutiny clamoured that they lacked not only uniforms but also powder and bullets. They feared that the local population, overburdened by free quarter, might rise against them. Richard Cokayne, Bunyan's commanding officer, thought there would have been a mutiny if money had not arrived in August 1645. Sir Samuel Luke, commander of the garrison, was equally alarmed. In September soldiers from the garrison were helping themselves to deer from Lord Bruce's park, near Newport Pagnell.[10]

The Luke family had been well known in Bedford for over a century. In 1597 an Oliver Luke was MP for the town. Sir Samuel lived only four miles away, and was a burgess and JP of the town. In 1640 he was elected its MP. (Bedford had a wider franchise than most towns: all adult male inhabitants were entitled to vote). Since elections to both the Short and the Long Parliaments in 1640 were disputed we have much information about them. In both contests Luke was elected in preference to the court candidate, who in April objected to the fact that seven labourers, some servants, and a cottager were among the more than 600 voters: eighty received some form of charity. Luke was clearly the popular candidate: he had the support of nonconformists, including at least seven future members of the congregation which Bunyan was to join.[11] Brown suggested that Bunyan's uncle Edward was confidential servant to Luke's father, Sir Oliver. Sir Samuel commanded a troop of horse at the battle of Edgehill in 1642. After the recapture of Newport Pagnell from the royalists in October 1643 the Earl of Essex appointed Luke its Governor. Its fortifications were strengthened, the money appropriately coming from fines on two judges who had

[9] Luke, *Letter-Books*, 258, 413, 422, 548; *The Journal of Sir Samuel Luke*, ed. I.G.Philip, Oxfordshire Record Soc. (1950), i. 47–8; *The Civil War Papers of Sir William Boteler, 1642–1655*, ed. G. H. Fowler, PBHRS 18 (1936), 22–3, 28. The royalist army was said to be in no better state (Luke, *Journal*, loc. cit.).

[10] Luke, *Letter-Books*, 514–15, 110, 304; Roundell, 'Garrison of Newport Pagnell', 307–9, 369; Fowler, *Sir William Boteler*, 24.

[11] Godber, *The Story of Bedford*, 48, 55; D. Hirst, *The Representative of the People? Voters and Voting in England Under the Early Stuarts* (Cambridge UP, 1975), 98–100, 123–4.

voted against Hampden in the Ship Money case. Luke was one of Essex's warmest friends and political supporters; he became Scoutmaster-General to Essex's army.[12]

Luke was as alarmed by sectaries in and around his garrison as by incipient mutiny. When he suppressed their meetings in the town, they met two or three times a week 'not far off'. One conventicle in Newport itself was attended by a captain at whose social origins Luke sneered: 'such a villain, formerly a silk-weaver', who refused on conscientious grounds to take the Solemn League and Covenant. In March 1645 Robert Nicholls of Potton was discharged from the garrison 'for disaffection to the service and perverseness to all religious exercises.' Luke's continued complaints of the danger from sectaries met with no response from London, and he became increasingly hysterical. It was, he told his father, 'far easier to breed people up to wickedness than to godliness, especially when under profession of the latter they may with allowance practice the former.'[13]

Sir Samuel did his best. In October 1644 there were seven divines in Newport Pagnell, two sermons every Sunday, another every Thursday. Each morning before changing the guard there were prayers and a chapter of the Bible read. Yet all to no avail. Writing to Cornelius Holland, MP for New Windsor, Luke reported that in Newport Pagnell 'women can be delivered of children without knowing men (if they belie not themselves) and men and women can take one another's words and lie together and insist it not to be adultery.' 'If I stay here', he continued with growing excitement, 'I must have liberty to free the town of [sectaries] lest God in his wrath deal with them as he did with Sodom and Gomorrah.'[14] Did Luke merely have different lower-class matrimonial customs forced on his attention, or were antinomian sectaries of the type later known as Ranters at work?

On 26 June 1645 Luke was deprived of his command under the Self-Denying Ordinance. He remained on duty for a couple of months and appears to have asked for a commission as captain of horse, but unsuccessfully. Many were Luke's gibes at the lower-

[12] Brown, 41; *VCH Bedfordshire*, ii. 44–6; Roundell, 'Garrison', 230; Luke, *Journal*, vi–vii.
[13] Luke, *Letter-Books*, 42–3, 49, 77, 193, 215.
[14] F. W. Bull, *History of Newport Pagnell* (Kettering, 1900), 165; Luke, *Letter-Books*, 192.

class officers of the New Model. In his own regiment, he boasted, 'I have not chosen beggars . . . to places of command, but such as can with their credits sustain their companies three months from mutinies.' This perfectly makes the case for the creation of the New Model, in which 'plain russet-coated captains' were promoted for military ability and devotion to the cause rather than for birth. It also makes the case for the financial reorganization which was the necessary condition for the regular pay which 'this poor despised army', as Rushworth had called it just before Naseby, was to receive.[15]

We hear every now and then of radical preachers visiting Newport Pagnell. The near-Ranter William Erbery was there, Thomas Edwards tells us, probably late in 1645.[16] Another notorious figure, Captain Paul Hobson, was passing through Newport Pagnell with Captain Beaumont on 15 June 1645 when Luke ordered a church parade to celebrate the Parliamentary victory at Naseby the previous day. Hobson organized a different sort of celebration at an Independent meeting, where he 'preached openly'. This meeting, Luke complained, 'left the church empty'. He had 'tailor Hobson' and 'druggist Beaumont' arrested and sent them to Fairfax for punishment. Luke declared that they were 'Anabaptists, who cannot consent with magistracy or government', though he also denounced Hobson as an atheist. To Luke's fury, Fairfax insisted on their release, and on the cashiering of the officers who had treated them rather roughly *en route* to him. (Hobson was a captain in Fairfax's own regiment, which was 'one of the chiefest praying and preaching regiments in the army'.) Provocatively, Hobson returned to Newport Pagnell and preached again.[17]

Sir Samuel protested vainly to his kinsman Charles Fleetwood. Then, time expired on 26 June, he handed over to his second-in-

[15] Luke, *Letter-Books*, 264, 267, 274–5, 311, 317, 566, 571; cf. 279; Roundell, 'Garrison', 309.

[16] Edwards, *Gangraena*, Pt. I (1646), 78. My attention was drawn to this by the Alberta D.Phil. thesis by Aileen Ross, *Millenarianism in the Works of John Bunyan* (1986), 73, which I am grateful to her for allowing me to read. For Erbery see *WTUD*, 192–8.

[17] Luke, *Letter-Books*, 323–4, 328–9, 582–3; Roundell, 'Garrison', 357, 359; Edwards, *Gangraena*, i. 89–91. Edwards' sharp eye had spotted Beaumont too. Not only was he heretical himself, but his soldiers were alleged, with his approval, to have christened a horse 'Esau' in the parish church at Yakesly, Bucks. (*Gangraena*, iii. 18). This was a traditional form of plebeian irreverence, practised in Bedfordshire and elsewhere long before the civil war. Cf. pp. 25–6 above.

command, Richard Cokayne. Cokayne was lobbying hard to succeed Luke as Governor of Newport Pagnell, and he accepted that Fairfax's was 'a demand not to be denied'. But Luke was determined to make a test case of it. He had Hobson rearrested and sent to a Parliamentary committee in London. He wrote to his friends in Parliament. For his part Hobson threatened, or was alleged to have threatened, to 'make this business the leading case of the kingdom for all the godly party'. The Parliamentary committee released him; the period immediately following Naseby was no moment to challenge the New Model. Nor did Cokayne get Luke's job; on Fairfax's recommendation it went to Charles D'Oyley, who had distinguished himself at Naseby but in July 1647 was to side with the Presbyterians in Parliament against the Army.[18]

The incident is symbolic of the power and radicalism of the New Model. In 1648 the millenarian Mary Cary suggested that the day the Army marched forth corresponded to the resurrection of the Two Witnesses in Revelation—a portentous moment in the approach of the millennium. Oliver Cromwell's had been a lone voice when in 1644 he wrote to his commanding officer, 'The man is an Anabaptist? . . . Admit he be, shall that render him uncapable to serve the public?' This attitude had now been adopted by the Commander-in-Chief of the triumphant New Model Army. Luke's sneers at the social status of Hobson and Beaumont were typical of conservative resentment of the New Model,[19] whose social radicalism was from the start stressed by its enemies. Fairfax was the son of a peer, Cromwell a son of the younger branch of a great landed family; but the Army which they commanded was from the start committed to a quite novel radicalism.

Luke's day was over. The commander of the garrison of Newport Pagnell and Scoutmaster-General to Essex's army disappeared into civilian life. In December 1648 he was purged from the Long Parliament by Colonel Pride, and retired to cultivate his garden. He became 'a nice florist', who exchanged plants with the

---

[18] Luke, *Letter-Books*, 588, 622; Edwards, *Gangraena*, i. 90–1; cf. ii. 68; Firth and Davies, i. 46–7.

[19] My *Antichrist in Seventeenth-Century England* (Oxford UP, 1971), 107; *Writings and Speeches of Oliver Cromwell*, ed. W. C. Abbott (Harvard UP, 1937–47), i. 278; Luke, *Letter-Books*, 267, 269, 274–5, 279, 284, 311, 317, 320, 513, 566, 571. For radicalism in the New Model Army see Appendix.

royalist Dorothy Osborne. Luke took no part in public life until he was offered a militia command on the eve of the restoration.[20] He was elected to the Convention Parliament for Bedford in 1660. He enjoyed a perhaps unwelcome immortality as Sir Hudibras in Samuel Butler's poem. Luke died in 1670.

Newport Pagnell was then a hotbed of radical discussion, in which Bunyan almost certainly participated. In August 1646 there were stories of a mutiny. How did all this affect the young Bunyan? We can only guess. But there are some indications. Thirty-five years after Luke's horrified cries about parthenogenesis in Newport Pagnell, Bunyan was to recall hearing a man say 'when he was tempting a maid to commit uncleanness with him — it was in Oliver's days — that if she did prove with child' she should say, 'when you come before the judge, that you are with child by the Holy Ghost.'[21] It would seem an odd conversation for Bunyan to have overheard anywhere except in the army.

The Hobson affair must have been the talk of Newport Pagnell, and Bunyan would know of it. The fact that Hobson's hastily arranged rival meeting could leave Luke's official service in the parish church 'empty' tells us a lot about opinion among the army rank and file. Bunyan had many things to say later about the arrogant interference of 'little gentlemen' with the religious rights and liberties of ordinary Englishmen. Such political loyalties as Bunyan and his like later had were not to Parliament, still less to the Parliamentarian gentry, but rather to the Army which had guaranteed them freedom to meet, worship and organize. As Hobson's case had shown in 1645, and as Bunyan learnt from his own experience in 1660, the obstacle to this freedom was the gentry rather than the government; Hobson was alleged to have said in 1645 that when the Cavaliers were defeated it might be necessary to turn their arms against persecutors on the Parliamentarian side.[22]

Bunyan retained many friends in Newport Pagnell, including

[20] Roundell, 'Garrison', 361; *Letters from Dorothy Osborne to Sir William Temple*, ed. E. A. Parry (Wayfarers' Library, n.d.), 73.

[21] *The Diary of John Harington, MP, 1646–1653*, ed. Margaret F. Stieg, Somerset Record Soc. (1977), 33; *Mr. B.*, Offor, iii. 613. A Ranter lady was alleged to have claimed to be pregnant by the Holy Ghost. See Anon., *The Ranters Monster* (1652), quoted in J. G. Turner, *One Flesh: Paradisal Marriage and Sexual Relations in the Age of Milton* (Oxford UP, 1987), 84–5.

[22] Edwards, *Gangraena*, i. 90.

the bookseller who shared in printing his first three works. His
Bedford congregation later had close relations with John Gibbs's
church at Newport. Gibbs was vicar there until he was ejected in
October 1659 for not administering communion to all parishioners. In 1653 he joined Bunyan and others in signing a letter
welcoming the summoning of Barebone's Parliament. He contributed a preface to Bunyan's very class-conscious *A Few Sighs from
Hell*: Gibbs himself was accused of hostility to the gentry, and was
active in opposing the restoration. In August 1659 it was he who
rode up to London bringing the good news that the fugitive leader
of an ineffective royalist rising, Sir George Booth, had been
captured at Newport Pagnell in women's clothes. After the restoration Gibbs continued to minister to a congregation of 'inferior
tradesmen and mechanical people'. He was one of those whom the
Bedford church consulted in December 1660 when they had to
choose a successor to John Burton as pastor. Later Gibbs joined
Bunyan in Bedford jail.[23]

ii. Paul Hobson

Bunyan must have known of Hobson's exploits at Newport Pagnell. Hobson was a signatory of the Particular Baptists' Confession
of Faith in 1644. In December of that year he was denounced as a
heretic by Sion College, in the good company of John Milton,
Roger Williams, John Goodwin, and William Walwyn. Two years
later Edwards noted him as a dangerous sectary. Lawrence Clarkson the Ranter testified to the eloquence of Hobson's preaching:
and he was something of a connoisseur of the art. Indeed Clarkson
found Hobson so exciting on 'the in-comes and out-goes of God'
that he joined his company at Yarmouth. In 1647, to counter
charges of blasphemy, Hobson printed the Newport Pagnell
sermon that had got him into trouble. There are many passages in
it with which Bunyan would later have agreed. They only are fit to
declare Christ, Hobson said, who understand him from enjoy-
ment. It is like the distinction between studying foreign countries
on a globe and actually going to them. 'He and he only is fit to

[23] Tibbutt, *Minutes*, 31, 207; Brown, 133; Bull, *History of Newport Pagnell*, 138–40;
M. F. Hewett, 'John Gibbs, 1627–1699', *Baptist Quarterly*, NS 3 (1927), 317–20;
Tindall, 69, 104, 138.

declare truth whose spirit is crucified by the power of the truth.' A church exists for 'the exchanges of experience that may refresh the souls of each other'; 'external declarations about external administrations' are irrelevant to church membership.[24]

In his Newport Pagnell sermon Hobson spoke of the church as 'A Garden Inclosed', taking as his text Canticles 8: 13, 'which of all Scriptures is so full of the saints' glorious privileges in Christ.' The church is enclosed not just by a 'bare internal discipline' but also by 'the special love and power and sweetness of Christ, to secure them from the evil that is in the world.' Such a church could only be a small group: the Church of England with its parishes, by contrast, was no garden but 'a confused wilderness'. More special fruit grew in the enclosed garden, more care was taken of it by special watching; it gave 'sweet refreshings', and Christ took satisfaction and content in it. We shall find Bunyan developing this idea of the congregation as garden.[25]

Hobson concluded his sermon on an ominous note: 'our time is short, and oppositions increase, we not knowing how soon we may be called to suffer for truth.' Popish bishops under Queen Mary had persecuted protestants, who in their turn persecuted more radical reformers; 'and what if those that were more pure reformers than their persecutors should get power and persecute them that endeavour to walk more exactly than themselves?'[26] In a treatise published in 1645 or 1646, *Christ the Effect not the Cause of the Love of God*, Hobson argued that 'Christ came not to reconcile God to man but man to God.' 'The gospel . . . is life through the death of Christ. . . . Christ did not pay a ransom to love and so purchased it; but he being purchased by love was made able in the strength of that love to pay a ransom to a law.' If Bunyan read this tract after his conversion he may have noted some of these ideas. But he would have rejected Hobson's view that 'election and

[24] Edwards, *Gangraena*, i. 89–91, ii. 161, iii. 49–50; Clarkson, *The Lost sheep Found* (1660), 9–10; P. Hobson, *A Garden Inclosed: and Wisdom Justified only of her Children* (1817), 6–8, 17–18 (1st pub. 1647). For Hobson see *Biographical Dictionary of British Radicals in the Seventeenth Century*, ed. R. L. Greaves and R. Zaller, ii (Brighton, 1983), 95–7, and Greaves, *Saints and Rebels: Seven Nonconformists in Stuart England* (Mercer UP, 1985). Surprisingly, Hobson finds no place in *DNB*.

[25] Hobson, *A Garden Inclosed*, 5–7, 17–18, 20–30; cf. Bunyan, *The Barren Fig-tree* (1673), MW v. 20; *A Discourse of the House of God* (1688), in *Poems*, 278–90. See also *Christian Behaviour* (1663), MW iii. 10, 54, and pp. 91–2 below.

[26] Hobson, *A Garden Inclosed*, 49; *Wisdom Justified only of her Children*, 67.

reprobation ... are not to be preached', still more Hobson's repudiation of the doctrine of Christ's satisfaction.[27]

Bunyan would have found Hobson's ecumenism attractive. Those who limit their affections to 'such as are brought up to, or brought over to, the same form of worship or practice of ordinances with themselves ... have forgotten where they first met with God.' Hobson reminded Presbyterians, Independents, and 'those also which are falsely called Anabaptists' that 'the prodigal's father ran to meet him.'[28]

Hobson opposed the offer of the crown to Oliver Cromwell in 1657. After the restoration he had a spectacular career, plotting incessantly. In 1660 he fled to the Netherlands. On his return he was arrested in 1661. He was involved in the Yorkshire Plot of 1663 and was imprisoned again, without trial. He was released only in 1665, on condition that he emigrated. Flamboyant to the last, he was involved in a scandal: two women members of William Kiffin's congregation were disciplined for wanton conduct with Hobson and another man. Hobson died, still in England, in 1666. He may or may not have influenced Bunyan at a susceptible time in the mid-1640s. But he is a representative of the radical antinomian and ecumenical Particular Baptists whose thought always had its attractions for Bunyan: though he never fully identified himself with it.[29]

iii. Back to Elstow

Bunyan was in the army from at least November 1644 to July 1647. Two and a half years is a long time when one is in one's teens; the six years between demobilization and conversion — eighteen and a half to twenty-five — were even longer. And what years! In June 1647 Agitators from the New Model Army had seized the captive Charles I. As Bunyan was returning to Bedfordshire the GHQ of the Army was meeting at Bedford for discussions with the King at

[27] Hobson, *A Garden Inclosed*, 6–15; Greaves, *Saints and Rebels*, 136, 155.
[28] Hobson, *The Prodigals Entertainment with the Father Discovered* (1820), 23–4 (1st pub. 1652).
[29] Greaves, *Saints and Rebels*, 148–53; id. *Deliver Us from Evil* (Oxford UP, 1986), 95, 166, 182. In 1654 Hobson had acknowledged to the Hexham church 'his own evil committed in those days of wantonness' (*Records of the Churches of Christ Gathered at Fenstanton, Warboys and Hexham, 1644–1720*, ed. E. B. Underhill, Hanserd Knollys Soc. (1854), 356; cf. 352–72, *passim*).

Woburn. Then came the rendezvous of the Army, acceptance of the Declaration that 'we were no mere mercenary army' which justified a march on London. A few months later, when the General Council of the Army discussed the future constitution of England in Putney church, an Agitator, whom the shorthand scribe called simply 'Bedfordshire man', was swayed by only one imperative: to give 'away nothing from the people that is the people's right'.[30] He was probably not much older than Bunyan. There followed the second civil war, purges of Parliament, the trial and execution of the King, proclamation of the Commonwealth, abolition of the House of Lords; and then suppression of Army democracy and the Leveller party.

The radical discussions of the interregnum are essential for understanding *Grace Abounding*, and indeed many of Bunyan's writings. The total breakdown of authority in the 1640s made possible wide-ranging debates on religion, politics, and morals, and encouraged the most optimistic utopian hopes. Soldiers in Wallingford in 1643, according to Sir Samuel Luke, were said to believe 'that Christ shall come into the world and destroy King Charles.'[31] Anything might happen.

For a brief period in the 1640s, then, a clean break with the past must have seemed possible. Bacon had seen new prospects confronting humanity as the world was opened up to European trade and plunder; as the heavens were reinterpreted by Copernicus and Galileo; as printing made possible a wider diffusion of ideas. Human beings might at last be able to control their own destiny. Bacon's works were widely read in the 1640s and 1650s; the millenarian ideas of those who hoped to bring about Christ's kingdom on earth momentarily converged with the optimism of scientists who thought that within a generation or two nature could be brought under human control. 'All sorts of people dreamed of an Utopia and infinite liberty, especially in matters of religion,' wrote an ejected royalist divine.[32] Levellers wanted to

---

[30] *Puritanism and Liberty*, ed. A. S. P. Woodhouse (1938), 18.

[31] Luke, *Journal*, i. 76.

[32] C. Webster, *The Great Instauration: Science, Medicine and Reform, 1626–1660* (1975), *passim*; [R. Chestlin], *Persecutio Undecima* (1681), 4 (1st pub. 1648); G. E. Page, 'Baptist Churches in the Bedford Area', *Baptist Quarterly*, NS 14 (1951–2), 271; Sharrock, 13; Fox, *Journal*, ed. N. Penney (1901), i. 3; Clarkson, *The Lost sheep Found* (1660), 24.

establish political democracy and equality, Diggers to establish economic equality as well. Ranters and Diggers wanted to abolish priests and sin, in the interests of a new human equality.

The soldiers who returned to Bedfordshire in 1647 had therefore much political experience behind them. But so had those who had remained at home. Bedfordshire had its religious radicals. In 1643 there was a Baptist meeting in Bedford. There were petitions against tithes from the county in 1647, against tithes and copyhold in 1659. The General Baptist Henry Denne made a preaching tour of the county in or around 1644; so did Lawrence Clarkson at some later date. George Fox 'stayed awhile' at Newport Pagnell before June 1644. There were Digger colonies at the old radical centre of Dunstable, and at Wellingborough, both less than twenty miles from Bedford, and probably another at Husbands Bosworth, a few miles further across the Leicestershire border. Digger emissaries from Surrey visited Bedford on a propaganda mission in 1650, on their way from Dunstable to Newport Pagnell. It was near Dunstable that in October 1647 Paul Hobson's regiment mutinied and refused to march northwards, allegedly at the instigation of Agitators. Thomas Gataker speaks in 1655 of a Leveller insurrection in Bedfordshire, but I have found no other information about that.[33] There was Leveller activity in the neighbouring county of Buckinghamshire.

Soon after his return to Elstow Bunyan married, we do not know exactly when. We know virtually nothing about his first wife, not even her name. The marriage is not recorded in the Elstow parish register, and she does not seem to have been a local girl. Bunyan did not know her parents. He may have met her in the army, or on his progresses as a tinker. It is possible — though this is the merest speculation — that she was previously unknown to Bunyan's father and that he disapproved of the match. Bunyan's first daughter was baptized on 20 July 1650, suggesting that the marriage took place not later than October 1649, and so before he was 21. This is considerably earlier than demographers think he ought

[33] K. V. Thomas, 'Another Digger Broadside', *P. and P.* 42 (1969), 57–68; ed. G. H. Sabine (Cornell UP, 1941), *The Works of Gerrard Winstanley*, 440–1; O. Lutaud, *Winstanley, socialisme et christianisme sous Cromwell* (Paris, 1976), 453–4; 'The Tower of London Letter-Book of Sir Lewis Dyve, 1646–47', ed. H. G. Tibbutt, *PBHRS* 38 (1958), 94; Woolrych, *Soldiers and Statesmen*, 228–9, 257–8, 282; Gataker, *His Vindication of the Annotations by him published* (1653), 12.

statistically to have married. Assuming they are right, it is worth asking what reasons Bunyan might have had for early marriage.

He was a self-assertive, fully adult Parliamentarian when he returned in the summer of 1647 to the house of his father and his stepmother. The brother who had been christened 'Charles' was dead. 'The Prodigal's father ran out to meet him', Paul Hobson wrote in 1652.[34] Perhaps John's father was less welcoming. If there were any political strains in the Bunyan household, they would not be lessened during the first two years after John's demobilization, when the King was a prisoner in the hands of the Army, to be tried and executed in January 1649. So there could be reasons for Bunyan wanting to set up a separate household. His description of the poverty of himself and his wife (no doubt exaggerated) may suggest that his father had not helped him to establish his independence.

It must have been a come-down to return from the army and the great world to tinkering and Sunday tipcat on the village green. But to his Elstow acquaintances the demobilized John Bunyan would seem a very sophisticated and dashing young man. 'A brisk talker', he called himself, 'a great sin-breeder'. He appears to have taken the lead among a group of irreverent, sceptical youngsters, who could be called Ranters for want of a better word. He said later that he had 'infected all the youth of the town where I was born with all manner of youthful vanities.' His best friend was 'a most wicked creature for cursing, swearing and whoring.' Ultimately Bunyan shook him off and rebuked him, receiving the reply, 'What would the devil do for company if it were not for such as I am?' Bunyan admitted to being a great swearer himself, though he claimed to have been chaste after his marriage: he does not say which marriage. (His first wife died in 1658, and he married his second, Elizabeth, in 1659.) Bunyan had found the Ranter idea of perfectibility, which meant you could do what you would, seductive, 'I being but a young man, and my nature in its prime.' But the libertinism of the Ranters may have attracted him less than their political attitudes – Clarkson's denunciation of the rule of the gentry, Coppe's attack on the rich generally. Bunyan's account of his own desperate wickedness is no doubt exaggerated with the hindsight of conversion. But the scraps of conversation which he

[34] See p. 55 above.

records ring true. He went through phases of conventional piety which failed to satisfy him, and experienced long periods of 'a very great storm', in which his internal dialogue with Satan continued that with his former Ranter friends.[35]

Bunyan had economic as well as theological problems. He was not well off, and his first daughter, Mary, was blind. Was this some sort of punishment? he must have wondered, as Milton did about his blindness. Between 1649 and 1652 the whole power of the dominant groups in society had been mobilized against Levellers, Diggers, and Ranters, and it was clear that a clean break with the past was not politically possible. The radical moment was over; specious Ranter recantations showed the superficiality of their posturings. The great hopes of turning the world upside down, of elevating the poor above the rich, vanished. Bunyan, like rank-and-file Parliamentarian supporters generally, was left to come to terms with a world which in the 1650s was slowly returning to its traditional posture, with the gentry and the rich on top. There is no evidence that Bunyan had shared the hopes of the political radicals, though his continuing solidarity with the poor against the rich is noteworthy. But he had been for several years in a milieu where such ideas circulated; he cannot but have been affected by them. He went on arguing with Ranters to the end of his life. Bunyan lacked the prior commitment which held Milton faithful to his radical republicanism. But enough questions had been asked for it not to be easy to return to the old certainties and habits. 'What shall I do?' his pilgrim was to ask. 'What shall I do to be saved?'[36]

This may help to explain the virulence of Bunyan's early tracts against Quakers, when he was defending traditional securities of belief. But soon he had to defend the newly won *right* to organize publicly in sects, to *discuss* salvation in meetings and in print. The uncharted seas of unbelief and continuing scepticism and questioning, to which Ranters had pointed, were too dangerous and too socially unsettling. Such was the conclusion of men like Milton, John Owen, William Dell, and Hobson as well as of Marchamont Nedham and Francis Osborne. Who shall say they were wrong? It is in fact a silly question to ask. They were

[35] *The Jerusalem Sinner* (1688), MW xi. 36; *GA*, 11, 16–17, 31–2.
[36] *PP*, 8–9.

right because the dreams of Ranters were socially impossible, inchoate . . . dreams.

Yet traces of radical ideas continued to plague Bunyan long after he had finished settling accounts with the Quakers. They recur, as we shall see, in *The Pilgrim's Progress* and in *Mr. Badman*. He was to be damned as a Ranter himself. All this suggests that Ranters continued to exist not only in Bunyan's mind but also in the society around him.[37]

[37] See pp. 132, 192 below.

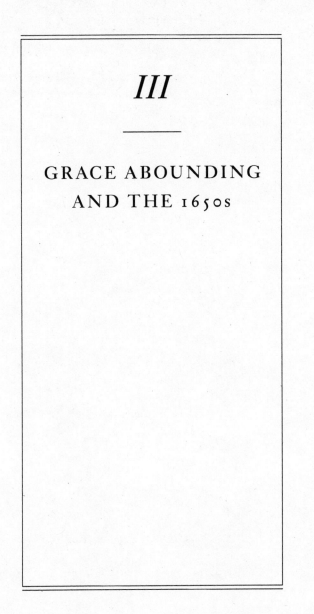

III

***

GRACE ABOUNDING
AND THE 1650s

6. *Grace Abounding to the Chief of Sinners*

Where sin, sore-wounding, doth oppress me
There grace abounding doth redress me.

JOHN DOWLAND[1]

Of sinners, I am the chief.

ABIEZER COPPE[2]

Until I came to the state of marriage, I was the very ringleader of
all the youths that kept me company in all manner of vices and
ungodliness. . . . In these days the thoughts of religion was very
grievous to me.   BUNYAN[3]

i. Spiritual Autobiography

GRACE ABOUNDING was not published until 1666, but
it must be discussed here because it tells us much about
Bunyan's spiritual development in the 1650s—as he saw it in
retrospect. *Grace Abounding* was written after the collapse of the
Commonwealth and the restoration of Charles II, after religious
toleration had been brutally ended and Bunyan himself had been
imprisoned. It is our principal source for the years between
Bunyan's return to Elstow in 1647 and his move to Bedford in
1655, when he was accepted into full membership of the Bedford
congregation. Even the assiduous John Brown found very little
other material relating to these years.

Grace Abounding is an unsatisfactory document for the biographer. It is a spiritual autobiography, describing the events which
led up to Bunyan's conversion. The chronology is at best imprecise, at worst chaotic. Any references to external events in
Bunyan's life during this period are quite accidental. We may
assume that after demobilization he worked with his father in
Elstow as a brazier, or tinker, until he set up on his own after his
marriage. The job would involve journeying round the countryside mending pots and pans.

---

[1] From the madrigal *A Pilgrim's Solace* (1612) in *English Madrigal Verse*, ed. E. H.
Fellowes (3rd edn., Oxford UP, 1967), 497.
[2] *Copps Return to the wayes of Truth* (1651), in *Ranter Writings from the Seventeenth
Century*, ed. N. Smith (1983), 134.   [3] *GA*, 7.

In *Grace Abounding* Bunyan says nothing about his military service. This may be due to caution. Since he was in prison as a subversive, it would have been imprudent to draw attention to his active participation in the army which had defeated Charles I. The only (neutral) reference to a military experience was added in the third edition, published between 1672 and 1674 when he was out of jail (xxxvii. 18). But there is also very little about his first marriage, except that his wife brought with her Arthur Dent's *The Plaine Mans Path-way to Heaven* and Lewis Bayly's *The Practice of Piety*. There is virtually no mention of his children, of his first wife's death, or of his remarriage. It is almost impossible to establish the sequence of events. In *The Pilgrim's Progress* Christian's journey does not follow a straight geographical or chronological line, but reflects his psychological states; so the narrative of *Grace Abounding* appears to jump backwards and forwards as it describes Bunyan's long battle with Satan.

Since W. Y. Tindall published his trail-blazing *John Bunyan, Mechanick Preacher*, in 1934 it has been accepted that the spiritual autobiography as a literary genre dates from around 1649. This is perhaps a little too precise, and may conceal an optical illusion. Anticipations of spiritual autobiographies can be found in diaries (spiritual balance sheets), prefaces to the collected writings of preachers, or biographical appendices to funeral sermons. The revolutionary decades saw the *publication* of this new genre.[4] Spiritual autobiographies of ordinary people could not have got into print before the breakdown of censorship and the establishment of effective religious toleration. Tawney, when asked about 'the sufferings of the peasantry in the sixteenth century', is said to have boomed back, 'The sufferings of the peasantry in the sixteenth century are due to the invention of printing.' The prevalence of a literature of despair and conversion during the English Revolution may be the result of unprecedented freedom of publication.

Members of the congregations which everywhere sprang up discussed one another's conversion experiences, and recorded them to help others: as congregations became settled, an account

---

[4] O. C. Watkins, *The Puritan Experience* (1972), 24–9. Cf. R. J. W. Evans, 'Calvinism in East Central Europe: Hungary and her Neighbours', in *International Calvinism, 1541–1715*, ed. M. Prestwich (Oxford UP, 1985), 189. Dr Evans tells me that spiritual autobiographies in Hungary date from after 1660 (personal communication).

of experience of grace was often required as a condition of full admission to the church. By 1651 the famous Hugh Peter — former New England minister, ex-Army chaplain — was calling for a collection of 'cases of conversion' to be printed.[5] There had been upper-class conversions earlier, naturally, which were sometimes recorded; but published discussions of the subject seem to occur only below the élite level. The novelty lay in sharing such experiences. There are no Laudian spiritual autobiographies. Despair leading to conversion was no doubt frequent, though rarely recorded, before 1640. We recall the two attempted suicides and ultimate conversion recounted by the London turner Nehemiah Wallington. If he had been born a little later he might have been tempted to publish some of the voluminous autobiographical writings which he composed from the 1620s onwards.[6]

A standard pattern for spiritual autobiographies soon took shape, but we should not therefore assume either that the saints copied from one another, or that their feelings became wholly conventional. In those critical times men and women had to face agonies of temptation and despair, as Bunyan did, alone. Knowledge that others had suffered the same devastating experience, and freedom to communicate and discuss, must have been a wonderful relief. What could be a more important subject than the experience of conversion? It became privileged as a rite of passage to elect status, and was therefore of intense interest to all potential saints. What more necessary than to be able to identify a 'true' conversion? It was only relatively late, in 1678, that Bunyan thought it necessary to warn against stereotypes of conversion. It was not even essential, he suggested, to roar aloud with the guilt of sin. 'If God will deal more gently with thee than with others of his children, grudge not at it.' The depth of the sense of sin proves nothing: witness Cain, Balaam, Judas.[7] Quakers were moderating their own external 'signs' and gestures at about the same time.

We are not therefore necessarily bound to accept everything in *Grace Abounding* as autobiographical truth. The object of the work is to convey a message. But the emotional intensity of the writing carries its own conviction:

---

[5] Peter, *Good Work for a Good Magistrate* (1651), 74–5.
[6] Watkins, *Puritan Experience*, 32–3, 99, and ch. 13, *passim*; P. S. Seaver, *Wallington's World: A Puritan Artisan in Seventeenth-Century London* (1985), *passim*.
[7] *Come, and Welcome* (1678), MW viii, 354–5; Talon, 27.

God did not play in convincing of me, the devil did not play in tempting of me, neither did I play when I sunk as into a bottomless pit, when the pangs of hell caught hold upon me; wherefore I may not play in my relating of them, but be plain and simple and lay down the thing as it was (3–4).

That perceptive critic Alick West pointed out that few books before *Grace Abounding* speak so energetically in the first person singular. Montaigne perhaps: but none addressed by a mechanic to his fellow artisans.[8]

Bunyan's primary object in writing *Grace Abounding* was pastoral. He aimed not to convert but to convince the elect that they were indeed saved, whatever their doubts and temptations. 'The Philistines understand me not.' The local touch was all-important for his purposes. 'Remember . . . how you sighed under every hedge for mercy. . . . Have you forgot the close, the milk-house, the stable, the barn and the like, where God did visit your soul?' (3) Intimations of grace occurred in normal daily life. 'One day, as I was travelling into the country. . . . At another time, as I sat by the fire in my house, and musing on my wretchedness . . .' (36). 'One morning, as I did lie in my bed . . .' (43). 'Once as I was walking to and fro in a good man's shop . . .' (52). 'One day, as I was in a meeting of God's people, full of sadness and terror . . .' (65). 'As I was passing in the field . . .' (72). It was when Bunyan was 'in the midst of a game at cat . . . just as I was about to strike it the second time, a voice did suddenly dart from heaven into my soul' (10; cf. 29, 58, 61, 81).

A powerful feature of Foxe's *Book of Martyrs* was its careful accuracy and attention to homely detail. It did not derogate from the dignity of the martyrs to portray them as ordinary lower-class Englishmen—like most of Foxe's readers. In stressing the familiarity of 'the thing as it was', Bunyan showed how even a saint, a martyr for the faith, could go through years of struggle with Satan, long after his apparent conversion. The theological need for precise and detailed observation contributed to literary realism.

ii. The Battle of the Texts

At first Bunyan tried to escape from the Scriptures, as so many of his Ranter-influenced contemporaries did. But he could not. So he tore through the Bible, desperately trying to find authoritative

---

[8] Alick West, *The Mountain in the Sunlight* (1958).

assurance that he was saved, just as Milton had done to find justification for divorce. To Bunyan the texts appeared contradictory, but there must be a resolution, and it must be found in the protestants' infallible book.

One of the astonishing features of *Grace Abounding* is the audibility of the exchanges between Bunyan and the tempter. Texts are hurled backwards and forwards like mountains in Milton's War in Heaven. 'The words began thus to kindle in my spirit, "Thou art my love, thou art my love", twenty times together, and still as they ran thus in my mind, they waxed stronger and warmer.' 'I was much followed by this scripture, "Simon, Simon, behold Satan hath desired *to have* you (Luke XXII. 31)". And sometimes it would sound so loud within me and as it were call so strongly after me, that once above all the rest, I turned my head over my shoulder, thinking verily some man had, behind me, called to me' (30–1). 'Then would the text cry . . . aloud with a great voice, "Return unto me, for I have redeemed thee"' (52). A text which Bunyan heard could silence 'all those tumultuous thoughts that before did use, like masterless hell-hounds, to roar and bellow and make a hideous noise within me' (53). 'I had no sooner said it but this returned upon me, as an echo doth answer a voice, "This sin is not unto death"' (59). 'These words did sound suddenly within me; . . . that piece of a sentence darted in upon me.' 'These words did, with great power, suddenly break in upon me' (64–5). 'Suddenly this sentence fell upon my soul . . .' (72). 'That word of God took hold of my heart. . . . I suddenly felt this word to sound in my heart' (80, 82). And when Bunyan was on trial in 1661,

while he [Judge Kelyng] was speaking these words, God brought that word into my mind, in the eighth of the Romans, at the 26th verse. I say God brought it, for I thought not on it before; but as he was speaking it came so fresh into my mind and was set so evidently before me, as if the Scripture had said, 'Take me, take me'. (115)

Texts fight against texts. 'As I strove to hold by this word, that of Esau would fly in my face like to lightning' (60). 'The Scriptures could not agree in the salvation of my soul' (72). 'This made me, with careful heart and watchful eye, with great seriousness, to turn over every leaf, and with much diligence, mixed with trembling, to consider every sentence' (77). At last 'I durst venture to come nigh unto those most fearful and terrible Scriptures, with which all this

while I had been so greatly affrighted, and ... had much ado an
hundred times to forebear wishing them out of the Bible, for I
thought they would destroy me' (69–70). Sometimes two rival
texts 'bolted both upon me at a time, and did work and struggle
strangely in me for a while.' 'At last, that about Esau's birthright
began to wax weak, and withdraw, and vanish.' 'Oh, what work did
we make! It was for this in John (6: 37) ... that we did so tug and
strive; he [Satan] pulled and I pulled; but, God be praised, I got the
better of him' (67–8). Finally, 'those dreadful scriptures of God left
off to trouble me' (72).

So, in the course of his years of agony, Bunyan came to know the
Bible better than most even in that Biblical age. He could nearly
always out-text a disputant. The textual slogging match with Satan
prepared him to become a great preacher and controversialist.

Sometimes the texts hurled at Bunyan were not from the Bible.
He searched for one 'above a year' before he found it in the
Apocrypha, Ecclesiasticus 2: 10 (62–3; cf. 72). On another perplexing occasion he asked his wife, 'Is there such a scripture, "I
must go to Jesus"?' She did not know, but Hebrews 12: 22–4 'came
bolting in upon me', and he slept happily (82).

iii. The Lost Inheritance

Sociological and psychological historians have not got very far in
explaining why there was so much despair in the late sixteenth and
early seventeenth centuries, leading some to suicide, some to
atheism, some to conversion. It seems to have been at its height in
the hectic middle decades of the seventeenth century. It may be
that anxiety was especially prevalent in this period because they
were the years of the great economic divide, in which the lucky few
might prosper whilst the mass of their neighbours were plunged
into deeper poverty. Predestinarian theologies both stimulated
anxiety and offered relief. Conversion perhaps played a role like
that of the drug culture in our similar age of economic crisis,
personal insecurity, and degradation.[9]

---

[9] *The Jerusalem Sinner Saved* (1688), MW xi. 63–6; cf. *The Acceptable Sacrifice* (1689),
Offor, i. 700, 713. See ch. 16 below. In *WTUD* I listed numerous examples of
doubts and despair in the late 1640s and 1650s, affecting such representative figures as
John Rogers, John Saltmarsh, William Franklin, Isaac Penington the younger, Anna
Trapnel, Abiezer Coppe, Jacob Bauthumley, Mrs Richard Baxter, Thomas Traherne,
William Deusbury, Edward Burrough, John Crook, George Fox, Archibald Johnston
of Wariston (171–5, 182–3).

Where was certainty to be found after the breakdown of the 1640s and 1650s? Some looked for it in the teaching of a prophet like John Reeve, who claimed that God had given him greater knowledge of the Scriptures than to any other man. In the same year, 1651, Hobbes offered certainty through surrender to Leviathan, the mortal God. But that was not for the godly. Conversion was one answer: Bunyan's future pastor, John Gifford, was converted in the early 1650s. Luther escaped from a similar spiritual crisis by wrestling with God until he won faith. Like Luther, Bunyan combined phenomenal moral toughness with his neuroses. He *had* to break through. But it took a long and exhausting struggle before Bunyan, like his contemporary Pascal, cast himself on to the God of Abraham, of Isaac, and of Jacob.

Bunyan convinced himself that he had committed the sin against the Holy Ghost, and so put himself outside God's mercy. The analogy which recurs in *Grace Abounding* is Esau's sale of his birthright and his inability to recover it. 'He found no place of repentance, though he sought it carefully with tears (Heb. XII, 16–17)'. Bunyan returns to that text a score of times (42–71). He was afraid that he had 'disinherited my poor soul'. In the seventeenth century the words 'inheritance' and 'birthright' normally referred to landed property. Jack Lindsay suggested that Bunyan's obsession relates to his family's sales of land in the sixteenth and early seventeenth centuries, their birthright whose loss had necessitated the wandering life of tinkers. 'The whole earth, therefore', Crowley had written over a century earlier, '[by birthright] belongeth to the children of men. They are all inheritors thereof by nature.'[10] Levellers, Diggers, Army radicals, and the Quaker Edward Burrough emphasized the importance of Englishmen's birthright freedom, and had striven unsuccessfully to recover it by political means. Winstanley and other Diggers used the story of Esau and Jacob in this context. Kingly government ('Esau') 'took his younger brother's creation birthright from him', Winstanley wrote.[11] We have no reason to suppose that Bunyan

---

[10] Lindsay, *John Bunyan*, chs. 8 and 9; Robert Crowley, *An Information and Peticion agaynst the Oppressours of the Pore Commons of this Realme* (1548), sig. A 8.

[11] Edward Burrough, *Good Counsel and Advice Rejected* (1659), in *Works* (1672), 563; Winstanley, *The Law of Freedom and Other Writings* (Cambridge UP, 1983), 306; *The Works of Gerrard Winstanley*, ed. G. H. Sabine (Cornell UP, 1941), 673–5; cf. 353. See also my 'Pottage for Freeborn Englishmen: Attitudes to Wage-Labour', in *Change and Continuity in Seventeenth-Century England* (1975), and ed. A. S. P. Woodhouse (1938), *Puritanism and Liberty*, 53, 69.

supported such political campaigns. By 1649–50 they had been defeated, by 1666 they were a distant memory. But he must have known about them.

The birthright which Bunyan was tempted to sell was access to salvation. Esau's 'birthright signified regeneration', 'the birthright to heaven.' The saints were '"heirs of God!" God himself is the portion of the saints' (71–81); theirs was 'the church of the first-born'. For what was Bunyan tempted to sell this birthright? *Grace Abounding* never makes this entirely clear. 'To exchange him for the things of this life, for anything', Bunyan says (41). For acceptance of the unequal social order re-established in the 1650s and confirmed in 1660? – a society in which tinkers should know their place? For a life aimed at worldly success and wealth? *The Life and Death of Mr. Badman* was to show the possibilities here even for small men if they were unscrupulous enough. Or for acceptance of a life of averagely decent behaviour, no better and no worse than one's neighbours, but abandoning the struggle to wring eternal life from an inscrutable God? The only clues we have are contained in Bunyan's own writings – in *Grace Abounding* itself, in *The Pilgrim's Progress*, *Mr. Badman*, and *The Holy War*. But the idea of selling out, of betraying one's own convictions, of getting by at a low but accepted level of achievement, of self-love rather than self-denial, remained to haunt Bunyan throughout his life.

In *The Pilgrim's Progress* Christian seeks 'an inheritance ... laid up in heaven'. For 'such as sell their birthright, with Esau', there is a 'by-way to hell, a way that hypocrites go in at'. Christian and Hopeful have their only serious dispute when Hopeful suggests that Little-faith (who had been robbed) might have sold or pawned some of his jewels. Christian slaps him down with a tartness that takes Hopeful aback. 'Esau sold his birthright', Hopeful expostulates, '. . . his greatest jewel; and if he, why might not Little-faith do so too?' Christian thereupon lectures him on the allegorical significance of the jewels, which seemed to have escaped Hopeful.[12]

The Barren Fig-tree (1673), *The Strait Gate* (1676), and the posthumous *The Heavenly Foot-man* all return to Esau's sale of his birthright and subsequent despair.[13] Bunyan reverted to the

---

[12] *PP*, 11, 122, 127–8.
[13] MW v. 23, 49, 100, 175; cf. *Profitable Meditations* (1663?), in *Poems*, 6, 9.

question of losing one's inheritance in *The Advocateship of Jesus Christ*, one of the last books he published (in 1688).

The man in Israel that, by waxing poor, did sell his land . . . in Canaan should not by his poverty lose his portion in Canaan for ever. The Lord, their head, reserved to himself a right therein. . . . 'The land is mine' (for ye are strangers and sojourners with me. Levit. XXV. 23–5). The law of grace has provided that the children shall not for their sin lose their inheritance in heaven for ever, but that it shall return to them in the world to come. . . . Your profuseness and prodigality shall not make him [Christ] let go his hold that he hath of you for heaven. . . . A spendthrift though he loses not his title may yet lose the present benefit. But the principal will come again at last. . . . When our evidences are taken from us because of a present forfeiture of this inheritance . . . they are not ordinarily got . . . again but by the help of a lawyer, an advocate. Thus it is with the children of God. . . . Jesus Christ our advocate is ready . . . to send us from heaven our old evidences again.

Such analogies appear to support Lindsay's conjecture: Bunyan's attention had been caught by the ability of poor Israelites to recover alienated land in the year of Jubilee, which he equated with the day of judgment.[14]

For a time Bunyan had fallen in 'very eagerly with the religion of the times', going to church regularly. But he still indulged in Sunday sports or even work on the Sabbath, until pulled up by a sermon from his parson. Vavasor Powell was similarly impressed by a rebuke which he received at the age of around 20 for *watching* games on the Sabbath. That must have been just before 1640. Margaret Spufford quotes an eighteenth-century account of a man who used to play football on Sundays in the 1630s, despite his minister's admonitions. But when he heard the parson read the Book of Sports, and saw that iniquity was established by law, 'chill horror not to be described' descended on him. 'What judgments are to be expected upon so wicked and guilty a nation! What must I do? Whither shall I fly? How shall I escape the wrath to come? . . . I date my conversion from that time.'[15] Bunyan went home from hearing a sermon against Sabbath sports 'with a great burden upon

---

[14] MW xi. 183–6. See Lev. 25.

[15] [Anon.], *The Life and Death of Mr Vavasor Powell* (1671), 2; M. Spufford, *Contrasting Communities: English Villages in the Sixteenth and Seventeenth Centuries* (Cambridge UP, 1974), 231–2. This recalls the opening of PP, and may derive from it. Defoe had spoken of 'wickedness established by a law', *The Earlier Life and Works of Daniel Defoe*, ed. H. Morley (1889), 166.

my spirit'. But even a voice from heaven darting into his soul whilst playing tipcat had only a temporary effect, and led to a 'kind of despair' that 'heaven was gone already' (8–11).

Bunyan was rebuked for swearing by a woman shopkeeper, which made him wish 'with all my heart that I might be a little child again, that my father might learn me to speak without this wicked way of swearing.' He 'fell to some outward reformation', so that his neighbours 'did take me to be a very godly man, a new and religious man,' and were very impressed, as Bunyan presumably intended. But he still had trouble with bell-ringing and it was 'a full year' before he could quite stop dancing, though he was 'now a brisk talker in matters of religion' (11–16).[16]

A first turning-point came when 'the good providence of God did cast me to Bedford, to work on my calling; and in one of the streets of that town I came where there were three or four poor women sitting at a door in the sun, and talking about the things of God. . . . They spake as if joy did make them speak. . . . They were to me as if they had found a new world. . . . They were far above and out of my reach.' But as he went about his job, 'their talk and discourse went with me', and he began to appreciate the super-ficiality of his own apparent godliness. He made a point of 'going again and again into the company of these poor people, for I could not stay away.' They softened his heart, and bent his mind to meditate on what they had said (14–16).

The women in the sunlight were poor and unlearned. But they knew more than the Ranter-influenced 'brisk talker'. The symbol-ism is as powerful as the thawing of the ice in Tolstoy's *Resurrec-tion*. At crises in Bunyan's spiritual development he returned to the women, and they entered his dreams. 'I saw, as if they were set on the sunny side of some high mountain, there refreshing themselves with the pleasant beams of the sun, while I was shivering and shrinking in the cold.' There was a wall between him and them. After much searching he found a narrow gap through which with great efforts he managed to squeeze himself (19–20). This clearly prefigures the wicket gate in *The Pilgrim's Progress*. 'Oh that I had turned sooner! Oh that I had turned seven years ago!' Bunyan cried. Ultimately he began to 'break my mind to those poor people', who introduced him to their pastor, John Gifford (22–6).

---

[16] The point about bell-ringing and dancing was not made in the first edition.

But Bunyan's struggles were not yet over. He believed that he would never forget the joy given him by the words '"Thou art my love, thou art my love" in forty years'. He 'could have spoken of his love . . . even to the very crows that sat upon the ploughed lands before me. . . . But alas! within less than forty days I began to question all again' (30).

What kept Bunyan going was his fierce determination to be saved, his refusal to forget the promises, as Christian was to forget them in Doubting Castle, his refusal to despair. *The Pilgrim's Progress* is at many points a commentary on *Grace Abounding*. The pilgrims encounter Giant Despair late in their progress, long after their conversion. What is remarkable is Bunyan's isolation in his battle with Satan—at least as depicted in *Grace Abounding*. 'As yet I had in this matter broken my mind to no man', he observes (18). His wife is barely mentioned in this context, except when he asked her to identify a text. (She couldn't.) Even when 'with joy I told my wife "O now I know, I know"', his real longing was 'for the company of some of God's people' (82).

Bunyan alone knows fully of the despairing agonies he experiences as he battles with Satan and his old Ranter friends, as he pores in terrifying isolation over his Bible. Was his struggle really as lonely as that, or is this the way he wished to present it to his audience? Such questions arise continually when we try to use *Grace Abounding* as historical evidence. The quest for salvation was indeed a lonely one, perhaps always so for followers of the lonely Luther, but especially for those who had lived through the English Revolution, in which all traditional certainties were called in question. The old episcopal church collapsed in 1640, and no one seemed to mind very much. What survived was protestantism, any threat to which, real or imaginary, could unite Englishmen of the most divergent views. But in the free-for-all of discussion in the 1640s it was revealed how very varied the views of protestant Englishmen were. Not least in the Army, as Bunyan experienced.

What should protestant Englishmen do to be saved? Who was to help them? The Reformation had abolished priestly mediators. The episcopal church under Laud seemed to be reverting to popery. The Presbyterian state church which replaced it had very little popular appeal. The Army guaranteed religious toleration, but could provide no agreed religious settlement. Bunyan himself

experienced and participated in bitter wrangling between orthodox Puritans and Baptists, between Baptists, Ranters, and Quakers.
'I never cared to meddle with things that were contentious and in
dispute amongst the saints', he tells us, truthfully enough (87).
Bunyan was driven back to the individualistic foundations of
protestantism, to Luther — 'an ancient godly man's experience,
who had writ some hundreds of years before I was born.' Bunyan
regarded Luther's *Commentary on Galatians* as second only to the
Bible, 'most fit for a wounded conscience' (40–1).[17] But the Ranter
presence remains all-pervasive in *Grace Abounding*, as it had been in
the Army and apparently was in Bedfordshire in the early 1650s.
Behind Ranters and Army radicals was the traditional sceptical
materialist anti-clericalism that went back at least to the Lollards.
Such ideas, and criticisms of the authenticity of the Bible, had been
canvassed in Ralegh's and Marlowe's circles in the late sixteenth
century, and were refuted by Arthur Dent in 1601. Mrs Attaway,
Walwyn, Winstanley, Roger Crab, and Ranters like Clarkson and
Coppe gave them new publicity.[18]

There are — for myself at least — moments of tedium in the
repetitiveness of Bunyan's temptations, but also moments when
the intense emotional power of his elation or despair carry us with
him. And even the *longeurs* tell us much about Bunyan's insecure
personality. How did he develop after 1660? There have been so
many ups and downs in the story that we are left with less certain
conviction than Bunyan seems to feel that his doubts and temptations are all behind him. The book ends with his establishment as
a highly successful preacher for the Bedford congregation. Theoretical doubts seem to have been resolved in practice: all his
conflicts are turned outwards. *Grace Abounding* was written in jail,
and looking back after six years of imprisonment Bunyan writes
with the confident conviction of one whose elect status has been
confirmed by martyrdom.

[17] This passage was not in the first edition.
[18] Dent, 294–315; *MER*, 308–9, 313.

7. *Ranters and Quakers*

How if all our faith, and Christ, and Scriptures, should be but a
think-so?   BUNYAN[1]

BUNYAN came to hate Ranters and Quakers because he had
so nearly been convinced by them. Their ideas attracted him,
but failed to give him what above all things he sought — assurance
of his own salvation. For a long time Bunyan was assailed by
blasphemous thoughts. They were Ranter commonplaces —
doubts about the existence of God and the historical Jesus Christ,

and whether the holy Scriptures were not rather a fable and cunning story
than the holy and pure Word of God. . . . How can you tell but that the
Turks had as good Scriptures to prove their Mahomet the Saviour, as we
have to prove our Jesus is? And, could I think that so many ten thousands,
in so many countries and kingdoms, should be without the knowledge of
the right way to heaven; if there were indeed a heaven, and that we only,
who live in a corner of the earth, should alone be blessed therewith?
Everyone doth think his own religion rightest, both Jews and Moors, and
Pagans! and how if all our faith, and Christ, and Scriptures, should be but
a think-so too? . . . Paul . . . being a subtle and cunning man, might give
himself up to deceive others with strong delusions. (31–2)

And Bunyan had many even worse thoughts, 'which at this time I
may not nor dare not utter' (31–2; cf. 76, 102). One wonders what
they were.

The Koran had been translated into English in 1649, with
upsetting effects. A mid-sixteenth-century Italian translation gave
rise to similar anxieties.[2] Bunyan remained very conscious of
radical criticisms of the Bible's authenticity, 'written by some
politicians, on purpose to make poor ignorant people to submit to
some religion and government.' He made a damned soul in *A Few
Sighs from Hell* (1658) remember calling it 'a dead letter, a little ink
and paper of 3 or 4 shillings price.' He had preferred 'a ballad, a
newsbook, *George on horseback* or *Bevis of Southampton*'. Hell existed
only in men's consciences.[3]

---

[1] *GA*, 31.
[2] C. Ginzburg, *The Cheese and the Worms* (Eng. trans., 1980), 30, 43, 101.
[3] M W i. 333, 342–3; cf. *Some Gospel-truths*, ibid. 19–23.

Of all the temptations which Bunyan experienced, he thought that 'to question the being of God, and the truth of his gospel, is the worst, and worst to be borne.' Sometimes 'the whole Bible has been to me as dry as a stick.' The first of seven abominations which he found in his heart was 'inclining to unbelief'. Even in prison he still suffered from doubts about the afterlife. In *Prison Meditations* (1663) he counters the Ranter idea that the Bible was 'devised by cunning men'. In *One Thing is Needful* (1665) he refers to scepticism about heaven and hell as 'that trick of youth', presumably referring to his own.[4]

Bunyan was tempted to solve his problems by settling for the belief that there was no such thing as a day of judgment, no resurrection, and 'that sin was no such grievous thing'. If you are damned you are damned: worrying will not help you. He would possess his mind 'with some such conclusions that Atheists and Ranters do help themselves withal' (49). The Ranter Lawrence Clarkson taught that sin existed only in the imagination: Bunyan, like Clarkson, 'found within me a great desire to take my fill of sin, still studying what sin was yet to be committed, that I might taste the sweetness of it' (11).

Even when Bunyan had been admitted to fellowship with the Bedford church he was tempted to blaspheme the ordinance of holy communion 'and to wish some deadly thing to those that then did eat thereof' (79). He felt, but overcame, similar temptations to blaspheme from the pulpit in his early preaching days (90). In the posthumous *Christ a Complete Saviour* he returned to the subject: 'some of those that are coming to Christ' have 'many strange, hideous and amazing blasphemies'. It is 'common to such . . . to have some hellish wish or other against God.' In *The Pilgrim's Progress* Christian fails to realize that the 'many grievous blasphemies . . . which he verily thought had proceeded from his own mind' were in fact whispered to him by a devil.[5] Did Bunyan cease to have such thoughts?

Since it has recently been alleged that there were no Ranters,[6] it is interesting that so many of the opinions which Bunyan encountered were commonplaces of Ranter libertinism. Bunyan names the Ranters only in the third edition of *Grace Abounding* (1672–4) (16–17, 49), though from the first edition his reference is clearly to

---

[4] *GA*, 102; *Poems*, 44, 64.   [5] *Christ a Complete Saviour*, Offor, i. 210; *PP*, 63–4.
[6] See Appendix.

their doctrines. In 1656 he had spoken of 'a company of loose Ranters'. Perhaps by the early 1670s he distinguished more distinctly between Ranters and Quakers than he wished to do in 1666. He tells us that he met a great many Ranters in Bedfordshire, and 'some Ranter books that were put forth by some of our countrymen, which books were also highly in esteem by several old professors.' Bunyan's one 'religious intimate companion ... turned a most devilish Ranter, and gave himself up to all manner of filthiness, especially uncleanness.' He would deny the existence of God, angels, and spirits. 'He told me ... that in a little time I should see all professors turn to the ways of the Ranters.' Bunyan 'left his company forthwith', but on his travels (as a tinker, presumably) he met several people who, 'though strict in religion formerly, yet were also swept away by these Ranters. These would ... condemn me as legal and dark; pretending that they only had attained to perfection that could do what they would and not sin.' (This again was Clarkson's doctrine.) 'These temptations were suitable to my flesh', Bunyan adds, 'I being but a young man' (16–17).[7]

We already know of Ranters in more than twenty counties.[8] Further local research might well reveal more, and so put into perspective the legislative and other measures directed against them in 1650–1. These were so effective, at least in driving Ranter heresies underground, that historians have perhaps too easily assumed that the legislation was superfluous because dealing with an insignificant phenomenon. The long history of views like theirs, before and after the Revolution, suggests otherwise. Ranters – unlike Bunyan, unlike Quakers – recanted easily under threat, because they expected no reward in heaven for martyrdom; but they almost certainly remained of the same opinion still.

For the rest of Bunyan's life he continued to wage battle against Ranter ideas. 1665 saw *The Holy City* attacking 'Ranting opinions'; *The Resurrection of the Dead* is throughout concerned with mortalism, 'the chief doctrine of the Ranters', 'the faith of Ranters, not of Christians', which had earlier tempted Bunyan (49, 76). Ranters are everywhere in *Grace Abounding*. In Bunyan's allegories their

---

[7] MW i. 16–20; cf. 99, 112, 138–9.
[8] A. L. Morton, *The World of the Ranters* (1970), ch. 4; *WTUD*, 227–30; J. F. McGregor, 'Ranterism and the Development of Early Quakerism', *Journal of Religious History*, 9 (1977).

ideas and practices continued to be a major concern. *Mr. Badman*
has many Ranter qualities; Carnal Security and Atheism in *The
Holy War* appear to be Ranters. So perhaps are the Doubters.
Bunyan thought it a knock-down argument against separate meetings for women of his church that Ranters and Quakers favoured
them.[9] In his *Exposition on . . . Genesis*, on which he was still working
when he died, Bunyan wrote 'the first thing that God made was
time: I say it was time.' God created time before he created man,
indeed before he created matter, the heavens, or the earth. The
philosophic nature of the statement is outside Bunyan's range: he
must have taken it over from somebody, though I do not know
from whom. But the heavy emphasis which he lays on it attracts
attention. It had been anticipated in Part II of *The Pilgrim's
Progress*, where Matthew gives Prudence the right answer to the
first question she asks when she catechizes him. Was there, she
inquires, 'ever anything that had a being antecedent to or before
God?' 'No', Matthew replies, 'for God is eternal, nor is there
anything excepting himself that had a being until the beginning of
the first day. For in six days the Lord made heaven and earth, the
sea and all that in them is.'[10]

Bunyan is refuting the traditional heresy, which Ranters took
over from popular sceptical materialism, that matter was eternal,
that God did not create the universe. Bunyan regarded this as
atheism; refuting it was essential to his refutation of Ranterism. If
no creation, there would be no afterlife, no rewards and punishments, no sense of sin, no hierarchy, degree or order on earth.
That Bunyan was still attacking such ideas at the very end of his life
suggests that Ranterism was not dead in the areas which he knew
best, Bedford and the surrounding countryside, and London.
They still seemed to Bunyan to offer a real threat.

The crucial fact in Bunyan's life was the conviction that he was
one of the elect, which came to him around 1653. The nearest he

[9] MW iii. 157, 228, 247; cf. pp. xxii–xxiii, xlvi, 199, 269–70; Offor, ii. 417; *The
Resurrection of the Dead* (1665), Offor, ii. 106; *The Heavenly Foot-man* (posthumous),
MW v. 152–3, 156; *Mr. B.*, Offor, iii. 646, 653; *HW*, 121, 155, 275; *A Case of Conscience
Resolved* (1683), Offor, ii. 664. Cf. *Some Gospel-truths*, MW i. 16–20, 99–112; *A Few
Sighs from Hell* (1658), ibid. 381–2; *Law and Grace* (1659), MW ii. 156–8, 170–1, 194;
Light for them that sit in Darkness (1675), MW viii. 128; *Saved by Grace* (1676), ibid.
208–9; *A Treatise of the Fear of God* (1679), MW ix. 105; *The Greatness of the Soul* (1682),
ibid. 221–2; *The Pharisee and the Publican* (1685), MW x. 135.

[10] Offor, ii. 417; *PP*, 226; cf. Bunyan's Traherne-like poem, 'Upon Time and
Eternity', in *A Book for Boys and Girls* (1686), *Poems*, 268.

gets to giving a date is 'just before the men called Quakers came into the country' – a significant way of putting it.[11] Ranters were then being persecuted out of existence, and Quakers were picking up many of them. Bunyan's first publications were directed against Quakers. For this there are two reasons. First he did not differentiate them from Ranters. Many of his contemporaries confused the two, just as they confused Levellers and Diggers; and indeed lines of division were not always clear-cut. There was no Ranter organization at all, and although Quakers had many personal connections with one another, there was at this date no way of identifying a Quaker. A large penumbra of unorganized radicals, libertines, and others hung around the movement.

We think of Quakers as wholly serious, courageous men and women of pacifist principle. But the habits of early Quakers were disturbing. They were not pacifists; they indulged in symbolic actions like going naked for a sign (with only a loincloth about their middles, for decency's sake), or disrupting religious services; they wrote large tomes to prove that the Bible was not the Word of God. For Bunyan all this must have seemed the height of frivolous irresponsibility. And in 1659–60 the Quakers played politics with the Commonwealth government. 'We look for a new earth as well as a new heaven,' Burrough told Parliament.[12]

Bunyan's earliest tracts against Quakers seem to us wrongheaded; they were certainly ill-tempered. He was defending the Bible to which he owed his conversion and the congregation which had given him a sense of security, of belonging. But his attitude towards Quakers mellowed after he had shared Bedford gaol with fifty of them. Their unflinching courage under persecution won the admiration of many who did not agree with them. It was particularly likely to impress Bunyan. One contemporary critic suggested that in his refusal to attach symbolic importance to baptism Bunyan came close to the Quakers: 'I walk according to my light with God.' Bunyan's release from gaol in 1672 is said to have been due to Quaker mediation.[13]

---

[11] *Law and Grace* (1659), MW ii. 157–8; *The Jerusalem Sinner Saved* (1688), MW xi. 63–6; cf. *The Acceptable Sacrifice* (1689), Offor, i. 706, 713.

[12] Edward Burrough, *To the Parliament of the Commonwealth of England* (1659–60), 3. See Barry Reay, *The Quakers and the English Revolution* (1985), ch. 5.

[13] Bunyan, *A Confession of My Faith* (1670–1), Offor, ii; H. J. Cadbury, 'John Bunyan and the Quakers', *Journal of the Friends' Historical Soc.*, 52 (1968), 47. See p. 292 below.

A second reason for Bunyan's hostility to Quakers was their sudden and successful propaganda campaign in Bedfordshire. In 1654 William Deusbury, 'the Quaker Apostle of Bedfordshire', converted John Crook, a county magistrate who had been a captain in the Parliamentary army. In 1653 Crook was proposed as a member of Barebone's Parliament; the following year William Dell recommended him for election to Parliament, remarking that he was 'against the paying of tithes and taxes'. Crook was in prison in 1656. His house, Beckrings Park, became a Quaker centre, the Swarthmore Hall of the Midlands. In 1658 the first Quaker yearly meeting took place there. In 1659 there was a disturbance at a Quaker meeting at Crook's house, caused by 'many of Bunyan's people'. (The phrase is incidental evidence of Bunyan's prominence in popular estimation: he was not pastor of the congregation until twelve years later.) From 1656 onwards there were clashes between Quakers and the Bedford congregation; they led to Bunyan's attacks. As early as 1654–5 the Quakers Thomas Stubbs and Thomas Storey were making conversions around Dunstable, a former Digger centre. Deusbury won supporters at the same time in Wellingborough, which also had maintained a Digger colony. Fox held 'a great meeting there' in 1655. Quakers appear to have looked especially to Baptist congregations for converts. By 1669 there were more Quakers than Independents in Bedford.[14]

There was much which shocked Bunyan in the beliefs of Ranters and Quakers. Most Ranters were mortalists — i.e. they believed that the soul dies with the body, and does not revive until the final resurrection — if then. They regarded the resurrection as a symbolic rather than a historical event: 'nothing but the resurrection from a sinful to a holy state in this life'. Bunyan attributed mortalism and denial of the resurrection of the body to Quakers. Mortalism could lead to atheism, which Bunyan also attributed to Ranters — 'if there be such a thing as an atheist in the world'. He came to share the wholly conventional view that denial of rewards

[14] H. G. Tibbutt, 'John Crook, 1617–99: A Bedfordshire Quaker', *PBHRS* 25 (1947), 110–16; W. C. Braithwaite, *The Beginnings of Quakerism* (1912), 152, 186; ed. N. Penney, *First Publishers of Truth* (1907), 6–7, 194; Fox, *Journal*, ed. Penney (1901), i. 250; MW i. p. xxiv. Crook was for a time in the 1660s to follow the Quaker heretic, John Perrot (*Early Quaker Writings, 1650–1700*, ed. H. Barbour and A. O. Roberts (Grand Rapids, Mich. 1973), 512).

and punishments after death would 'open a flood-gate to all manner of impiety'.[15]

Ranters denied the Scriptures to be the Word of God; so did the Quaker Samuel Fisher. Ranters thought the Bible was a historical document to be criticized like any other. Many of them denied the historical existence of Jesus Christ, or at least held with Gerrard Winstanley the Digger that 'the mystery' was more important than 'the history', Christ within us more important than the Christ who died at Jerusalem. Ranters were sceptical about Christ's Second Coming, regarding it too as a metaphor for transformations within believers — as Winstanley had done. Bunyan attributed 'mocking at the Second Coming of the man Christ' to Quakers as well as to Ranters.[16] Ranters rejected baptism and holy communion — 'and are not you the same?' Bunyan asked Quakers.[17] The Ranters Clarkson and Coppe extended antinomianism to cover sexual licence and promiscuity. The practice of some on the fringes of the Quaker movement made it easy to accuse all Quakers of similar immoralism.

Bunyan believed that

the opinions that are held at this day by the Quakers are the same that long ago were held by the Ranters. Only the Ranters had made them threadbare at an ale-house and the Quakers have set a new gloss upon them again, by an outward legal holiness or righteousness.

The Baptist Thomas Collier said something similar though less striking in the same year, 1657; Richard Baxter and many others were to echo it later. For Bunyan the authenticity of the Bible, the doctrine of justification by faith, Christ's historical existence and his sacrifice on the cross, had been fundamental factors in his conversion. To call them in question was to tear up the roots of his faith.[18]

In *Grace Abounding* Bunyan suggested that Quaker opposition to

---

[15] MW i. 123-4, 138, 183, 217; *Mr B.*, Offor, iii. 627; *HW*, 121; *The Resurrection of the Dead*, MW iii. 214. Francis Osborne agreed that atheism was impossible (*Miscellaneous Works, Essays*, 28).

[16] *A Few Sighs from Hell* (1658), MW i. 333, 343; *Some Gospel-truths* (1656), ibid. 99, 112; *A Vindication* (1657), ibid. 138.

[17] *Some Gospel-truths*, MW i. 16-20; *A Vindication*, ibid. 138-40, 217; cf. *A Few Sighs from Hell*, ibid. 381-2.

[18] *A Vindication*, ibid. 139; [T. Collier], *A Looking-Glasse for the Quakers*, 7; *Reliquiae Baxterianae* (1696), i. 77; cf. E. Pagitt, *Heresiography* (5th edn., 1654), 143-4; *Law and Grace* (1659), MW ii. 156-8, 170-1, 194.

God's truth, as he saw it, meant that 'God did the more confirm me in it, by leading me into the Scriptures' (39). Ranters and Quakers 'knowingly, wilfully and despitefully' rejected the atonement of Christ, his resurrection, and Second Coming. Their errors, he said in *The Strait Gate* (1676), meant that they 'will seek to enter in, and shall not be able'.[19] Edward Burrough, a leading Quaker, replied to *Some Gospel-truths*, and again to Bunyan's *A Vindication*. He rightly corrected Bunyan's confusion of Quakers with Ranters. The exchange was very abusive on both sides. Burrough referred to Bunyan's 'carnal sottishness', his 'sinful, wicked, devilish nature', 'his damnable doctrines and errors' – 'a man given up to wickedness'. Bunyan retorted in kind against Burrough's 'railings', 'deceit', 'lame arguments', 'like a blind man in a thicket of bushes', 'raging expressions', 'bawlings'. There was much slinging of texts backwards and forwards. Quakers, Bunyan said, were 'the greatest enemies to the Christ of God without.'[20]

Burrough replied by accusing John Burton, pastor of the Bedford congregation, of preaching for hire: he did in fact hold a living in the state church until 1660, which Burrough estimated at £150 per annum, and thought Bunyan got some of it. 'Bunyan is railing against the priests, and runs up into the pulpit himself', George Fox snorted when he intervened in the dispute in 1659. Much of the disagreement was semantic. Neither Bunyan nor Burrough tried to understand the different ways in which the other used words like 'light' and 'Christ'; each accused the other of confusion for not using words in his sense. Burrough claimed that at a meeting at Pavenham on 12 April 1656 Bunyan had said, 'there is nothing in me nor in any man to be taken notice of.' That sounds like an agreeable piece of modesty. But Burrough interpreted it to mean that Bunyan was 'a reprobate and without Christ in him, one that hath denied Christ in him, or else thinks Christ not worth taking notice of.' Bunyan did not reply to Burrough's second tract, nor to Fox's *The Great Mistery of the Great Whore*. Thomas Collier joined in on Bunyan's side against Burrough in 1657.[21]

---

[19] *Law and Grace*, MW ii. 209–10; *A Vindication*, MW i. 123–9, 176–7; *The Strait Gate* (1676), MW v. 127.

[20] Burrough, *Works* (1672), 136–52, 275–309; MW i. 145–6, 159, 165, 175, 195.

[21] Burrough, *Works*, 302–7; cf. 151; MW i. 59–61, 73, 85–6, 99, 114–15, 123–33, 217; G.F., *The Great Mistery of the Great Whore Unfolded* (1659), 8–13, 52, 205–11. The 374 pages of this folio tome are wholly concerned with answering hundreds of critics of Quakerism; Collier, *A Looking-Glass for the Quakers*, 4.

Bunyan regarded the Quaker inner light as simply that 'law of nature' which 'is universal in every individual man in the world'. But unregenerate man is without Christ. Bunyan was no doubt even more indignant with Quaker disparagement of ministers who 'preach up sin'. If sin and salvation and the historical Christ are not real, Bunyan thought, we can rely only on our own righteousness. Ranters and Quakers dismissed the fears and scruples which overwhelmed Bunyan.[22]

Like Milton, Bunyan had to hold on to the Bible, and the historical Christ. Ranters demonstrated how rudderless men could become once the Bible was discarded. Milton was prepared to interpret the Bible, drastically and Jesuitically; but never to jettison it. The Quaker Samuel Fisher's scholarly tome arguing that the Bible was so internally inconsistent and contradictory that it could not be the Word of God was published only in 1660, too late to make an impact on popular opinion. It was left to Spinoza and other philosophers to follow up this lead.[23] The sceptical moment had passed. Yet Bunyan's fury against the Quakers showed how insecure this questioning of the foundations had made him. Why was the Bible more authoritative than the Koran, if wide acceptance of the former was a main argument for its authenticity? If the inner light, the Christ inside one, was supreme, then how could there be agreed interpretations of the Bible – or of anything else? This made way for Hobbism.

The Quakers were to grapple with these problems, painfully, after 1660. They proclaimed pacifism and abstention from politics, and withdrew from making the sort of antisocial gestures to which the spirit had moved the first generation. They reinstated sin and the Bible. They came nearer to Bunyan as he came nearer to them.

For Bunyan – historically correctly – the Bible in English was the basis of popular protestant culture, won in two-and-a-half centuries of struggle by Lollards, Marian martyrs, and separatists. Calling the Bible in question would seem to him to call in question all the achievements of the people of the Book. There had always

---

[22] Bunyan, *Questions about the Nature and Perpetuity of the Seventh-Day Sabbath* (1658), Offor, ii. 362; MW i. 24–6, 211.

[23] R. H. Popkin, 'Spinoza, the Quakers and the Millenarians, 1656–1658', *Manuscrito*, 6 (Brazil, 1982), 132; 'Spinoza and the Conversion of the Jews', *Spinoza's Political and Theological Thought*, ed. C. de Deugd (Amsterdam, 1984), 174; *WTUD*, 266–7.

been tension in protestantism, between the individual conscience and the authority of the church, or the state, or accepted norms of social behaviour. But now norms were changing; and individual consciences were necessarily the vehicles of change. There was no final solution to that problem: only temporary halting-places on the way. Hence Bunyan's ecumenism, his impatience with squabbles about ceremonies, once the essentials were agreed on. But how difficult to extend that agreement beyond a small group!

8. Early Writings

Be not offended because Christ holds forth the glorious treasure
of the Gospel to thee in a poor earthen vessel, by one who hath
neither the greatness nor the wisdom of this world to commend
him to thee.... Not many wise men after the flesh, not many
mighty, not many nobles are called: but God hath chosen the
foolish things of the world, etc. This man is not chosen out of an
earthly but out of the heavenly University ...

JOHN BURTON[1]

i. Anti-Quaker Pamphlets, 1656–1657

THROUGHOUT his two anti-Quaker pamphlets Bunyan's
stress was on his opponents' lack of a sense of sin, of the total
unworthiness of man before God, which was the essential preliminary to effectual calling. 'If all the Quakers and Ranters in the
world were but under the guilt of one sinful thought, it would make
them to cry out with Cain, "My punishment is greater than I can
bear"' (71; cf. 156–60). We recall Samuel Fisher's mockery of
priests whose 'trick is for money to declare against sin', and Fox's
'now they have gotten our money they hope we will not look for
perfection ... while we are upon earth, ... for we must carry a
body of sin about us.... Oh deceivers!'[2]

Bunyan believed that Satan tries first of all to keep men in love
with their sins and pleasures, to prevent them listening to those
who warn against them. If this fails, his second ploy is to persuade
the sinner that his anxieties about his soul are 'but a melancholy fit',
calling for physic (14). Ranters, Walwyn, and Winstanley had
explained religious melancholy leading to despair in medical
terms; for them too physic was the answer. Mr. Badman's phys-
ician gave him the same advice.[3] Satan's third attack was to use
consciousness of sin to reduce the sinner to despair of his own

---

[1] 'To the Reader', prefixed to *Some Gospel-truths Opened* (1656), Bunyan's first
published work (MW i. 11).

[2] S. Fisher, *The Testimony of Truth Exalted* (1679), 650 (1st pub. 1660); Fox, *Epistles*
(1662), 222, quoted in R. B. Schlatter, *The Social Ideas of Religious Leaders* (Oxford UP,
1940), 242. (Figures in brackets in this section refer to pages in MW i.).

[3] *Mr. B.* (1680), Offor, iii. 651.

prospects. Finally his fourth line was 'to make thee rest upon thy own righteousness', to think that heaven can be earned. It was here that Ranters and Quakers could delude 'unstable souls' who 'were shaking in their principles'. They made them 'slip into high notions', till they became 'puffed up' in their fleshly minds, priding themselves on their knowledge of the Scriptures (13–16).

Ranters and Quakers, in short, responded to the special needs of sincere Christians confused by the collapse of old standards and lack of agreement among the godly on anything to replace them; and they appealed to complacent 'notionists' whom the possibility of the coming of a better society had given what Bunyan saw as excessive self-confidence. They ignored what Bunyan regarded as facts: the existence of sin, of a predestined elect saved not by their own efforts or for their own abilities or notions, but by Christ alone. At this point we may recall Victor Kiernan's remark about predestinarian theories: that they often appealed to the poor and unprivileged, who might or might not be saved, but who felt themselves distinct from the rich. The latter have their good times on earth; few indeed of them could hope for salvation.[4] The would-be intellectualism, as Bunyan saw it, of Ranters and Quakers put them with the privileged, the educated élite who were almost certainly damned. The plausibility of their notions to natural human reason was merely evidence of their satanic origin. Bunyan's hostility to Quakers diminished as they came to share persecution. But Bunyan did not forget. Among the Delectable Mountains lie the unburied bones of those who denied the resurrection. He was still attacking Quakers in the posthumous *Israel's Hope Encouraged.*[5]

The conservative Richard Baxter said he had known learned men who were Arminians; but antinomians, he thought, were normally of 'the vulgar sort', uneducated.[6] Bunyan often skirted near antinomianism; his hatred for Arminian Quakers (and for Latitudinarians) is perhaps tinged with a social distaste for pseudo-intellectuals. Moreover, Quakers allowed women a liberty in church worship of which Bunyan disapproved.

---

[4] V. G. Kiernan, 'The Covenanters: A Problem of Creed and Class', in *History from Below: Studies in Popular Protest and Popular Ideology in Honour of George Rudé*, ed. F. Krantz (Montreal, 1985), 111.

[5] *PP*, 121; Offor, i. 613–14; cf. 611.

[6] W. Lamont, *Richard Baxter and the Millennium* (1979), 143.

The political atmosphere was already becoming more conservative in the late 1650s. We must see Bunyan's personal spiritual
crisis against this social background. The optimistic libertine
speculations of the late 1640s had proved mere 'notions'; the state
church had not recovered its prestige and authority: nothing had
taken its place. Many concluded 'there are so many sects and
judgments in the world, that we cannot tell which way to take'
(126). Bunyan no longer wanted to be perfect. He had seen too
many who did, with – as he thought – disastrous consequences. He
wanted to be saved. His own conversion, he said, came after he had
been 'killed by the authority of the holy Scriptures' (53–4). It
released him from the overwhelming sense of sin, of worthlessness
before God. Bunyan had been horrified at the light-heartedness
with which Ranters liberated men and women from sin, apparently
oblivious to the possible consequences. In a world dominated by
the ungodly rich, the sense of sin gave a tougher courage to endure.
Bunyan thought Quakers were more dangerous than Ranters just
because they were more morally virtuous, more courageous in
their resistance to persecution.

Yet Bunyan still believed that 'the coming of the Lord Jesus
Christ is . . . nigh, even at the doors' (99). His sense of sin and of
the coming millennium encouraged a desire to separate from the
godless mass of mankind, to turn inwards, but also to reject the
dominance of the rich, the university-educated opinion-formers of
the society, who had never even been troubled by the doubts and
hopes to which Ranters and Quakers had responded. Bunyan now
saw Ranters and Quakers as seducers on the side of Satan, the
established church, and the rich. It was no accident that in the
1660s he was to equate Latitudinarian with Quaker ideas. But in
the 1650s it was a gut reaction: 'I do know they are the poor that
receive the Gospel' (145).

ii. *Dives and Lazarus*

That 'the poor receive the Gospel' was one of the few points on
which Bunyan agreed with Edward Burrough. After disposing of
the Quakers, Bunyan's next publication was *A Few Sighs from Hell*
(1658), an expansion of a sermon which he had preached on the
parable of Dives and Lazarus, the rich man and the beggar. The
theme is that which underlies Bunyan's controversy with the

Quakers: the urgent necessity of bringing home to men and women the parlous state of their souls until they become convinced of their depravity. But the parable, made familiar by the Elizabethan *Book of Homilies*, was regularly employed, mostly by radicals, to make social points.[7] Bunyan thought the parable reveals 'the sad condition of those that are for the most part rich men.' Rich men 'are most liable to the devil's temptations, . . . most liable to be puffed up with pride' and other sins: God's own 'are most commonly of the poorer sort' (253–4). 'God hath chosen the poor, despised and base things of this world.' Lazarus is 'a scabbed creep-hedge'. But it is 'better to hear the Gospel under a hedge than to sit roaring in a tavern' (304, 307). Bunyan seems almost to have had someone in mind when he observed how 'the great ones of the world will go strutting up and down the streets' (252), 'hunting and whoring, . . . dancing and playing' (279). 'They will build houses for their dogs, when the saints must be glad to wander and lodge in dens and caves of the earth.' They eject their godly tenants, or 'pull down the house over their heads' (257; cf. 315). 'So far from parting with any worldly gain, . . . they are still striving, by hook or by crook, as we say, by swearing, lying, couzening, stealing, covetousness, extortion, oppression, forgery, bribery, flattery, or any other way, to get more' (340).

In *A Few Sighs from Hell* the state clergy are shown as no better than the rich. They are patterns to their flocks not of godliness but of pride, wantonness, drunkenness, covetousness (127). Bunyan speaks alliteratively of the 'flatteries and fawning of a company of carnal clergymen' (307). They preach 'for filthy lucre's sake' (314; cf. 306). Bunyan included gentry, clergy, and the universities in a brilliantly dismissive phrase when he said that God's little ones 'are not gentlemen, . . . cannot, with Pontius Pilate, speak Hebrew, Greek and Latin' (304; cf. 345).

A Few Sighs from Hell may have been one of the sermons which, Bunyan modestly tells us, had considerable success and won him no small reputation. His vigorous response to a congenial theme

---

[7] *Sermons or Homilies Appointed to be read in Churches* (Oxford UP, 1802), 75, 179; see for instance Lilburne, Walwyn, Winstanley, the Baptist John Pendarves, the Ranters Lawrence Clarkson and George Foster, the Quakers Parnell, Fox, Farnsworth, Nayler, the anonymous *The Husbandmans Plea against Tithes* (1647) and *England's Troublers Troubled* (1648) and the millenarian John Mason. See also Tindall, 110–11, 253–4. It started perhaps in the early fifteenth century with the Lollard *Dives and Pauper*.

cannot have endeared him (or the religious toleration which made such a sermon by a tinker possible) to the well-to-do citizens of Bedford or to 'the pretty gentry' in the town and its immediate neighbourhood.[8] Threats were uttered. 'Would the creatures do as some men would have them, the saints of God should not walk so quietly up and down the streets, and other places, as they do' (258). Bunyan felt personally menaced. 'The world rages, they stamp and shake their heads and fain would be doing: The Lord help me to take all they shall do with patience.' He asked for his readers' prayers 'that God would fit me to do and suffer what shall be from the world or devil inflicted upon me' (248; cf. 399).

The gentry were already preparing for the revenge which was to be theirs after 1660. Bunyan knew that he was a marked man, and he was ready for his ordeal. In attacking Quakers he had been going with the tide; but in *A Few Sighs from Hell* he set himself resolutely against it.[9] 'Unless the over-ruling hand of God in goodness do order things contrary to their natural inclination, they will not favour you so much as a dog' (259). But 'there is a time coming, O ye surly dogged persecutors of the saints, that they shall slight you as much as ever you slighted them. . . . In your greatest need and extremity they shall not pity you. The righteous . . . shall wash his feet in the blood of the wicked' (284). Such violent and provocative language made it unlikely that the gentry would pity Bunyan if they had the opportunity to silence him.

[8] *The Journeys of Celia Fiennes*, 340–1.
[9] Ironically, in attacking the vices of the rich Bunyan found himself in agreement with Quakers.

9. *Bunyan and the Bedford Congregation*

> Our time is short, and oppositions increase, we not knowing how
> soon we may be called to suffer for truth.   PAUL HOBSON[1]

i. The Congregation

BUNYAN was accepted by the Bedford congregation in 1653.
In April 1654 he took advantage of the establishment of civil
registration of births to have his second daughter registered as
'born', not baptized in the parish church. His third and fourth
children, born before 1658, do not even seem to have been
registered.[2] Bunyan was baptized and became a full member of the
church in 1655, shortly before its founder, 'holy Mr Gifford', died.
John Gifford had been a royalist officer during the civil war, and
was converted after it. He was a powerful personality, who left his
mark on the congregation. A group of godly persons had come
together in Bedford before his time. They were 'not embodied into
fellowship according to the order of the Gospel; only they had in
some measure separated themselves from the prelatical superstition and had agreed to search after the nonconforming men,
such as in those days did bear the name of Puritans.' Gifford
insisted on ecumenism, 'without respect to this or that circumstance or opinion in outward and circumstantial things', and on
social equality.[3]

In a letter which he wrote to the congregation from his deathbed
Gifford exhorted them to 'avoid all disputes which gender to
strifes, as questions about externals and all doubtful disputations.'
Separation from the church because of any externals, including
baptism, psalm-singing, etc., was to be avoided as a great evil. This
was a point on which Bunyan was later to insist. In other respects
we can see Gifford's influence on Bunyan. Gifford urged his flock
to take no truth on trust from any man (37). 'It is very expedient

---

[1] *A Garden Inclosed* (1647), 49.
[2] *GA*, 171; Brown, 87, 92, 222; J. Hobson Thomas, 'Bunyan the Baptist', *Baptist
Quarterly*, 4 (1928), 97–8.
[3] Tibbutt, *Minutes*, 15, 20; Brown, 89.

that there should be heresies among us', Bunyan wrote in 1657, 'that thereby those which are indeed of the truth might be made manifest.' The more truth is opposed, he agreed with Milton's *Areopagitica*, 'the more it will clear itself'. 'Let no respect of persons be in your comings together', Gifford wrote. 'When you are met as a church, there's neither rich nor poor, bond nor free, in Christ Jesus.' Hence pews should not be rented – one of the ways in which the sects were apt to finance themselves, lacking the state church's income from tithes and fees. But 'the necessities of those who are in want' must be met by the congregation: rich members must be more generous than they had been.[4]

Bunyan took over, perhaps from Paul Hobson, the metaphor of the church as garden. God Almighty first planted a garden, in Eden, and put Adam into it. Bunyan interpreted the Genesis story as meaning that God took the church out of the wilderness and enclosed it. To this foundation Bunyan added Gifford's principles of fellowship and ecumenicism. In *Christian Behaviour* (1663) he wrote that 'Christians are like the flowers in the garden, that stand and grow where the gardener hath planted them.' 'They have upon each of them the dew of heaven, which being shaken with the wind, they let fall their dew at each other's roots, whereby they are jointly nourished, and become nourishers of one another.'[5] Mutual self-help and encouragement, especially for the frailer members of the congregation, was especially stressed in Part II of *The Pilgrim's Progress* in 1684.

Bunyan insisted on the orderliness of the garden. Christians must keep their rank, relation, and station. Faith is planted by God in his garden. Presumption grows up only outside 'where other wild notions abound'. But the garden is enclosed from 'the wide and open field' and ministers 'water the plants of the Lord'. In *The Pilgrim's Progress* the Interpreter explains that, although in his garden 'the flowers are divers in stature, in quality and colour, and smell, and virtue, . . . where the gardener has set them, there they stand, and quarrel not one with another'.[6]

A small community of flowers which drop dew upon one another necessarily involved careful selection of church members.

---

[4] Tibbutt, *Minutes*, 17, 19–20; *Some Gospel-truths*, MW i. 134.

[5] Genesis, Offor, ii. 425; *Christian Behaviour*, MW iii. 10, 54; cf. *The Barren Fig-tree* (1673), MW v. 20, 64. See pp. 53–5 above.

[6] *The Jerusalem Sinner* (1688), MW xi. 67; cf. *Genesis*, Offor, ii. 425–6; *PP*, 202.

Admission came after a period of probation, and after the candidate had satisfied the congregation as to his state of grace. It was impossible to be sure on earth who were saints: some 'creep in unawares' by means of 'a show of repentance and regeneration'.[7] 'Visible saints' were those who had an appearance of grace, who were of suitable conversation, and had satisfied the church as to their soundness of doctrine by a confession of faith and repentance of their sins. This is represented in *The Pilgrim's Progress* when at the Palace Beautiful 'one of the virgins . . . will, if she likes your talk, bring you into the rest of the family, according to the rule of house.' Church membership was not essential for salvation; but 'church fellowship, rightly managed, is the glory of all the world', as an aid to spiritual growth, Bunyan wrote in *The Desire of the Righteous Granted* (posthumous). He insisted, following Gifford, that baptism was not a necessary condition for admission to the church, provided the candidate gave a satisfactory account of his faith. Even preachers and pastors might fall from grace.[8]

Contemporaries always assumed — at least after 1660 — that dissenting congregations were composed of socially inferior people. In 1669 Bunyan's meeting was described as Anabaptist, having about thirty members of the 'meanest sort' — shopkeepers and craftsmen, hatters, cobblers, heelmakers.[9] The founding members were certainly not socially inferior, artisans though they may have been. They included two men who had been mayors of the town, John Grew and John Eston. Together with another former member of the church, Arthur Harington, they had defended their Puritan Vicar against Laud's commissary in 1640. In 1647 Grew spoke up for the unorthodox Captain Francis Freeman, a near-Ranter, against Colonel Okey, himself an Anabaptist. In 1651 Grew and Eston had demonstratively refused to wear gowns in common court, and the rule was voided – though it came back after the restoration. They were also JPs, and Grew a militia commissioner. When he died in 1661 he was described as

---

[7] *The Barren Fig-tree*, MW v. 15, 20, 44; cf. Gordon Campbell, 'The Theology of *The Pilgrim's Progress*', Newey, 252.

[8] *PP*, 46; Campbell, 'Theology', 251–3; Offor, i. 757–8, ii. 449–50, 605–6.

[9] Brown, 203, 205; M. Mullet, 'The Internal Politics of Bedford, 1660–1688', PBHRS 59 (1980), 6; cf. M. F. Hewett, 'John Gibbs, 1627–1699', *Baptist Quarterly*, NS 3 (1927), 319; G. R. Cragg, *Puritanism in the Period of the Great Persecution, 1660–1688* (Cambridge UP, 1957), 159–60.

a gentleman. Two members of the congregation were Triers for the Cromwellian state church. Richard Cooper, mayor in 1657, was also a member of the church.[10] We shall see later that Bedford politics were closely linked with national politics; the congregation was deeply involved in both. In 1640 several future members of the church had supported the election of Sir Samuel Luke to what was to be the Long Parliament. In 1653 Gifford and other members of the congregation welcomed Cromwell's forcible dissolution of the Rump of the Long Parliament, and the decision to call a nominated assembly. The signatories included Eston, Grew, Thomas Gibbs, and John Bunyan, as well as John Gibbs of Newport Pagnell and William Dell.[11]

The signatories suggested names of two possible members for the nominated assembly, one of whom actually sat in Barebone's Parliament. In 1657 *The Humble and Serious Testimony of many hundreds of godly and well-affected people in the county of Bedford and parts adjacent*, protesting against the proposal to revive monarchy in the house of Cromwell, was circulated by Dell and the regicide Colonel Okey. We 'still remain faithful to the Good Old Cause', declared the signatories, who included several members of the Bedford church — Grew and Eston, Richard Cooper, and John Fenn. The practice of circulating petitions on national affairs dated from 1641; it had been extensively used by Levellers later in the 1640s, who printed their petitions. *The Humble and Serious Testimony* of 1657 was printed and led to arrests and to the examination of Eston and Fenn among others, as well as possibly to dissension in the Bedford congregation.[12]

After this petition the church set a day apart 'to seek God about the affairs of the church, the affairs of the nation, and the work of God in the world.' When Cromwell, under Army pressure, rejected the offer of the crown, the church held a day of praise to God

---

[10] Brown, 13, 77, 81–5, 102, 202–3, 205; *The Minute-Book of Bedford Corporation 1647–1660*, ed. G. Parsloe, PBHRS 26 (1949), p. xxxii; Sharrock, 29; *Colonel John Okey, 1606–1660*, ed. Tibbutt, PBHRS 35 (1955), 50–1, 56 n. For Freeman see *WTUD*, 200–1.

[11] Parsloe, *Minute-Book*, p. xxiv; Brown, 95–6. There were other John Bunyans in Bedfordshire, and it has been argued that the tinker was too socially inferior to have signed. But the consensus of opinion seems now to be that it was in fact our John Bunyan.

[12] Tibbutt, *Okey*, 86–9; Brown, 101–4; MW i. pp. xxvi, 399.

for his goodness in delivering them out of their late troubles. In the ensuing six months they sought God about the affairs of the nation no less than four times. At the end of October 1659 the church set apart Guy Fawkes Day 'to bless God for our late deliverance' from Sir George Booth's royalist rising against the Commonwealth. In the next six months many days were given up 'to seek the Lord, especially upon the account of the distractions of the nation'. Just before the restoration they prayed for the nation and God's work; just after it they prayed God to direct their governors.[13] Apart from a reference in August 1661 to the increase of their troubles, they then lapsed into a prudent silence on the political matters which had hitherto so much concerned them. That was what the restoration had been about.

ii. Millenarianism

The English Revolution gave a new stimulus to the idea that the end of the world is approaching, that the kingdom of God is at hand. Such millenarian ideas recurred constantly in medieval heresies, peaking at times of economic or political crisis. They had been greatly encouraged by the Reformation. Protestants identified the Pope with Antichrist. There had been a convergence of scholarly opinion, based on intensive study of the prophecies of Daniel, Revelation, and elsewhere by Napier, Brightman, Mede, that the last days were to be expected in the seventeenth century, probably in the 1650s.[14] Arthur Dent in 1603 thought that his was the 'last age', which would see the heat of the war 'betwixt the armies of Christ . . . and of Antichrist'. Rome would be destroyed 'within the age of a man'. He gave this doctrine a democratic twist when he insisted that it must be 'made known to the common people' among the godly. Every minister of the gospel was bound to preach this doctrine to 'all the Lord's people whatsoever, . . . men and women, young and old, rich and poor'.[15] Forty years later Parliamentarian propagandists would make much of this approach. In 1643 William Prynne, no radical, declared that the

---

[13] Tibbutt, *Minutes*, 10–37.
[14] Marjorie Reeves, *The Influence of Prophecy in the Later Middle Ages* (Oxford UP, 1969), *passim*. See my *Antichrist in Seventeenth-Century England* (Oxford UP, 1971), ch. 1; '"Till the Conversion of the Jews"', *Religion and Politics in Seventeenth-Century England* (Brighton, 1986), ch. 13.
[15] Dent, *The Ruine of Rome*, sig. aa–aa2, 262; cf. sig. aa3.

Earl of Essex was 'General of the Lord of Hosts' to set up Christ's kingdom. Army rumour transformed this into a claim that Essex was John the Baptist, preparing for Christ to come and destroy King Charles.[16]

Millenarian ideas were developed by radicals and sectaries; many believed that in the millennium the saints would rule and judge the earth.[17] As Dent showed, millenarianism linked naturally with John Foxe's evidence that the lower classes were the staunchest foes of Antichrist. 'The voice that will come of Christ's reigning', proclaimed the anonymous *A Glimpse of Sions Glory* in 1641, 'is like to begin from . . . the vulgar multitude, the common people'.[18] The rule of Antichrist is maintained, said John Goodwin in 1642, 'by doctrines and tenents excessively advancing the power of superiors over inferiors.' It was men 'of ordinary rank and quality' who were to execute God's judgments upon Antichrist and to vindicate and maintain 'the just rights and liberties and privileges of those . . . under authority and subjection to others.' 'The *vox populi*', Stephen Marshall told the House of Commons even more alarmingly in December 1641, 'is that many of the nobles, magistrates, knights and gentlemen and persons of great quality are arrant traitors and rebels against God.'[19]

The Digger Winstanley carried this democratic millenarianism to its extreme by arguing that the imminent millennium will not take the form of a descent of Christ from the clouds but of Christ rising within sons and daughters. They would learn the reasonableness of co-operation and would establish a communist society. There will be no other Second Coming. For Winstanley, Antichrist was associated with the gentry.[20]

Fifth Monarchists and Quakers preached a less secular millenarianism, but they too linked the millennium with social justice and

---

[16] W. Prynne, *The Popish Royal Favourite* (1643), sig. 2; *The Journal of Sir Samuel Luke*, Oxford Record Soc. (1950), i. 76.

[17] For instance William Aspinwall, John Brayne, Edward Burrough, John Canne, Mary Cary, Thomas Collier, John Cook, William Erbery, George Fox, Thomas Goodwin, Hanserd Knollys, John Milton, Isaac Penington, Hugh Peter, Robert Purnell, John Sadler, William Sedgwick (*MER*, 282, 304; my *The Experience of Defeat* (1984), 52–3, 181).

[18] *Puritanism and Liberty*, ed. A. S. P. Woodhouse (1938), 234.

[19] John Goodwin, *Anti-Cavalierisme* (1642), 31, in *Tracts on Liberty in the Puritan Revolution, 1638–1647*, ed. W. Haller (Columbia UP, 1933), ii; Marshall, *Reformation and Desolation* (1642), 45.

[20] *Religion and Politics in Seventeenth-Century England*, ch. 11.

sometimes with social subversion. Mary Cary in 1651 expected a
material heaven on earth 'before twenty or ten or five years pass'.
The saints then will join in judging 'all the workers of iniquity'. Fox
echoed Winstanley on property: a rich man is 'the greatest thief',
since he got his wealth 'by cozening and cheating, by lying and
defrauding'. The Fifth Monarchist John Rogers attacked 'corrupt
and naughty nobles'. John Tillinghast thought that 'the present
work of God is to bring down lofty men.' Christopher Feake saw in
aristocracy 'an enmity against Christ'; in the millennium there
would be 'no difference betwixt high and low, the greatest and the
poorest beggar'. The anonymous preacher of the funeral sermon
for John Simpson, Fifth Monarchist, declared that 'the nation is
more beholding to the meanest kitchen maid in it that hath in her a
spirit of prayer than to a thousand of her profane and swaggering
gentry'.[21]

Such views were widely circulated and discussed in the revolutionary decades. As Professor Greaves sagely pointed out, millenarian discourse, with its imagery of war and destruction, had
potential political overtones whether or not the speaker intended
them. It is not surprising that the authorities found it difficult to
distinguish between passive millenarians, waiting for the Second
Coming, and those who intended actively to hurry the day along.
John Cook and John Milton both thought the trial and condemna-
tion of Charles I was an anticipation of the judgment of the saints.[22]

Professor Greaves has recently emphasized the millenarian
connections of the Bedford congregation in the 1650s and later. It
was in correspondence with the Fifth-Monarchist congregation of
Peter Chamberlen in London. It was close to Henry Jessey, John
Simpson, and George Cokayne, all open-communion Baptists.
Gifford had used millenarian language at the beginning of the
Bedford church book, and on his deathbed in 1655 he urged the
congregation 'forget not your brethren in bonds', which Roger
Sharrock plausibly relates to Christopher Feake and John Rogers,

---

[21] M. Cary, *The Little Horns Doome and Downfall*, 133, 201, 238, 285–317; Fox, *Newes
Coming up out of the North* (1654), 11; Rogers, *Ohel* (1653), 11, 22–3; *Mr Tillinghasts 8
Last Sermons* (1655), 219; Edwards, *Gangraena*, iii. 148; *Thurloe State Papers*, v. 755;
[Anon.], *The Failing and Perishing of Good Men* (1663), 13–14. I owe many of these
references to B. S. Capp, *The Fifth Monarchy Men: A Study in Seventeenth-Century
English Millenarianism* (1972), 143.
[22] *MER*, 282.

then in jail.[23] In 1657 a millenarian petition from Bedfordshire, hoping for 'the full destruction of Antichrist's kingdom' and the advancement of the kingdom of Christ, was signed by two of Bunyan's friends (John Fenn and Richard Cooper). In the same year John Child, a silk-weaver of Bedford, then one of Bunyan's closest colleagues, was described as a Fifth-Monarchist agent.[24] Child was one of the signatories of a Preface to Bunyan's *Vindication of Some Gospel-truths* (1657).

The Bedford congregation's agreement to set apart a day for special prayer in 1657 was part of a national campaign, instigated by the millenarian Henry Jessey. When John Child showed signs of wishing to withdraw from the congregation in 1658, it was to Jessey that its members turned for help. And when Gifford's successor, John Burton, was ill towards the end of 1660, the church sought advice from John Simpson[25] (who had been an active Fifth Monarchist at least until 1658) and from George Cokayne, a Bedfordshire man.

Cokayne, a powerful and popular preacher, had preached to the House of Commons on 29 November 1648, a week before Colonel Pride purged it. He took his text from Isaiah 65: 16–18: 'Behold, I create a new heaven and a new earth.' Cokayne insisted that 'God at last will judge all the causes of the sons of men' mediately by the saints, picking out perhaps 'the meanest of his people' for this duty. But he made it clear he was addressing MPs when he said, 'the Lord is risen in you and will judge the world by you.' He hinted unambiguously that the King should be brought to trial. 'Think not to save yourselves by an unrighteous saving of them who are the Lord's and the people's known enemies.' He anticipated the arguments of those who would flinch from such a dénouement: 'if God do not lead you to do justice upon those that have been the great actors in shedding of innocent blood, never think to gain their love by sparing of them.' They will take vengeance if you leave them the chance. He warned too against MPs failing to do their duty 'because of some unwonted interruptions of your proceedings'. When he wrote his Epistle Dedicatory to the Com-

---

[23] Greaves, *Deliver Us from Evil* (Oxford UP, 1986), 228 and *passim*; MW xi. p. xxxix; *HW*, pp. xii–xiii. For Jessey and Simpson see Greaves, Index.

[24] MW xi. p. xxxix; Greaves, 'John Bunyan and the Fifth Monarchists', *Albion*, 3 (1981), 84.

[25] Tibbutt, *Minutes*, 29–30.

mons on 11 December, the unwonted interruption had taken place five days earlier, and Cokayne was clearly upset by it. But he insisted that what he had told them was 'still an unchangeable truth. . . . Your privileges are indeed broke . . . but let not this lay a foundation for breach of truth.' Cokayne was later reported to have said that Charles deserved his fate. Cokayne was a friend both of the Leveller John Wildman and of Bulstrode Whitelocke. He must often have discussed with Bunyan the great events in which he had been involved.[26]

Cokayne was active in Fifth-Monarchist politics in the early 1650s and again in the 1660s. But in 1661 he, like Bunyan and Henry Denne, repudiated Venner's Fifth-Monarchist rising. Cokayne and Jessey were probably joint authors of *Mirabilis Annus* (1661). Cokayne may have been responsible for *Mirabilis Annus Secundus*. He was said to have visited Bunyan in prison in 1664, the year in which Cokayne was again arrested and his house searched for seditious literature. In the 1670s there was intercommunion between the Bedford congregation and Cokayne's church in Southwark. In 1672 an elder of the Bedford church was licensed to preach at Cokayne's house in Cotton End, Bedfordshire. In 1682 and again in 1683 Cokayne was fined for preaching. He wrote a Preface for Bunyan's posthumous *The Acceptable Sacrifice*, and he may have preached Bunyan's funeral sermon. John Strudwick, at whose house in London Bunyan died, was a member of Cokayne's congregation. Cokayne may have been the author of *A Continuation of Mr Bunyan's Life*.[27]

Millenarianism was to play a part in all Bunyan's thinking. For him as for others writing under censorship, Antichrist became a useful, because imprecise, symbol. Antichrist can be anyone who persecutes the children of God. 'Opposing Antichrist . . . in the world' Bunyan equated with opposing Cain. This was a long-standing radical tradition. That persecution was Antichristian had

---

[26] Cokayne, *Flesh Expiring and the Spirit Inspiring in the New Earth: Or God Himself supplying the room of withered Powers* (1648), 14–18, 26–8; Ruth Spalding, *The Improbable Puritan: A Life of Bulstrode Whitelocke, 1605–1675* (1975), 142, 238–9, 248, 294–5. For Whitelocke see pp. 189n., 290 below.

[27] MW xi. pp. x–xli; *Thurloe State Papers*, vi. 87; Tibbutt, *Minutes*, 29–30; MW i. p. xxiv; *Calamy Revised*, 'Cokayne'; Greaves, *Deliver Us from Evil*, 57, 62, 97, 125, 211; C. B. Cockett, 'George Cokayn', *Trans. Congregational Historical Soc.*, 12 (1935), 225–30; Offor, i. 686–8. Cokayne was chaplain to Bulstrode Whitelocke and Charles Fleetwood. Whitelocke was elected MP for Bedford in 1654, but chose another seat.

been taught by Wyclif, Tyndale, the Geneva Bible, the Baptists Thomas Helwys and Leonard Busshor, John Bastwick, Roger Williams, Thomas Taylor, John Owen and other preachers of Fast Sermons to Parliament, Overton and other Levellers, Henry Denne, Edward Burrough, George Wither, and John Milton. Bunyan stated the doctrine in *The Holy War*. For John Goodwin, Milton, Colonel Goffe, Levellers, John Canne, John Spittlehouse, monarchy was Antichristian. The royalists in the civil war were 'the Antichristian party'; for Coppe Antichrist's was 'a kingdom of gain, hire and self-interest', just as for Milton Antichrist was 'Mammon's son'.[28]

Bunyan shared and retained much of this radical millenarianism. In *The Advocateship of Jesus Christ* (1688) he referred to a time when 'I did use to be much taken with the sect of Christians' who called Christ 'the blessed King of Glory'. Greaves suggests that this refers to the Fifth Monarchists in the 1650s. In *Some Gospel-truths* (1656) Bunyan spoke of 'the last days. . . . The coming of the Lord Jesus Christ' was 'so nigh, even at the doors'. He criticized 'all those that mock the Second Coming, as Quakers, Ranters, drunkards and the like.'[29] *A Few Sighs from Hell* (1658) drew to a conclusion with the words 'God's hand is up. . . . The judgment-day is at hand.'[30]

[28] *Of Antichrist and his Ruin*, Offor, ii. 53–4, 79; *Genesis*, Offor, ii. 419; *HW*, 275; see my *Antichrist in Seventeenth-Century England*, 5–6, 41–2, 48, 57–9, 93–6, 109–10, 119–20, 131, 144, 147; cf. 47, 74–5; *MER*, 237, 281, 307; Owen, 'A Discourse about Toleration', annexed to *A Sermon Preached to . . . the House of Commons, 31 Jan. 1649*, 93.

[29] MW xi, pp. xxxvii, 194; cf. xl–xli; MW i. 84, 99; cf. 82: 'his coming will be very shortly'. Bunyan would no doubt have added Diggers to those who mock at the Second Coming if he had read Winstanley.

[30] MW i. 362.

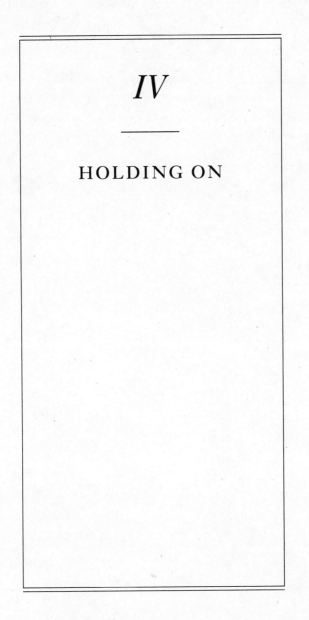

IV

HOLDING ON

10. *Preaching and Imprisonment*

For I offended have
  Nobles of high degree;
What favour can I crave
  For life and liberty?

[ANON.][1]

THE penultimate section of *Grace Abounding* is headed 'A Brief Account of the author's call to the work of the ministry'. It is the culmination of Bunyan's spiritual autobiography. Preaching was a continuation of the struggle against Satan by other means: the internal battle was externalized. Preaching helped Bunyan to find his way out of his spiritual crisis: it was a kind of therapy. In denouncing Quakers/Ranters he was continuing his own dialogue with Satan and with himself. Instead of tearing himself to pieces, he attacked an external enemy in order to help others on the path to salvation. He could go straight into the pulpit and preach on that subject, with little preparation. Hence the violence of his language: it was directed not only against Quakers but also against Satan in himself. The necessity of personal salvation from outside, his voice and texts, were all turned against Ranters and Quakers. Before Bunyan found his vocation as a writer, he had won it as a preacher. Writing came secondarily and consequentially.

The Bedford congregation saw that God 'had given me utterance to some measure, to express what I saw to others for edification.' This was in 1656, a year after his admission to full membership. First he preached outside Bedford, 'in the darkest places in the country', then in the town itself. He preached 'in Paul's steeple-house in Bedford town' on 23 May 1656, Edward Burrough records. Bunyan was still 'most sorely afflicted with the fiery darts of the devil concerning my eternal state'. 'The terrors of the law, and guilt for my transgressions, lay heavily on my conscience. I preached what I felt, what I smartingly did feel, even that under which my poor soul did groan and tremble to astonishment.' 'I went myself in chains to preach to them in chains; and carried

---

[1] *The Wofull lamentation of Edward Smith, a poore penitent prisner in the jayle of Bedford* (1613–33?), *The Roxburghe Ballads*, ii, ed. W. Chappell (Hertford, 1874), 465–9.

that fire in my own conscience that I persuaded them to beware of.'[2] His pent-up moral energy flowed out like lava.

Bunyan himself thought of preaching not as therapy, but as a talent which the Holy Ghost insisted should be exercised. 'When I have been to preach, I have gone full of guilt and terror even to the pulpit door, and there it hath been taken off, and I have been at liberty in my mind until I have done my work.' His own internal dialogue continued. 'Sometimes . . . when I have been preaching, I have been violently assaulted with thoughts of blasphemy, and strongly tempted to speak the words with my mouth before the congregation.' But now he was fighting the Lord's battles, conscious that he was doing good; and he was rewarded by success. For two years he cried out against men's sins, and their fearful state because of sin. After that, being more settled in his own soul, he broadened his subject-matter. So the fierce controversial manner which he adopted against the Quakers in 1656–8 disappeared. Henceforth 'I never cared to meddle with things that were controversial' among the saints: 'an awakening word' was what he hoped to convey.[3] His horizons widened still further when his fame spread to London and he began preaching there to great acclaim.

In common with most Puritans Bunyan regarded preaching as the principal means of salvation. In *The Pilgrim's Progress* it is Evangelist the Preacher who starts Christian on his pilgrimage, and who exhorts him and Faithful before they enter Vanity Fair, where Faithful was to be martyred.[4]

We know too little of Bunyan's preaching techniques,[5] but some things can be guessed. It would appear that all his writings published before *Grace Abounding* derived from sermons: and probably most of what he published later. He seems to have relied on continuous repetition of key phrases, a technique no doubt very effective in the pulpit. 'Begin at Jerusalem' forms a kind of refrain echoing through *The Jerusalem Sinner*, whilst 'Every one of you', 'stand thou with the number of the biggest sinners' are repeated

[2] Burrough, *Truth (the Strongest of all) Witnessed forth . . . against all deceit* (1657), in *Works*, 304; *GA*, 84–91, 164.
[3] *GA*, 83–92.
[4] *PP*, 10, 86; *Law and Grace*, MW ii. 135; *Instruction for the Ignorant* (1675), MW viii, 32–3; *GA*, 29.
[5] But see now Midgley's Introduction to MW v. pp. xxii–xxxvii.

staccato in shorter passages. In *The Strait Gate* (1676) 'Strive to enter in', and in the posthumous *The Heavenly Foot-man* 'So run', have the same effect. In *Grace Abounding* there is an early example. '"Yet", thought I, "I will pray". "But", said the tempter, "your sin is unpardonable". "Well", said I, "I will pray". "It is to no boot", said he. "Yet", said I, "I will pray".' This looks forward to repetitions of '"I will in no wise cast out", says Christ' in *Come, and Welcome*, and of the word 'stand' in *The Pilgrim's Progress*.[6] George Fox's incantatory style achieves something of the same effect.

What we cannot tell is how much racier and more personal Bunyan's spoken words may have been than those which he prepared for publication. His great reputation as a popular preacher, and the indignation of the Bedfordshire gentry and Edward Fowler at what the latter regarded as his 'licentious and destructive principles', his criminal subversion,[7] suggest that he may have been less restrained and circumspect when the word of God came to him in the pulpit. We may also suppose that the colloquialisms, the homely touches which survive in the dignity of print, may have played a larger part in his spoken words. His first published treatises, attacking Quakers, abound in oversimplified accusations, in mere abuse. The subject-matter of *A Few Sighs from Hell* may not have seemed controversial among the saints; others might think differently.

In 1660 Bunyan was arrested: he remained in jail for twelve years. Many have regarded his imprisonment as unjustified, an over-reaction: that is the impression Bunyan himself intended to give us. It is true that the restored royal government and the restored gentry were nervously uncertain of the stability of their regime. Venner's Fifth-Monarchist rising, which terrorized London in January 1661, two months after Bunyan's arrest, showed the possible dangers; and the government reacted violently. The fact that we know the end of the story enables us to speak of over-reacting. But the situation was by no means stable. Quakers proclaimed the peace principle only after Venner's revolt had failed. In the late 1650s they had expanded rapidly and advocated very radical policies: they offered their service (on terms) to the

---

[6] *The Jerusalem Sinner*, MW xi, *passim*; *The Strait Gate*, MW v. 80–8, 147–8; *GA*, 63; *Come, and Welcome* (1678), MW viii. 340–1.

[7] [Anon.], *Dirt wipt off* (1672), title-page.

republican government in 1659. Men of property regarded them, not without reason, as socially subversive.[8]

We know too that Baptists on the whole were to adopt a pacifist and non-political stance, but not all, and not immediately. W. T. Whitley, in a disapproving article, collected much evidence of Baptist plotting after 1660, and this has been confirmed by the researches of R. L. Greaves. Bunyan was no plotter, no politician. But his preaching may well have been regarded by the Bedford-shire gentry as dangerous rabble-rousing. He saw their insistence that he abandon preaching and return to his calling of tinker as an invitation to betray his Master, to neglect the gifts with which he had been endowed. The teaching of Bunyan and his like may well have seemed to the jittery rulers of Bedfordshire as supplying the ideological back-up for revived republicanism. Bunyan had been politically active in the '50s. He certainly did nothing to ensure the stability of the restored monarchy. If one sees politics as class struggle, there was logic in Bunyan's imprisonment. Only regicides and outstanding political figures like Major-General Lambert, Colonel Hutchinson, and James Harrington were treated with greater severity. Bunyan's sentence, Professor Greaves pointed out, was 'a striking exception, not the norm'.[9] The account which he wrote of his trial and imprisonment could not be published in his lifetime.

Bunyan had already been indicted for preaching as early as February 1658. He 'saw what was a-coming' a year before he was arrested in November 1660.[10] He was charged under the 1593 act for holding 'unlawful meetings and conventicles', 'calling together the people'. But both he and his accusers knew that he was being penalized for his *preaching*: this is what both sides emphasize. Preaching was not in itself an offence under that act, nor under any other, though it was soon to be made illegal. Bunyan ironi-cally offered to preach in public if private meetings were objected to, or to hand over notes of all his sermons. But it was the *act* of preaching, as well as the content, that offended. Mussolini's prosecutor said of Gramsci in 1928: 'For twenty years we must stop that brain from working.'[11] So with Bunyan: it was

[8] Barry Reay, *The Quakers and the English Revolution* (1985), Pt. III.

[9] Whitley, 'Militant Baptists, 1660–1672', *Trans. Baptist Historical Soc.*, 1 (1908–9); Greaves, *Deliver Us from Evil* (Oxford UP, 1986), 15, and *passim*.

[10] *GA*, 93, 97, 165; see also *A Few Sighs from Hell*, MW i. 248, 258.

[11] A. Gramsci, *The Modern Prince and Other Writings*, ed. L. Marks (1957), 55.

necessary to silence him. In neither case was the objective achieved.

For Bunyan preaching was his God-given vocation, which he must carry out. God had told him that 'I have something more than ordinary for thee to do.' For his enemies, attacking the rich inevitably seemed related to the aims of Venner's Fifth-Monarchist rebels. Paul Cobb specifically referred to the 'glorious pretence' of this revolt when in April 1661 he tried to persuade Bunyan to submit. When Bunyan – remarkably – managed to 'go to see Christians at London' whilst still imprisoned, it was not surprisingly argued that he 'went thither to plot and . . . make insurrection.'[12]

For the Bedfordshire gentry Bunyan's preaching, even if it did not directly incite to rebellion, fanned the discontent that many felt with the restored regime and church. Subjectively, Bunyan could honestly deny subversive intentions. Objectively, his refusal to promise not to preach was threatening. The very claim that preaching was his vocation was subversive; his vocation was being a tinker. Mechanic preaching had been the cause of all the trouble in the 1640s and 1650s. Now was the gentry's chance at last to put mechanics back in their place. Bunyan 'could not be released unless I would promise to preach no more.'[13] He was convicted in January 1661.

The gentry knew their enemies, as was shown when they conducted a purge of Parliamentarians from town corporations in 1662. Sir Matthew Hale, an ex-Cromwellian judge from outside the county, seems to have been the only person connected with Bunyan's trial who was not fiercely hostile to him. But even he may have been alienated by Elizabeth Bunyan's final magnificent explosion: 'because he is a tinker and a poor man, therefore he is despised and cannot have justice.' It confirmed the view of her husband as potentially subversive. For it was a familiar radical point. In 1646 Lilburne had complained 'because we are poor . . . and not able to fee lawyers', he and his fellow-Levellers could not have justice. 'For if we had moneys, . . . we should no ways doubt the gaining of our liberties.' 'The law is the fox, poor men are the geese', Winstanley added; 'he pulls off their feathers and feeds

---

[12] *GA*, 84–5, 91–2, 120, 130; *Law and Grace*, MW ii. 158.
[13] *GA*, 126.

upon them.'[14] 1661 was no time for a former Commonwealth judge to err on the side of lenience.

Bunyan had to promise to give up preaching, or face an uncertain fate. He did not lack advisers who urged him to submit. One was Paul Cobb, a local gentleman who held the office of Clerk of the Peace in Bedford. Cobb addressed the prisoner condescendingly as 'goodman Bunyan', 'neighbour Bunyan'; Bunyan addressed him as 'Sir'. Cobb would have no appreciation of Bunyan's belief in his divine call to preach, and no sympathy with his politico-religious position. (Cobb was to be mayor of Bedford in 1681 when Charles II purged the corporation.) But the law was uncertain, the gentry were on the rampage, and arbitrariness was to be expected: Cobb's failure to produce Bunyan for trial at the assizes in 1662 has been attributed to a desire to save him from provoking a death sentence. It may be so; or it may have been the easiest way to ensure that he stayed in prison, in case a judge from outside showed too much sympathy. 'He is a pestilential fellow, there is not such a fellow in the country again', declared Sir Henry Chester, a local justice.[15]

In the heated political atmosphere of 1661 Hale could not stand up to the bullying judge John Kelyng, who lived within eight miles of Bedford and so had first-hand knowledge of Bunyan. Kelyng had been imprisoned in Windsor Castle from 1642 to 1660 for his royalist activities. He had grounds for feeling vengeful. Kelyng was knighted immediately after Bunyan's trial. He took part in the proceedings against the regicides. He was elected MP for Bedford to the Cavalier Parliament, where he was largely responsible for drafting the Act of Uniformity (1662). In the same year he acted as prosecutor against Sir Henry Vane, who though not a regicide was executed because he was thought to be a dangerous republican. In 1664 Kelyng and two other judges tried participants in the Northern Plot to overthrow the government, twenty-one of whom were executed. Three years later he was up before the House of Commons for fining and imprisoning juries which would not return the verdicts he wanted. This was declared illegal. Kelyng

---

[14] Ibid. 128; Lilburne, *Liberty Vindicated against Slavery*, in *Leveller Manifestoes of the Puritan Revolution*, ed. D. M. Wolfe (Princeton UP, 1944), 11; Winstanley, *Fire in the Bush* (1650), in *The Law of Freedom and Other Writings* (Cambridge UP, 1983), 239.

[15] E. Stockdale, 'A Study of Bedford Prison, 1660 to 1877', PBHRS 61 (1982), 8; *GA*, 120–2, 127.

was alleged to have called Magna Carta 'magna farta'. The phrase has also been attributed to Oliver Cromwell, and it is not untypical of his irreverence even for his own side's shibboleths. But Cromwell was not a judge responsible for maintaining the law, and if he did use the phrase it was not on a formal legal occasion. Kelyng shared the determination of his fellow gentry, most of them ex-royalists, to force Bunyan to stop preaching, either by voluntary agreement or by sending him to jail.[16]

So Bunyan was sentenced to perpetual banishment, and remained in jail for what turned out to be twelve years. He contemplated the possibility of a death sentence. His acceptance of martyrdom for God's cause, at a time when weaker vessels broke, must have strengthened the resolve of his co-religionists, as he intended. But it must also have confirmed to Bunyan that he was indeed in a state of grace. Next to the Bible, Foxe's *Book of Martyrs* was his staple reading-matter in prison. We cast no doubts on his sincerity by suggesting that it influenced his ringing declarations of constancy. He admitted to fearing he might show fright on the ladder if he was executed. 'Only this was some encouragement to me, I thought I might now have an opportunity to speak my last words to a multitude, which I thought would come to see me die.' (Bunyan may have recalled the last speeches of the regicides, executed in 1661–2. These had been published and widely read. Or he may even have thought of Charles I.) If 'God will but convert one soul by my very last words', he continued, 'I shall not count my life thrown away or lost.' 'It was for the Word and way of God that I was in this condition,' he told himself, and

I was engaged not to flinch a hair's breadth from it. . . . It was my duty to stand to his Word, whether he would ever look upon me or no, or save me at the last; wherefore, thought I, I will leap off the ladder even blindfold into eternity, sink or swim, come heaven come hell, Lord Jesus, if thou wilt catch me, do; if not I will venture for thy name.[17]

It is a little histrionic, written up years after the event. But it

[16] Stockdale, 'Sir John Kelyng, Chief Justice of the King's Bench, 1665–1671', PBHRS 59 (1980), 46–50; *The Diary of John Milward*, ed. Caroline Robbins (Cambridge UP, 1938), 159–60, 163, 166–70, 187; G. Burnet, *The History of My Own Time*, ed. O. Airy (Oxford UP, 1897), i. 326; Greaves, *Deliver Us from Evil*, 191; Brown, 142; Clarendon, *The History of the Rebellion* (Oxford UP, 1888), vi. 93. Bob Owens kindly helped me with Kelyng.

[17] *GA*, 95, 99–100, 118–19, 122–3.

confirms the effect that Bunyan's success as a preacher had in stabilizing his conviction not only that he was one of the elect but that God had special tasks for him to perform. And it incorporated into the tradition of the romance literature, on which Bunyan and his public had been brought up, a Puritan ethos. Now the heroism consists not in the military virtues but in steadfast endurance. Milton at exactly the same time was making the same point in *Paradise Lost*. Not 'wars, hitherto the only argument / Heroic deemed' but 'the better fortitude / Of patience and heroic martyrdom / Unsung'. Bunyan's was not unsung; and that too has its historic significance. Before the Revolution no mere tinker could have won such publicity for his fortitude, however heroic; or so publicly have associated himself with God's cause. The emphasis on standing fast under the gravest danger is one that we shall meet again.

11. *Adapting to the Restoration*

Unjust tribunals, under change of times.

MILTON[1]

God's people are (as it hath always been, Ezra 4. 12–16) looked
upon to be a turbulent, seditious and factious people.

BUNYAN[2]

i. *'Normality' Restored*

CONTEMPORARIES saw clear social issues behind the
disputes about religion and religious toleration, behind the
restoration. In 1653 the great Parliamentarian preacher Stephen
Marshall amused Dorothy Osborne, a Bedfordshire lady, by saying
from the pulpit that 'if there were no kings, no queens, no lords, no
ladies, nor gentlemen nor gentlewomen in the world, 'twould be
no loss to God Almighty.' 'I had the most ado', she admitted, 'to
look soberly enough for the place I was in that ever I had in my
life.'[3]

Dorothy Osborne and her like had no doubt of the absurdity and
indeed wickedness of such democratic views. They became increasingly alarming to the well-to-do. A poem published in 1659
boasted that:

> We have a people now,
> Blue-apron blades-men that know how
> To keep the gentry under.

That appeared in a volume entitled *England's Changeling, Or The
Time Servers Laid open in their Colours*.[4] It is hardly surprising
that, as an anonymous pamphlet of the same year tells us, 'the
old spirit of the gentry' was 'brought in play again'; its 'earthly,
lordly rule' threatened 'the growing light of the people of God'.

---

[1] *Samson Agonistes* (1671), l. 695.
[2] *I will Pray with the Spirit* (1662?), MW ii. 253.
[3] *Letters from Dorothy Osborne to Sir William Temple*, 143.
[4] HW, op. cit., quoted in J. Frank, *Hobbled Pegasus: A Descriptive Bibliography of Minor
English Poetry, 1641–1660* (New Mexico UP, 1968), 398. 'Blue-apron' indicates
craftsmen, artisans. For 'apron-men' see *Coriolanus*, iv. vi. 27.

The Buckinghamshire county election of 1659 was fought between 'the gentlemen' and 'the Anabaptist party'. The gentlemen won. In February 1660 the command of the militia all over the country was taken from 'persons of no degree and quality' and restored to 'the government of the nobility and principal gentry'.[5]

Post-restoration legislation confirmed the exclusion of 'those of no degree and quality'. The Act of 1661 against tumultuous petitioning forbade the collection of more than twenty signatures to any petition to King or Parliament which had not been approved by three or more JPs. This put an end to the sort of political petitioning that members of the Bedford congregation had engaged in during the 1650s. The Clarendon Code (Corporation Act, 1661, Act of Uniformity, 1662, Conventicle Act, 1664, Five Mile Act, 1665) had as its object the exclusion of nonconformists from any share in central or local government. The Settlement Act of 1662 immobilized the working population, protected London and corporate towns from a surplus of labour, and left labour cheap in the countryside, where there had been many complaints of high wages in the late 1650s. It also deprived political or religious opposition of any chance of organizing. It increased the dependence of poor husbandmen.

'None are so servilely dependant', said Richard Baxter, as poor husbandmen 'are on their landlords. They dare not displease them lest they turn them out of their houses or increase their rent.' A Quaker imagined a JP saying in 1660, 'Now we may do what we will, and who shall control us?' Cottagers were being evicted from their holdings on the waste, as nonconformist ministers were being evicted from their livings. (We may compare Bunyan's phrase in *Mr. Badman*, 'in danger to be moved like a cottage'.)[6] There was a simultaneous campaign against customary rights like wood-gathering, turf-cutting, and other means by which the poor maintained themselves; new and severe laws protected game, and there were no more pamphlets against enclosure such as had proliferated in the 1640s and 1650s. The object of the legislation was to restrict

[5] [Anon.], *The Cause of God and of These Nations* (1659), ch. 1, *passim* and p. 13, quoted in A. Woolrych, MCPW, vii. 22; *Memoirs of the Verney Family*, ed. F. P. and M. M. Verney (1892–9), iii. 444; Clarendon, *History of the Rebellion*, vi. 176.

[6] My *Reformation to Industrial Revolution*, 140–1, 178; *Mr. B.*, Offor, iii. 593. The reference is to Luke 24: 20.

mobility, to tie men and women to their villages where they would work as wage-labourers, with all the uncertainties and risks which such employment entailed. In *A Few Sighs from Hell* (1658) Bunyan had denounced landlords who would eject tenants of whose religion they disapproved, 'or pull down the house over their heads rather than not rid themselves of such tenants.' 'The ungodly love their dogs better than the children of God.'[7]

Richard Baxter in 1659 noted that 'the rabble hate both magistrates and ministers'. A letter writer at about the same time agreed that between the gentry and the 'ordinary sort of people' there was 'a natural animosity, of late years infinitely increased'. The last clause is the interesting one: it gives force to the denunciation in Venner's Fifth-Monarchist manifesto of 1661 of the 'old, bloody, popish, wicked gentry of the nation'. Many could accept that description without sharing Venner's theology. The Earl of Aylesbury, James II's agent in Bedfordshire, emphasized that 'the commonalty hate the yeomen' and that the latter 'care but little for their gentlemen'.[8]

New taxes introduced during the Revolution gave rise to inequities which were enhanced after 1660. At the beginning of the Parliament of 1661 an observer wrote, ''tis the general opinion of some that this Parliament, being most of all landed men and some few traders, will never take away the excise, because their own burdens will thereupon become greater.' (The excise was voted to Charles II in return for confirmation of the abolition of feudal tenures, from which the gentry alone benefited. The excise fell mainly on the food and drink of the poor.) 'The acceptance in the seventeenth century of the doctrine that the poor should pay taxation', wrote its historian, 'is one of the landmarks in English political opinion' — the opinion of the classes whom Parliament represented, of course. 'The nobility and gentry are the necessary if not the only support of the crown', said Sir John Holland in 1668; 'if they fall that must.' He was attacking the land tax. Parliamentary elections, Sir William Petty estimated, 'are gov-

---

[7] MW i. 256–7; cf. Offor, iii. 699, 712, 714. For increased enclosure in Bedfordshire after 1660 see Joyce Godber, *History of Bedfordshire, 1066–1888* (Bedfordshire County Council, 1969), 255.

[8] Baxter, *The Holy Commonwealth* (1659), 226–7; *Thurloe State Papers*, vi. 704; Thomas Venner, *A Door of Hope* (1661), 8; *Memoirs of Thomas, Earl of Ailesbury* (Roxburghe Club, 1890), ii. 442.

erned by less than 2000 active men'. It is hardly surprising that in
1679 'the entire dissenting party' was believed to be against 'the
gentry and their interest'. As for 'the poorer and meaner people',
the Duke of Albemarle declared in 1671 that they 'have no interest
in the commonwealth but the use of breath. These are always
dangerous to the peace of a kingdom.'[9]

From his adolescence until he was about 30 years old, Bunyan
had never experienced organized religious persecution such as
prevailed in England before 1640 and after 1660. Older men
remembered Laudian times, and Quakers had suffered in the
1650s. But till the late 1650s others of the godly had existed side by
side in argumentative peace. They had been free to organize, to
meet for discussion, to preach. In 1658 Bunyan had observed that
many would *like* to persecute the sectaries; and he had threatened
persecutors with hell-fire.[10] But he must have been emotionally
unprepared for the challenge which faced him in 1660: stop
preaching or go to jail.

Francis Osborne had written against toleration in 1656. 'Will
not such proceedings incline to anarchy? And that proving loath-
some to all, make room for the old or some more acceptable family,
if not for conquest by a foreign nation?'[11] 1660 proved him right.
His view has won increasing acceptance from historians. The
memory of Levellers (suppressed 1649), Diggers (suppressed
1650), Ranters (suppressed 1651) lived on and coloured the attitude of members of the propertied classes to Quakers. Quakers
refused to doff their hats to gentlemen or magistrates; they used
the familiar 'thou' instead of the deferential 'you' when addressing
social superiors. This social egalitarianism was accompanied by a
belligerent millenarianism and readiness to take part in political
activity: pacifism and abstention from politics were adopted only
after 1660. The debates on the case of the Quaker James Nayler in
Parliament in 1656 show the social panic which many MPs felt
when they contemplated the sudden rapid expansion of the
Quaker movement. It was very loosely structured; but it had a

---

[9] E. Hughes, *Studies in Administration and Finance* (1934), 124; W. Kennedy, *English
Taxation, 1640–1799* (1913), 67; *Petty Papers*, ed. Lansdowne (1927), i. 7; Monck,
Observations upon Military and Political Affairs (1671), 145–6.
[10] *A Few Sighs from Hell*, MW i. 258, 284, 295–6, 399; Brown, 113, 120.
[11] Osborne, *Miscellaneous Works*, i. 94.

national organization of sorts, as the Levellers and Diggers were beginning to have when they were suppressed in 1649 and 1650. And Quaker doctrines were, to alarmed conservatives, not very clearly distinguishable from those of Levellers, Diggers, or Fifth Monarchists who had revolted in London in 1657 and were to do so again in 1661.

Barry Reay has documented definitively the overwhelming desire of the men of property to suppress freedom of organization and of discussion for those below the political nation. A major objective of the restoration was the re-establishment of a single state church controlled from above, and silencing all those who did not accept it.[12] Bishops and clergymen extruded during the Revolution came back with Charles II; only now the church was controlled by Parliament rather than by the King. The initiative in the persecution of the 1660s came from Parliament: Charles, for his own political reasons, would have preferred a more tolerant policy. So Bunyan's trial and sentence to prison was less a judicial than a political act. Bunyan was no Quaker; but he was a millenarian who had Fifth-Monarchist associations. Above all, his preaching had a bias against the gentry. His mere claim to the right to preach was for them a social outrage.

R. L. Greaves's important book, *Deliver Us from Evil*, establishes that after 1660 there was 'no cessation of revolutionary thinking or activity'. He shows us an England bitterly divided, seething with discontent, in which the discontented were collecting arms and preparing for revolt. Secretary Nicholas spoke in April 1661 of 'a general desertion in point of affection in the middle sort of people in city and country from the King's interest.' In 1663 the government received reports of 'surreptitious radical activity from one end of the country to the other', as well as from Ireland and Scotland. Nor were the plotters merely desperate fanatics, expecting divine intervention, like Venner's men of 1661. They included ex-Army officers, clergymen, land purchasers ruined by the restoration, and men of substance in their localities like George

---

[12] Barry Reay, 'The Quakers, 1659, and the Restoration of the Monarchy', *History*, 63 (1978); id., 'Popular Hostility towards Quakers in Mid-Seventeenth-Century England', *Social History*, 5 (1980); id., *The Quakers and the English Revolution* (1985); Ronald Hutton, *The Restoration: A Political and Religious History of England and Wales, 1658–1667* (Oxford UP, 1985), follows Reay.

Blackburne, the wealthy Huddersfield clothier who thought that 'the gentry were insupportable to the people'.[13]

Until recently, denominational historians tended to underestimate the political and social radicalism of the precursors of post-restoration nonconformist sects. The researches of R. L. Greaves and Richard Ashcraft suggest that a similar reassessment of the attitudes of post-restoration dissenters is called for. It seems likely that more of them participated in, or were aware of, conspiracies against the government than used to be thought. Much work still remains to be done; but it is intrinsically improbable that all dissenters at once abandoned politics, even revolutionary politics, after 1660. Not even the Quakers did that.

This is the background against which the government tended to regard *any* illegal meeting as potentially seditious. There were those in the government, including Charles himself, who thought that toleration for genuinely pacifist nonconformists would isolate the militants; but the majority in the House of Commons and some bishops preferred a policy of mere repression.

We may ask why all this clandestine activity in the 1660s produced only one or two minor and isolated revolts? One reason is that potential rebels were united only by dislike of monarchy and bishops, divided by memories of the fierce disputes of the 1650s which had led to the downfall of the republic. Some wanted a Presbyterian discipline, others religious toleration for all protestants, others the rule of Jesus Christ through his saints; some wanted a republic, some the restoration of the house of Cromwell. Bunyan's controversy with the Quakers illustrated these divisions, which brought persecution on all dissenters. He himself came to regret them, as Milton did.[14]

Secondly, the government had picked off potential leaders of revolt. The regicides and Vane had been executed; Lambert, Hutchinson, and Harrington were in jail. Others like Ludlow were in exile. The government made extensive use of informers and *agents provocateurs*; it was helped by divisions between and within sects as they adjusted to the new situation. A providential view of history inclined many to see the restoration of monarchy and episcopacy as a divine judgment on a sinful people, and to conclude

[13] Op. cit. 3, 67, 159, 197, and *passim*.
[14] *MER*, 369.

that Christ's kingdom was not of this world. From 1661 the Quakers adopted the peace principle and abjured political activity, though it was long before all members of the Society of Friends accepted the new line. Quakers were active in the Northern Plot of 1663, and as late as 1685 some Quakers fought for Monmouth in his rebellion against James II.

Charles II often flirted with the idea of using the royal prerogative to allow toleration for protestant dissenters, partly in order to obtain toleration for Roman Catholics as well, partly to free himself from dependence on the Church of England and the House of Commons. He was defeated in 1662, but he tried again in 1672. Most sectaries gratefully accepted his Declaration of Indulgence; the Bedford congregation registered as 'Congregational'. But the relief was short-lived. Charles had to withdraw the Declaration.

Uncertainties in government policy led to inconsistency in execution of the laws against dissenters. When Parliament was in session they tended to be enforced more severely than when it was in recess; under the Declaration of Indulgence they were not enforced at all. Much would depend on the attitude of local JPs. But even when they wanted to enforce the laws against nonconformists, they could not do so without the co-operation of lesser officials, themselves liable to be influenced by local opinion. Where dissent was strong, blind eyes might be turned to religious meetings, or neighbourly feelings shield potential victims of persecution. Thus in Bedford in 1670, when an attempt was made to enforce the second Conventicle Act, constables refused to raid an illegal meeting. When churchwardens tried to levy fines they were pursued by a hostile crowd, who fixed a calf's tail on the back of one of them. Porters who were supposed to carry off goods distrained from dissenters disappeared, saying 'they would be hanged, drawn and quartered before they would assist in that work.' Even with the help of 'a file of soldiers' the officials proved incapable of breaking up a meeting of the congregation, and were told to call on the help of 'certain gentlemen of the town'. 'Most of the traders, journeymen, labourers and servants' either left the town or hid. With the gentry's help the law was enforced. John Fenn, hatter, in whose house the meeting had been held, lost all his hats and his household goods. A weaver at Cotton End was fined £19, and all his possessions, including the implements of his trade, were distrained. It is a significant, if propagandist, vignette of politics in and around Bedford in 1670.[15]

There are many other examples of local support for dissenting congregations. 'The country people . . . generally', exclaimed a JP in 1677, 'are so rotten that they will not complain of them [dissenters], though they see and know of these seditious meetings before their eyes daily.' It was in areas where dissenters were heavily outnumbered that desperation led to the most dangerous conspiracies. It is hardly surprising that many nonconformists pursued a waiting policy, expecting 'a sudden change in the state of public matters'. That was Seth Ward writing to Archbishop Sheldon in 1664. In the same year Elias Ashmole told his Presbyterian brother-in-law that 'nonconformity could be nothing but in expectation of a change'.[16]

During his twelve years' imprisonment Bunyan had to wait too. At first he was occasionally able to get out, either to go to London or to attend to his pastoral duties in and around Bedford. People could come to see him, and there were no doubt lively discussions between the prisoners. But he must have felt cut off from what was going on in his world, able to contribute only from afar to nonconformist politics.

So we need not think of Bunyan as a particularly political person to be confident that he regretted the restoration. His writings make it clear that he looked back nostalgically to the revolutionary decades. He was too prudent to say that the restoration had been a political disaster. But he suggested this more than once, cautiously, in *The Pilgrim's Progress*. In *Advice to Sufferers* (1684) he wrote: ''Tis a sad sight to see a man that has been suffering for righteousness restored to his former estate, while the righteousness for

---

[15] [Anon.], *A true and impartial narrative of some Illegal and Arbitrary Proceedings by certain Justices of the Peace and others, against several innocent and Peaceable Nonconformists in and near the Town of Bedford* (1670). Brown thought this pamphlet was printed by Francis Smith, Bunyan's printer. See also Brown, 205–9; Offor, ii. 216; M. Mullet, 'The Internal Politics of Bedford, 1660–1688, PBHRS 59 (1980), 3–6; G. E. Page, 'Baptist Churches in the Bedford Area', *Baptist Quarterly*, NS 14 (1951–2), 325.

[16] Sir Peter Leicester, *Charges to the Grand Jury at Quarter Sessions, 1660–1677*, ed. E. M. Halcrow, Chetham Soc., 3rd Ser. v (1953), 91; cf. 93; Greaves, *Deliver Us from Evil* (Oxford UP, 1986), 12; J. Simmons, 'Some Letters from Bishop Ward of Exeter, 1663–1667', *Devon and Cornwall Notes and Queries*, 21 (1940–1), 285. I owe this reference to the unpublished Exeter D.Phil. thesis by P. W. Jackson, *Nonconformity and Society in Devon, 1660–1689* (1986), 124; H. Newcome, *Autobiography*, ed. R. Parkinson, Chetham Soc. (1852), 145.

which he suffered remains under locks and irons.' His resentment was directed especially towards those who, in his view, had
turned their coats in order to profit by the restoration. In *Prison
Meditations* (1663) he wrote of:

> that which our foes expect,
> Namely our turning the postate
> Like those of Judas' sect. . . .
>
> Good men suffer for God's way
> And bad men at them rage. . . .
> Here we see also who turns round
> Like weathercocks with wind. . . .
>
> The politicians that profest
> For base and worldly ends,
> Do now appear to us at best
> But Machivillian friends.[17]

The great moral example came to be Brother John Child, a leading
member of the Bedford church in the 1650s, who conformed to the
state church in 1660 for fear of persecution and ultimately hanged
himself. He is thought to be the despairing Man in the Iron Cage in
The Pilgrim's Progress.[18]

Bunyan looked back, beyond the revolutionary decades, to the
heretical succession to which radicals had always appealed—
Lollards, 'Hus, Bilney, Ridley, Hooper, Cranmer'. Their light and
knowledge were great, but revelation is progressive, and the saints
of Bunyan's day had more of it even than the martyrs. This must
have been a deeply consoling thought, particularly in view of the
humbler social status of seventeenth-century English saints than
that of sixteenth-century bishops. The point was put forcefully and
effectively in a sermon preached to the House of Commons in
November 1646 by Bunyan's friend William Dell.[19]

But things seemed very different to the nervous rulers of
England, who equated obstinate refusal to conform to the state
church with sedition and rebellion. Jailbirds like Bunyan had to be
especially careful. So we should not expect outspoken political
comment in his writings; nor were politics his main concern. But

---

[17] MW x. 63; *Poems*, 47. 'Profest' means 'made profession of religion'.
[18] *GA*, 164–5; *PP*, 34–5.
[19] *The Holy City* (1665), MW iii. 154; Dell, *Several Sermons and Discourses* (1709), esp.
138.

circumstances forced him to think about the ecclesiastical and
political organization of the society in which he lived. 'Oftentimes
when the wicked world hath raged most' against dissenters, there
had been 'souls awakened by the Word. I could instance particu-
lars, but I forbear', he added prudently. In *Of the Resurrection of the
Dead* (1665) Bunyan wrote, 'I am this day . . . persecuted by . . . an
hypocritical people [who] will persecute the power of those truths
in others which themselves in words profess.' And he spoke, less
guardedly, of 'the very heart of Cain the murderer, of Judas the
traitor.' But at last they would be judged, 'be thou King or Keser'.
In the posthumous *Israel's Hope Encouraged* he spoke again of the
'greatness' of 'men of a persecuting spirit'. There are plenty of
hints like these if we read between the lines.[20]

   In *The Holy City* (1665) Bunyan saw that 'the saints are yet but as
an army routed'. Want of light had led to 'that crossness of
judgment and persuasion that hath been found among the saints'.
Bunyan expected better times; but meanwhile he had to confront
those who 'murmur and repine at God's hand, at his dispensations,
and at the judgments that overtake them, in their persons, estates,
families, or relations. . . . A murmuring spirit is such an one as
seems to correct God, and to find fault with his dispensations', to
claim to detect 'a failure in the nature and execution of things'. The
restoration had indeed given the godly grounds for questioning
God's justice, or his mercy, or both. 'Have you not hard thoughts
of God', Colonel Okey was asked on his way to execution as a
regicide, 'for this his strange providence towards you?' Okey
proclaimed his belief that the Good Old Cause would revive;[21] but
the question remained unanswered.

ii. In Jail

Seventeenth-century jails were run by private enterprise, with the
abuses that naturally follow. Fees had to be paid; privileges could
be bought. Bunyan was not well off, and he had a wife and five
surviving children (four by his first wife). The eldest of these, his

---

   [20] *GA*, 89; *The Resurrection of the Dead*, MW iii. 204–5, 261, 275; *Israel's Hope
Encouraged*, Offor, i. 581.
   [21] *The Holy City*, MW iii. 136–40; *A Treatise of the Fear of God* (1680), MW ix. 121;
Advice to Sufferers (1684), MW x, *passim*; Brown, 166–7; *Colonel John Okey, 1606–1660*,
ed. Tibbutt, PBHRS 35 (1955), 154.

'poor blind child, . . . lay nearer my heart than all I had besides.'
Elizabeth's first child died when she was 'smayed at the news' of
her husband's arrest. He had to 'tag laces' to earn a few pennies for
them. When he emerged from prison, 'he found his temporal
affairs were gone to wreck, and he had as to them to begin again'
(*GA*, 98, 128).

We should not forget how appalling prisons could be. Satan can
make 'a jail look like hell itself', wrote Bunyan many years later.
Insanitary conditions, lack of heating, and overcrowding, led to jail
fever and other diseases. The early Quaker leadership was deci-
mated by deaths in prison. Fox, like Bunyan, was exceptionally
tough, and both survived. The plague of 1665 raged around
Bedford jail, claiming forty victims. A pest-house was set up in the
town.[22]

The severity of Bunyan's imprisonment varied from time to
time, with the political situation. At one time he 'had by my jailor
some liberty granted me more than at the first', and even was able
to follow 'my wonted course of preaching', visiting and exhorting
'the people of God'. He went as far afield as London. This was not
exceptional. Lawrence Clarkson when in prison in the 1640s could
'sit at the street-door' and 'go abroad'. But when Bunyan's enemies
heard what was happening they 'almost cast my jailor out of his
place' and tightened up Bunyan's imprisonment. From October
1661 to October 1668 he is not recorded as attending meetings of
the Bedford congregation. In 1666 he was released for a few
months, but since he persisted in preaching he was rearrested. In
jail Bunyan had only the Bible to read, we are told, until he bought
a copy of Foxe's *Book of Martyrs*. Yet he was able to obtain and
read William Penn's *The Sandy Foundations Shaken* and Edward
Fo\ ler's *The Design of Christianity* soon after they were published
in 1668 and 1671 respectively.[23]

Access to the imprisoned Bunyan seems to have been easy.
George Cokayne apparently had no difficulty in visiting him. A
woman who had robbed her Wellingborough master of a considerable sum came to seek his advice. Bunyan offered to send for

---

[22] Paul Slack, *The Impact of Plague in Tudor and Stuart England* (1985), 225. For
conditions in jails see G. R. Cragg, *Puritanism in the Period of the Great Persecution,
1660–1688* (Cambridge UP, 1957), ch. 4; Godber, *The Story of Bedford: An Outline
History* (Luton, 1978), 97.

[23] *GA*, 128–30; Brown, 154, 158–60; Sharrock, 46; *Israel's Hope Encouraged*
(posthumous), Offor, i. 581. See pp. 130–5 below.

her master and endeavour to make her peace; but she was too frightened of being hanged. He had other similar visitors. He and his brethren preached to one another on Sundays, 'in our prison chamber'. Bunyan has a touching story of one occasion when 'it being my turn to speak', he was 'so empty, spiritless and barren that I thought I should not have been able to speak among them so much as five words of truth with life and evidence.' Providentially his eye fell on Revelation 21, which produced not only a sermon but, 'after we had well dined, I gathered up this basketful . . . of the fragments that were left' – amounting to 294 pages of *The Holy City* (1665).[24]

In the winter and early spring of 1660–1 there were more than fifty Quakers in prison with Bunyan; and there were more later. Overcrowding may indeed have accounted for his unofficial leave of absence. Other fellow-prisoners, at one time or another, included Nehemiah Coxe of his congregation (for preaching); John Gibbs of Newport Pagnell; John Dunne or Donne, ejected minister of Pertenhall; five men of Blunham, imprisoned for conventicles; John Fox, accused of murder. Elizabeth Pratt, Bedford's last alleged witch, died in prison in 1667 before she came to trial.[25]

Enforced acquaintance with Quakers in jail may have modified Bunyan's hostility to them, and theirs to him. In any case, the emphasis of Quaker doctrine had shifted since his controversies of the 1650s. The Quaker John Rush and his mother were released from Bedford jail at the same time as Bunyan. Bunyan's name was included in a list of prisoners to be freed in 1672 at the instance of the Quaker George Whitehead. Both parties seem to have learnt the lesson which Bunyan drew in his *Confession of my Faith and a Reason of my Practice* – that divisions among the godly had 'greatly prevailed to bring down these judgments which at present we feel and groan under'. They were, he added, 'a cause thereof'.[26]

---

[24] Greaves, 'John Bunyan's *The Holy War*', *Baptist Quarterly*, 26 (1975); *Mr. B.*, Offor, iii. 610. The story of the woman visitor is told by Mr. Wiseman, but the experience was clearly Bunyan's.

[25] E. Stockdale, 'A Study of Bedford Prison, 1660 to 1877', PBHRS 56 (1977), 14–16, 70–1; Fox, *Journal*, ed. Penney (1901), 358. Nehemiah was son of Benjamin Coxe who ran a congregational meeting at Bedford in 1643. The son, a cordwainer or shoemaker, was licensed to preach as a Baptist at Maulden in 1672 (Page, 'Baptist Churches in the Bedford Area', 271, 276, 327).

[26] H. J. Cadbury, 'John Bunyan and the Quakers', *Journal of the Friends' Historical Soc.*, 52 (1968), 47; cf. ibid. 10 (1915), 290–1; Offor, ii. 614; cf. 634. Published in 1683, probably written *c.*1670–1.

Greaves has drawn attention to an unexpected consequence of Bunyan's imprisonment. At one time or another he was joined in jail by at least nine men who were to play a leading part in spreading dissenting congregations in and around Bedfordshire in the 1670s. Finding themselves 'aside from the lumber and cumber of this world', they had not much else to do but talk to one another. It seems reasonable to conclude that they planned there the rapid expansion and co-operation of churches which took place after 1672 under the Indulgence.[27] The prisoners must have seen this frustration of the intentions of their Antichristian persecutors as providential.

One other thing that Bunyan was able to do in prison, rather surprisingly, was to write. Like George Fox, Bunyan took full advantage of his enforced leisure. Within the first six years of his imprisonment he produced a number of books — *Grace Abounding*, published in 1666; *Of the Resurrection of the Dead* and *The Holy City* (both 1665). The latter derived from the sermon which Bunyan preached to his fellow-prisoners. It is a large work about the New Jerusalem, with millenarian overtones. He experimented with verse — *Profitable Meditations* (1661) and *Prison Meditations* (1663), *One Thing is Needful* and *Ebal and Gerizzim* in 1665. During the six years after 1666 he published nothing. He was probably writing *The Pilgrim's Progress*, and perhaps *The Heavenly Foot-man*, an account of life as a foot-race, which could have led on to *The Pilgrim's Progress*. It was not published in Bunyan's lifetime. It is just possible that others of his posthumously published works may date back to these years, though none have been positively identified. A more likely explanation for non-publication before 1678 is that the political atmosphere was unfavourable. This was a period of persecution during which the Bedford church seems to have met only in secret. The shop of Bunyan's publisher, Francis Smith, was raided in 1666 and many books were seized, including almost certainly some of Bunyan's. Smith named him as a highly suspect author. So either no other publisher would touch him, or Bunyan himself may have felt discretion to be the better part until his release in 1672 coincided with the Declaration of Indulgence which enabled the Bedford congregation to meet legally again.

[27] *The Holy City* (1665), MW iii. 77; Greaves, 'The Organizational Response of Nonconformity to Repression and Indulgence: The Case of Bedfordshire', *Church History*, 44 (1975), 1–13.

In prison Bunyan must have added to his mastery of the Bible; he may have completed his own concordance. He may also have collected his considerable knowledge of the law and of litigation. Greaves has suggested that the analogy which Bunyan develops at length in *The Advocateship of Jesus Christ*, and the legal knowledge assumed, must mean that it was intended by Bunyan primarily for the literate and well-to-do London dissenting community, and for their counterparts in other areas.[28] But Clive Holmes has recently argued that such knowledge may, of necessity, have been more common among yeomen and artisans than we are accustomed to think. The point is reinforced from the other side by Wilfrid Prest, who emphasizes that lawyers' clients are found among classes well below the gentry.[29] Bunyan's own legal expertise no doubt derived from his own experience as a defendant. But his frequent use of legal technical terms suggests an assumption that his readers will understand them. Was such knowledge common among yeomen and artisans? Or had dissenters learnt from their experience of persecution, as Holmes's fenmen learnt from their communal action against fen drainers?

[28] Newey, 110; *Law and Grace* (1659), MW ii. 139 (*praemunire*, replieve), 143 (indenting), 161 (throw over the bar); *The Advocateship of Jesus Christ* (posthumous), MW xi (replevy), 154 (*supersedeas*), 164 (demur), 169 (nonsuit), 184 (feoffee in trust), 190 (*in forma pauperis*), 160–1 (litigation); *A Relation of My Imprisonment*, GA, 107, 112–13 (*mittimus*, bill of indictment, writ of error); *The Pharisee and the Publican* (1685), Offor, ii. 239 (*caveat*); MW xi. p. xxxiv; *HW*, 265 n.

[29] Holmes, 'Drainers and Fenmen: The Problem of Popular Political Consciousness in the Seventeenth Century', in *Order and Disorder in Early Modern England*, ed. A. Fletcher and J. Stevenson (Cambridge UP, 1985), 166–95; Prest, 'The English Bar, 1550–1700', in *Lawyers in Early Modern Europe and America*, ed. Prest (1981), 71–2; Prest, *The Rise of the Barristers*, ch. 2.

12. The Tinker and the Latitudinarians

> The Bible in English under every weaver's and chambermaid's arm hath done us [royalists] much hurt. . . . For controversy is a civil war with the pen which pulls out the sword soon afterwards.
>
> THE DUKE OF NEWCASTLE (TO CHARLES II)[1]

> Be not offended at his [Bunyan's] plain and downright language. . . . Though his outward condition and former employment was mean, and his humane learning small, . . . he hath laid forth himself to the utmost of his strength, taking all advantage to make known to others what he himself hath received of God: and I fear this is one reason why the archers have shot so sorely at him.
>
> I.G. (PROBABLY JOHN GIBBS)[2]

i. The Subversive Bible

THERE is much to be found in the Bible about the iniquities of the rich and powerful and the virtues of the poor and humble, which not all Christians emphasize equally at all times. But in the 1640s, and 1650s, with the poor more able to speak for themselves than had been usual, their case had been stressed by Levellers, Diggers, Ranters, Quakers, Fifth Monarchists, and many others. Bunyan inherited this theme and expounded it with gusto.

The main support for separatist congregations came from artisans, the middling and poorer sort. John Brown collected much evidence to demonstrate that in Bedfordshire the majority of persons up before the church courts for nonconformity in the 1660s came from this social class. Those who attended conventicles were described as 'the meaner sort', 'the scum of the people'. There is an element of conventionality in such phrases: no doubt those who seemed 'the scum of the people' to JPs and ecclesiastical officials were respectable citizens to their neighbours. Brown gives evidence of support, protection, and warnings given to nonconformists by their neighbours.[3]

Bunyan in *A Few Sighs from Hell* wanted to persuade sinners that,

---

[1] A. S. Turberville, *A History of Welbeck Abbey and its Owners*, i. *1559–1715* (1938), 60, 173–6.

[2] (To the Reader), prefixed to Bunyan's *A Few Sighs from Hell* (1658).

[3] *WTUD*, 19–24, 331, 348–9, 354; Brown, 202–3, 208, 215, 396, 411–12.

predestination notwithstanding, salvation is potentially accessible to all if they will only turn towards Christ. The poor and humble indeed have a better chance than the rich and great. Bunyan denounced 'rich ungodly landlords, that so keep under their poor tenants, that they dare not go out to hear the Word, for fear their rent should be raised, or they turned out of their houses.' The phrases tell us a great deal about patriarchal aspects of the society which Bunyan especially disliked. 'Oh I dare not for my master, my brother, my landlord. I shall lose his favour, his house of work, and so decay my calling.' What Bunyan respects, and expects, is independence, the ability to stand on one's own feet without kowtowing to employers. He pities those who are 'poorer than they that go with flail and rake'. Bunyan's metaphors make the same point. Under the Law, men never know whether they will be paid wages or not. 'They work for they do not know what, even like a poor horse that works hard all day, and at night hath a dirty stable for his pains.'[4]

After 1660 a cautiously political note enters in. It was the rich, the aristocracy, who backed the regime which was persecuting those whom Bunyan believed to be the elect of God. 'Look into the gaols of England', he wrote, 'and into the ale-houses; . . . and I believe you will find those that plead for the spirit of prayer in the gaol, and those that look after the forms of men's inventions only—in the ale-house'. In the first day of the Gospel the poor, the halt, the lame, the blind, were those who responded. Only in the latter day will God take hold of kings. But when Jerusalem was being built after the captivity, 'their nobles put not their necks to the work of the Lord (Nehemiah III. 5).' 'All their princes shall be nothing, saith the prophet, and when they call their nobles to the kingdom, none shall be there.'[5]

Those who expect God to have too much respect for their 'noble race' to send them to hell should reflect on the fate of the rebel angels,

> though of higher race
> Than thou, and also put in higher place,
> Yet them he spared not.

[4] MW i. 315, 336, 340, 373; MW ii. 46. Cf. ch. 23 (iii) below.
[5] *I will Pray with the Spirit* (1662?), MW ii. 284; *The Holy City* (1665), MW iii. 165–9, 85, 138.

One might suppose that Bunyan was tilting at windmills here. But in 1682 the diarist John Evelyn clearly admired a brutal murderer who declared on the scaffold that he 'hoped and believed God would deal with him like a gentleman'. In *Israel's Hope Encouraged* (posthumous) Bunyan summed up his resentment at his own persecution and imprisonment with a memory of the radical reliance on the traditional laws of England. 'The old laws, which are the Magna Carta, the sole basis of the government of a kingdom, may not be cast away for the pet that is taken by every little gentleman against them.'[6]

The Pilgrim's Progress and *The Holy War* are full of this sort of class awareness. The evil characters are all carefully described as lords and gentlemen: Christian is a poor itinerant. In *The Holy War* the Diabolonians are peers and vagabonds. In *Of Antichrist and his Ruin*, Antichrist is described as a gentleman, who 'takes a pet' against the people of God. Here once more Bunyan may be close to popular literature: Dr Capp cites a chap-book of 1670 in which the devil appeared 'like a brave gentleman'.[7]

Tindall suggested that Bunyan took less account of social tensions as he himself became better off.[8] This is not the impression I get from the works of the 1680s or of those which Bunyan left unpublished at his death, no doubt for prudential reasons. 'He that is poor and needy' shall have life, he wrote in *Come and Welcome to Jesus Christ* (1678). Christ 'has life to give away to such as want it, and that hath not a penny to purchase it; and he will give it freely.' This is the obverse of the commercial society of Vanity Fair and of *Mr. Badman*; 'the poor, because they are poor, are not capable of sinning against God as the rich man does (Ps. XLIX. 6)'. Poverty brings positive spiritual advantages. 'The poor can more clearly see himself preserved by the providence of God than the rich, for he trusteth in the abundance of his riches.' Bunyan becomes eloquent in spurning 'things far lower, more base, but much more easy to obtain, as crowns, kingdoms, earldoms, dukedoms, gold, riches or the like.' 'God has refused to give his children

---

[6] *Ebal and Gerizzim* (1665?), in *Poems*, 177; Evelyn, *Diary*, 10 Mar. 1682; Offor, i. 600.
[7] *HW*, 91, 121–3; Offor, ii. 54; Capp, 'Popular Literature', in *Popular Culture in Seventeenth-Century England*, ed. B. Reay (1985), 220.
[8] Tindall, 105.

the great, the brave and glorious things of this world, a few only excepted', Bunyan explained, 'because he hath better things for them'.[9] *The Pharisee and the Publican* (1685) returns to the theme of Dives and Lazarus, 'the potentates of this world' and 'one of the vilest of men'. In 1688 Bunyan, with the pride of a skilled craftsman, spoke disparagingly of the idle rich, who 'know not how to turn their hand to do any things so'; 'for all their lofty looks' craftsmen were their betters, and had to 'come and mend their work'.[10]

God was 'preparing mansions for those his poor ones that are now by his enemies kicked to and fro, like footballs in the world; and is not that a blessed sight?' 'I am apt to think sometimes', wrote Bunyan in *The Heavenly Foot-man*, 'that more servants than masters, . . . more tenants than landlords, will inherit the kingdom of heaven. . . . Many of them are wiser than you in the things of the world to come.' 'The poor receive the gospel; not many rich', said Bunyan in *Paul's Departure and Crown*, also posthumous.[11]

Take *The Jerusalem Sinner*, also not published in Bunyan's lifetime. Here Bunyan repeats that Christ rejects 'the great ones that were the grandees of the world', and struggles hard 'for hedge-creepers and highwaymen'. On Calvary 'he took the thief away with him to glory'. Bunyan adapts the theme to criticize ministers who have social aspirations. We must:

lay aside our foolish, worldly, carnal grandeur: let us not walk the streets, and have such behaviours as signify we are scarce for touching of the poor ones that are left behind; no, not with a pair of tongs. . . . Why not familiar with sinners, provided we hate their spots and blemishes? . . . Why not fellowly with our carnal neighbours? Practical love, which stands in self-denial, in charity to my neighbour, . . . is counted love.

Jesus Christ would have mercy offered in the first place to the biggest sinners.[12] The starting-point of *The Advocateship of Jesus Christ* (1688) is that Christ is said to plead the cause not of the rich but of the poor and needy. I shall be looking in chapter 26 at the

---

[9] MW viii. 373; *Mr. B.*, Offor, iii. 594, 618–19, 624, 632–3, 638, 644; *The Greatness of the Soul* (1682), MW ix. 236. Cf. *PP*, quoted on p. 224 below.

[10] MW x. 115–16, 184; *The Advocateship of Jesus Christ*, MW xi. 205–6.

[11] *The Desire of the Righteous Granted* (posthumous), Offor, i. 759; MW v. 177; cf. 165; Offor, i. 735.

[12] MW xi. 29, 80–1. Bunyan finds it necessary to add that such doctrine does not lead to looseness.

similar social lessons which Bunyan drew from the first ten chapters of Genesis.

Bunyan's congregation in 1669 consoled Brother Harrington, Sister Foxe, and Sister Hustwhat with 'the ease and peace of another world': the first-named had been driven from his family to avoid arrest as a dissenter. 'Troubles for Christ's sake', Bunyan wrote in the posthumous *House of the Forest of Lebanon*, 'are but like the prick of an awl in the tip of the ear, in order to hang a jewel there. . . . I am now in rags', but soon '£200 a year comes into my hand'. Israel was led through the wilderness to the promised land.[13]

There is a lot of history behind Bunyan's awareness of class. He could have learnt it from Dent, Bayly, Bernard, or Dell; or direct from the Bible. Dent had insisted that aristocrats were as liable to damnation as anyone else, and has many eloquent passages against the rich. Bayly, in a Biblical phrase which Bunyan echoed, said, 'not many wise, . . . not many mighty, not many noble are called'. Bernard was equally severe against the gentry, denouncing oppression of the poor and covetousness, longing for 'good neighbourhood'. Dell's sermons contained much criticism of the rich.[14]

I use the phrase 'class-awareness' rather than 'class-consciousness' in deference to those who dislike applying the latter phrase to the seventeenth century because of its nineteenth-century Marxist associations. My suggestion is not that Bunyan looked for class solidarity against his enemies (what classes would he have looked to?) but that he spoke for the poor against the rich, for 'us' against 'them', for peasants, artisans, and small merchants against the gentry. Anti-landlord feeling was traditional, but it now had a new edge. The abolition of feudal tenures in 1645 (confirmed 1656 and 1660) had established absolute property rights for the gentry in their lands, but no such security of tenure for copyholders, lesser landholders. So the agricultural revolution of the later seventeenth century was made at the expense of tenants who could now be more easily evicted when this was convenient for their landlord. Traditional customary rights beneficial to the peasantry were being eroded. All these developments imposed new

---

[13] Tibbutt, *Minutes*, 57–60; Offor, iii. 537.
[14] Dent, esp. 189–210; Bayly, esp. 116–18; Bernard, *The Isle of Man* (1803), esp. 70–5, 150–62, 178–85 (1st pub. 1627); Dell, *Several Sermons and Discourses* (1709), 87–91 and *passim*.

stresses on relations between rich and poor, those whose property rights were protected by law and those whose customary rights were ceasing to be legally enforceable. Of these strains Bunyan was very much aware: and his sympathies were whole-heartedly with the poor.

ii. Bunyan and Edward Fowler[15]

Latitudinarians regarded themselves as liberal, rational, middle-of-the-road men. Bunyan disliked them as much as he disliked Quakers, perhaps more. He regarded the two as theologically linked. His particular bête noire was Edward Fowler, Rector of Northill, just outside Bedford, who in 1670 published The Principles and Practices of certain Moderate Divines of the Church of England. This was a defence of the Latitudinarians, against high flyers in the Church of England as well as against dissenters. Fowler spoke of 'the reasonableness of the Gospel precepts', denouncing the absolute decrees of predestinarian theology and 'the antinomian opinion of imputed righteousness'. Bunyan held that men and women were saved by Christ's imputed righteousness, though he did not regard this as an antinomian opinion. But Fowler's treatise was not merely theoretical. He arrived at the practical conclusion that dissenters 'ought not to be esteemed or dealt with as men of tender consciences'.[16]

Fowler followed this up in 1671 with The Design of Christianity. Here he further provoked by declaring that no serious person could rationally arrive at the antinomian error arising from the doctrine of imputed righteousness. The object of The Design of Christianity was to establish that a holy and moral life was possible for everyone, because the principles of such a life were written in the hearts of all men. Bunyan thought that Fowler's theology 'is the self-same which our late ungodly heretics the Quakers have made such a stir to promote.' Fowler's book reminded him of the Quaker William Penn's The Sandy Foundations Shaken (1668). In his Defence of the Doctrine of Justification (1672), Bunyan rejected Fowler's optimistic view of the potentialities of human nature, his

[15] In what I say about Latitudinarians I am not trying to give a balanced account of their views, but to explain the reasons for the fierce mutual antipathy between them and Bunyan. For a sympathetic contemporary opinion see G. Burnet, The History of My Own Time, ed. O. Airy (Oxford UP, 1897), i. 334–41.

[16] Op. cit. 75, 143, 199, 333. Bunyan's younger brother, Thomas, lived at Northill.

failure to insist on the sinner's absolute dependence on divine grace. Bunyan claimed to be more orthodox than the beneficed Anglican parson, citing three of the Thirty-nine Articles in order to demonstrate that 'I quarrel not with him about things wherein I dissent from the Church of England.' The quarrel was about Fowler's advocacy of 'a heathenish and pagan righteousness'. For Bunyan, the elect and Christ 'are united in one.... They ... receive of that inward quality, the grace and holiness that was in him at the day of his rising from the dead.'[17]

An additional reason for disliking Latitudinarians arose from their behaviour at the restoration. Fowler was ejected from his living in 1662, as were his father and elder brother. Both the latter remained dissenters; but Edward Fowler, on second thoughts, conformed. Other future Latitudinarians had retained their livings throughout the revolutionary decades and declined to become martyrs in 1660–2. They were 'ignorant Sir Johns ... persons who have for the love of filthy lucre, and the pampering of their idle carcasses, made a shipwreck of their former faith.' They 'hop from Presbyterianism to the prelatical mode; and if time and chance should serve you, backwards and forwards again.' 'A glorious Latitudinarian that can, as to religion, turn and twist like an eel on the angle; or rather, like the weathercock that stands on the steeple.'[18]

Bunyan's indignation was roused especially by Fowler's insistence that whatever things 'are commanded by the custom of the place we live in, or commanded by superiors, or made by any circumstance convenient to be done, our Christian liberty consists in this, that we have leave to do them.' Anyone who thought otherwise was guilty of 'conceited, pragmatical, ... contentious and unpeaceful behaviour', based on exaggerated ideas of his own worth. 'How then', Bunyan asked, 'if God should cast you into Turkey, where Mahomet reigns as Lord?' Bunyan had thought his way through such possibilities before his conversion, and now he regarded Fowler's position as mere Hobbism: he claimed to have

---

[17] Fowler, *The Design*, 274–7; Bunyan, *A Defence of the Doctrine of Justification* (1672), Offor, ii. 286, 292, 296–301, 305–6, 323–4, 331–4; MW viii, p. xliii; cf. 395–9, and Offor, i. 614: *Israel's Hope Encouraged*.

[18] *A Defence*, Offor, ii. 304, 313–14, 322; cf. *Prison Meditations* (1665?), in *Poems*, 46–7, quoted on p. 119 above; *The Strait Gate* (1676)–'the temporizing Latitudinarian', 'his religion turning this way and that way' (MW v. 125–6). Cf. a contemporary ballad, *The Turn-coat of the times*, in *The Roxburghe Ballads*, iv. 517.

'broken the head of your Leviathan'. Part of Fowler's object, Bunyan insisted, was 'clawingly [to] insinuate . . . Christ's loyalty to the magistrate', in order to imply disloyalty on the part of nonconformists. As L. J. Trinterud puts it, 'Rational religion and the repression of troublemakers' went together in the restoration period.[19]

Fowler's writings were the more disturbing because they represented a follow-up of Samuel Parker's *Discourse of Ecclesiastical Polity* (1669). Parker had been an Independent but turned his coat at the restoration, and was now chaplain to the Archbishop of Canterbury. He demanded that his former co-religionists should be cut off as 'enemies and outlaws to human society', and should be punished 'with the severest inflictions'. His treatise, which caused great alarm among dissenters, was answered by John Owen and many others. Bunyan was not alone in seeing Latitudinarians as Hobbists. 'Virtually all the dissenters charged Parker with being a Hobbist,' wrote Professor Ashcraft.[20] *Britannia and Rawleigh* (1674–5?), often attributed to Marvell, made the same accusation against the Church of England generally. If Marvell was the author, he may have been thinking particularly of Samuel Parker.

Fowler (or his curate writing on his behalf) gave as good as he got. He denounced Bunyan as 'a downright Ranter', 'a shameless abuser and perverter of the holy Scriptures'. His vocabulary is a useful reminder that Bunyan and the Quakers had no monopoly of violent language: 'so very dirty a creature', 'folly and wickedness', 'brutish barkings', 'scurrilous and vile language', 'ignorant fanatic zeal', 'insufferable baseness', 'spitting his venom', 'hideous nonsense', 'insolent pride', 'turbulent spirit', 'most hellish and devilish'. The title-page cited two texts: 2 Peter 2:12 against those that are not afraid to speak evil of dignities. 'These as natural brute beasts' are 'made to be taken and destroyed'. The second was Proverbs 18: 6: 'A fool's lips enter into contention, and his mouth calleth for

[19] *A Defence*, Offor, ii. 281, 319, 322; L. J. Trinterud, 'A.D. 1689: The End of the Clerical World', in *Theology in Sixteenth and Seventeenth Century England*, ed. W. Hudson and L. J. Trinterud (Los Angeles, 1971), 41; cf. D. D. Wallace, *Puritans and Predestination: Grace in English Protestant Theology, 1525–1695* (N. Carolina UP, 1982), 127.

[20] Parker, *Discourse*, pp. vi. 18, 221; *A Defence and Continuation of the Ecclesiastical Polity* (1671), 541. For reactions to Parker see R. Ashcraft, *Revolutionary Politics and Locke's Two Treatises of Government* (Princeton UP, 1986), ch. 2. Ashcraft argues that refuting Parker's arguments played a great part in the evolution of Locke's political thought (ibid. ch. 3).

strokes.' At the end of the pamphlet the author made explicit a call for Bunyan's exclusion from the benefits of the Declaration of Indulgence: 'I now appeal to Authority, whether this man ought to enjoy any interest in his Majesty's toleration, and whether letting such firebrands and most impudent malicious schismatics go unpunished doth not tend to the subversion of all government.'[21] He made his position clear.

In a pamphlet quaintly entitled *Peaceable Principles and True* (1673?) Bunyan snorted: 'Say what you will or can, though with much more squibbing frumps . . . than hitherto you have mixed your writing with.'[22] From Bunyan's point of view, Fowler was not only theologically unsound but was also a turncoat whose 'latitudinarianism' applied only inside the Church of England. There was to be no tolerance for those outside. He called for use of the power of the law against his former colleagues. The Quakers at least were in no position to persecute. It was this refusal to permit lay preaching which Bunyan found intolerable. A state church with toleration outside it was acceptable: Bunyan and his congregation took advantage of Charles II's Declaration of Indulgence in 1672. But not to be allowed to preach against sin, even or especially in the rich, was to ask Bunyan to abandon his vocation. He had spent twelve years in jail rather than do that.

Bunyan was not unique in disliking Latitudinarians. The contempt — no other word will do — that men so different as Andrew Marvell, Henry Stubbe, Samuel Butler, and especially the Earl of Rochester felt for the Latitudinarians derived in part from their reputation as turncoats: 'Cromwellian renegadoes', 'renagado-presbyterian turned Latitudinarian'. Their sweet reasonableness was not wholly divorced from an eye to the main chance. Fowler became Bishop of Gloucester — though it must also be said that he acquitted himself well in 1688, refusing to read James II's Declaration of Indulgence.[23] Whether Bunyan would have approved at the time is another question.

---

[21] *Dirt wipt off . . .* [against] *John Bunyan, lay-preacher in Bedford* (1672), 40, 70, and *passim.*

[22] Offor, ii. 654. The reference was not to Fowler.

[23] Marvell, *The Rehearsal Transpros'd*, ed. D. I. B. Smith (Oxford UP, 1971), esp. 42, 92, 96, 107, 310–11; J. R. Jacob, *Henry Stubbe: Radical Protestantism and the Early Enlightenment* (Cambridge UP, 1983), 140–1; Rochester, *Complete Poems*, ed. D. M. Veith (Yale UP, 1968), 75–6; my *Writing and Revolution in Seventeenth-Century England* (Brighton, 1985), 283–4, 302–4; Brown, 355.

Tindall and Sharrock compare Ignorance in *The Pilgrim's Progress* to Fowler. Ignorance is 'a brisk lad', like Bunyan in his Ranterish phase. He is satisfied that he had 'a good heart and a good life, according to God's commandments'. Ignorance 'soon got over' the River of Death, like Mr. Badman, but was sent down to hell just when he expected to enter heaven. Mr. Worldly Wiseman, Mr. By-ends, and the latter's friends also have Latitudinarian characteristics. 'Since God has bestowed upon us the good things of this life', argued Mr. Hold-the-world, 'he would have us keep them for his sake.' All these characters illustrate how Bunyan thought the church and society had been corrupted by the restoration. 'We never strive against wind and tide', said By-ends.[24]

'The generality of those who live most pleasantly in the world', wrote John Wilkins, a more pleasing Latitudinarian than Fowler, 'are the most religious and virtuous part of mankind.' Religion obliges men to 'diligence, caution, etc.': those who lack these virtues have only themselves to blame if poverty results. Bunyan was still inveighing indignantly against the 'first principles', 'dictates of human nature', of the Latitudinarians in his posthumous *Israel's Hope Encouraged*.[25]

In the long run latitudinarianism was to replace Calvinism as the dominant strain in English protestantism: Bunyan was fighting a losing battle on behalf of the predestinarian doctrines which had predominated for the 150 years after the Reformation. Latitudinarianism points forward to the new world of deism and rationalism. But the Latitudinarians also helped to reconcile the workings of the capitalist market with Christianity. Innumerable sermons which Pepys and Evelyn report show London preachers easily persuading their congregations that 'righteousness is a surer moral way of being rich than sin and villainy'; 'sanctified riches were marks of favour from God'; 'how piety and religion contributed to thriving and happiness even in this world'. George Bull thought

---

[24] *PP*, 99, 102, 123–5, 144–9, 162–3; Tindall, 62–3; Sharrock, 18, 92–3, 191. Ignorance has much in common with the character Antilegon in Dent's *The Plaine Mans Path-way*. Hold-the-world's speech was added in the third edition of 1679.

[25] Wilkins, *Of the Principles and Duties of Natural Religion* (1675), Bk. II, 342, 383. This posthumous work was edited by Tillotson. (I owe this reference to Dr Isabel Rivers); Offor, i. 617.

that to serve God without thought of reward amounted to antinomian fanaticism.[26]

'The most historically significant contribution of the Latitudinarians', Margaret Jacob suggested, 'lies in their ability to syn-
thesize the operations of a market society and the workings of
nature in such a way as to render the market society *natural*'.[27] So it
made sense for a radical like Henry Stubbe to oppose the alliance of
latitudinarian bishops and gentry in Parliament and in the Royal
Society—no less than an enemy of science like Samuel Butler, or
than Bunyan. Shame in *The Pilgrim's Progress* complained of the
pilgrims' 'ignorance of the times in which they lived, and want of
understanding in all natural science' (72). Newton, the great
synthesizer of modern science, and Whig Master of the Mint,
symbolizes the triumph of the new modes of thought. We are
perhaps not quite so certain today that the victory of Newtonianism was an unmixed blessing for the world.[28]

iii. Tinkers, Education, and Literature

Bunyan's concern about his lowly social origins and his inadequate
education was not superfluous. The bill of indictment of 1660 had
described him as 'labourer'. Like his father, he called himself
'brazier' rather than tinker: the names for the occupation seem to
have been interchangeable. A tinker was an emblem of lower-class
non-respectability and immorality. The drunken lecher Christopher Sly in *The Taming of the Shrew* claimed that the Slys 'came in
with Richard Conqueror', as the Bunyans may have come in with
William.[29] Prince Hal in *1 Henry IV* showed his outrageous

[26] Wallace, *Puritans and Predestination*, 170–1. See Pepys, *Diary*, 23 Aug. 1668;
Evelyn, *Diary*, 12 Jan. 1672, 23 May 1688; cf. 9 July 1675, 30 Mar. 1690; Bull, *Works*
(Oxford UP, 1846), i. 357–71.

[27] M. C. Jacob, *The Newtonians and the English Revolution, 1689–1720* (Hassocks,
1976), 51; J. R. Jacob, *Henry Stubbe, passim*. See now M. C. Jacob, *The Cultural Meaning
of the Scientific Revolution* (New York, 1988) chs. 3 and 4: 'Christianized self-interest'
(p. iii).

[28] See for instance Carolyn Merchant, *The Death of Nature: Women, Ecology and the
Scientific Revolution* (San Francisco, 1980), *passim*; and Brian Easlee, *Witch-Hunting,
Magic and the New Philosophy: An Introduction to Debates of the Scientific Revolution*
(Brighton, 1980), *passim*.

[29] *GA*, 112; Shakespeare, *The Taming of the Shrew*, Induction, i. 'Richard Con-
queror' no doubt relates to Manningham's anecdote about Shakespeare and Burbage:
'William the Conqueror was before Richard the Third', *Diary*, ed. J. Bruce, Camden
Soc. (1868).

abandonment of respectable standards by being ready to drink with any tinker. Two Archbishops of Canterbury agreed with Shakespeare about tinkers. Bancroft attacked Presbyterians who, he said, assumed that Christ's kingdom was 'nowhere acknowledged or to be found but where half a dozen artisans, shoemakers and tinkers ... do rule the whole parish.' Laud elegantly and charitably remarked that ''tis superstitious nowadays for any man to come with more reverence into a church than a tinker and his bitch come into an ale-house.' Sir Thomas Overbury agreed that the tinker is usually to be found 'where the best ale is'; 'the companion of his travels is some foul sunburnt quean.'[30] The author of *The Tinker of Turvey* (1630), writing for 'all strolling tinkers and all brave metal-men that travel on the hoof', described himself as a hard-drinking bachelor itinerant, 'my drab by my side'. 'Many a tinker's trull have I bum-fiddled'.

> From fair to fair we amble,
>   Our doxies pranking by us'.[31]

Turvey was only a few miles from Elstow.

In the 1640s Bancroft's point about artisans running churches was worked to death. 'Those venerable and reverend Fathers, Master Cobbler, Tinker and Button-maker', 'rising from the very dunghill, beating the pulpits.' 'Cobblers, tinkers, peddlars, weavers, sowgelders and chimney sweepers.' 'Cobblers and tinkers' were said to be governing Chelmsford in 1642: they had appropriately subversive social views, despising learning and wishing to abolish universities. The lists became common form,

---

[30] Shakespeare, *1 Henry IV*, II. iv. 15–20; Richard Bancroft, *Dangerous Positions* (1593), 44; Laud, *Works* (Oxford UP, 1847–60), vi, pt. i. 57; Sir Thomas Overbury, *Characters* (1614), in *Character Writings of the Seventeenth Century*, ed. H. Morley (1891), 53–4.

[31] [Anon.], *The Tinker of Turvey* (1630), in *Short Fiction of the Seventeenth Century*, ed. C. C. Mish (New York, 1963), 118–22; cf. *A Jovial Tinker* (1616), *The Pepys Ballads*, ed. H. E. Rollins (Harvard UP, 1923), i. 102–8; Brown, 29–30. The drunkenness of tinkers is emphasized by Henry Glapthorne (*The Lady Mother* (1635), I. i; III. i) and in ballads (J. A. Sharpe, 'Plebeian Marriage in Stuart England: Some Evidence from Popular Literature', TRHS, 5th Ser. 36 (1986), 79). One version of *The Taming of the Shrew* (1594) ends with tinker Sly shown as unable to control his own wife (Lisa Jardine, *Still Harping on Daughters: Women and Drama in the Age of Shakespeare* (Brighton, 1983), 136). 'Tinker's dog' was the ultimate abuse hurled at a village constable delivering a summons (Joan R. Kent, *The English Village Constable, 1580–1642: A Social and Administrative Study* (Oxford UP, 1986), 255).

but tinkers were always on them.[32] An indignant royalist in the South-West during the civil war denounced Parliament, unplausibly, as 'a company of tinkers and peddlars'.[33] John Cleveland and many others sneered at 'Tinker Fox', the Birmingham blacksmith who led his own contingent against the royalists in the early years of the civil war and seemed to be setting himself up as an independent third force in the Midlands until the New Model Army took over. On the other side Richard Overton declared that 'bellows-menders, broom-men, cobblers, tinkers or chimney sweepers . . . are all equally freeborn with the loftiest.'[34] He drew the opposite political conclusion, but he too lumped tinkers with the lowest of the low.

George Gascoigne, born a century earlier than Bunyan within half a mile of his birthplace, may have started what became a traditional joke that tinkers made more holes than they repaired.[35] John Davys, in his Preface to Hobbes's *Of Liberty and Necessity* (1654), slandered the clergy in the most offensive way possible: 'blackcoats . . . are a sort of ignorant tinkers, . . . making and soldering men's consciences'; but they 'made more holes than they found'. At the trial of the Fifth-Monarchist Benjamin Keach the judge said 'this fellow would have ministers to be . . . tailors, peddlars and tinkers'.[36] Charles Goodall complained that radicals wanted medicine thrown open to tinkers, 'tailors to invade the bar and jugglers the pulpit'. In 1681–2 the Whigs were accused of appealing to 'any porter, cobbler or tinker', 'tinkers and

[32] [Anon.], *The Country-Mans Case And the Citizens Feare* (1641), 3–4; John Taylor, *A Swarme of Sectaries and Schismatics* (1641), 27; Ryves, *Angliae Ruina*, 27; *Mercurius Elencticus*, 21 Apr.–8 May 1649: 'cobblers, tinkers, broom-men, button makers'; *Mercurius Pragmaticus*, 5–12 June 1649: 'base brewers, tinkers, mechanic slaves'; [Anon.], *England's Murthering Monsters*, c.1650: 'tinker and tailor'; *Mercurius Fumigosus*, 21–28 Mar. 1655: 'broom-men, draymen, tinkers, porters and the meanest mechanics'. All the above are quoted in Tindall, 245.
[33] Quoted in David Underdown, *Revel, Riot and Rebellion: Popular Politics and Culture in England, 1603–1660* (Oxford UP, 1985), 180.
[34] Cleveland, *The Character of a London Diurnal*, in *Works* (1687), 91. See also J. W. Willis-Bund, 'A Civil War Parliament Soldier: "Tinker Fox"', *Associated Architectural Societies' Reports and Papers*, 25 (1899–1900), 373, 403; Overton, *An Arrow against All Tyrants* (1646), 19–20; cf. *The Araignement of Mr. Persecution* (1645), 18; E. Chillenden, *Preaching without Ordination* (1647), 6–7.
[35] Gascoigne, *The Steele Glas* (1576); Overbury, *Characters*, 54; cf. Samuel Butler, *Hudibras* (1662), Pt. I, canto ii; [Anon. (?T. Smith)], *A Gagg for the Quakers* (1659), uses the jest against Bunyan.
[36] Hobbes, *English Works*, ed. Sir W. Molesworth (1839–45), iv. 235–6; Tindall, 7.

broom-men', just as Parliamentarians had been forty years earlier.[37]

In 1691 Richard Baxter predicted that 'if any would raise an army to extirpate knowledge and religion, the tinkers and sow-gawters and crate-carriers and bargemen and all the rabble that cannot read, nor ever use the Bible, will be the forwardest to come into such a militia.' The extruded incumbent of St John the Baptist church in Bedford, demanding his living back after the restoration, did not fail to emphasize that it had been given to Bunyan a tinker and Burton a coachsmith. In 1685 'Cummins the tinker' was preacher to the church of Gamlingay, Cambridgeshire, associated with the Bedford congregation. It was therefore courageous but not very plausible when Charles Doe said of tinkers (after Bunyan's death) 'commonly' they are Anglicans.[38]

So Bunyan had reason for his sensitivity about being a tinker, though he seems to have ceased to work at the trade after his imprisonment. He was left in no doubt about its social aura. If it was wrong for artisans to preach or write, it was doubly intolerable for a mere tinker to do so. This perhaps goes some way to explain the fierceness of Bunyan's early controversial methods, though it is fair to say that his first adversary, Edward Burrough, did not attack him with this particular weapon. Quakers too opposed university learning as a prerequisite for preaching the Word of God.

Even Bunyan's friends, even when defending him, must have rubbed salt into his wounds. Henry Denne (MA Cantab.) rebuked people for being surprised that the tinker mended souls as well as kettles and pans. ('As soon find a true minister of the Gospel in the University of Newgate' as from Oxford or Cambridge, Denne said.) William Dell, Master of Gonville and Caius College, Cambridge, after inviting Bunyan to preach in his church on Christmas Day 1659, said 'he had rather hear a plain countryman speak in the church than the best orthodox minister that was in the country.'

[37] Goodall, The Royal College of Physicians (1672), sig. A4; cf. The Royal College of Physicians Vindicated (1676); John Eachard, The Grounds and Occasions of the Contempt of the Clergy (1670), 74; Ashcraft, Revolutionary Politics, 301.

[38] Baxter, The Poor Husbandman's Advocate to Rich Racking Landlords, ed. F. J. Powicke, Bull. of the John Rylands Library, 10 (1926); Colonel John Okey, 1606–1660, ed. Tibbutt, PBHRS, 35 (1955), 80; M. Spufford, 'Dissenting Churches in Cambridgeshire from 1660 to 1700', Proceedings of the Cambridgeshire Antiquarian Soc., 61 (1968), 88; C. Doe, The Struggler (1691), in Offor, iii. 765.

Both were no doubt kindly meant; but they cannot have been balm to the self-conscious preacher and author, smarting from Professor Smith's crude dismissal of his views and refusal to argue because Bunyan did not know the forms in which to conduct an academic discussion.[39]

So although Bunyan became a person of some standing in Bedford, he never quite got over the need to proclaim, without apologizing for it, that he was a plain unlearned man, who did not get his ideas from other people's books.[40] A proud assertion of low birth and lack of education was one way of claiming divine inspiration. Radical hostility to academic learning goes back a long way – at least to the heretic 'free-willer' Henry Hart in the reign of Edward VI. It links up with the uneducated man's distrust of print, and to education as a class privilege. Shakespeare, whose ear in these matters is impeccable, made Jack Cade say, 'Because they could not read, thou hast hanged them.' Before the sixteenth century an educated man was almost necessarily a priest or a gentleman; only the Reformation emphasis on Bible-reading made possible, and economic circumstances demanded, a rapid spread of literacy. Cade was referring to benefit of clergy, a clerical privilege which survived the Reformation and allowed men who could read to escape the penalties of a first felony. It helped the well-to-do and penalized the poor: women were not fully eligible for benefit of clergy until 1692.[41]

The 'educational revolution' of the sixteenth century, it has been suggested, may have widened the cultural gap between the increasing number of the middling sort who could afford education, and the populace who could not. 'The hostility to the universities which exploded in the freer atmosphere of the sixteen-forties', Professor Morgan perceptively observed, may have been a consequence of the 'educational revolution'.[42] The contempt of

---

[39] *GA*, 170; Denne, *The Quaker no Papist* (1659), sig. A 2; *Fenstanton Records*, 377; Brown, 117–18; *The Holy City* (1665), MW iii. 171–2; *Solomon's Temple Spiritualized* (1688), Offor, iii. 464. Cf. the epigraph to this chapter.

[40] *A Few Sighs from Hell*, MW i. 304; *Light for them that sit in Darkness* (1675), MW viii. 49–51; *HW*, 251.

[41] J. W. Martin, '"The first that Made Separation from the Reformed Church of England"', *Archiv fur Reformationsgeschichte*, 77 (1986), 290; 2 *Henry VI*, iv. vii; Susan Staves, *Players' Scepters: Fictions of Authority in the Restoration* (Nebraska UP, 1979), 184.

[42] J. Morgan, *Godly Learning: Puritan Attitudes towards Reason, Learning and Education, 1560–1640* (Cambridge UP, 1986), 130.

clerical academics for 'mechanic preachers' was one of the lasting legacies of the Revolution.

Universities trained the clergy who exacted tithes from the peasantry. A chorus of radical voices – Cobbler How, Walwyn, Winstanley, Dell, John Webster, Thomas Tany, John Reeve, Edward Burrough, George Fox – had joined in denouncing the universities' presumption that classical learning was a necessary part of the training of a preacher. Antichrist, said William Dell, 'chose his ministers only out of the universities'.[43] Dons sneered at Bunyan's aspirations to preach; he in his turn resented their claims to a learning which he regarded as superfluous, and to a social status above his. *A Few Sighs from Hell* (1658) attacked 'carnal priests . . . who muzzle up your people in ignorance with Aristotle, Plato and the rest of the heathenish philosophers.'[44]

In another early work Bunyan told his readers that he wrote without 'fantastic expressions, . . . light, vain, whimsical scholar-like terms' because 'I never went to school, to Aristotle or Plato, but was brought up at my father's house, in a very mean condition, among a company of poor countrymen.' If those who knew Greek were alone capable of understanding the Scriptures, he exploded, 'then but a very few of the poorest sort should be saved.' Bunyan had found true wisdom in three or four poor women sitting at a street door. In the early 1670s Nehemiah Coxe, a cordwainer, was associated with divisions in the Bedford congregation. Bunyan would not be impressed, as many others were, at the cordwainer's ability to plead before the magistrates in Greek and Hebrew. In *The Holy War* three academic types switched from El Shaddai to Diabolus as soon as the latter appeared to be winning.[45]

In 1673 Bunyan was incensed because even William Kiffin, whom he regarded as 'my brother', disdained Bunyan's 'person because of my low descent among men, stigmatising me for a person of THAT rank, that needed not to be heeded or attended unto.' He quotes the very rich Kiffin as saying, 'I had not meddled with the controversy at all, had I found any of parts that would divert themselves to take notice of YOU.' Justifiably indignant, Bunyan retorted:

---

[43] See *WTUD*, 303; *MER*, 423–4; *Religion and Politics*, 44–5, for more on this; Dell, *Several Sermons*, 246; cf. 264, 273, 297, 516, 600.

[44] MW i. 345. I have ventured to substitute 'muzzle' for the text's 'nuzzle'.

[45] *Law and Grace* (1659), MW ii. 16; *GA*, 3; *PP*, 335; *HW*, 51–2.

What need you, before you have showed one syllable of a reasonable argument in opposition to what I assert, thus trample my person, my gifts and graces, have I any, so disdainfully under your feet? What kind of a YOU am I? And why is MY rank so mean, that the most gracious and godly among you may not duly and soberly consider of what I have said?

He quoted 'Is not this the carpenter?' and 'His bodily presence is weak and his speech contemptible, I Cor. X. 10.' The social and educational slur still obviously rankled. 'The Latin I borrow', he self-consciously explained in Part II of *The Pilgrim's Progress*.[46]

The reputation of a tinker could thus become a challenge and even an asset for Bunyan. Continuing the tradition of the mechanic preachers of the 1640s he could – like Winstanley – reject academic learning and proclaim that Scripture alone was the source of his thinking. This appealed to the middling and meaner sort who formed the bulk of his audience. But Bunyan also wanted to show that he could beat the academics at their own game, that he knew his Luther and the Thirty-nine Articles. Against Ranters, Quakers, and Latitudinarians he clung to the predestinarianism which had been the strength of protestantism since the Reformation. Bunyan's theological conservatism also appealed to middle-of-the-road dissenters, who prided themselves on preserving the true traditions of the Church of England against intellectual innovations. It fitted the in-turning, the provincialization, of dissent after 1660.

But critics have too easily accepted Bunyan's self-image of the unlettered simple man. Since the publication of Midgley's edition of Bunyan's *Poems* this can no longer be maintained. In *The Pilgrim's Progress* Bunyan gives 'a surprising display of the technical terms' which fill seventeenth-century discussions of fiction and truth, pleasure and memorability, delight and faith.[47]

Bunyan may have got his apparent echo of Lovelace via a ballad, as Midgley suggests. One can think of many ways by which Mr Valiant-for-the-truth could have become acquainted with Amiens's song in *As You Like It*, which is recalled by Bunyan's best-known lyric, 'Who would true valour see'. Ian Donaldson noted remarkable echoes of Ben Jonson's *Bartholomew Fair* in *The*

---

[46] *Differences in Judgment about Water Baptism, No Bar to Communion* (1673), Offor, ii. 617–18; *PP*, 229.
[47] *Poems*, xix.

Pilgrim's Progress.[48] What looks like knowledge of *Paradise Lost* in *The Pilgrim's Progress* may well come via Benjamin Keach's *War with the Devil* (1673). The song of Christian and Hopeful from the Delectable Mountains is reminiscent of Sydney Godolphin's 'Lord when the wise men came from far'; but that is no doubt a coincidence.[49] Bunyan's introductory verses to *The Pilgrim's Progress* repeat a fairly common convention: they recall Bernard's *The Faithful Shepheard* (1609), and his Apology at the end of *The Isle of Man* (1629). Bunyan may have read both. But what are we to make of the similarities to Thynn's *Pride and Lowliness* which some have seen? Thynn wrote of events in a dream:

> I purposed to write them in a book.
> Yet therewithal I had this fantasy,
> They will but laugh at me that on it look.[50]

Or the epilogue to Middleton's *The Roaring Girl* (1611)? ('Some said ... others said ... Others cried "No"'.) Echoes could be heard of Marlowe's *Faustus* in *The Heavenly Foot-man*, of Webster's *Duchess of Malfi* in *Mr. Badman*, of Glapthorne's *The Lady's Privilege* in *The Exposition on . . . Genesis.*[51]

This list demonstrates the folly of looking for influences or echoes. Once a poem or a song is in print, and perhaps before, it becomes common property; we cannot hope to trace its circulation.

But Bunyan did own some books—the Dent and the Bayly which his first wife brought him as her dowry; Foxe's *Book of Martyrs*, Dod and Cleaver on the ten commandments, Andrewes's *Sermons*, Fowler's *Design of Christianity*, and Penn's *The Sandy Foundation* (both for controversial purposes), Danvers and Paul on baptism. At one time or another he mentions writings by Origen, Machiavelli, Luther, Tyndale, Cranmer, Ainsworth, Samuel Clarke's *A Mirrour and Looking-glass for both Saints and Sinners* (1646), Owen, Baxter, Jessey, and the Koran. He may refer to Hobbes in *A Defence of the Doctrine of Justification* (1672). Bunyan seems to be acquainted with the possibility of the existence of other

---

[48] Ibid. xxxiii, 143, 320; *PP*, 295, 351; Donaldson, *Notes and Queries*, NS 29 (1982), 142–3. For Lovelace see p. 267 below.

[49] Godolphin, *Poems*, ed. W. Dighton (Oxford UP, 1931), 28–9; *PP*, 123.

[50] Francis Thynn, *The Debate between Pride and Lowliness*, ed. J. P. Collier (1841), 65–6. Collier dates this poem before 1568.

[51] Offor, iii. 385, 65. For Glapthorne see pp. 136n. above, 326 below.

worlds, an idea which may derive—however indirectly—from John Wilkins.[52] If he had read as much as other men Bunyan might have written as little. But knowledge of the right kind matters. In *The Pilgrim's Progress* Ignorance is the character who suffers the most deplorable fate of all.

[52] MW ii, p. xiv; Offor, i, p. lxvii; ii. 281, 319; Tindall, 193–5; *PP*, 7, 313; *HW*, 5. 254.

13. *The Church after the Restoration*

Christ's church is an hospital of sick, wounded and afflicted
people.   BUNYAN[1]

It is disgraceful and disgusting that the Christian religion should
be supported by violence.   MILTON[2]

i. Bunyan and his Congregation

GRACE ABOUNDING contains the last autobiographical
information we have about Bunyan. So we are denied the
answers to some interesting questions. Did he remain secure in his
faith after his imprisonment? What, if any, spiritual conflicts
recurred? Was he still tempted by the urge to blaspheme? In *Grace
Abounding* Bunyan feared making a bad end and so bringing
disgrace on God's cause; Christian was afraid to cross the River of
Death; and the lengthy discussion arising from Mr Badman's
peaceful end shows that the subject was still in Bunyan's mind. We
would welcome revelations of the type that *Grace Abounding* gives,
however much we may discount them.

After 1660 we have only Bunyan's posthumous London biographers. There is remarkably little from local sources. There are
legends, some of them plain wrong, or distorted—like putting
Bunyan's jail on Bedford bridge. We should not read too much
into this absence of local material: Bunyan had become a national
figure. But it remains a fact.

In the 1650s the Bedford congregation had been able to remain
part of the Church of England. Presentation to the living of St
John the Baptist was in the hands of the mayor and corporation of
Bedford, who in 1653 presented Gifford. When he died in 1655,
after some manœuvring they were pressurized by Oliver Cromwell
to present John Burton, the congregation's nominee. This gave
Burrough the opportunity to sneer at Burton (and, he implied,
Bunyan as well) as a 'hireling'.[3]

---

[1] *Justification by an Imputed Righteousness* (posthumous), Offor, i. 327.
[2] *Christian Doctrine* (posthumous), *MCPW*, vi. 123.
[3] Brown, 83, 96; Joyce Godber, *The Story of Bedford: An Outline History* (Luton,
1978), 71–2; Burrough, *Works*, 151, 280, 302, 307.

After 1660 'the persecution that always attends the Word' fell upon the Bedford church. Persecution of dissenters was erratic in the 1660s, varying with central and local circumstances. But it intensified after 1669. The Archbishop of Canterbury observed in 1670 that conventicles were spreading from cities and greater towns to villages and hamlets. At the restoration seven ministers were ejected from their Bedfordshire livings; when in 1672 Charles issued his Declaration of Indulgence to dissenters, twenty-four took out licences. The county had a higher proportion of licensed dissenting congregations in proportion to area than any other in the country. The Bedford church bought a barn as a permanent meeting-place.[4]

The Declaration had a polarizing effect. Most protestant dissenters accepted it gladly, including Bunyan's church, which was listed as Congregational. Parliament opposed the Declaration because it included papist as well as protestant dissenters, and because the Commons held the royal claim to suspend the operation of Parliamentary penal statutes by prerogative to be illegal. But the Declaration created the possibility of new alignments, new alliances between protestant dissenters and some Anglicans.

The Bedford congregation perforce existed semi-legally until 1672. One of its members, Samuel Fenn, yeoman, was in trouble in 1669 for saying the King was not head of the Church of England: but a jury returned an ignoramus verdict. In the following year Nehemiah Coxe, cordwainer, recently admitted to the congregation, was accused of saying 'the Church of England as it now stands is an Antichristian church.' He repeated the remark in the presence of the mayor.[5]

Bunyan's view of the Anglican establishment was no more favourable. In 1657 he had written of the 'loose conversation' and 'wicked walking' of preachers of the state church, who 'harden their hearers in their sins'. 'Would a parishioner learn to be proud? he or she need look no further than to the priest, his wife and family.' Would they learn to be wanton, drunkards, or covetous, 'they need but look to their ministers' — 'riding and running after great benefices and parsonages by night and by day.' Next year in

---

[4] *A Holy Life* (1683), MW ix. 290; cf. 260; W. T. Whitley, 'Militant Baptists', 198; T. Richards, *Wales under the Penal Code, 1662–1687* (1925), 9; Godber, *History of Bedfordshire, 1066–1888* (Bedfordshire County Council, 1969), 237.

[5] M. Mullet, 'The Internal Politics of Bedford, 1660–1688', PBHRS 59 (1980), 4–5, 37. Coxe was in trouble with the church four years later.

A Few Sighs from Hell he attacked 'the carnal priests' who 'tickle the ears of their hearers with vain philosophy and deceit, and thereby harden their hearts against the simplicity of the Gospel.'[6]

It was not always easy after 1660, in view of the censorship, for Bunyan to be open about his rejection of the state church. But in 1662, in *I Will Pray with the Spirit*, Bunyan attacked 'trencher chaplains' in 'great men's families', 'whose great business is their own bellies', and denounced the set forms of the Antichristian prayer book. 'A good sense of sin, and the wrath of God, with some encouragement from God to come unto him, is a better Common Prayer Book than that which is taken out of the papistical Mass-Book.'[7]

In *The Holy War* Diabolus set up his own church, a sufficient ministry with lecturers, preaching a holy law unto which the inhabitants must conform. And in *Antichrist and his Ruin*, which Bunyan prudently did not publish, he cautiously but clearly criticized the surviving rags of Antichrist in the Church of England, its convocations, church courts, and lordships, and warned against the danger of a return to popery. Ministers should not rule, he wrote in *A Discourse of the Building . . . of the House of God* (1688); they should be waiters at table.[8]

Erratic enforcement of the laws against nonconformity may in part be explained by the sympathy which local residents felt for their more godly neighbours. But the uncertainty helped to increase the deterrent and destabilizing effects of persecution. Two Bedford men who were sentenced to deportation in 1668 were still in England four years later, when they were pardoned.[9]

Meetings of the congregation were correspondingly erratic. There are no entries in the church book for early 1661, late 1662, and almost all of 1663, and none at all between 1664 and late 1668, when the Conventicle Act expired and nonconformists won some relief. Persecution was renewed when the second Conventicle Act (1670) encouraged widespread use of informers; it empowered a single JP to take punitive action against nonconformists. But even in 1668–9 1,400 cases of prosecution of dissenters had been

[6] *A Vindication*, MW i. 127, 345; cf. 307.
[7] MW ii. 239, 273, 285; the Common Prayer Book is not commanded in the Word of God.
[8] *HW*, 84; Offor, ii. 51, 76, 78, 80; *Poems*, 285.
[9] Mullet, 'Internal Politics', 3.

recorded in the Archdeacon's court for Bedford and Bedfordshire. Many of the congregation's meetings went unrecorded when it met in villages outside Bedford. Members of the congregation had to flee from their houses. In 1669 Brother Merrill backslid so far as to charge the church with rebellion, with having their hands in the blood of Charles I.

Two years later Robert Nelson was cast out 'because he was openly baptized after the Antichristian guise of the Church of England.' Many members withdrew from communion 'in these troublous times', and attended 'at the superstitious and idolatrous worship that with force and cruelty is maintained in opposition to the true worship and worshippers of God.' 'While the world are continuing their persecution and spoil of us', to cite the words of the church book, the pamphlet *A True and Impartial Narrative of some Illegal and Arbitrary Proceedings . . . in and near the town of Bedford* gave a vivid account of actions in 1670, when church members were fined and their goods distrained. When the church was licensed there were a number of applications to join or rejoin. But this licence was revoked in 1675.[10]

In 1672 Bunyan had accused Edward Fowler of overthrowing three of the Church of England's Thirty-nine Articles. We may compare Milton's quotation of the Thirty-nine Articles in *Of True Religion, Heresy, Schism, Toleration and what means may be used against the Growth of Popery* (1673). Milton no doubt had his tongue in his cheek in this attempt to align protestants against popery. But Bunyan expressed the genuine sentiments of those protestant dissenters who looked back approvingly to the church of Grindal and Abbott. Marvell's *Account of the Growth of Popery and Arbitrary Government in England* (1677), William Penn's *One Project for the Good of England* (1679), and William Dell's *The Increase of Popery in England* (1681) all had the same political objective.[11]

In 1675 Bunyan was summoned to appear before the Archdeacon's Court for failing to attend services at his parish church. He went into hiding rather than obey the summons. The case was transferred to the secular arm. A warrant was issued for

---

[10] *Elstow Moot Hall Booklet*, No. 2; Brown, 186, 190, 200, 205–9; Tibbutt, *Minutes*, 7, 38–42, 52, 62–3.

[11] *A Defence of the Doctrine of Justification by Faith*, Offor, ii. 278; *MER*, 219, 229. Dell had tried to publish his book in 1667, but it was suppressed, and now appeared posthumously.

Bunyan's arrest, with what Brown noted as 'a formidable and unusual list of names' of thirteen Bedfordshire JPs attached. Bunyan was still regarded as a dangerous man. From December 1676 to June 1677 he suffered his second imprisonment. Nonconformists reacted to this new wave of persecution by organizing a series of lectures on the dangers of popery at Pinners' Hall, Old Broad Street, to which Bunyan contributed.[12] These lectures attracted much attention and won respect from staunchly protestant members of the Church of England.

From the start the Bedford congregation had a deep sense of the corruption of the society in which it had to exist, of the dangers of *formal* righteousness. Life seemed to have gone out of the old Puritans, *a fortiori* out of the state church. Much of *Grace Abounding* is concerned with this problem of the inadequacy of mere morality. Hence in 1665 Bunyan declared that church organization was necessary for the saints to meet and edify each other, and also meet their God, by whom they are blessed and refreshed. To abandon outward gospel-worship looked to Bunyan 'too like Ranting opinions', to the danger of which he was always alert. With a little poetic hyperbole he wrote in 1688:

> What though some slight it, it a cottage call,
> Give't the reproachful name of beggars' hall,
> Call it an alms-house builded for the poor:

it is still the House of God. Vagabonds, highwaymen, fornicators, liars, debtors can all be received into the church[13] – though one suspects they would have got short shrift if they had relapsed into these bad habits after joining the church.

The congregation retained the power of excommunication, after appropriate private advice and public warnings. 'This tremendous sentence' was God's. The church preferred decisions to be unanimous rather than by majority, and the pastor had no formal superiority, though no doubt his views would normally count for more than those of most members.[14]

The gathered congregation was thus in one sense a defensive

---

[12] *Instruction for the Ignorant* (1675), Prefatory letter; Brown, 267–8; *The Greatness of the Soul* (1683), 'first preached in Pinners' Hall' (title-page), MW ix. 135.

[13] *The Holy City* (1665), MW iii. 65–6; *Poems*, 275, 280–1.

[14] *A Reason of my Practice in Worship* (1670–1?), Offor, ii. 615; Tibbutt, *Minutes*, 50, 55, 127; *Poems*, 308–17.

rearguard against the world. It turned in on itself, protected and helped its poor and its weaker brethren, purged inadequate professors, but tried not to drive away its well-to-do members. It worked out a new casuistry to adjust to life as it had to be lived in an increasingly commercial world. As we shall see, the covenant theology, with its suggestion that by conscious effort we could almost choose to be saved, was well suited to enhance the self-respect of artisans, small men at sea in a troubling world. We could 'roll upon free grace', so long as this doctrine did not lead to antinomian ideas that God was within his elect.[15]

So Bunyan's harsh theology of the 1650s and early 1660s, aimed against the competition of Quakers and Latitudinarians, yielded to a more compassionate theology in the 1670s and 1680s, combined still with severity against smug professors. The millenarian hope had prevailed in a society which it had seemed possible to transform. Now individuals and small communities had to accept that sinful society and strive to live the best lives they could within it. The church gave a sense of solidarity and comradeship, of shared risks and sufferings for shared belief. It provided support in adversity, and gave consolatory assurances of incomparably better times to come, possibly in this life, certainly in the hereafter.

In the 1670s and 1680s Bunyan ministered to his own congregation in Bedford, and to affiliated churches in Bedfordshire, Huntingdonshire, Hertfordshire, and Cambridgeshire[16] — so far as was possible in the intermittent persecution of those years. 'Some, though in jeering manner, no doubt, gave him the epithet of Bishop Bunyan' in consequence of his preaching and pastoral visits to remote congregations. The church also had links with London congregations — with George Griffith's church in Addle Street, and with George Cokayne's in Southwark. Bunyan preached frequently in London, at John Owen's church and especially at Cokayne's, to crowded congregations. 'If there were but one day's notice given', his devoted follower Charles Doe tells us, 'there would be more people come together to hear him preach than the meeting house could hold.' He speaks of thousands of hearers. Bunyan almost certainly preached at the Independent Stepney

---

[15] *Ebal and Gerizzim* (1665?), *Poems*, 110; cf. *One Thing is Needful* (1665?), *ibid*. 68.

[16] Kempston, Maulden, Cotton End, Edworth, and Gamlingay were daughter-churches.

church of Matthew Meade, a Bedfordshire man who had the largest congregation in the London area.[17]

When Bunyan preached at Newington Green in the early 1680s, 'some . . . if not all' of the students at Charles Morton's dissenting academy went to hear him. This despite the fact, the Revd Samuel Wesley tells us with the prim sectarianism of the lapsed nonconformist, that he had 'no form of ordination'. Bunyan's reputation as a preacher must have been sensational for Charles II—of all people—to have heard of him and to ask John Owen about him. Two Londoners stood surety for Bunyan when he was released from prison in 1677.[18]

ii. Millenarianism Again

Attempts were made to boost the sagging morale of the godly party by illegal publications like the anonymous *Mirabilis Annus* tracts, which in 1661–2 recorded signs and portents of God's wrath against the restored monarchy. Bunyan's friends Henry Jessey and George Cokayne were probably the authors, and the tracts were printed by men whom Bunyan patronized. The Great Plague of 1665, the Great Fire of London in 1666, and the Dutch invasion of the Medway the year after, all seemed to confirm God's displeasure.[19]

In the posthumous *Of Antichrist and his Ruin* Bunyan regretted:

the forwardness of some . . . who have predicted concerning the *time* of the downfall of Antichrist, to the shame of them and their brethren; nor will the wrong that such by their boldness have done to the church of God be repaired by them nor their works. . . . I shall not therefore meddle with the times and seasons.

[17] *A Continuation of Mr. Bunyan's Life*, *GA*, 169. Cf. R. L. Greaves, 'The Organizational Response of Nonconformity to Repression and Indulgence: The Case of Bedfordshire', *Church History*, 44 (1975), 1–13; Charles Doe, 'The Struggler', Offor, iii. 766–7; P. Earle, *Monmouth's Rebels: The Road to Sedgmoor, 1685* (1977). For Meade see pp. 313, 371 below.

[18] [S. Wesley], *A Letter from a Country Divine to his Friend in London concerning the Education of the Dissenters in their Private Academies* (1703), 4–7. Samuel Wesley, father of John and Charles, was himself at Morton's Academy in the early '80s. See p. 371 below, and for Charles II, p. 167.

[19] Greaves, *Deliver Us from Evil* (Oxford UP, 1986), 211–15, 221.

Who can tell? 'Let Christians beware that they set not times for God, lest all men see their folly.' But in *Solomon's Temple Spiritualized* (1688) Bunyan recognized that the saints were impatient. Christ 'accomplished all the first part of his priesthood in less than forty years'; but now 'he has been above in heaven above sixteen hundred years, and yet has not done.' This, Bunyan admitted, calls for 'faith and patience'. Saints have often been mistaken in their 'guesses' at the time of the Second Coming, he observed in *Of Antichrist and his Ruin*. But if it was wrong to try to fix a date (as Owen agreed with Bunyan in thinking) the millennium always remains a possibility, when God decides. If we cannot foretell the time, we can read the signs of the fall of Antichrist, some of which are now visible: the slaying of the Witnesses does not 'seem to be a great way off'. Of that point Bunyan remained convinced from the time of his first published work.[20]

In *Prison Meditations* (1663) Bunyan foresaw the saints reigning with Christ, an idea which he often repeated. In *The Resurrection of the Dead* (1665?) he insisted that the saints will 'be set upon the throne with Christ, as kings and princes with him, to judge the world'. The rule of the saints will continue until Christ's kingdom itself shall wither away, 'that God may be all in all'. This vision had been familiar in the 1640s and 1650s, shared by John Canne, Mary Cary, Milton and George Cokayne among many others. The Shining Ones recall it to Christian and Hopeful at the end of *The Pilgrim's Progress*: 'the saints also shall have a voice in that judgment, because they were his and your enemies'.[21]

This is a waiting, not an active millenarianism; it is the millenarianism of the Quakers after 1660, and of Milton. Millenarianism had been closely linked to the separatist principle. In the heady days when the millennium seemed 'at the door' it was right to separate from the Antichristian state church. When the millennium came, the saints would displace the present rulers in church and state. But as it became painfully clear that the millennium was not imminent, the saints had to adapt themselves to life in a world in which the ungodly had recovered their hold on the levers of

[20] Offor, ii. 54–62, 68, 72–9, 480–1, iii. 507; MW i. 84; Owen, *Works*, ix. 510.
[21] *Poems*, 49; MW iii. 229, 289–91; *PP*, 160. For Cary and Cokayne see pp. 51, 95–6, and 96–8 above.

power and were unlikely to be dislodged except by violence.[22] After 1661 it would clearly be folly to advocate such a policy. So the whole rationale of the coexistence of sects with a hostile state church had to be thought out anew, with all the problems of conduct and discipline which this raised. And now all the cards were held by Antichrist's representatives.

Henry More in 1664 sneered at 'the rude and ignorant vulgar' who 'have so fouled' the words Antichrist and Antichristian that they are now 'unfit to pass the lips of any civil person'. In their 'mad mistaken zeal' they denounce 'every legitimate magistrate' as Antichrist, 'and every well ordered church' as the Whore of Babylon.[23] Those very revealing remarks, taken in conjunction with what Owen and Bunyan had to say about 'the wrong done to the church of God' by rash predictions of the millennium, confirm that the early 1660s were not a favourable moment for discussing the last times.

Bunyan, however, published his most millenarian tract in 1665, *The Holy City*. With the caution appropriate for a jailbird writing under strict censorship, he depicted the church returning out of a long Antichristian captivity, which he sometimes dates from soon after the days of the Apostles, sometimes from Constantine. The holy city, the New Jerusalem, will be built only after Antichrist is overthrown. 'The western part of the world . . . will be the last part of the world that will be converted.' Meanwhile the saints are 'disputing about the glorious state of the church in the latter days' with 'crossness of judgment and persuasion'. Bunyan had a vivid and disturbing picture of dissent in restoration England. 'The saints are yet but as an army routed, and are apt, sometimes through fear, sometimes through forgetfulness, to mistake the word of their Captain-General, . . . the Son of God.' They

---

[22] W. Lamont, 'Pamphleteering, the Protestant Consensus and the English Revolution', in *Freedom and the English Revolution: Essays in History and Literature*, ed. R. C. Richardson and G. M. Ridden (Manchester UP, 1986), 86; George Fox the Younger, *A Noble Salutation . . . unto thee, Charles Stuart* (1660), in *Early Quaker Writings, 1650–1700*, ed. H. Barbour and A. O. Roberts (Grand Rapids, Mich., 1973), 403; *MER*, 466; *Religion and Politics in Seventeenth-Century England* (Brighton, 1986), 303–4.

[23] H. More, *A Modest Enquiry into the Mystery of Iniquity* (1664), sig. A 3v, 185–7. I owe this reference to the unpublished Open University D.Phil. thesis by W. R. Owens, *A Critical Edition of John Bunyan's Posthumously Published Treatise, Of Antichrist and his Ruin*. I am grateful to him for giving me a copy. I also owe him thanks for much help in interpreting Bunyan's thinking about the last times.

are 'too prone to shoot and kill even their very right-hand man.'[24]

The church 'hath lain now in the danger of Antichrist for above 1000 years.' But 'the . . . time is near, yea very near'. 'Dominion . . . shall be given to the people of the saints of the Most High', who will exact vengeance against 'the high ones, lofty ones, haughty ones and the proud.' 'The implacable enemies of God' will 'shrink and creep into holes', to the contentment of 'such men that have for several years been held in the chains of affliction.' 'Our Antichrist' treads down the church. But though 'Satan and Antichrist have had their day in the world, and by their outrage have made fearful havoc of the souls of sinners', yet the church of Christ will obtain 'a complete conquest and victory over the world', and will subdue her enemies and rule over their oppressors on earth. When it comes to building the New Jerusalem, 'most of the kings and great ones of the earth will be found employed and taken up in another work than to fall in love with Mount Sion'; they prefer Mistress Babylon. Meanwhile Bunyan, writing from jail, thought it necessary to add reassuringly that the church is not a 'rebellious city'; it will not meddle with the property of the governors of this world. It is not 'destructive to kings and a diminisher of their revenues'. Bunyan left it an open question whether his generation will see the New Jerusalem. But in the posthumous *Exposition on Genesis I–X* he hoped that 'some of us shall live to see it'. As Brown observed, *The Holy City* is not about 'the life beyond' but about living on earth, now.[25]

After *The Holy City* Bunyan published no overtly millenarian works until *The Holy War* (1682). Here he accepted that Mansoul could be liberated only by military power. Something very like the army of the saints of the 1640s must do the job. In *Antichrist and his Ruin*, probably written in the early 1680s, but not published because of the censorship, Bunyan insisted that Antichrist—like Diabolus in *The Holy War*—has set up his own church government, officers, and discipline. Interference with freedom of worship, by penal laws and constraints, indeed persecution of any sort, is Antichristian.[26] He did not say that this government must be overthrown, but the conclusion was inescapable.

---

[24] MW iii. 79–80, 94; cf. *The House of the Forest of Lebanon* (posthumous): 'The many petty divisions and names amongst us', Offor, iii. 524.

[25] MW iii. 89, 92, 95–6, 132, 138, 165–9, 171; Brown, 166.

[26] See pp. 98–9 above.

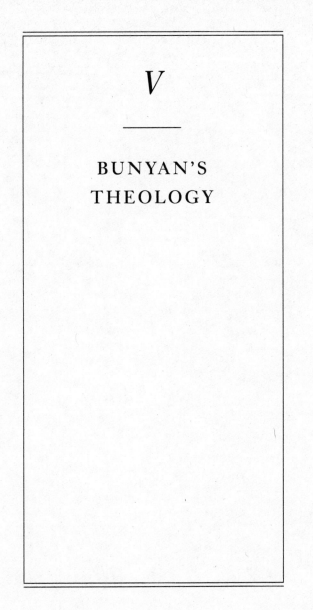

V

BUNYAN'S
THEOLOGY

14. *Some Influences*

Our famous and holy worthies, that before us have risen in their place, and shook off those relics of Antichrist that entrenched upon the priestly office of our Lord and Saviour, even worthy Wyclif, Hus, Luther, Melanchthon, Calvin and the blessed martyrs in Queen Mary's days, etc., with the rest of their companions . . .

                                                                BUNYAN[1]

i. *Luther and Foxe*

WE know tantalizingly little about early influences on Bunyan. His first wife brought with her Arthur Dent's *The Plaine Mans Path-way to Heaven* and Lewis Bayly's *The Practice of Piety*. Martin Luther's *Commentary on Galatians* made a great impression on him, and he studied Foxe's *Book of Martyrs* in jail. It is likely that he had read Richard Bernard's popular *The Isle of Man*. He must have been well acquainted with Puritan covenant theology from sermons and discussions. The most likely single influence here, in his later life at least, is his friend John Owen. Bunyan had encountered some radical theology in the army, preached for example by Paul Hobson and William Dell. Ranters and Quakers had provoked him to think in opposition to their ideas. I shall not be trying to assess fully the writings of any of those whom I mention in this chapter, only to pick out aspects of their thought which seem to me to have bearings on Bunyan's theological development.

Bunyan admitted to learning from Dent and Bayly, but he claimed Luther as second only to the Bible. The difference in tone is significant. Luther changed his life, or so he thought. In the depth of his spiritual despair, as Bunyan struggled against his sense of sin, and against the sceptical libertinism of the Ranter milieu which tempted him to 'blasphemy, desperation and the like', he longed 'to see some ancient godly man's experience who had writ some hundreds of years before I was born', who had gone down himself 'into the deep'. And 'God . . . did cast into my hand' Luther's *Commentary on Galatians*.[2]

There is an interesting piece of history here. Bunyan bought John Foxe's *Book of Martyrs* when he was in prison, and was reading

---

[1] *The Holy City* (1665), MW iii. 134.   [2] *GA*, 41.

it when he wrote *Grace Abounding*. From Foxe Bunyan got his assurance that the Pope was Antichrist (confirmed by Bayly), and that God's Englishmen had been in the forefront of the struggle against him throughout the ages. He would learn the especially congenial fact that it was humble Englishmen — artisans like himself — who had been most steadfast in adherence to their faith under the Marian persecutions, when gentlemen and clergymen either conformed or fled into the safety of exile. Faithful's torments in Vanity Fair derive from Foxe. Bunyan was no doubt aware that Laud was accused of refusing to allow Foxe to be reprinted after the edition of 1632–3, as well as of suppressing Luther's *Table Talk* and Bayly's *Practice of Piety*.[3]

Foxe was a devotee of Luther. 'It was almost entirely due to Foxe', writes Patrick Collinson, 'that Luther lived on in the English religious consciousness, above all as the author of the ever-popular *Commentary on Galatians*.'[4] Luther on Galatians was a favourite of Bayly's. Bunyan came to prefer it, after the Bible, 'before all the books that ever I have seen, as most fit for a wounded conscience.' Luther surprised Bunyan by showing that 'the law of Moses as well as the devil, death and hell hath a very great hand' in his own temptations. Like Bunyan, Luther had had to face 'fond heads, . . . bragging of the spirit, of revelations, of dreams'. He too had confronted arguments drawn from the Koran and from the strength of Mohamedanism.[5]

Bunyan learnt from Luther the absolute dichotomy between law and grace, the impossibility of fallen man obeying the law; and he accepted Luther's solution, that the elect could escape from the despair which the wrath of the law entailed only by the imputed righteousness of Christ. The law makes carnal men worse sinners; it leads them to blaspheme and despair. 'A Christian', Luther had written, 'is not he who is without sin but he to whom God does not

[3] Bayly, 445, 455. Foxe was reprinted again in 1641, in three volumes. A copy of this edition, with Bunyan's name and the date 1662, is in the Pierpont Morgan Library. But it is uncertain whether the name is in Bunyan's hand (I owe this information to Bob Owens). For Bunyan's use of Foxe see MW ii. 239, viii. 98, 203, 383; Offor, ii. 78, iii. 532.

[4] P. Collinson, 'England and International Calvinism, 1558–1640', in *International Calvinism, 1541–1715*, ed. M. Prestwich (Oxford UP, 1985), 215. Foxe was responsible for three other translations of Luther following *Galatians*.

[5] Bayly, 407; cf. 105–12, 120, 338; *GA*, 40–1; Luther, *A Commentary on St Paul's Epistle to the Galatians* (1807 repr. of the 1575 trans.), i. 40, 44. This was the translation which Bunyan used.

impute sin.' The saints cannot escape from 'the dregs of their natural corruption'. But once they recognize that they can be saved by Christ's imputed righteousness, then 'that fiery law' which was previously so terrifying can become the delight of the inward man, who 'would always be walking in it'. 'There is no law to come in against the sinner that believes in Jesus Christ, for he is not under that.' The second covenant is not between man and God but between Jesus Christ as a public person and God; so the elect cannot break the covenant. This was the version of the covenant theology that Bunyan was to adopt.[6]

Luther's recognition that the commandments cannot be kept had great liberating force for the laity. It revealed the whole ecclesiastical apparatus of penance, absolution, indulgences, etc. as a clerical conspiracy whose object was money-making. The direct telephone line which Luther set up between man and God was outside clerical supervision. Lutheranism thus expressed the consciousness of educated laymen who could study the Scriptures for themselves. It was less immediately attractive for the uneducated. If we ask what functions are left for protestant pastors? the answer seems to be: to edify the elect élite and to control the less fortunate.

Luther proclaimed that Christ was liberty. 'A Christian man is both righteous and a sinner, . . . an enemy of God and yet a child of God.' He anticipated Perkins's argument that God accepts the will for the deed:

How can I be holy, when I have and feel sin in me? I answer . . . it is one step of health, when the sick man doth acknowledge and confess his infirmity . . . To apprehend that Son by faith . . . and with the heart to believe in him given unto us and for us of God, causeth that God doth account that faith, although it be unperfect, for perfect righteousness. . . . Wherefore let every man so practice with himself, that his conscience may be fully assured that he is under grace, and that his person and works do please God. And if he feel in himself any wavering or doubting, let him exercise his faith and wrestle against this doubting, and let him labour to attain more strength and assurance of faith. . . . When I have laid hold of him by faith, I wrestle against the fiery darts of the devil. . . . I am made righteous already by that righteousness which is begun in me'.[7]

---

[6] Bunyan, *Justification by an Imputed Righteousness* (posthumous), Offor, i. 317; Luther, *Galatians*, i. pp. xxx–xxxii, 170–2, 304; cf. 177; Bunyan, *Law and Grace*, MW ii. 126–30, 154–7, 166; *Christian Behaviour*, MW iii. 58.

[7] Luther, *Galatians*, i. 244–6; ii. 80, 187.

So the activity which Bunyan (and Luther) needed was restored: 'these things be not rightly understood, but when they be put in practice'. Faith is the most difficult of all works. Consciousness of divine grace enables one to resist even the Biblical texts which the devil hurled at a terrified Bunyan. 'I come with the Lord himself, who is above the Scripture and is made unto us the merit and price of righteousness and everlasting life.' For Luther 'a new creature is the work of the Holy Ghost, which cleanseth our heart by faith. . . . It is the renewing of the mind by the Holy Ghost, after the which followeth a change of the members and senses of the whole body.' Not only the senses are renewed: 'the mind also approveth, loveth and followeth another thing than it did before.'8

'Luther had great fears', Lady Brilliana Harley told her son in 1639, 'till he had thoroughly learnt the doctrine of justification by Christ alone'.9 The greatness of these fears must have appealed to the suffering Bunyan. Luther showed him a human way out from the rigorous predestinarian logic which stressed God's sovereign will rather than man's predicament. 'Not one sinner who came to Christ for mercy went ever away without his errand', Lewis Bayly assured the doubtful; 'not sinners . . . but they who are un-willing to repent of their sins' are debarred from communion with God. For Luther too impenitence was the unpardonable sin.10

William Dell, an early patron of Bunyan's, also praised Luther as 'that chosen vessel of God'. He picked out for especial approval Luther's attack on uniformity. Dell was thought to have anti-nomian tendencies. Richard Baxter accused Bunyan of the anti-nomian heresy, and Bunyan himself was aware that on occasion he came uncomfortably close to it. Luther was regularly cited by anti-nomians in the 1640s. Samuel Rutherford in his lengthy *Survey of the Spiritual Antichrist* (1648) filled scores of pages explaining that Luther was not really the antinomian he appeared to be.11

---

8 Luther, *Galatians*, i. 284; ii. 187–8, 299–300; *Reformation Writings of Martin Luther*, ed. B. L. Woolf (1952), i. 259.

9 *Letters of the Lady Brilliana Harley*, ed. T. T. Lewis, Camden Soc. (1854), 20. Luther, Lady Harley added interestingly in view of Bunyan's approach, 'was instructed in the truth by an old man'.

10 Bayly, 338; cf. Greaves, *John Bunyan* (Abingdon, 1969), 117–18, 154–7; Luther, *The Bondage of the Will*, trans. H. Cole (1823), 23.

11 Dell, *Several Sermons and Discourses* (1709), 290–1; Rutherford, op. cit. 87–163. See my *Religion and Politics in Seventeenth-Century England*, ch. 10, *passim*, and *Change and Continuity in Seventeenth-Century England* (1975), 90.

ii. *Arthur Dent* (d. 1607)

Dent's best-selling *The Plaine Mans Path-way*, significantly, was originally published in 1601 not in England but in Amsterdam, a safer place to print material not wholly acceptable to the English ecclesiastical authorities. It ran to twenty-five editions before 1640. By 1704, when it was in its fortieth edition, it had sold 100,000 copies. *The Pilgrim's Progress* was to exceed that figure, but few other seventeenth-century books did. Dent's main influence on Bunyan may have been in literary technique, in his use of dramatic dialogue to diversify his traditional guide to godliness.[12] But there is much in Dent which Bunyan was to echo later, whether consciously or not. Dent's sensitivity to social problems, for instance, must have attracted Bunyan. The theologian in Dent's dialogue insists that virtue is far more important than birth; dukes, lords, and ladies are not exempt from original sin. But this does not exonerate the poor. 'The cause that many do want outward things . . . is in themselves, because they want faith.' Though God's children may want, yet they are never utterly forsaken, Dent said reassuringly if implausibly; poverty is sent to try them. We are not free from afflictions, but 'from all hurtful afflictions'. He gave many examples of economic oppression: the remedies included 'contentment'.[13]

Nevertheless, Dent is refreshingly honest about the inadequacies of the godly themselves. 'Many who are not regenerate do in some things excel the children of God' — for instance in learning, discretion, justice, temperance, prudence, patience, liberality, affability, kindness, courtesy, good nature, etc. It is a long list. Bunyan was later to make similar points about self-righteous members of his Bedford congregation. Few are saved, Dent thought; but it is unprofitable to speculate whether one in a hundred or one in a thousand. Regeneration is impossible without the aid of the Word preached, and of the Spirit. Salvation is attainable, but 'if you will not believe Moses and the prophets', Dent's theologian said, neither will you believe someone who

[12] M. Hussey, 'Arthur Dent's *Plaine Mans Path-way to Heaven*', *Modern Language Review*, 44 (1949), 26; '*Mr Badman* would have been impossible without Dent', said Roger Sharrock, 98; cf. 112.
[13] Dent, 5, 22, 116, 132–3, 203–19. Nehemiah Wallington was so impressed by Dent on the use of afflictions that he copied out many pages (Seaver, *Wallington's World*, 6; cf. 134).

comes from the dead to inform you. Bunyan repeated this Biblical phrase. Dent had much to say about the horrors of the last judgment, and of hell.[14]

Idleness is for him the mother of all sins; the idle include gentlemen and rich citizens, and especially their wives. Lying is the particular vice of shopkeepers. Covetousness is a sin of rich and poor alike. 'That which you call covetousness', asserted Dent's Antilegon, 'a caviller', 'it is but good husbandry' – a phrase which Bunyan remembered. Dent lists a large number of offences to which craftsmen and merchants are liable, including breach of the Sabbath. His theologian denounced especially the sin of swearing, one of Bunyan's favourite vices before his conversion. 'There are sworn in this land a hundred thousand oaths every day in the year.' Philagathas, an honest layman, interestingly takes the lead in criticizing breaches of the Sabbath.[15]

The caviller Antilegon anticipated many of the views of Ranters whom Bunyan encountered – all are saved, there is no hell except in the conscience, we can serve God without preachers; the Scriptures are men's inventions. Since we cannot resist God's will, why should he be angry with us for sinning? The doctrine of predestination leads men to despair – as it nearly did Bunyan. Antilegon recommended the reading of merry books as a cure for the fear of hell which is a form of melancholy.[16] Bunyan was to reject with what seems excessive rigour the 'merry books' which he had enjoyed reading in his younger days. Dent's *The Ruine of Rome, Or, An Exposition upon the whole Revelation* (1603) would also have interested Bunyan if he read it.

iii. Lewis Bayly (d. 1631)

Lewis Bayly had an interesting career. He was chaplain to Prince Henry, the patron of defenders of an aggressive protestant foreign policy. Bayly dedicated *The Practice of Piety* to the Prince in 1612.

---

[14] Dent, 25, 33–4, 267, 289–94, 386–407; Bunyan, *The Strait Gate* (1676), MW v. 103–21 – few professors saved.

[15] Dent, 77, 107, 121–4, 136, 138, 157, 174, 189–99.

[16] Ibid. 294–320, 408. L. B. Wright rightly stresses Dent's importance in his *Middle-Class Culture in Elizabethan England* (N. Carolina UP, 1935), 54–6.

In the same year Bayly accused some members of the Privy Council of popery—true but tactless. However, it did not prevent him becoming chaplain to James I, and Bishop of Bangor in 1616—an appointment which some regarded as banishment. In 1619 he was reprimanded for praying for Princess Elizabeth and her husband as King and Queen of Bohemia before the English government had recognized them. Two years later Bayly was imprisoned for denouncing Prince Charles's proposed Spanish marriage, and he had a 'hot encounter' with James I concerning his opposition to the royal Book of Sports. The King also objected to *The Practice of Piety*, which nevertheless reached its third edition by 1613, its twenty-fifth before Bayly's death in 1631, its forty-third by 1640, and its fifty-ninth a century later. He 'amplified' it considerably in later editions. *The Practice of Piety* had the honour of being quoted in Congreve's *The Old Batchelor* and Farquhar's *The Constant Couple*, as well as of being suppressed by Archbishop Laud and placed on the Roman Catholic Index. It was naturally popular with Puritans. Earle's 'She precise hypocrite' was addicted to it.[17]

But there is another side to Bayly's character. In February 1626 he was a little too grateful to God that 'I am now again in extraordinary favour with the Duke of Buckingham.' Later that year he was accused in the House of Commons of simony, bribery, extortion, licensing incestuous marriages, and of 'incontinency the most palpably proved that ever I heard'. It was no doubt in reference to this that John Bastwick called him 'my Lord Bangwhore', an early Puritan example of the word 'bang' used in a sexual sense. Worst of all, an attempt was made after the restoration to deprive him of the authorship of *The Practice of Piety*. The nonconformist Louis du Moulin alleged that the work had been written by a Puritan minister, and 'a bishop not altogether of a chaste life did after the author's death bargain with his widow for the copy, which he received but never paid her the money.' 'Afterwards, by interpolating it in some places, he published it as his own.'[18]

[17] J. E. Bailey, 'Bishop Lewis Bayly and his *Practice of Piety*', *Manchester Quarterly*, 2 (1883), 204, 208–12; Earle, *Microcosmography* (1628) in *Character Writings of the Seventeenth Century*, ed. H. Morley (1893), 195.

[18] Bailey, 216; *CSPD, 1625–1626*, 355; Paul Christianson, *Reformers and Babylon: English Apocalyptic Visions from the Reformation to the Eve of the Civil War* (Toronto UP, 1978), 160; Louis du Moulin, *Patronus Bonae Fidei* (1672), quoted in Bailey, 210–11.

One hopes that Bunyan heard none of these libellous stories. There was much in *The Practice of Piety* that he would have found congenial. 'Read Luther on Galatians, chapter 5', Bayly recommended. 'We are fallen into the dregs of time', he told Prince Charles in his Epistle Dedicatory, 'which being the last must needs be the worst days'. 'Never was the judge nearer to come.'[19]

Grace is given especially to sinners, Bayly argued, provided they are repentant. Good works are not necessary to justification, but justification is always accompanied by good works: 'every true Christian, as soon as he is regenerate, begins to keep all God's commandments in truth, though he cannot in absolute perfection.' God 'accepteth their good will and endeavours, instead of perfect fulfilling of the law.' Bayly conveniently lists and disposes of those Biblical texts which appear to contradict the doctrine of predestination. His 'Meditations on the misery of the body and soul in death' may have impressed Bunyan. So would the remark 'despair is nothing as dangerous as presumption.'[20]

Bayly was a severe social critic. 'For the most part the poor receive the gospel, . . . not many mighty, not many noble are called. . . . Few rich men shall be saved.' It is greatly to be feared that the 'outrageous swearing, adultery, drunkenness, oppression, profaning of the Sabbath' of 'many nobles and gentlemen' will provoke the Lord to vengeance. (Men 'think that to swear is gentleman-like', Wiseman was to say in *Mr. Badman*.) Bayly asked to be led 'to these chief pillars, whereupon the realm standeth, that I may pull the realm upon their heads' like Samson. Bayly had much to say about 'household piety', the 'special charge' which 'God gives to all householders, and especially their duties on the Sabbath'. 'Time spent in prayer never hindreth, but furthereth and prospereth a man's journey and business.' 'Esteem . . . the loss of time one of the greatest losses; . . . use not sleep as a means to satiate the soggy litherness of thy flesh', but as a medicine. Like Dent, Bayly gave examples of vices disguising themselves as virtues — covetousness as thrift, gluttony as hospitality — a trick that Bunyan was later to use.[21]

[19] Bayly, 407, sig. A 3v–A4.

[20] Ibid. 45–54, 101–12, 120, 338.

[21] Ibid. 115–18, 157, 178, 180, 192–3, 271–2; *Mr. B.*, Offor, iii. 601. My edition of Bayly reads 'foggy' for 'soggy'.

iv. *Richard Bernard* (1567–1641)

A further influence, especially on *The Pilgrim's Progress*, is *The Isle of Man* (1627) of Richard Bernard. Bernard—who only just failed to become a separatist—published in 1617 *A Key of Knowledge For the opening of the secret mysteries of . . . Revelation*, in which he demonstrated twenty-two ways of making the number 666 spell 'the Pope', in various languages. He thought England was the nation divinely appointed to overthrow Rome.[22] His *Look beyond Luther* (1627) was an answer to the papist question, Where was your church before Luther? The answer was of course in Wyclif and the Lollards, Hus and the Hussites. In *The Bible Battels: Or, The Sacred Art Military For the rightly wageing of warre according to Holy Writ* (1629), dedicated to Charles I, Bernard aimed 'to write an History of Holy Warres'.[23] His *Threefold Treatise of the Sabbath* (1641), dedicated to the House of Lords and the House of Commons, looked back to times when 'certain vain men, profane enough' (i.e. the Laudians), had attempted to degrade the Sabbath. But 'now, blessed be God', the 'honourable wisdom, goodness, power and authority' of MPs had restored its glory. The King is not mentioned.[24] Bernard criticized 'hangers-on who bray of their gentry' and will not work, 'contrary to God's injunction that men should labour, contrary to the practice of all the godly.' No one should live merely in 'the calling of a gentleman'. 'The Lord chooseth most of such as be poor for his people', and few of the rich.[25] In the same year he published *A Short View of the Prelaticall Church of England*, also dedicated to Parliament. This work contains a very comprehensive analysis of abuses, political, judicial, and financial, with proposed remedies.[26] So Bernard was tolerably radical in his outlook.

In *The Isle of Man*, an allegory, Sin and his confederates are put on trial. They are mostly gentlemen, including Sir Worldly Wise, Sir Luke Warm, and Sir Plausible Civil. The accused object to the jury named to try them: 'hardly any one of them is of any account with men of great estates.' They ask instead for 'gentlemen

---

[22] H. F. Sanders, 'Early Puritanism and Separatism in Nottingham', *Trans. Congregational Historical Soc.*, 12 (1933–6), 101; Bernard, *A Key of Knowledge*, 341–3, 128–9.

[23] Op. cit. sig. ¶ 5   [24] Op. cit. sig. a 2v–3.

[25] *Ruth's Recompense* (1628), reprinted in 1865 with R. Stock and S. Torshell's *Commentaries upon Malachi*, 35–7; cf. 56–8.

[26] Op. cit. (by John Barnard?, 'newly corrected with additions by Richard Bernard').

freeholders of great means'. Bernard repeated Dent and Bayly's joke about Covetousness going under the name of Good Husbandry. Covetousness's sons include Thrifty and Pinch, Advantage and Holdfast, Cunning and Catch. Bernard attacks covetousness in all its forms—sale of offices (cf. Vanity Fair), monopolies, enclosure, and racking of rents, making religion a cloak. Covetousness destroys good neighbourhood.[27]

v. William Dell (?1607–1669)

William Dell was born in Bedfordshire. In 1642 he succeeded the notorious Laudian Dr John Pocklington as Rector of Yelden, and retained this living until his ejection in 1662. He was Master of Gonville and Caius College, Cambridge, from 1649. He attracted attention and criticism in 1646 by his radical preaching to the Army at Oxford. He attacked the rich, 'the great men of the kingdom, to whom every poor man is a prey.' 'A poor mean Christian that earns his bread by hard labour is a thousand times more precious than . . . a gentleman, or a knight, or a nobleman, or a king' who is unregenerate. 'The power is in you, the people', he told the soldiers; 'keep it, part not with it'. In the same year he urged the House of Commons to regard 'the oppression of the poor and the sighing of the needy'.[28] Despite his headship of a Cambridge college Dell rejected the accepted idea that universities should be 'the fountain of the ministers of the Gospel.' 'All the clergy must be quite taken away ere the church of Christ can have any true reform.' Antichrist 'chose his ministers only out of the universities'. Philosophy, arts, and sciences are useless to ministers. Dell would 'rather choose to be in fellowship with poor plain husbandmen and tradesmen who believe in Christ . . . than with the heads of universities and highest and stateliest of the clergy'.[29] Hence his invitation to Bunyan to preach at Yelden.

Dell had an imaginative programme for reform of the whole educational system. He wanted universities or colleges to be set up in every great city in the nation, through which students could

---

[27] *The Isle of Man*, 70–1, 74–8, 128–9, 158–87. See Wright, *Middle-Class Culture*, 397–9.

[28] L. F. Solt, *Saints in Arms, Puritanism and Democracy in Cromwell's Army* (Stanford UP, 1959), 12, 90.

[29] E. C. Walker, *William Dell, Master Puritan* (Cambridge, 1970), 22–3; cf. Brown, 74–6, 118; Dell, *Several Sermons*, 87, 91, 256, 273, 303, 316–18, 325, 327–8, 391, 396, 440–58, 467; my *Change and Continuity*, 137–43.

work their way whilst still living at home.[30] He opposed kingship and tithes. He looked back to Wyclif, Hus, and the heretical tradition, but also shared Bunyan's high opinion of Luther. Dell was an antinomian to the extent of thinking that we are free from the law and from sin. He taught that 'all churches are equal, as well as all Christians.' Union with the church flows from our union with Christ, not vice versa. The churches of men are all more or less the habitations of Antichrist. Civil ecclesiastical reform only changes externals. Bunyan would appreciate Dell's insistence that men of worldly power or place should not be chosen as elders. His ecumenism and denigration of water baptism by comparison with the baptism of the spirit would also appeal to Bunyan.[31]

Dell played a significant part in Bedfordshire politics, making recommendations for MPs in 1654 (Okey, Crook, and three others — 'good men and against the paying of tithes'). He and Okey sponsored the petition against kingship for Cromwell in 1657. His parishioners reported in 1660 that Dell had said Charles I 'was no King to him, Christ was his King'. A republic was good enough for Venice and Holland, why not England?[32]

vi. *John Owen* (*1616–1683*)

If John Owen was an influence on Bunyan, it was a late one. The former Vice-Chancellor of Oxford University told Charles II that he would gladly exchange his learning for the tinker's power in the pulpit. Owen often invited Bunyan to preach to his congregation in Moorfields, which the Puritan aristocracy attended. Owen himself 'preached in all plainness and simplicity'. Owen is said to have persuaded his former tutor Bishop Barlow of Lincoln to release Bunyan from jail in 1677;[33] he may have introduced Bunyan to Nathaniel Ponder, Owen's own publisher.

Owen was a millenarian. In April 1649 he spoke of 'these latter days'. Like Milton, he stressed that the Second Coming would

[30] Dell, *Sermons*, 642–8.
[31] Walker, *Dell*, 113–16; Dell, *Sermons*, 290, 590–4, 610–12, 620–2.
[32] Tibbutt, 'John Crook', 112; *Calamy Revised*, 'Dell'.
[33] Brown, 241, 366. Barlow was described by the Earl of Aylesbury, no impartial witness, as hostile in principle to prelacy, 'being a downright Calvinist' (*Memoirs of Thomas, Earl of Ailesbury*, i. 229). Barlow was one of the last seventeenth-century Anglican bishops to denounce the Pope as Antichrist (my *Antichrist in Seventeenth-Century England* (Oxford UP, 1971), 153).

mark the end of 'antichristian tyranny'. Like Bunyan, Owen later came to regret 'how woefully and wretchedly' men had been mistaken in their computations of the time of the end. Owen was also a political radical. He was selected to preach to the House of Commons on 31 January 1649, 'a day of solemn humiliation', the day following Charles I's execution. In 1657 he drafted the decisive petition from London officers which persuaded Oliver Cromwell not to accept the crown. Owen opposed the creation of a second chamber, and was held by Baxter to be largely responsible for the overthrow of Richard Cromwell in 1659.[34]

Owen had played a major part in creating the Cromwellian church. But from at least 1657 he turned against the idea of 'an authoritative national church consisting solely in the power and interest of the clergy.' In a work written in or soon after 1665, though not published till the safer year 1680, Owen argued that the post-restoration Anglican church depended on the monarchy and might tend to support absolutism. It was 'no less glorious in the sight of God', Owen declared, 'to suffer in giving testimony against the abominations of the apostate, Antichristian church-state than to suffer for the Gospel itself in opposition to idolatrous paganism.' 'Grasping temporal power upon a spiritual account' was 'the greatest badge of Antichrist'. Owen was a covenant theologian, and held that nonconformists were the true Church of England in doctrine.[35]

After the restoration Owen seems to have engaged in several plots against the government. In 1661, just after Venner's unsuccessful rising, six or seven cases of pistols were found in his house at Stadhampton. Later in the same year an informer accused Owen of preparing men for revolt in connection with Yarranton's plot. He became recognized as one of nonconformity's leaders. In the 1670s he was prominent in combating Samuel Parker's call for persecution of dissenters. In 1683 he had the honour of having a book condemned to be burnt by the University of Oxford, in the good company of Hobbes, Milton, and Baxter.[36]

---

[34] Owen, *Works* (1850–5), viii. 256–64; cf. 129, 374, 409; ix. 510; W. Lamont, *Richard Baxter and the Millennium*, 220–1.

[35] Owen, *Works*, iii. 243–5; v. 166, 174; vii. 74–6, 133, 244; viii. 386; xi. 25; xiv. 519–27, 555; cf. xv. 143, 230–61.

[36] R. L. Greaves, *Deliver Us from Evil*, (Oxford UP, 1986), 54, 75; cf. 30, 126. See also my *The Experience of Defeat* (1984), ch. 6, sect. 1.

vii. The Bible

Throughout Bunyan's is a *Biblical* theology. From his first published work, *Some Gospel-truths Opened* (1656), he carefully builds
up his argument on a basis of texts, rather as Milton was doing at
the same time in the *De Doctrina Christiana*. 'He that believes the
Scriptures to be the Word of God', wrote Bunyan in *A Few Sighs
from Hell* (1658), and finds a text which appears to exclude him
from the promises, 'will not be contented' till he finds that his 'state
is good'.[37] The believer must rely on his own experience, but this
experience must be carefully checked against the Bible.

The Bible is Bunyan's sheet-anchor, his defence against despair
and atheism. He would have been lost if he had abandoned it. This
accounts for what seem today some of the less attractive features of
Bunyan's thinking—his emphasis on hell-fire, on the inherent
sinfulness of children, his racism and sexism. When necessary he
explains away a difficult text, though not as cavalierly as Milton. He
could apply critical methods, as when, like Sir Walter Ralegh, he
tried to ascertain the tonnage of Noah's ark. Earlier radical
protestants had used the Bible as a negative-critical authority:
institutions and practices not to be found in the Bible were
unlawful. Bunyan himself rejected the Book of Common Prayer
because it was not commanded in the Word of God. But when the
institutions of his own choice were questioned, the Bible, as he
interpreted it, was to be accepted as the final and incontrovertible
authority. He so used it to reject separate women's meetings.[38]

Bunyan seems to have quoted the 'Puritan' Geneva Bible equally
with the Authorized Version throughout his career. Of some thirty
instances which Offor noticed in which he cited a text from the
Geneva Bible, twenty came after 1672—half-way through his
publishing career. He refers once to Tyndale's version.[39]

[37] *A Few Sighs from Hell*, MW i. 358–9.
[38] *A Vindication*, MW i. 184–5; *Law and Grace*, MW ii. 166; Offor, ii. 464, 658.
[39] *The Acceptable Sacrifice* (1689), Offor, i. 695.

15. *Covenant Theology*

> Only doers shall be saved, and by their doing though not for their
> doing. . . . The profession of religion is no such gentleman-like
> life or trade, whose rents come in by their stewards, whether they
> sleep or wake, work or play. . . . A man of good estate knows it is
> the way to maintain it, often to look into his debt books, and cast
> up his reckonings; but a bankrupt hath no heart to this busi-
> ness. . . . Nothing is more industrious than saving faith; it looks so
> to the end, which is salvation, as it is most diligent in the means.
>
> THOMAS TAYLOR[1]

i. *The Protestant Heritage*

THE origins of the covenant theology are to be found in
Luther. It was developed in England by the Lutheran
Tyndale, and later by Perkins, Preston, Sibbes, Thomas Taylor.
By the 1640s it had become accepted Puritan theology. There is no
reason to suppose that Bunyan had read any of the great English
covenant theologians: he must have heard the doctrine in countless
sermons from his youth onwards. It was to be found in popular
emblem books like Thomas Jenner's *The Soules Solace* (1626, and
many later editions), *The Path of Life* (1656), and *The Ages of Sin*
(*c.*1656). It was often preached to the House of Commons — in
1646 by John Owen.[2]

The essence of this theology is the doctrine of the two cov-
enants. Adam failed to keep the original covenant of works, the
Law summed up in the Ten Commandments; in consequence his
whole posterity was corrupted by inherited original sin which
made it impossible for even the most virtuous man or woman to
observe the Law. In the second covenant, the covenant of grace,
Christ offered himself as a sacrifice to God's wrath by taking upon
him the sins of Adam and his posterity. In Bunyan's version of this
covenant there is no reciprocal element. The covenant is between
the Father and the Son: man takes no part. The elect are not saved

---

[1] 'The Jaylors Conversion', in *Works* (1653), 166–79. Taylor died in 1633, but 'the
iniquity of those times' prevented his works from being published under Laud.

[2] Luther, *Thirty Four Sermons*, trans. William Gace (1747), 143, 219; *The Emblem
Books of Thomas Jenner*, ed. S. Gottlieb (New York, 1983); Owen, *A Vision of Unchangeable free mercy* (1646).

because they believe: they believe because they are saved. A man may be justified by Christ's imputed righteousness 'even then when himself knoweth nothing thereof'.[3]

Covenant theology seems to have appealed especially to the laity.[4] It adopted the assumptions of laymen who worked in a world of bargains and agreements enforceable by law. For protestants the covenant replaced the mediation of saints. God now contracts directly with humanity's representative. Christ is the sole mediator. The relationship of the elect to God is conceived as a debtor–creditor relationship.

The elect are a small minority—perhaps one out of 1,000 men and one out of 10,000 women.[5] 'Most of the poor souls in the world,' Bunyan believed, are irrevocably condemned to an eternity in hell. 'Unless the great God, of his infinite grace and bounty, had voluntarily chosen me to be a vessel of mercy, though I should desire and long and labour until my heart did break, no good would come of it', Bunyan tells us in *Grace Abounding* that he had thought. Moors and pagans are apparently all damned; Dent had said that all papists were. The idea of universal salvation is something that can be held by 'no rational man'. Conclusions are drawn from this with legalistic logic. Men are damned not because they are not elected, but because they have sinned wilfully, knowingly, and desperately. The majority are guilty of 'horrid neglect'; 'where is one man of a thousand—yea, where is there two of ten thousand'—that do show that they care about their eternal state? Even among professors, 'but few . . . have been saved'.[6]

[3] *A Confession of my Faith* (1672), Offor, ii. 598; *The Pharisee and the Publican* (1685), MW x. 194.

[4] D. Zaret, *The Heavenly Contract: Ideology and Organization in Pre-Revolutionary Puritanism* (Chicago UP, 1985), 163, 203 and ch. 5, *passim*.

[5] *A Holy Life* (1683), MW ix, 282; cf. *The Greatness of the Soul* (1682), MW ix. 137: one of a thousand, one of five thousand; *Profitable Meditations* (1661), *Poems*, 28; *One Thing is Needful* (1665?), ibid. 76. Arthur Dent thought from one of a hundred to one of a thousand (289). Thomas Shepard suggested one of a thousand (*God's Plot: The Paradoxes of Puritan Piety*, ed. M. McGiffert (Massachusetts UP, 1972), 9); Lancelot Andrewes—the great majority (*Works* (Oxford UP, 1841), v. 191); John Spittlehouse—a quarter might be saved (B. S. Capp, *The Fifth-Monarchy Men: A Study in Seventeenth-Century English Millenarianism* (1972), 173); Donne, one in three (*Sermons*, ed. G. R. Potter and E. M. Simpson (Berkeley UP, 1953–63), viii. 372); Muggleton—a half (C. Hill, B. Reay, and W. Lamont, *The World of the Muggletonians* (1983), 120).

[6] *A Few Sighs from Hell* (1658), MW i. 245; *GA*, 21; *The Resurrection of the Dead*, MW iii. 274–81; Dent, *The Ruine of Rome*, 267; Bunyan, *Come, and Welcome, to Jesus Christ* (1678), MW viii. 243; *The Greatness of the Soul* (1682), MW ix. 105; *The Strait Gate* (1676), MW v. 103–21.

The logic of thus restricting the number of the elect is not clear, but it was traditional Augustinian orthodoxy which Luther and Calvin took over. Radical Arminians, Socinians, Ranters, and Quakers were beginning to challenge it in the seventeenth century. For Bunyan it was axiomatic. It is perhaps the mirror image of life in this world, in which a few enjoy wealth, idleness, luxury, and power; the vast majority live in labour and poverty. In the next life some positions will be reversed. Dives will look hopelessly up for help from Lazarus, but it will be too late. Hence theologies showing the predestination of a minority to eternal bliss attracted especially the unprivileged, and those of the poor who were sufficiently sophisticated and educated to realize that there was a wrong to be righted. A play performed in Kendal in 1621 showed hell filled with landlords and sheriff's bailiffs — and with Puritans as well.[7]

Those whom God intended to save had to be 'awakened', had to realize that they were saved; otherwise the deep sense of their own sinfulness, which was the beginning of salvation, might overwhelm them with despair. Hence the importance of preaching. Early in his career Bunyan realized that he had a gift for awakening; and most of his later work had this as its main object. In his sermons and treatises he is addressing the elect, some of whom are still ignorant of their fortunate status. Others, conscious of their salvation, have to be kept up to the mark. They will not be saved by works, but if they are truly saved they will lead virtuous lives.[8]

In The Doctrine of Law and Grace (1659), Bunyan's first and fullest exposition of covenant theology, he insists that the covenant of grace was between the Father and the Son. Grace comes by way of covenant or bargain to us, yet made with another for us. The bargain was struck before time began. The promise of salvation to the elect, and the choice of those to be saved, were also made before time. The elect are saved by belief in the sacrifice of Christ on the cross; but this belief they owe to divine grace, not to their own merits. 'It is God that worketh in thee to will and to come to Jesus Christ.' Bunyan's version of the covenant emphasizes the promises, as Tyndale had done before him. 'Without a promise

[7] Mildred Campbell, The English Yeoman Under Elizabeth and the Early Stuarts (Yale UP, 1942), 152.
[8] Midgley, Introd. to MW v. xiii–xxii; cf. Advice to Sufferers (1684), MW x. 59.

there can be no faith', Tyndale had declared. 'The devil hath no promise; he is therefore excluded from Paul's faith.'[9]

Because of the divine nature of the parties to the covenant, nothing could be more certain than the salvation of the elect. God bound himself by an oath. The conditions are fulfilled for man by the Son—as a legally binding covenant. Jesus Christ was 'bound as a surety, and stands engaged upon oath to see that all the conditions of the covenant . . . should be accomplished by him.' Bunyan gives the example of a sale of 10,000 sheep, for which cash is not paid down immediately. 'What though I have broke £1000 in my creditor's debt, yet if another will discharge the whole freely, what has the law to do with me as to that?' So we may come to Jesus Christ for anything we want 'of the things made mention of in the New Covenant', as to a common treasure-house, 'he having them all in his own custody by act of purchase.' Christ cannot go bankrupt, whatever happens to those for whom he stands surety. The saints 'ventured all upon his standing surety for them.' God has been given 'complete satisfaction . . . for the sins of the world'.[10]

As Bunyan wrote in 1659, to suppose 'that your repenting and promising to do so no more may . . . put you in a condition to attain the mercy of God by the Law; these thoughts do flow from gross ignorance.' It is impossible to live up to the Law's demands. Even 'to imitate Christ is to make him a Saviour not by sacrifice but by example.' All that matters is faith in his blood.[11] 'If holiness of life be preached as necessary to salvation, then faith is undervalued'; though the converse is also true. 'Many that pretend to be for holiness quite exclude the doctrine and motives that election gives thereto.' 'Many professors are no different from the greatest sinners except in externals.' Others think that 'because their

---

[9] MW ii. 26–8, 88; *Come, and Welcome*, MW viii. 391; *Justification by an Imputed Righteousness* (posthumous), Offor, i. 304, 327–30; *Christ a Complete Saviour* (posthumous), Offor, ii. 332; Tyndale, *Doctrinal Treatises*, Parker Soc. (Cambridge UP, 1848), *passim*. For the blend of Lutheranism, Calvinism, and antinomianism in Bunyan's covenant theology, see esp. R. L. Greaves, *John Bunyan* (Abingdon, 1969), 105–8; id., 'The Origins and Early Development of English Covenant Thought', *The Historian* (USA, 1968), 32–4.

[10] MW ii. xxv–xxviii, 90, 94, 97–101, 186, 192, 196–8; *Israel's Hope Encouraged* (posthumous), Offor, i. 618; cf. *HW*, 75, 78.

[11] *The Acceptable Sacrifice* (posthumous), Offor, i. 719; *Law and Grace*, MW ii. 31–44; cf. 57–61, 144, 147–51, 165–6, 170–1, 191–2, 199–201; *A Defence of the Doctrine of Justification* (1672), Offor, ii. 323, 330–1; cf. 278, 280–1, 333.

parents have been religious before them, and have been indeed the
people of God, . . . if they also do as to the outward observing of
that which they learnt from their forerunners, that God doth
accept them.' But grace is not by inheritance. That is why children
must be told 'betimes what cursed creatures they are . . . under the
wrath of God'.[12]

In his early writings, based on his own conversion experience,
Bunyan emphasized two points which recur in his theology. First,
grace will not come without profound *personal* conviction of the
utter worthlessness of one's own endeavours; second, the 'scabbed
hedge-creep' Lazarus is more likely to be among the chosen than
Dives. 'Mercy seems to be out of his proper channel when it deals
with self-righteous men; but then it runs with a full stream when it
extends itself to the biggest sinners.'[13]

ii. The Will for the Deed

If we are saved or damned from all eternity, it would seem that
nothing we can do will influence our fate. Yet Bunyan, and those to
whom he preached, could not be satisfied to leave it at that. How
are men and women to be saved from despair? 'This would still
stick with me,' Bunyan recalled in *Grace Abounding*: 'how can you
tell that you are elect? and what if you should not?' Some assurance
must be given to suffering souls genuinely seeking salvation. The
answer is contained in Perkins's phrase, God accepts the will for
the deed. 'He who desires to be righteous, is righteous', declared
John Downame; 'he that would repent, doth repent.' It would be
nice to think that Quarles was caricaturing this view when he
wrote:

> How easy is our God, and liberal, who
> Counts it as done, what we have will to do.[14]

---

[12] *A Holy Life* (1683), MW ix. 251–4, 262, 326; *The Barren Fig-tree*, MW v. 47; *I Will
Pray with the Spirit* (1662), MW ii. 76, 179–80, 268–9. See ch. 24 (iii), below.

[13] *The Heavenly Foot-man*, MW v. 140; cf. 153–5, 160–1; *The Advocateship of Jesus
Christ* (1688), MW xi. 121; *The Jerusalem Sinner* (1688), 26–8; cf. 38–40. *The Pharisee
and the Publican* (1685) picks up this theme.

[14] *GA*, 21; Downame, *Christian Warfare* (1604), 120; Quarles, *Divine Fancies* (1632),
in *Complete Works*, ed. A. B. Grosart (1880), ii. 223.

But I fear he meant it seriously. Henry Denne, on the other hand, snorted that 'the poor man can tell you that to be rich and to desire to be rich are two things.'[15]

Perkins's principle restores an element of conscious will to the process of salvation. We cannot be saved by our works, but our determination to be saved may—only may—be evidence that we are in fact in a state of grace. Bunyan urged the penitent to 'fly in all haste to Jesus Christ, ... secretly persuading thy soul that Jesus Christ standeth open-armed to receive thee.' 'If we come we shall be received.'[16] We would not be passionately concerned about our salvation unless we are in fact saved. 'Were I not elect, the Father would not draw me. ... Not one of the non-elect shall ever be able to say ... I did sincerely come to Jesus Christ'. Doubts and anxieties are 'a sign God has not quite left thee'. We must come boldly to God, taking it 'for granted that God will give us ... whatever we ask in the name of his Son.' 'In effectual calling there is ... faith, hope and repentance', a turning of the heart to God in Christ from sin and the devil. Effectual calling follows awakening to the evil of sin and unbelief. "'Tis not grace received', says a marginal note in *The Holy War*, 'but grace improved that preserves the soul from temporal dangers.'[17]

The sinner must:

work that I may have Christ, ... do the Law that I may have the Gospel; ... thou must believe, because thou canst not do, ... or else thou wilt never come to Christ as a sinner; and if so, then Christ will not receive thee. ... To keep off from Christ because thou canst not do, is to be kept off from Christ by the Law.

The contradictions are dialectical. 'Faith is a gift of God, or an act of ours, take it which way you will. ... Faith is a gift bestowed upon us by the gracious God, the nature of which is to lay hold on

[15] Denne, *A Conference between a sick man and a minister* (1643), 2; cf. Capp, *Fifth-Monarchy Men*, 94. Tobias Crisp and William Walwyn, among other antinomians, rejected Perkins's principle (Walwyn, *The Power of Love* (1643), 19–22, in W. Haller (ed.), *Tracts on Liberty in the Puritan Revolution, 1638–1647* (Columbia UP, 1933), ii. For Crisp see *Religion and Politics in Seventeenth-Century England* (Brighton, 1986), ch. 9. See also Burton, *Anatomy of Melancholy* (Everyman edn.), iii. 415, 421.
[16] Zaret, *Heavenly Contract*, 159–60; *Law and Grace*, MW ii. 17, 97–101, 196–8; cf. pp. xxxi–xxxii, 163, 169–71, 173–88; *Come, and Welcome* (1678), MW viii. 255–6, 291.
[17] *Come, and Welcome*, 352–3, 372, 391–2; *The Jerusalem Sinner* (1688), MW xi. 86–9; *Ebal and Gerizzim* (1665), *Poems*, 113; *Saved by Grace* (1675), MW viii. 225; *A Confession of My Faith* (1672), Offor, ii. 599–600; *HW*, 152.

Christ.' 'Dost thou want faith? Then come for it to the man Christ Jesus.' To be unable to pray 'is a good sign that thy prayers are more than bare words, and have some prevalence at the throne of grace through Christ Jesus.' 'Close in with this Jesus and accept of him; . . . be thou bond or free, wise or foolish, if thou close with him, he will say unto thee, "Well done, good and faithful servant"'. Faith seems to be an act of free choice on the sinner's part, an act of will. The 'fickle thoughts' of Lord Willbewill in *The Holy War* illustrate the will in action. Those who want to be saved by Jesus Christ cannot have committed the sin against the Holy Ghost.[18]

Bunyan draws very fine distinctions here. When the sinner says, 'I will labour to do what I can, and what I cannot do Christ will do for me', he is rebuked: 'This is the wrong way too, for this is to make Christ but a piece of a Saviour.' To the expostulation, 'Would you have us do nothing? Would you have us make Christ such a drudge as to do all, while we sit idling still?' The answer is, 'He that can make himself clean hath no need of Christ. . . . Your business is seriously to enquire whether you are under the first or second convenant; for unless you are under the second, you will never be regarded of the Lord.' There are some for whom the day of grace has passed. Some have wilfully, knowingly, and maliciously rejected Christ. But it is possible to help ourselves against Satan, to urge the promises at the throne of grace, to adopt 'a wrestling spirit of prayer'.[19]

It is no easy task. Luther had said that faith is the most difficult of all works. Bunyan agreed: 'he that undertakes to believe, sets upon the hardest task that ever was proposed to man', so corrupt is the human heart. 'Believing is sweating work.' 'Run for heaven, fight for heaven, labour for heaven, wrestle for heaven', wrote Bunyan in 1676, 'or you are like to go without it'. Too many of those who consider themselves the elect are passive. 'The text says Strive, and they sit and sleep; that says Strive to enter in, and they content themselves with a profession that is never likely to bring them

---

[18] MW ii. 80–1, 198–9, 211, 224; cf. 300; *The Jerusalem Sinner*, MW xi. 89; *HW*, 54 and *passim*; cf. *Poems*, 109–10, 114–15, 154.

[19] MW ii. 174–6, 201, 204; cf. 58–9, 66–8; *The Barren Fig-tree* (1673), title-page and MW v. 46–7; *The Heavenly Foot-man* (posthumous), MW v. 140; *Poems*, 30–1, 111–13, 281; *Israel's Hope Encouraged* (posthumous), Offor, i. 588.

thither.' 'Departing from iniquity' is a war, a continual combat.[20] 'They that will have heaven must run for it', Bunyan insisted. 'Not to run a little now and then, by fits and starts, or half-way, or almost thither; but to run for my life, to run through all difficulties, and to continue therein to the end of the race, . . . to the end of my life.' 'Man by nature is rather a hearer than a doer.' 'A man may read and hear, not to learn to do, though to know.' 'That love is little set by that breaks not through to practice.' The distinction between doers and mere talkers was common among Puritan activists. It is the basis of Cromwell's 'Trust in God and keep your powder dry'. The victory of God's cause may be inevitable, but it depends on his servants fighting effectively for it. The point was emphasized in *The Pilgrim's Progress*. Conversion means a total change of life, a self-dedication. In the post-restoration period, as Bunyan discovered, this involved a readiness to make any sacrifice rather than compromise, as the Latitudinarians did. It led, in however negative a way, to political action.[21]

In his posthumous *The Desire of the Righteous Granted* Bunyan asked 'Since I have lusts and desires both ways, how shall I know to which my soul adheres?' And the answer is, 'Which wouldst thou have prevail? . . . How art thou when thou thinkest that thou thyself hast grace?' If this gives feelings of great joy, then 'thy desires are only good; for that thou hast desired against thy sin, thy sinful self; which indeed is not thy self, but sin that dwells in thee.' 'If we have but grace enough to keep us groaning after God, it is not all the world can destroy us.'[22]

Christ came to save those who know they are the greatest of sinners. 'I never heard a presumptuous man in my life say that he was afraid that he presumed; but I have heard many an honest humble soul say, that they have been afraid their faith hath been presumptuous.' A glimpse may be enough: *all* men can turn towards Christ. 'Believing and coming was all one', Hopeful thought Christ had assured him.

[20] Luther, *Reformation Writings*, i. 259; *The Advocateship of Jesus Christ* (1688), MW xi. 116, 188; *Light for them that sit in Darkness* (1675), MW viii. 157; *The Strait Gate* (1676), MW v. 81–6; *A Holy Life* (1683), MW ix. 347; cf. *Justification by an Imputed Righteousness* (posthumous), Offor, i. 332–3; *The Pharisee and the Publican* (1685), MW x. 183–5.

[21] *The Heavenly Foot-man*, MW v. 148–9; *Christian Behaviour* (1663), MW iii. 52; *A Holy Life*, MW ix. 254, 257; *PP*, 79–80; Sharrock, 33; Talon, 102.

[22] *The Desire of the Righteous Granted* (posthumous), Offor, i. 758–9; cf. 769.

Coming to Christ is a moving of the mind towards him. . . . Christ's
receiving us to mercy depends upon our coming; and so our salvation by
Christ is conditional: if we come we shall be received; if not, we shall
not. . . . When God shuts the door upon men, he gives them no heart to
come to Jesus Christ. . . . But thou comest, therefore it is given to thee of
the Father. . . . If . . . the covenant of salvation is not broken, none can
show a reason why he that comes to Christ should be damned.[23]

This was approaching antinomianism.

In 1672 Bunyan wrote, 'There is no such thing in man by nature
as liberty of will, or a principle of freedom in the saving things of
the kingdom of Christ.' Yet he also wrote, 'I tell you the will is all:
that is one of the chief things which turns the wheel either
backwards or forwards. . . . Get thy will tipt with heavenly grace
and resolution against all discouragements, and then thou goest
full speed for heaven; but if thou falter in thy will, . . . be sure thou
wilt fall short at the last. . . . Heaven is prepared for whosoever will
accept of it.'[24]

Bunyan shares to the full what to modern ways of thinking seems
the rather disagreeable legalism of the covenant theologians.
'Mansoul is mine by right of purchase', Emanuel tells Diabolus in
The Holy War: 'I . . . became a surety to my Father, body for body,
life for life, blood for blood'. This is especially evident in *The
Advocateship of Jesus Christ* (1688). Christ acts as our attorney.
'God's law . . . did so seize upon the Lord Jesus, and so cruelly
handle him, and so exact upon him, that it would never let him
alone until it had . . . screwed his very heart blood out of his
precious heart.' 'Before that prisoner can be released, there must
be a full satisfaction given to [the Law of God], either by the man's
own life, or by the blood of some other man.' 'The soul that hath
eternal life, he must have it by right of purchase or redemption.'
On the other side, Christ's 'faithfulness to his threatenings would
not let him extend his mercy to me.' 'Satisfaction' – a word which
Bunyan admits 'will hardly be found in the Bible' – plays a large
part in this theology. 'Justice calls for satisfaction.' Christ hath

---

[23] *The Jerusalem Sinner* (1688), MW xi. 69; cf. 8, 57, 84–9; *Come, and Welcome*
(1678), MW viii. 255–6, 267, 270–1, 291, 340, 352–3, 391–2; cf. 372; *PP*, 143; *Christ a
Complete Saviour* (posthumous), Offor, i. 222; cf. Talon, 144.
[24] *A Defence of the Doctrine of Justification*, Offor, ii. 312; *The Heavenly Foot-man*
(posthumous), MW v. 165, 167; cf. *PP*, 295.

'paid the full price for us by his death'; he has 'done more than make satisfaction for our sin.'[25]

Contrariwise, 'the wicked shall lie down and be beaten with many stripes in the presence of Christ . . . and the holy angels.' God 'would falsify his Word, if after a time he should deliver them from hell, concerning whom he hath solemnly testified that they shall be there for ever.' Bunyan stressed 'with what delight' God 'will burn sinners in the flames of hell, for the easing of his mind and the satisfaction of his justice.' 'God is resolved to have the mastery, . . . the victory, . . . to break the spirit of the world, to make all men cringe and crouch unto him.' Bunyan knew as well as Milton did that the Eternal Decrees were being questioned, and that the ways of God to men had to be justified.[26]

One great difference between Bunyan's covenant theology and that of Perkins, Preston, Sibbes, Taylor, and their school is that the latter silently assumed the existence of a state church. They do not discuss the subject; it is taken for granted. In the circumstances in which they lived, they had decided against separation, whatever their ideal preferences might have been. The covenant theology helped to ward off Familism, antinomianism, and radical Arminianism.[27] Perhaps the censorship did not permit discussion of the subject in the abstract. Bunyan equally took for granted the independence and freedom of the congregation of the faithful. The state of affairs between 1657 and 1660, when the minister of the Bedford congregation held a living in the state church, had been exceptional.

There is nothing original in Bunyan here. His assumptions are those of his generation, shared by large numbers of Puritans who accepted the separatism which had become a viable alternative after 1640. Before 1640 the elect had been isolated men and women. They might recognize one another, form informal groups, discuss together, trade together; but separatist congregations

---

[25] *HW*, 75; *Law and Grace*, *MW* ii. 38–9, 58, 99–100, 128, 131, 189–90, 194; cf. 90, and *Justification by an Imputed Righteousness* (posthumous), Offor, i. 344; *GA, passim; Light for them that sit in Darkness* (1675), *MW* viii. 107–47, 194; cf. *The Defence of the Doctrine of Justification* (1672), Offor, ii. 301; *The Pharisee and the Publican* (1685), *MW* x. 214–15; *Israel's Hope Encouraged* (posthumous), Offor, i. 605.

[26] *The Greatness of the Soul* (1682), *MW* ix. 210–15, 219, 222; *Israel's Hope Encouraged*, Offor, i. 617; *The Resurrection of the Dead*, Offor, ii. 111, 123; *A Treatise of the Fear of God* (1679), *MW* ix. 121.

[27] See Zaret, *Heavenly Contract*, 15–16, 137–40.

could be formed only illegally or in exile. The combination of covenant theology with congregational independence had been worked out in exile by William Ames, Thomas Goodwin, Hugh Peter; and by John Owen in England in the 1640s. Bunyan simply took it over ready-made: the case no longer needed arguing. Yet the existence of congregational churches gave a different emphasis to the covenant theology. Part II of *The Pilgrim's Progress* is an allegory about the congregation, as Part I had been an allegory about the individual saint.

So Bunyan's theology assumes pluralism, as the theology of Perkins, Preston, Sibbes, and Taylor assumed unity. For Bunyan discussion is of the essence. Dell quoted Luther when opposing an enforced uniformity;[28] and Bunyan no doubt discussed such matters with Dell. Gifford's church in Bedford was founded on ecumenical principles.

In New England the congregational church preserved doctrinal unity under the aegis of a godly magistracy. In England in the 1640s toleration was forced on the churches by the need for unity against the intolerant Presbyterian church. When a broader state church was confirmed under the Protectorate of Oliver Cromwell, separatist congregations were tolerated outside it. Under Charles II, with gentry power rampant in the localities, congregations led a precarious existence. The threat of a return to the pre-1640 position of complete illegality always existed. But now there were too many separatists. The Church of England's refusal to allow Presbyterians to remain within the church meant that nonconformists were too economically and numerically powerful to be persecuted out of existence, however much some would have wished it.

iii. *The Metaphors of Bunyan's Covenant Theology*

Bunyan frequently made the connection between theology and everyday life by using commercial metaphors. Most are now familiar to readers of Perkins, Preston, and Sibbes — sureties, creditors, oaths, satisfaction, a public person.[29] We are redeemed by

---

[28] Dell, *Several Sermons and Discourses* (1709), 290–1; cf. p. 160 above.

[29] *The Doctrine of the Law and Grace Unfolded* (1659), MW ii. 97–101, 162, 196–8, 288; *GA*, 73. Bunyan used such metaphors in *Ebal and Gerizzim* (1665?), *Poems*, 112: he was to use them again in the posthumous *The Saints' Knowledge of Christ's Love*, Offor, ii. 34.

right of purchase: Christ paid for everything in advance. In *Grace Abounding* Bunyan rejoiced that 'all those graces of God that now were green in me, were yet but like those cracked groats and fourpence halfpennies that rich men carry in their purses, when their gold is in their trunks at home! Oh, I saw my gold was in my trunk at home!' The metaphor in *Prison Meditations* (1663) recalls Traherne – 'We change our drossy dust for gold'.[30]

In *The Pilgrim's Progress* Hopeful illustrates the folly of sinners thinking of getting to heaven by keeping the Law – 'If a man runs £100 into the shop-keeper's debt, and after that shall pay for all that he shall fetch, yet his old debt stands still in the book uncrossed' (139–40). When Bunyan returned in 1682 to the theme of Dives and Lazarus in *The Greatness of the Soul*, the thrust of his argument was rather different from that of *A Few Sighs from Hell* a quarter of a century earlier. Now he stressed the folly of Dives in venturing his soul for earthly pleasures, when he might have invested in the safe profits of the after life. 'Suppose so many cattle in a pound', wrote Bunyan in *The Advocateship of Jesus Christ* (1688), 'and one goes by whose they are not', he does not concern himself. 'But suppose at his return he should find his own cattle in that pound, ... he has interest here. ... If he finds them rightfully there, he will fetch them thence by ransom; but if wrongfully, he will replevy them and stand a trial at law with him that has thus illegally pounded his cattle.' 'The advocate ... pleadeth a price already paid. ... His credit, his honour, his glory and renown, flies all away if those for whom he pleads as an Advocate perish for want of worth in his sacrifice pleaded.' Bunyan varies the metaphor by illustrating from a poor man selling land.[31]

So Bunyan carefully adapted his metaphors to his audience. 'I have often observed', he wrote, 'that those that keep shop can briskly attend to a two-penny customer; but when they come themselves to God's market ...'. Most tradesmen 'will be more vigilant in dealing with a 12-penny customer than they will be with Christ.' The sacraments were ordained 'for men to travel and trade in, for the good and wholesome merchandise of heaven, as the men of this world do in the streets and open places of their cities and places of privilege.' God sets his distinguishing mark on the graces

[30] *Poems*, 48; cf. 50–1 – the wise merchant.
[31] *PP*, 139–40; MW, ix. 224; *The Advocateship of Jesus Christ*, MW xi. 132, 160. 183–6.

of the saints, 'as your great traders do with the goods that their chapmen have either bought or spoke for.' Just as money or estates are put into the hands of trustees, so God has put our salvation 'into the hands of the trusty Jesus'. Even if we have gone £1,000 into debt, Jesus Christ will 'keep us from writ, bailiff or jail'. 'For those that have halted, or may halt, the Lord has mercy in his bank.' The pastor, Bunyan explained in *The Building of the House of God* (1688), is like a steward who looks after the cash, an overseer. More sombrely, Lord Willbewill 'took Mr Letgoodslip one day as he was busy in the market', just like any one of us, 'and executed him according to law'.[32]

[32] *Paul's Departure and Crown* (posthumous), Offor, i. 729; *Christ a Complete Saviour* (posthumous), Offor, i. 214; *The Greatness of the Soul* (1682), MW ix. 201; *Israel's Hope Encouraged* (posthumous), Offor, i. 583–4; *The Jerusalem Sinner* (1688), MW xi. 78–9; *Poems*, 286; *HW*, 283.

16. *Social Uses of Hell-fire*

Canst thou think that such a muck-heap of sin as thou art shall be
lifted up to heaven?   BUNYAN[1]

Man crumbles to dust in the presence of God.

BUNYAN[2]

BUNYAN'S doctrine starts from the 'necessity of breaking the
heart in order to salvation'; 'a broken heart therefore suiteth
with the heart of God'. As early as 1658 Bunyan was speaking of
spiritual death and resurrection by the Scriptures. A sense of guilt
seems a necessary preliminary to the coming of grace. Bunyan
might have heard this familiar doctrine in Paul Hobson's sermon
at Newport Pagnell in 1645: 'he and he only is fit to declare truth
whose spirit is crucified by the power of truth.'[3] Hence Bunyan's
emphasis on the terror of judgment, of the bottomless pit. 'Hell-
fire, devouring fire, the lake of fire, eternal everlasting fire: O to
make thee swim up and down in the flames of the furnace of fire!'
'Canst thou drink hell-fire? Will the wrath of God be a pleasant
dish to thy taste?' He agreed with John Owen that threats of
the wrath to come are essential to social discipline: they form
'the great engine of the providence of God for the preserving
mankind from the outrageousness and unmeasurableness of
iniquity and wickedness which would utterly ruin all human
society.'[4]

The emphasis is on what Margaret Spufford called 'unabashed
use of fear as a lever to conversion': she was speaking of religious
chap-books. There is nothing unusual in this theological

---

[1] *The Strait Gate* (1676), MW v. 119.
[2] *A Treatise of the Fear of God* (1679), Offor, i. 439.
[3] *The Acceptable Sacrifice*, Offor, i. 702, 712; *A Few Sighs from Hell*, MW i. 353–8; cf.
324–8; *The Jerusalem Sinner* (1688), MW xi. 84–7; Hobson, *A Garden Inclosed*, 8.
[4] *The Pharisee and the Publican* (1685), MW x. 205–11; *Law and Grace*, MW ii. 226;
cf. *A Few Sighs from Hell*, MW i. 266–7, 272–6, 300–3, 371–2; *Justification by an
Imputed Righteousness*, Offor, i. 333–4; *The Strait Gate* (1676), MW v. 119, 121; *The
Resurrection of the Dead* (1665), MW iii. 286; *Poems*, 30–1, 93–7; Owen, *Works*
(1850–5), xii. 587.

approach. In 1650 Isaac Penington, in his Ranter phase, stressed the omnipotence of God who impartially destroyed the perfect and the wicked. Thomas Goodwin's posthumous *Discussion of the Punishment of Sin in Hell* (1680) started from the assumption that God is 'an enraged enemy'. Bunyan's emphasis on a vengeful God, and his aggravation of the sinner's offences, are nevertheless rather horrible.[5] They lead to a suggestion that the torments of hell justify the brutal sentences enforced by the law—'those petty judgments among men, as putting in the stocks, whipping or burning in the hand.' When in the afterlife 'the godly think of hell, it will increase their comfort'. When an objector remarks, in words that echo the Leveller William Walwyn, 'I cannot believe that God will be so severe as to cast away into hell fire an immortal soul for a little sin', Bunyan replied: 'It would be injustice to deliver those whom the Law condemneth.' If he did, God 'would falsify his Word'.[6]

Donald Davie observed that Bunyan's scheme of salvation in *The Pilgrim's Progress*, with 'its ferocious rigour', is 'such as few Christians to-day—not to speak of unbelievers—can stomach'.[7] True enough: but since most seventeenth-century theologians shared these traditional medieval Catholic ideas, this is hardly relevant to our purposes. Bunyan's contemporary Lodowick Muggleton envisaged the saints feeding with joy and delight upon the eternal damnation of those less fortunate than themselves.[8]

It was a commonplace that Calvinist doctrines of predestination could lead to despair; there was no reason why papists should despair, Robert Burton thought. The Baptist Helwys in 1611, the anonymous author of *Tyranipocrit Discovered* in 1649, the astrologer John Gadbury in 1658, Joseph Alleyn in 1671, Thomas Hobbes in 1679, all agreed on that. Jeremiah Burroughs in 1648,

[5] Spufford, *Small Books and Pleasant Histories*, 207; Penington, *Light or Darkness* (1650), 7–9; Goodwin, op. cit. 10, 78; Bunyan, *The Greatness of the Soul* (1682), MW ix. 167–9, 172–5, 181–5, 205–6, 239–45; *The Jerusalem Sinner* (1688), MW xi. 70–4; cf. 20–4 and *Instruction for the Ignorant* (1675), MW viii. 14–15; *Come, and Welcome* (1678), ibid. 322.

[6] *The Resurrection of the Dead* (1665), MW iii. 289, 291; *The Greatness of the Soul*, MW ix. 221–2; *Walwin's Wiles* (1649), in *The Leveller Tracts*, ed. W. Haller and G. Davies (Columbia UP, 1944), 296–7.

[7] Davie, *A Gathered Church: The Literature of the English Dissenting Interest, 1700–1930* (1978), 9–10.

[8] Muggleton, *A true Interpretation of all the Chief Texts . . . of the whole Book of the Revelation* (1665), 228.

possibly more realistically, cited sin and debt as causes of despair.[9]
Bunyan quoted the 1649 life of Francis Spira, in *Grace Abounding*,
The Barren Fig-tree, *The Heavenly Foot-man*, and *The Greatness of the
Soul*. Spira was notorious for relapsing from protestantism back to
popery; he died in despair. The seventeenth-century equivalent
was John Child, once a member of the Bedford congregation,
who conformed to the Church of England in 1660 and ultimately committed suicide in despair.[10] The economic crisis of
the early seventeenth century may have worked together with
Calvinism to induce a sense of desperation: it would be useless
to speculate which was the more operative cause.

Dr Spufford noted the familiarity of this subject in religious
chap-books: even children attempted suicide. She sensibly adduces
falling life expectancy and the crises of civil war, fire, and plague as
reasons. The congregational solidarity and mutual support of the
sects may have helped those who had been terrified by fears of
hell.[11] Perhaps from considerations of this sort, Bunyan went out
of his way to discourage sick-bed repentance. Mr. Badman's quiet
death was evidence of his sinfulness and carnal security.

John Downame devoted many pages to the anxieties caused by
Satan raising doubts about election, calling, sanctification. Lewis
Bayly thought 'despair is nothing so dangerous as presumption'.[12]
Nehemiah Wallington made a series of attempts to kill himself in
his teens, and was thought to be a suicide risk until he was in his
30s. He noted many other suicide attempts in London, some of
them successful. Around 1632 William Kiffin was saved by John
Goodwin from depression about the impossibility of fulfilling the
Law. In a sermon published in 1652 Robert Abbott instanced a

---

[9] Burton, *The Anatomy of Melancholy* (Everyman edn.), iii. 403–4; [Anon.], *Tyranipocrit Discovered* (Rotterdam, 1649), in *British Pamphleteers*, i, ed. G. Orwell and R.
Reynolds (1948), 89; A. C. Underwood, *A History of the English Baptists* (1947), 134; B. S.
Capp, *Astrology and the Popular Press: English Almanacs, 1500–1800* (1979), 148; Joseph
Alleyn, *An Alarm to the Unconverted* (repr. 1964), 59; Hobbes, *Behemoth: The History of
the Causes of the Civil Wars of England, English Works*, ed. Sir W. Molesworth,
(1839–45), vi. 194–6; Burroughs, *The Rare Jewel of Christian Contentment* (repr. 1964),
187.

[10] *GA*, 49; *MW* v. 58, 151, 173; ix. 167; *PP*, 318.

[11] M. Spufford, *Small Books and Pleasant Histories*, 203, 215–18; *The Jerusalem Sinner*,
MW xi. 57, 89. But see Michael MacDonald, *Mystical Bedlam: Madness, Anxiety and
Healing in Seventeenth-Century England* (Cambridge UP, 1981), esp. chs. 3 and 4.

[12] Downame, *The Christian Warfare: the Devill, World and Flesh* (4th edn., enlarged,
1634), Pt. I, Bks ii and iii; Bayly, 120.

young apothecary who committed suicide from despair. In the 1640s John Rogers, Vavasor Powell, Lodowick Muggleton, and others were in a similar condition. In the case of Anna Trapnel the alternative to suicide seemed to be 'those Familistical ranting tenents'. I listed above other representative figures who suffered from doubts and despair in the late 1640s and 1650s.[13] Many Quakers suffered temptations to despair—Fox himself in the 1640s, John Gratton 'in Oliver Cromwell's time', John Crook. John Burnyeat spoke of 'the horror and terror we were in ... because of the guilt of sin that was upon us' in 1653: the Quaker message came to save them.[14]

Bunyan then was competing with Quakers on the one hand, and Latitudinarians on the other, in analysing the dangers of despair. He thought that both minimized the problem in a facile and superficial manner. His solution was to push through despair to an awareness of human helplessness in the face of sin and guilt, which would lead to a true conversion. It was a remedy for strong characters. Bunyan himself never thought of suicide, so far as we know. Conscious of the dangers of despair and total loss of faith, he put his confidence in the Bible as a defence. The temptation to despair in Doubting Castle results from the Pilgrim's forgetfulness of the promises. In *The Holy War* Mr. Deceit recommended that — rather than tempting Mansoul to pride or to wantonness — 'if we could drive them into desperation, that might knock the nail on the head.' Diabolus shouted 'hell-fire' to scare the inhabitants of Mansoul, letting loose an army of Doubters, and especially election-doubters, in the hope that 'desperation shall thrust them down' into the pit. The election-doubters were Diabolus's life-guard. But 'we dare not despair', the Lord Mayor of Mansoul said, 'but will look for, wait for, and hope for deliverance still'. Despair,

[13] Seaver, *Wallington's World*, 16–25, 60, 204; cf. 222; William Orme, *Remarkable Passages in the Life of William Kiffin* (1823), 10–11; R. Abbott, *The Young Mans Warning-piece* (1652), *passim*; E. Rogers, *The Life and Opinions of a Fifth-Monarchy Man* (1867), 12–20; [Anon.], *The Life and Death of Mr. Vavasor Powell* (1671), 9–12; L. Muggleton, *Acts of the Witnesses* (1764), 10–35 (1st pub. 1699, relating to 1651); [Anna Trapnel], *The Cry of a Stone* (1654), 8–10; B. S. Capp, *The Fifth Monarchy Men: A Study in Seventeenth-Century Millenarianism* (1972), 95–8; M. R. Watts, *The Dissenters: From the Reformation to the French Revolution* (Oxford UP, 1978), 177. See p. 68 above.

[14] Fox, *Journal*, ed. N. Penney (1901), i. 4; *A Journal of the Life of . . . John Gratton* (1720), 5; *A Short History of the Life of John Crook* (1706), 10; Thomas Wight, *A History of the Rise and Progress of the . . . Quakers in Ireland* (4th edn., 1811), 155–6.

which might lead to atheism, was a worse fate than perishing under the enemy. Despair, Milton thought, falls on the reprobate alone.[15]

[15] *Some Gospel-truths*, MW i. 14; *A Vindication*, ibid. 185; *Profitable Meditations* (1661), in *Poems*, 19–21; *The Saints' Knowledge of Christ's Love* (posthumous), Offor, ii. 37; *Come, and Welcome*, MW viii. 340–2; *The Jerusalem Sinner*, MW xi. 63–6; *The Advocateship of Jesus Christ*, ibid. 188; *Justification by an Imputed Righteousness*, Offor, i. 317; *PP*, 115; *HW*, 167, 170, 186–7, 203, 211, 220; *MCPW*, vi. 659, quoting Gen. 4: 13.

17. *Antinomianism*

Thou art no captive, but a child and free;
Thou wast not made for laws, but laws for thee.

BUNYAN[1]

THE idea that the spirit from which we act is more important than the external form of the action had been essential to protestantism from the start. The orthodox were always having to defend Bunyan's favourite Luther from the charge of antinomianism. Mere ceremonies mean nothing in religion if they do not express the deepest feelings of the heart. At the day of judgment, Bunyan said, 'it is the principle as well as the practice that shall be enquired into, ... whether the spirit from which you acted was legal or evangelical.' Works therefore are valid only if done from faith. This was a reason for rejecting set forms of prayer. Without the Spirit, 'though we had a thousand Common-Prayer-Books, yet we know not what we should pray for as we ought.' One of the 'dying sayings' attributed to Bunyan was, 'When thou prayest, rather let thy heart be without words than thy words without a heart.' Popish ceremonies—penance, pilgrimages, flagellation, sackcloth, confession, indulgences—all arise from a slavish fear of God induced by priestcraft: the doctrine of justification by faith banishes this fear, and with it these ceremonies.[2]

Sometimes Bunyan expressed this rather slackly:

Sincerity! Grace is thereto entailed,
The man that was sincere, God never failed.

'He is already a bad man that doth bad deeds', proclaimed Mr. Wiseman in *Mr. Badman*. The essential basis for commercial morality was the spirit in which transactions were conducted. 'Every true Christian', Lewis Bayly had written, 'as soon as he is

---

[1] *Of the Building of the House of God* (1688), *Poems*, 294.
[2] See my 'Protestantism and the Rise of Capitalism', in *Change and Continuity in Seventeenth-Century England* (1975), *passim*; *Law and Grace* (1659), MW ii. 71; *I Will Pray with the Spirit* (1662?), ibid. 247–50, Offor, i. 65; *A Treatise of the Fear of God* (1679), Offor, i. 448, 483; cf. *A Defence of the Doctrine of Justification* (1672), Offor, ii. 325.

regenerate begins to keep all God's commandments *in truth*, though he cannot *in absolute perfection*.'[3]

Antinomianism was always potentially present in predestinarian theologies, as critics like Fowler did not fail to point out. Bunyan and his like rejected what they saw as the spiritual pride of those who believed they could be saved by their works; but they were in danger of slipping into the equally arrogant belief that the godly cannot sin. In the liberty of the 1640s many drew antinomian conclusions from the doctrine of justification by Christ's imputed righteousness. The word 'antinomian' indeed dates from that decade. Bunyan's friend George Cokayne wrote a preface for the posthumous *Christ Alone Exalted* of Tobias Crisp, the well-known antinomian whose father-in-law, Colonel Rowland Wilson, was a prominent member of Cokayne's church. 'In way of condition of the covenant', declared Crisp, 'you must do nothing'. 'Under Dr. Crisp's doctrine' Lawrence Clarkson was influenced towards the 'sect' of antinomians. But he was even more impressed by Paul Hobson.[4] Baxter said that Hobson was one of those responsible for spreading antinomianism in the New Model Army. Like Bunyan later, Hobson 'was once as legal as any of you can be. . . . But I am persuaded that when I used all these duties, I had not one jot of God in me.' Hobson believed that saints 'are admitted and have some entrance into heaven here; they live as saints, . . . they trade as saints.' John Owen in 1653 wrote a Preface recommending the antinomian William Eyre's *Justification without Conditions*.[5]

Bunyan knew that his theology tended towards antinomianism. He gave hostages to fortune. In *Law and Grace* he described a *new law* — an idea popular with antinomian radicals. Traditionalists thought there was only one law, and that the old one. It was Gerrard Winstanley who had published a treatise called *The New*

[3] *The Building of the House of God* (1688), *Poems*, 299; *Mr. B.*, Offor, iii. 627, 641; Bayly, 110.

[4] *OED* has 'antinomist' in 1632: David S. Lovejoy, *Religious Enthusiasm in the New World: Heresy to Revolution* (Harvard UP, 1985), 238; C. B. Cockett, 'George Cokayn', *Trans. Congregational Historical Soc.*, 12 (1933–6), 225–6; Crisp, *Christ Alone Exalted* (1643), i. 83 (Crisp died in 1643); Clarkson, *The Lost sheep Found*, 9–10. Wilson's widow became Bulstrode Whitelocke's third wife. Cokayne, who helped to bring about the marriage, was her chaplain (Spalding, *The Improbable Puritan*, 122, 142).

[5] *Reliquiae Baxterianae*, 111; Edwards, *Gangraena*, i. 90; Hobson, *Practical Divinity* (1646), 86–7; MW ii. p. xxxi; Wallace, *Puritans and Predestination: Grace in English Protestant Theology, 1528–1695* (N. Carolina UP, 1982), 120. For Eyre see my *Religion and Politics in Seventeenth-Century England* (Brighton, 1986), 153, 163.

Law of Righteousness in 1649. Bunyan, like Milton, stressed the *liberation* of the elect, in a way that verged on antinomianism. But unlike Clarkson and Ranters, Bunyan knew that liberated saints would want to maintain monogamous marriage and the work ethic. They could not possibly let consciousness of election open the doors to antinomian immorality. It was always a theoretical danger; but in practice the argument could be used only by those — Ranters — who were manifestly not godly.

Hence the apparent danger from Quakers, who appeared godly but seemed too uncritical in their reliance on the inner light: as Quakers themselves came to see after the Nayler case, after Perrot, after the Story-Wilkinson separation. Henceforward they differentiated themselves more sharply from Ranterism, established the peace principle and withdrawal from political activity, restored emphasis on sin and on the authority of the Bible, abandoned eccentricities like going naked for a sign. They approached normal sectarian behaviour, modified only by greater unwillingness to compromise on shared principles. In the 1650s they had been carried away by the intellectual release of being able to rely on the inner light, as well as by the apparent millennial possibilities. The test, for them as for Bunyan, as for Milton, came ultimately to be the preservation or not of the authority of the Bible. Bunyan emphasized the Law and the historical Jesus against what he saw as the anarchy of the inner light, which had tempted him in his youth. Quakers sobered down as their leaders aged; restoration persecution and the failure of the millennium to arrive forced discipline on them if they were to survive.

'All the power of God cannot shake anything that hath been done for us by the Mediator of the New Covenant', declared Bunyan. 'No sin is to be charged' against us. 'Stand fast in the liberty wherewith Christ hath made you free, and be not again intangled (nor terrified in your consciences) with the yoke of bondage.' To the objection 'then one need not care what they do, they may sin and sin again', Bunyan initially tried to avoid answering, but finally replied, rather testily, 'They that are in Jesus Christ are so far off from delighting in sin, that sin is the greatest thing that troubleth them . . .' 'The Covenant . . . doth allow of repentance, in case thou chance to slip or fall by sudden temptation.' 'Set the case thou hast committed abundance of treason, he hath by him abundance of pardons.' The greatest sinner can 'roll upon free grace'.[6] Later Bunyan wrote 'election is absolute, not conditional, and therefore cannot be overthrown by the sin of the man that is wrapt up therein. . . . No sin in us shall frustrate or make election void.' So concerned was Bunyan with the freedom of the elect and the dangers of legalism that he declared that sin

> will make a law, where God has made man free,
> And break those laws, by which men bounded be.

'Repent, believe and love' was still Bunyan's message in 1688.[7]

In 1674 Bunyan referred to 'those aspersions that the adversaries cast upon our doctrine, . . . that because we preach justification without the works of the Law, therefore they pretend we plead for looseness of life.' In the posthumous *The Jerusalem Sinner* Bunyan admitted again that 'the world, when they hear the doctrine that I have asserted, . . . that Jesus Christ would have mercy offered in the first place to the biggest sinners, will be apt, because themselves are unbelievers, to think this is a doctrine that leads to looseness and that gives liberty to the flesh.' Historically the critics had some justification. Tobias Crisp also held that the elect were saved from all eternity and so their salvation was totally unconditional. 'As soon as [a believer] hath committed this sin', he wrote, 'the Lamb of God . . . hath already taken away this very sin.' Coppe and Clarkson used this doctrine to justify libertinism.[8]

Though aware of the problem, Bunyan, like Crisp, Milton, and other antinomians, found it difficult to give an answer which would convince doubters – no doubt 'themselves unbelievers'. 'They surely did never come to God by Christ', he said in one attempt, 'that will from the freeness of Gospel grace plead an indulgence for sin.' Although antinomianism 'is a doctrine tending to looseness and lasciviousness, . . . the doctrine of free grace believed is the most sin-killing doctrine in the world', Bunyan asserted. It may well have been awareness that his own doctrines tended towards antinomianism that made Bunyan so anxious to dissociate himself

---

[6] *Law and Grace*, MW ii. 169–71, 186, 192; *Ebal and Gerizzim* (1665?), in *Poems*, 110; cf. ibid. 68.

[7] *The Advocateship of Jesus Christ*, MW xi. 121, 130; *A Caution to Stir Up to Watch against Sin* (1684), in *Poems*, 179; *Of the Building of the House of God* (1688), ibid. 293–5, and epigraph to this chapter. But see p. 304: against those who say we have no sin. Cf. Milton: 'the practice of the saints interprets the commandments' (*MCPW*, vi. 368).

[8] *Christian Behaviour* (1663), MW iii. 9; *The Jerusalem Sinner*, MW xi. 82; Crisp, *Christ Alone Exalted*, 6, 16–17, 28, 60, 89, 146–7, 452–3.

from Ranters. 'Thy desires are only good', he told believers, 'for that thou hast desired against thy sin, thy sinful self, which indeed is not thyself but sin that dwells in thee.' It is rather unfortunate that this precise phrase had become notorious from its alleged use by a servant girl who denied any responsibility for stealing because 'it was sin in her', as well as by the near Ranter, Robert Norwood.[9]

Bunyan was concerned above all with 'the great cheat that the devil and Antichrist delude the world withal, ... to make them continue in the form of any duty, the form of preaching, of hearing, of praying, etc.', accepting the form of godliness but denying the power. Holiness and liberty should be joined together, he argued in 1684: liberty to do good must not be resisted.[10] Antinomianism flourished in the revolutionary decades, fostered by the millenarian hope. Hobson, Dell, Denne, and Milton flirted with it, as well as Cokayne and Bunyan. But as the reign of Christ came to seem less imminent, so men expressed their antinomianism more cautiously.

Fowler (or his curate) asserted that the object of *The Design of Christianity* had been 'to root out the doctrine of antinomianism'. He must have annoyed Bunyan very much by saying that he was 'as rank and Ranting an antinomian as ever fouled paper'. 'This monstrous piece of impertinence saith that the saints on earth are as perfectly holy as Christ himself.' He attributed to Bunyan the view that 'he that hath but confidence enough strongly to believe (though he hath no more reason to do so than because he believes so) that his sins are forgiven, hath justifying faith.' 'Can any Ranter talk at a madder rate? ... How sottish is this Ranter!' Baxter, whom Fowler quoted with approbation, attacked *Law and Grace* as antinomian.[11]

One great objection to antinomianism was its appeal to the lower classes—servant girls, for instance. Richard Sibbes in 1639 called it 'an error crept in amongst some of the meaner, ignorant sort of people.' Similar points were made about antinomianism in

[9] *Christ a Complete Saviour* (posthumous), Offor, i. 217; *Saved by Grace* (1676), MW viii. 221; *The Desire of the Righteous Granted* (posthumous), Offor, i. 755; J. Trapp, *Commentaries on the New Testament* (Evansville, 1958), 501 (1st pub. 1647); Norwood, *A Declaration or Testimony* (1651), p. 4.

[10] *I Will Pray with the Spirit* (1662?), MW ii. 259, 281; *Advice to Sufferers* (1684), MW x. 29–34, 44–50.

[11] [E. Fowler], *Dirt wipt off* (1672), 17, 40, 45, 66–7; Baxter, *The Scripture Gospel Defended* (1690), sig. A2, published after Bunyan's death.

New England in the 1630s, in old England in the 1640s. Baxter observed that 'the vulgar sort are attracted to antinomianism, not the learned', who tended towards Arminianism. Antinomianism is 'so easy a way, which flesh and blood hath so little against, as being too consistent with men's carnal interest.' The antinomian doctrines coincided 'in almost every point' with what is 'naturally fastened in the hearts of the common profane multitude.' 'God doth not say, I love you if you be holy, but I love you to make you holy', wrote Hobson in 1640.[12]

It may be that the millenarian hope, so powerful in the 1640s and early 1650s, pushed believers either towards free grace and antinomianism, or to the God within, the God of Winstanley, Ranters, Quakers. Rejecting the Quakers' God within, Bunyan had difficulty in avoiding antinomianism; and the dilemma remained with him. Increasingly — as in *The Holy War* — he saw the millennium as something that would come from outside, from Emanuel's conquest, from kings and rulers. That had not really been the message of *The Pilgrim's Progress*. But Bunyan also rejected Winstanley's conviction that humanity must save itself, without relying on the vicarious sacrifice made by an external Saviour from above the sky. So he was forced into a harsh determinism, a 'waiting millenarianism' without a timetable.

Ultimately the hopes of those who had turned from Levellers to the Army Grandees on political realist grounds withered. Milton too appears to have come to expect liberation from outside, as in *Samson Agonistes*. Individual heroism might contribute to its coming, but the people who stood outside the temple were spared by miracle, through no merits of their own.

[12] Sibbes, *Works* (Edinburgh, 1862–4), ii. 316; my *Religion and Politics in Seventeenth-Century England*, 170, 174–5; *Richard Baxters Confession of Faith* (1655), 3; Lamont, *Richard Baxter and the Millennium*, 128, 143; Hobson, *Practical Divinity* (1646), 31.

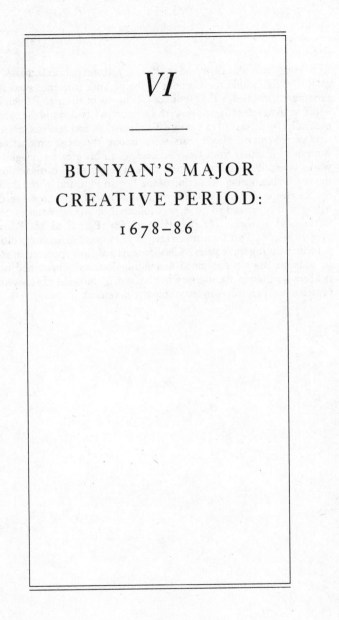

VI

BUNYAN'S MAJOR
CREATIVE PERIOD:
1678–86

The years between 1678 and 1686 saw intense political crisis. The campaign to exclude the Catholic Duke of York from the succession produced majorities in the House of Commons in all three Parliaments between 1679 and 1681, and powerful support in London and the country generally. Its defeat led to a severe Tory reaction, and renewed persecution of dissenters. These years were among the most productive of Bunyan's life: apart from *Grace Abounding*, all his greatest imaginative works were published then. In part this can be explained by relaxation of the censorship during the period of the Popish Plot, and by the lapse of the Licensing Act in 1679. *The Pilgrim's Progress*, written some time before it was printed in 1678, was followed by *Mr. Badman* in 1680, intended as a sequel; *The Holy War* in 1682, Part II of *The Pilgrim's Progress* in 1684. Part I was much revised and expanded for later editions published during these years. *A Book for Boys and Girls* appeared in 1686. In addition Bunyan continued to publish doctrinal works, and many treatises were left in manuscript when he died. In the midst of a busy life as preacher and pastor it is an astonishing achievement.

18. The Pilgrim's Progress

Take a carnal man, when he grows up in this world from a child, he is as a drop in that sea, he mingleth in that sea; and which way the sea goes, he goes with it; he finds them suitable to his principles, and the world finding him suitable to them hugs him, embraces him: and thus it comes to that mighty power and prevalency, especially Satan working together with it. And men are apt to please others, to live to the lusts of men, I Pet. IV. 2; to receive honour one from another, John V. 44, and the examples of the most: for what the most do, all will do. . . . It is a hard matter, therefore, my brethren, to be converted and turned to God; it is hard for a man to come out of this world, to swim against this stream. . . . Therefore, my brethren, take it for a certain sign of an unregenerate estate, to be carried thus along with the stream, and to be moulded to the same principles the generality of the most of men are; and the generality of the most of men are civil men. It is a sign, I say, of death.   THOMAS GOODWIN[1]

O what mists, what mountains, what clouds, what darkness! . . . But faith . . . taketh stomach and courage, fighteth, and crieth, and by crying and fighting, by help from heaven, its way is made through all the oppositions that appear so mighty . . . [until] it sweetly resteth after its marvellous tossings to and fro.

BUNYAN[2]

1. The Allegory and its Antecedents

PART I of *The Pilgrim's Progress* was written in jail, at almost exactly the same time as Milton, imprisoned by blindness, was writing *Paradise Lost, Paradise Regained,* and *Samson Agonistes.* Bunyan served two prison sentences – one from 1660 to 1672, with occasional remissions, the other in 1676–7. There has been disagreement about which of these two periods saw the actual writing of *The Pilgrim's Progress.* It doesn't matter much, but for what it is worth my preference would be for the earlier period. Although Bunyan claimed that the writing came to him easily and spontaneously, six months would have been a very short time in which to compose *The Pilgrim's Progress.* The allegory relates very closely to *Grace Abounding,* published in 1666. 'One Temporary in your

---

[1] *An Exposition of the Second Chapter of the Epistle to the Ephesians* in *Works* (Edinburgh, 1861–3), ii. 29.
[2] *The Pharisee and the Publican* (1685), MW x. 183–4.

parts', who deserted the cause 'about ten years ago' is clearly a reference to the restoration, suggesting that this passage was written not later than 1672. Similarly, the description of Giant Pope as 'grown crazy and stiff in his joints' seems more applicable to the 1660s than to the late 1670s. The danger appeared on the increase to Bunyan when he published Part II in 1684 (65, xxxiii).

To account for the delay in publication there are several considerations. First, Bunyan's introductory verses show he was genuinely worried about the propriety of writing fiction on so serious a subject. Or rather, he was worried about the reactions of the godly to its publication. He must have taken many opinions before deciding to publish, and not all his co-religionists approved. Some of the many spurious continuations of The Pilgrim's Progress claimed to be rectifying its theological impropriety and lack of seriousness; though one may suspect that this was not the only reason for trying to cash in on Bunyan's fame. Secondly, Bunyan's jail sentence of 1676–7 would have made immediate publication difficult then. The brief liberty after Charles II's Declaration of Indulgence in 1672 soon ended, and a period of renewed persecution followed. Most of Bunyan's books hitherto had been printed without licence, and there were things in The Pilgrim's Progress which might displease a captious censor. But by 1678 the government was being pushed on to the defensive by Whig Exclusionists, and publication was becoming easier. Bunyan was by now in touch with leading London Independents, and — probably on the advice of John Owen — switched to Owen's publisher, Nathaniel Ponder. Ponder no doubt hoped for and expected a wide circulation for The Pilgrim's Progress, and therefore wanted it to appear respectably licensed.

The opening of The Pilgrim's Progress is perhaps the most memorable scene in the book. The pilgrim, the man in rags with a burden on his back, runs away from the City of Destruction with his fingers in his ears, to prevent him hearing the cries of his deserted wife and children. He is started on the true path by Evangelist, the preacher, who reappears from time to time to advise and admonish. After surviving the Slough of Despond, the Pilgrim is admitted to the way by the wicket-gate. He visits the House of the Interpreter, who shows him a series of moral emblems. His burden falls off at the cross, he is stripped of his rags, clothed in fresh garments, and given a roll as a sort of identity card.

His name is changed from Graceless to Christian. He promptly loses his roll while sleeping, and has to go back to find it (28, 38, 45, 316, 321).

At the Palace Beautiful, signifying the congregation of the faithful, the pilgrim is given a sword and armour. The sword is of especial significance. It is of course the sword of the spirit. But it is also a social symbol. The armigerous bore arms in both senses. One of the dreadful things about the civil war was that ordinary people, people like Bunyan, got arms into their hands; and when the New Model Army was created it was officered by men who either were not gentlemen themselves or who lacked respect for hierarchy. I quoted above Luke's sneers at their social inferiority.

The sword and armour transform the man in rags into a warfaring saint. They put him on a more equal footing with Apollyon, whom he encounters immediately afterwards and 'by dint of sword did quickly make him fly' (54–60). So to the traditional story of Jack the Giant Killer Bunyan has added faith, the sword of the spirit. Courage alone is of no use against the superior arms of the gentry. But now the pilgrim—like the Parliamentarian soldier—could resist the onslaught of swordsmen.

Christian passes through the Valleys of Humiliation and of the Shadow of Death. Faithful joins him, and they are arrested in Vanity Fair, where Faithful is tried and executed. Hopeful, inspired by Faithful's martyrdom, joins Christian. But Christian, over-confident, leads them out of the way, and they are captured and imprisoned by Giant Despair. Escaping, they proceed to the Delectable Mountains from which shepherds show them the Celestial City. Finally they reach the River of Death, and cross it to enter the City.

In *The Pilgrim's Progress*, as in the contemporary *Hudibras* and the earlier *Don Quixote*, exciting action is tempered by conversation. Christian has long and improving discussions with fellow-pilgrims, with false pilgrims, and with those like Mr. Worldly Wiseman who try to persuade him to give up. Part I ends with Ignorance, who has pestered them *en route*, knocking confidently at the gate of the Celestial City and being led off to hell.

Part II appeared in 1684, provoked to some extent by Bunyan's indignation at a number of spurious sequels which were circulating; partly, we may suppose, in order to be able to express second thoughts—e.g. on Christian's desertion of his family. Part II describes the journey of Christian's wife, Christiana, their four sons, and a young girl, Mercy, following the same route. Their neighbours try to dissuade them, as Christian's had done, but they persist, inspired by his memory. They are given Mr. Great-heart as guide and to do the fighting for them.

Their journey is more leisurely than Christian's had been. They stay for a month at the Palace Beautiful, more than a month at Gaius's inn, 'a great while' at Vanity Fair, now far less dangerous for pilgrims. Marriages take place, children are born. They are joined by several fellow-pilgrims — Mr. Honest, Mr. Fearing, Mr. Feeble-mind ('true of heart though weak in graces' (172)), Mr. Ready-to-halt, Mr. Valiant-for-the-truth, and Mr. Stand-fast. When they come to the River of Death, Christiana soon crossed, and most of the others follow. But Christiana's boys, with their wives and children, are still on the bank when the story ends.

Part II is in some respects a more ecumenical, more tolerant book than Part I. It was, however, tolerant only of godly protestants. Bunyan's hostility towards catholics and persecution had if anything hardened since Part I. But Part II does reflect his liberal attitude towards controversies over baptism and intercommunion. Part I deals with an individual fighting alone to save his soul, which is his and only his. Part II deals with a family, a community, on the way to the heavenly city. They are second-generation professors, who have benefited from the experience and example of the lone pioneer Christian. In 1672 Bunyan had become pastor to the Bedford congregation. Part II handles problems and solutions which he had encountered in that role. In particular it deals with the defects, the hypocrisies, of godly members of a gathered church.[3]

I had originally intended to treat Part II of *The Pilgrim's Progress* as a separate work. It was probably written fifteen or so years after Part I. Chronologically it belongs much more with *Mr. Badman* and *The Holy War*. But the two parts are closely interlocked. Part I as we know it today has been extensively revised and added to: many of the revisions and additions relate to Part II and can hardly be discussed separately. So I have treated the two parts together, but I have tried to make it clear when I am quoting from Part II, or from an addition to Part I, and I hope the reader will keep the

---

[3] Cf. Sharrock, 74, 92, and chap. 24 below.

chronological distinction in mind. (In the Oxford University Press edition, Part II begins at p. 165.)

Allegory was traditionally a way of circumventing the censor, of speaking to an audience fit though few. Sidney had both preached and practised this, and Spenser practised it. Fulke Greville under-lined its usefulness, and the Spenserian poets – Daniel, Drayton, Browne, Sylvester, Wither, Milton – continued to make use of it. Bunyan was well aware of the advantages of allegory for this purpose. The giants personify persecution, the House Beautiful the illegal separatist congregation.

Much printer's ink has been spilt in the search for antecedents for *The Pilgrim's Progress*. I refer the interested reader to John Brown, J. B. Wharey, and Harold Golder.[4] I shall merely try to summarize what I take to be present opinion. The concept of life as a pilgrimage goes back far into the Middle Ages, if not further. All attempts to tie Bunyan down to a single model have failed. The idea was common property in the fifteenth to seventeenth cen-turies, as Wharey rightly emphasizes. The dream framework, the Valley of the Shadow of Death, giants who challenge wayfarers to duels: all these are traditional.[5] Pilgrimage of course was rather popish, but the theme had been passed on by the radicals of Edward VI's reign, and received a new lease of life from popular Puritan preachers in the early seventeenth century. Later it seemed particularly appropriate to the post-revolutionary sense that the utopian millenarianism of the radicals had failed. Now that the big bang had not materialized, gradualism came into fashion, wayfaring rather than warfaring.

The idea of abandoning all for Christ, including one's own family, had especial relevance to the mobile world of vagrant soldiers and ex-soldiers of the 1640s and 1650s. Consider the following:

I was at the plough, meditating on the things of God, . . . and suddenly I heard a voice saying unto me, Get thee out from thy kindred and from thy father's house; and I had a promise given with it. . . . Having neither taken

---

[4] Brown, 272–6; J. B. Wharey, *A Study of the Sources of Bunyan's Allegories* (Baltimore, 1904), esp. 67–77, 102–3. For Golder see following note. G. R. Owst, *Literature and Pulpit in Medieval England* (Cambridge UP, 1933), 109.

[5] H. Golder, 'Bunyan's Valley of the Shadow', *Modern Philology*, 27 (1929), 65–6; id., 'Bunyan's Giant Despair', *Journal of English and Germanic Philology*, 30 (1931), esp. 374; cf. id., 'John Bunyan's Hypocrisy', *North American Review*, 223 (1926), 326–32.

leave of wife or children, nor thinking then of any journey, I was commanded to go into the West. . . .

The promise was 'that God would be with me'. That was the beginning of the itinerant ministry of the Quaker James Nayler. The Quaker Richard Hubberthorne also claimed to have been called from the plough, like Elisha, by the Word of the Lord.[6] George Fox's *Journal* records a solitary pilgrimage away from this world.

Thanks to Golder and Margaret Spufford, we now know something of the significance for Bunyan of chap-book romances. Like Perkins before him, Bunyan refers disparagingly to those who preferred 'a ballad, a newsbook, *George on horseback* or *Bevis of Southampton*' to the Bible; but he seems to include some of the godly among chap-book readers.[7] His own early reading left its mark on him. Golder suggests that he first came to the Bible after demobilization, and that he then read it through the spectacles of the romances. Like Baxter, he was initially attracted by the historical books of the Bible.[8] Bunyan's *Exposition on Genesis*, giants, battles, and all, fits in with this interest. So does the history of Old Testament massacres shown to Christian in the Interpreter's house (54). Christiana is told that 'the name of her husband, . . . his travels and wars, . . . rings all over these parts of the world'. He was the model Christian-chivalric hero (248).

L. B. Wright suggested that what Spenser accomplished in the romance tradition for the courtly reader, the prose romances which Richard Johnson published in the early seventeenth century did for the plain citizen.[9] Following up this perception, Nick Davies has pointed to analogies between Johnson's stories and *The Pilgrim's Progress*. Johnson, like Bunyan, intersperses his prose

---

[6] Nayler, *Sauls Errand to Damascus* (1654), 30; [R. Hubberthorne], *A True Testimony of Obedience to the Heavenly Call* (1654), 4–6.

[7] L. B. Wright, *Middle-Class Culture in Elizabethan England* (North Carolina UP, 1935), ch. 4, *passim*; M. Spufford, *Small Books and Pleasant Histories*, chs. 7–9, *passim*; Perry Miller, *The New England Mind: The Seventeenth Century* (New York, 1939), 86; *A Few Sighs from Hell*, MW i. 332–3. The note in MW i. 400 suggests that *George on horseback* is likely to refer to Richard Johnson's *The Seven Champions of Christendom* (1597, and many later edns.).

[8] Spufford, *Small Books and Pleasant Histories*, 7–8, 74; Golder, 'Bunyan's Valley of the Shadow', 65–8; *Reliquiae Baxterianae*, 2; *GA*, 14.

[9] L. B. Wright, *Middle-Class Culture in Elizabethan England* (N. Carolina UP, 1935), 100.

with occasional verses. His heroes, like Bunyan's, are saints as well as knights. Among the conventional features of romance that Bunyan echoed are the unheeded warning; the resisted temptation to return; the useless sword; dark and dangerous valleys; the distant glimpse of a far-off city or country; the arming of the hero; his imprisonment; the castle on a height defended by lions, against whom innocence is a protection; the unwitting failure of loyalty; the magical healing of the wounded hero with leaves from a tree; the prevalence of riddles; the overriding power of destiny.[10]

In Bunyan's poem before Part II of *The Pilgrim's Progress* he tells Christiana how to respond to those who:

> love not the method of your first,
> Romance they count it, throw't away as dust.

He does not take the accusation too solemnly, but replies:

> Some love no cheese, some love no fish, and some
> Love not their friends, nor their own house and home.

Let them take it or leave it is in effect Bunyan's confident retort (171–2).[11]

In *The Pilgrim's Progress* Pope, Persecution, Despair are all giants. Apollyon, the power of sin, is a dragon: lions represent persecutors. Christ 'had been a great warrior'; men were harnessed out 'for the service of their Lord' (50, 54). There are many duels, and some unexpected chivalry, as when Mr. Great-heart allows Giant Maul to recover after felling him to the ground (245). There is not much chivalry in *The Holy War*, apart from the white garments in which Emanuel clothed the people of Mansoul as 'my livery, and the badge by which mine are known from the servants of others'.[12] But there is much military display and celebration. The most remarkable example of influence of the romances comes in 'Of the Spouse of Christ', in *A Book for Boys and Girls*. The church is represented as a beggar maid, cast out of doors, naked,

---

[10] I have drawn on Golder's writings here (see p. 201 n. 5 above); Davis, 'The Problem of Misfortune in *The Pilgrim's Progress*', Newey, 186, 188, 190, 195–7; Nick Shrimpton, 'Bunyan's Military Metaphor', ibid. 211–14. The notes to *PP* give parallels for many other details from Richard Johnson.

[11] I am grateful to Bob Owens for drawing my attention to this point.

[12] *HW*, 146.

'the day that she was born'. But a great King becomes enamoured of her:

> His cheeks like flowers are, his mouth's most sweet.
> As for his wealth, he is made heir of all,

and this lady becomes joint-heir with him.

> Thou, of an outcast, now art made a queen . . .
> Barefoot, but now as princes' daughters shod.[13]

Another source has often been seen lurking in the background, though specific links are difficult to establish — Langland's *Vision of Piers Plowman*. Coulton thought that 'very probably Bunyan had read him' or at least heard tales from him, and that 'here we have the origin of Giant Despair and Doubting Castle'. Coulton quotes Langland:

> 'By Christ', quoth Conscience then, 'I will become a pilgrim,
> And walk on, as wide as the world lasteth,
> To seek Piers the Plowman, that Pride may be destroyed, . . .'
> And then he groaned after Grace, till I 'gan awake.[14]

I think it very improbable that Bunyan had read Langland. But from Edward VI's reign onwards Langland — like Chaucer — had been misinterpreted as a Wycliffite, and had been co-opted into the heretic tradition. Not only his works but others relating to Piers Plowman had been widely disseminated. One feature of the Piers Plowman inheritance was its strong bias in favour of the poor, who were far more likely to be saved than the rich — a point which Latimer echoed and Foxe seemed to express, and which is central to Bunyan's thinking.[15]

The theme of pilgrimage became commonplace — in the Homily *Against the Fear of Death*, in Stephen Batman, *The Travayled Pilgrim* (1569), G.B.'s *The Shipps of Safe-guard* (1569), Geoffrey Whitney, *Emblemes* (Leyden, 1596), William Broxup, *St. Peters Path to the Joyes of Heaven* (1598); so did the dangerous journey

---

[13] *Poems*, 257–9.

[14] G. C. Coulton, *Medieval Panorama: The English Scene from Conquest to Reformation* (Cambridge UP, 1945), 543, 553.

[15] H. C. White, *Social Criticism in Popular Religious Literature* (New York, 1944), Ch. 1, 'The Piers Plowman Tradition', *passim*, esp. 24–32; J. N. King, *English Reformation Literature: The Tudor Origins of the Protestant Tradition* (Princeton UP, 1982), 37, 51–2, 322–47, 446–7, and *passim*; Newey, 229.

occurring in a dream (Humphrey Gifford, *A Posie of Gilloflowers*, 1580; Francis Thynn, *The Debate between Pride and Lowliness*).[16] Hendrik Niclaes's *Terra Pacis* (Eng. trans., 1575, repr. 1649) has been seen as a source for *The Pilgrim's Progress*. It depicts a perilous spiritual pilgrimage from 'the wildernessed lands' to Paradise on earth. ('Fly now!' H.N. exhorts his readers.) Property was common in the Land of Peace.[17]

Nearer home, we find the pilgrimage theme in the greatest English Puritan, William Perkins. There is a strait and narrow gate, leading to two cities. Bunyan appears to imitate many of Perkins's tricks of style: 'Is Christ . . . ? Then . . . .', and of content: 'What professors shall be saved?' John Preston thought a Christian's life was 'like a walk . . . from place to place', from sin to salvation – or to hell. This life is the ground, Christ the way: his is the shortest and plainest, but we must expect to meet obstacles *en route*. John Downame compared the Christian to a pilgrim or traveller, whose life is 'a tedious and painful pilgrimage', on which 'he meeteth with few friends and many dangers'.[18]

William Browne in *Britannia's Pastorals*, like Perkins, shows two paths of life stretching before the sinner, and calls on the Muses to be profitable to him in his pilgrimage. Thomas Taylor in *The Pilgrims Profession* compared the life of the saint to a traveller returning home through a strange country. 'Christ himself lived in the flesh as a pilgrim', observed Fynes Morison; all our life is a pilgrimage. *Purchas his Pilgrimes* also insisted on life as a pilgrimage: the Apostles were pilgrims.[19]

Later prototypes of *The Pilgrim's Progress* show that the theme was popular. Thus Sir William Denny's *The Pilgrimes Passe to the Land of the Living* (1653) declared that life 'is a long journey on

[16] *Sermons or Homilies* (1802), 78–9; *Select Poetry . . . of the Reign of Queen Elizabeth*, ed. E. Farr, Parker Soc. (Cambridge UP, 1845), i. 205, 209–10, 218–21; ii. 388–90; Thynn, 7–10, 65–6. Thynn defended the profitability of his apparently frivolous subject-matter, rather as Bunyan did in his Prologue to *PP*.

[17] [H.N.], *Terra Pacis, A True Testification of the Spiritual Land of Peace* (1649), 11, 21–2, 185, and *passim*; R. M. Jones, *Studies in Mystical Religion* (1909), 43; J. Moss, *'Godded with God': Hendrik Niclaes and His Family of Love*, Trans. American Philosophical Soc., 71 (1981), 32.

[18] Perkins, *Works* (1616–18) iii. 227, 245, 465–6, 366–7 (2nd pagination); Preston, *The New Covenant, or the Saints Portion* (5th edn., 1630), 181–208; Downame, *The Christian Warfare against the Devill, World and Flesh* (4th edn., enlarged, 1634), sig. §. 2.

[19] Browne, Bk. 1, song 5; Bk. 11, song 1; S.C. Chew, *The Crescent and the Rose* (New York, 1937), 34; cf. William Pulling, *The Christians Trade* (1619), 150.

foot'. 'Though the way be rugged it is direct.' 'Presumption may as dangerously overthrow thee as desperation was like to . . . undo thee.' 'Wade through the slough! This thawed clay! That mires, this tires!' Samuel Pordage's *Mundorum Explicatio* (1661) manages to anticipate (in content though not in skill) both Milton and Bunyan, the Fall and the theme of pilgrimage.[20]

Others come so late that they need only be mentioned. Vavasor Powell's *A Christian Pilgrimage* was published in *The Bird in the Cage, Chirping*, when he was in prison in 1661.[21] Powell was like Bunyan in his religious and political outlook. So was Benjamin Keach, whose *Warr with the Devil* (1676) was a very popular allegory. Simon Patrick is sometimes misleadingly mentioned in this context, but he had nothing in common with Bunyan. He was a Latitudinarian, and his *The Parable of the Pilgrim* (1664) contains little allegory and much didacticism, designed to show the superiority of the established church.

If it is difficult to pinpoint specific sources for *The Pilgrim's Progress*, it is easy to demonstrate that the idea of conversion as a journey was familiar in the seventeenth century. More important than any influence is the milieu in which seventeenth-century Puritans lived, the problems and tensions which they had to face in their lives. Arnold Kettle observed that 'a persecuted minority is likely to express and maintain its faith in allegorical rather than realistic terms, partly for tactical reasons, but also because its *thinking* will be in those terms.' And he movingly described Bradford's *History of Plymouth Plantation* as 'a spiritual pilgrimage, conceived essentially in terms of allegory.' 'The pilgrims', Bradford's or Bunyan's, 'need to see themselves in terms of allegory in order to survive.'[22]

As Sharrock emphasized, perhaps the most significant prototype of *The Pilgrim's Progress* is *Grace Abounding*.[23] The state of desperation in which the Pilgrim finds himself at the beginning of the story (9) mirrors that of Bunyan throughout *Grace Abounding*. The

---

[20] [Sir William Denny], *Peleconicidium; or the Christian Adviser against Self-Murder. Together with A Guide, and the Pilgrims Passe to the Land of The Living* (1653), sig. A 4v, 35–6, 194, and *passim*; my *The Experience of Defeat*, 234–9.

[21] Op. cit. (2nd. edn., corrected and enlarged, 1662), 26–46.

[22] Arnold Kettle, 'The Precursors of Defoe: Puritanism and the Rise of the Novel', in B. S. Benedikz (ed.), *On the Novel: A Present for Walter Allen* (1971), 211–13.

[23] Sharrock, 104; *PP*, p. xxxiv. Most of the examples that follow are drawn from Sharrock's notes.

wicket-gate had been anticipated in Bunyan's dream of his
exclusion from the company of the godly in Bedford (*GA*,
20–1). The Slough of Despond recalls Bunyan finding himself 'as
on a miry bog that shook if I did but stir' (*GA*, 28). Christian's fear
that Mount Sinai would fall on his head recalls Bunyan's fear that
the church bells or steeple might fall on him whilst watching
bell-ringing (*GA*, 15). The blasphemies whispered to Christian by
a devil in the Valley of the Shadow of Death echo those which
Bunyan himself had been tempted to utter. Hopeful is as influenced as Bunyan had been by the text 'My grace is sufficient for
thee' (63–4; *GA*, 32, 79, 65).

The 'very brisk lad' called Ignorance, and Mr Brisk in Part II
(123, 226–8), remind us that Bunyan himself had been a brisk
talker in matters of religion (*GA*, 11–14, 19, 27). Hopeful seems to
have had Ranter tendencies, as at one time Bunyan did. Hopeful
'delighted much in rioting, revelling, drinking, swearing, lying,
uncleanness, Sabbath-breaking and what not.' Like Bunyan, he
'could not tell how to part with mine old companions, their
presence and actions were so desirable unto me.' Mr. Self-will in
Part II sounds Ranterish too, and perhaps Vain-confidence in Part
I (137–8, 255–7, 348–9; 112, 330). Faithful suspected that Talkative had nothing else but 'notions', a usual phrase for Ranter ideas.
Atheist had 'been seeking this city this twenty years', which would
take him back to the Ranter epoch (84, 135, 326).

Or indeed, as Olivier Lutaud suggested, we might find the main
source for *The Pilgrim's Progress* in the Bible – a Bible read through
romantic spectacles, Exodus and the return from Babylonian Exile,
pilgrimage to the Promised Land or to Zion – 'the way for the
wayfaring men'. 'All saints shall walk . . . even in one street, in one
way and in one light. It is Antichrist that hath brought in all those
crossings, bye-lanes and odd nooks that to this day many an honest
heart doth greatly lose himself in.'[24]

One other antecedent should be mentioned – popular dialogue
and trial scenes. These were developed from Dent and Bernard by
Levellers and other radical pamphleteers during the Revolution. I
take one example – not as a source for *The Pilgrim's Progress*, but to
illustrate the loosening up of prose and of ideas which had

[24] O. Lutaud, *Les Deux révolutions d'Angleterre: Documents politiques, sociaux, religieux*
(Paris, 1978), 80; Bunyan, *The Holy City* (1665), MW iii. 151.

occurred in Bunyan's youth. Richard Overton's *The Araignement of Mr. Persecution* came out in April 1645, whilst Bunyan was at Newport Pagnell. It must have been widely read and appreciated by those in the Army who were enjoying the religious liberty which Overton defended in this tract.

Bunyan had his own experience of trials, so he had nothing to learn from Overton in that respect. After 1660 the saints themselves were in the dock, whereas in the 1640s they could hope to put their enemies on trial.[25] Overton, like Bunyan, draws on an old tradition in his use of descriptive names – Sir Symon Synod and Sir John Presbyter,[26] who are prosecuted by Mr. Gods-vengeance of the town of Impartiality in the county of Just-judgment. Gods-vengeance has forborne for some time, persuaded by 'his kinsman Mr. Long-sufferance (an honest peaceable gentleman, unwilling his enemy should perish)', but finally he obtains a warrant from Lord Chief Justice Peace-with-all-men for the Constable, Mr. Reward-of-tyranny, to attach Persecution. The latter is then tried by the judge Lord Parliament, together with Reason, Humanity, and Conformity, Justices of the Peace, and before twenty-five jurors with appropriate names like 'Gospel', 'National-loyalty', 'Liberty-of-the-subject', and 'Innocent-blood'. We may compare 'our well-beloved uncles, Cardinals False-heart, Would-have-wit, . . . and Dr. Corrupt-doctrine' in Overton's *The Last Will and Testament of Superstition* (1642).[27]

Overton's tract recalls Dent's and Bernard's use of name-changing. Mr. Persecution had gone under the names of Spanish Inquisition, High Commission, Classical Presbytery, and now claimed to be called Present-Reformation. Overton's delightful irony frequently anticipates Bunyan. Mr. Persecution had been 'of all the universities of Christendom'. He asked for a new jury because 'my breeding, nature and course of life is not so well known unto [the jury selected] as unto divers other gentlemen.' Sir Symon on Mr. Persecution's behalf proposed a new jury, including

---

[25] I owe this point to Bob Owens.

[26] 'Sir John' was the familiar contemptuous nickname for an inadequate priest of the episcopalian Church of England, and so particularly offensive here, suggesting that new Presbyter was but old priest writ large. Cf. p. 131 above.

[27] Overton, *The Araignement*, 1–3, in *Tracts on Liberty in the Puritan Revolution*, ed. W. Haller (Columbia UP, 1933), iii; Marie Gimelfarb-Brack, *Liberté, Égalité, Fraternité, Justice! La Vie et l'œuvre de Richard Overton, Niveleur* (Berne, 1979), 513.

Satan, Antichrist, Council-of-Trent, Sir John Presbyter, and Rude-multitude.[28]

Overton's tract drew on covenant theology, and advocates toleration for Roman Catholics and Jews as well as for Anabaptists, Independents, and antinomians. Samson, he pointed out, lived peaceably among the Philistines. The rebellion in Ireland, Overton declared flatly, was caused by intolerance, which is a mark of Antichrist. Bunyan would not have gone as far as that, and he would certainly have rejected Overton's defence of mortalism and commendation of his own treatise, *Mans Mortalitie* (1644).[29]

ii. Sweating Work

Christian is revealed as one of the predestined elect the moment he enters the wicket-gate: those who enter by other, surreptitious, routes do not survive till the end of the journey. One of the significant paradoxes of *The Pilgrim's Progress* is that nevertheless one feels that the Pilgrim is making free choices all the time, deciding for himself. The journey itself is a matter of choice. Christian has to do a great deal of knocking at both the wicket gate and the Interpreter's House before either is opened (25, 28; cf. 188). Mr. Badman and the citizens of Mansoul appear also to be free agents. It is the paradox of all predestinarian protestantism, and no doubt of Islam and Marxism as well.[30] 'If we be truly willing to have it [salvation]', Christian tells Plyable, 'he will bestow it upon us freely.' 'Believing and coming was all one', Christian assures Hopeful. 'They that must be saved' are 'those that accept of his salvation', Joseph informs Prudence, to her satisfaction (141, 143, 225). Repentance is always possible for the saints, and will never be rejected (118, 232). The fact that Christian is predestined to salvation, whether he knows it or not, gives him the courage to go on believing and so to face the horrors of life's pilgrimage. This point is made in Mr. Valiant-for-the-truth's song:

> Hobgoblin nor foul fiend
>   Can daunt his spirit;
> He knows he at the end
>   Shall life inherit   (295)

[28] Bernard, *The Isle of Man*; Overton, 1, 3, 31, 40. Cf. pp. 162, 164, 166 above.

[29] Ibid. 20, 26–7, 11–13, 15, 22–3, 28–30.

[30] Cf. R. T. Kendall, *Calvin and British Calvinism to 1649* (Oxford UP, 1979), 123–4, 134, for the theory: preparationism; P. S. Seaver, *Wallington's World*, 104, 232, for examples of the practice.

Election sets Christian apart, with his band of comrades, and enables him to distinguish between true and false pilgrims. Yet all through *The Pilgrim's Progress*, throughout Bunyan's writings, there is an emphasis on activity, *willed* activity, on the struggle to achieve sanctification. 'The soul of religion is the practic part', says Christian. 'At the day of doom men shall be judged according to their fruits. It will not be said then Did you believe? but, Were you doers, or talkers only?' (79–80; cf. 82). Christian's escape from the Slough of Despond, and his victory over Apollyon ('as God would have it') (59) seem no less acts of his own will and courage than did Abdiel's stand against Satan and his legions in *Paradise Lost*. 'Often at the resting-places', observed Mr. Great-heart, 'some pilgrims in some things come off losers', and Christian lost his roll, the token of his salvation (217). Bunyan hoped that this allegory 'will make the slothful active be' (6–7).

There is no miraculous divine intervention for the pilgrims. Evangelist advises and warns, as do the Interpreter and the ladies at his house. In Doubting Castle it is Christian himself who ultimately remembers that he has had the key of escape all the time. The burden falls off at the cross, very early in the journey. Christ is the way, the road, and is spoken of as a great warrior who defeated God's enemies. But he himself is relatively absent from the allegory. There is little about his redemptive suffering—by contrast with *Profitable Meditations* of 1661, in which we are repeatedly urged to look 'upon his side, his hands, his feet'. In this *The Pilgrim's Progress* recalls *Paradise Regained* and *Samson Agonistes* rather than *Grace Abounding*. The subject of Bunyan's allegory is Christian, his experience, his struggles, temptations and decisions, defeats and victories: not the vicarious sacrifice on the cross which Bunyan had insisted on in *A Vindication* and *Law and Grace*, and was to stress again later. *The Pilgrim's Progress* is all thoroughly this-worldly. Bunyan 'never imagined heaven or hell without reference to the earth.'[31]

'Be careful then in little things', wrote Bunyan in his posthumous *Exposition on . . . Genesis*. The words recall Adam's summary of Michael's teaching at the end of *Paradise Lost*:

    [31] *Poems*, 11, 15; *A Vindication*, MW i. 186–7; *Law and Grace*, MW ii. 107–8, 124; *A Defence of the Doctrine of Justification* (1672), Offor, ii. 330–1; *Light for them that sit in Darkness* (1675), MW viii. 100, 151–3; *Israel's Hope Encouraged*, Offor, i. 610–15; Newey, 24: cf. 30–2.

> by small
> Accomplishing great things, by things deemed weak
> Subverting worldly strong, and worldly wise
> By simply meek.[32]

There was no reason why Adam should wish to subvert 'worldly strong', though many why Milton should. Bunyan, like Milton, was 'deemed weak' in restoration England.

With Milton the word 'stand' is crucial. 'Sufficient to have stood though free to fall' applies to the rebel angels as well as to Adam and Eve.

> Stand fast: to stand or fall
> Free in thine own arbitrament it lies.

'They also serve who only stand and wait.' 'I sing . . . unchanged.' The climax of *Paradise Regained* comes when Satan places the Son of God on the pinnacle of the temple, and challenges him to stand there. '"Tempt not the Lord thy God", he said, and stood.'[33] So too for Bunyan. In *Grace Abounding* he had written 'O how happy now was every creature over I was! For they stood fast and kept their state, but I was gone and lost.' William Sedgwick had described the New Model Army as 'Valiant for truth'.[34] In Part II of *The Pilgrim's Progress* Mr. Stand-fast and Mr. Valiant-for-the-truth are key figures. 'No man could ever make him face about', Bunyan said of Valiant-for-the-truth in his prefatory verses (173). 'He would not go back', says Great-heart repeatedly about Mr. Fearing (249–51). Gifford's last letter to his church concludes, 'Stand fast: the Lord is at hand.' Christian decides not to flee before Apollyon because his armour offered protection only against frontal attack. 'In the description of the Christian armour', Bunyan repeated in *The House of the Forest of Lebanon* (posthumous), 'we have no provision for the back. So our men in the church in the wilderness are supposed to be more stout.' Emanuel's last words in *The Holy War* echo those of Gifford: 'Hold fast till I come.'

When Faithful is done to death in Vanity Fair, Hopeful takes his

---

[32] Offor, ii. 484; *Paradise Lost*, xii. 566–9.

[33] *Paradise Lost*, iii. 98, vi. 911, vii. 24, viii. 640–1; cf. Satan's emphasis on his constancy in Bk. I; Sonnet XVI; *Paradise Regained*, iv. 560. Cf. A. Sinfield, *Literature in Protestant England, 1560–1660* (1983), 40–3.

[34] *GA*, 59; Sedgwick, *A Second View of the Army Remonstrance* (1649), 12–18.

place by Christian's side. In the ebullient 1640s faith in the coming millennium had fortified the morale of Parliamentarian troops: a less-assured hope for the ultimate coming of the Lord strengthened the godly remnant's dogged resistance in the darker 1660s and 1670s. 'None can make him to forsake what he has received of God', Bunyan reminded 'sufferers' in 1684: 'a commandment to hold fast'.[35] 'Who knows', Hopeful tells Christian, 'but that God that made the world may cause that Giant Despair may die?' (115); the words were written by Bunyan after many years of incarceration in Bedford jail. Despair does not die (in Part I); but the pilgrims escape from his clutches.

iii. From this World to That Which is to Come

Running through *The Pilgrim's Progress* is a strong sense of the superiority of the poor to the rich. The traditional pilgrimage-romances which Bunyan inherited were about Everyman: *The Pilgrim's Progress* is about one of the elect. But the Pilgrim, like the whole book, is firmly set in a lower-class ambiance. The Dreamer who tells the tale is an itinerant—a tinker, perhaps—who is sleeping rough on his travels, as Quaker missionaries did. He kips down for the night in a 'den', which is normally identified with Bedford jail, but might be any cave or hovel. Part II starts with the author 'on his wonted travels', sleeping for the night in a wood and dreaming again. The judge in Vanity Fair denounces the pilgrim Faithful as a 'runagate', a vagabond, just as in *A Few Sighs from Hell* Dives had described Lazarus as 'a scabbed creep-hedge'.[36] The pilgrim is related not only to Lazarus but also to the publican in *The Pharisee and the Publican*. Christian and all his fellow-travellers are 'foot-men'. The hero of the ballad, *A Jovial Tinker* (1616):

> walked about the country
> With pike-staff and with budget.

The ordinariness of the participants in the dialogue of *Mr. Badman* is established by the fact that they meet out walking in the early morning.[37] Behind *The Pilgrim's Progress* are the literal wanderings

[35] Tibbutt, *Minutes*, 21; Offor, iii. 526; *Advice to Sufferers*, MW x. 77–8.
[36] MW i. 304.
[37] *The Pepys Ballads*, ed. H. E. Rollins, i. (Harvard UP, 1929), 102–8; *Mr. B.*, Offor, iii. 595.

of itinerant craftsmen or beggars, as well as the spiritual pilgrimage of seekers passing through all sects.

The word 'pilgrim' is regularly used in contemporary ballads to describe roving vagabonds. The protagonist of *The Distressed Pilgrim*, dated *c.* 1676 or earlier, wanders 'from place to place, from town to town'. 'I once had land', he tells us, but now 'I'm grown exceeding poor. . . . Let patience work for me.' *The Contented Pilgrim*, possibly a few years earlier, declares that 'There's nothing here but care and strife with the poorer sort we see. . . . To save our souls, let's strive for that.' Middlesex J Ps in 1684 ordered all unlicensed itinerant peddlars to be taken up as vagrants. It is perhaps one-sided to speak of *The Pilgrim's Progress* as 'the epic of the itinerant'. But it originates in a society in which there had been a clamp-down on the lower-class mobility which had characterized the revolutionary decades. In Elizabeth's reign itinerant catholic priests had been denounced as runagates, vagabonds.[38] The Settlement Act of 1662 was directed against both vagabonds and itinerant preachers.

When we first see him the Pilgrim is in rags — allegorical rags, to be sure, but they also represent his real poverty. ('You must also own religion in his rags', Christian later tells Mr. By-ends (100).) The Pilgrim is a 'labouring man', of 'base and low estate and condition'. (In 1661 Bunyan had been indicted as a labourer.) The Pilgrim had been 'driven out of his native country'; the pilgrims are 'strangers in the world' (90). Like any seventeenth-century vagabond, the Pilgrim has no property ties: he is free to leave home, his wife, and children; they are free ultimately to follow him.

'The man in rags', as G. M. Trevelyan observed, had been a familiar symbol since Wyclif. The 'great burden upon his back' was Bunyan's addition, recalling Humphrey Gifford's unemployed 'country clown', who:

> went up and down
> With fardell on his back.[39]

The Pilgrim had acquired his burden by reading the Bible (17–18). In *Grace Abounding* Bunyan had 'a great burden upon my spirit'. 'I

[38] *The Roxburghe Ballads*, viii. 93–4, 98; Fletcher, *Reform in the Provinces*, 211; W. T. MacCaffrey, *Queen Elizabeth and the Making of Policy, 1572–1588* (Princeton UP, 1981), 484.

[39] *GA*, 113; Trevelyan, *Clio, A Muse and other Essays* (1930), 52; Gifford, *Poems* (1580). I cite from *Miscellanies of the Fuller Worthies Library*, ed. A. B. Grosart (1870), 94.

was a burden to myself.' Thomas Taylor had spoken of sin as a
burden like an actual load on a man's back.[40] The burden on the
back was the symbol of the lowest grade of itinerant, just as the
sword was the outward sign of social superiority.

The social lowliness of the Pilgrim is shown by the way he is
addressed, and addresses others. Mr. Wiseman, who 'looked like a
gentleman', calls him 'good fellow', and 'thous' him throughout;
Christian replies with the deferential 'you' and 'Sir' (17, 21, 24).
Paul Cobb had with equal condescension called Bunyan 'goodman', 'neighbour', when trying to persuade him to promise to give
up preaching; Bunyan 'sirred' him while refusing.[41] The Latitudinarian divine Edward Fowler 'thees' and 'thous' Bunyan from time
to time. In *The Holy City* (1665) Bunyan addresses the 'learned
reader' as 'Sir'; 'the godly reader', and even 'the captious reader',
presumably from Bunyan's own class, are 'friends'.[42] Initially
Evangelist 'thous' the pilgrim, and he replies with 'you' and 'Sir';
but when Evangelist comes to warn Christian and Faithful about
Vanity Fair they 'thou' each other (9–10, 86). Apollyon and Giant
Maul 'thou' the pilgrims (56–7, 244). Although Demas at the Hill
Lucre is 'gentleman-like', Christian 'thous' him as a sign of
contempt, as Great-heart was to 'thou' Giant Despair (106–7,
282), as indeed Sir Edward Coke had said to Ralegh at his trial 'Lo!
I thou thee, thou traitor!'

The character Shame protests that 'but few of the mighty, rich
or wise' are ever of Faithful's opinion. He 'objected the base and
low estate and condition of those that were chiefly the pilgrims.'
Religion 'made a man grow strange to the great, . . . and made him
own and respect the base'—another snide comment on the restoration. Many pilgrims were 'beggars born, and their original had
been the dunghill' (72–3, 52–3; cf. 153–4).[43] This recalls what
Bunyan had written in *A Few Sighs from Hell* and was to write in *The
Heavenly Foot-man*. 'Give me not riches' had been the Interpreter's

---

[40] *GA*, 10, 45, 50; Taylor, *Highway to Happiness* (1633), quoted by Greaves, MW
viii. p. xlvi.

[41] *GA*, 119–24. On the other hand, when Bunyan visited 'an honest woman' at her
house, and she called him 'Goodman Bunyan', this was equal talking to equal (*The
Acceptable Sacrifice*, Offor, i. 701).

[42] MW iii. 69–72.

[43] 'None but mean persons' were Puritans, Mary Springett testified from her own
experience (M. Webb, *Penns and Penningtons of the Seventeenth Century* (1867) 13, 18).

prayer (200). 'The ungodly who prosper in the world', said Mr. Wiseman in *Mr. Badman*, 'they increase in riches'.[44]

Undesirable characters in *The Pilgrim's Progress*, as later in *The Holy War*, are almost obsessively labelled as lords and ladies, gentlemen and gentlewomen. In addition to Worldly Wiseman, Formalist and Hypocrisy are gentlemen; so is Giant Pope. Evangelist is one of the very few good characters described as a gentleman (a tribute to the ministry?); Mr. Sagacity, whose narrative starts off Part II, was 'an aged gentleman' (174–5). Madam Bubble, 'the Mistress of the world', is a gentlewoman (300–3), Madam Wanton 'an admirably well-bred gentlewoman' (185). In *The Holy City* (1665) the Whore of Babylon is 'this gentlewoman'; in the posthumous *Of Antichrist and his Ruin* Bunyan described Antichrist as a gentleman.[45] Mr. By-ends had become 'a gentleman of good quality', related to Lord Turnabout, Lord Timeserver, and 'the parson of our parish, Mr. Two-tongues', as well as married to Lady Faining's daughter. His friends Mr. Hold-theworld, Mr. Money-love, and Mr. Save-all are all gentlemen (99–103). When Faithful is brought up for trial in Vanity Fair it is for slandering several of the nobility and 'most of the gentry of our town'. ('Sins are all lords and great ones' adds the marginal note, in case we should miss the point.) The judge is Lord Hate-good. The 'gentlemen of the jury' think Faithful a 'rogue', a 'sorry scrub'. All the witnesses against him are lords or gentlemen, and he was punished according to 'their law' (94–7). (We recall the gentry who had to be introduced into the government of Bedford after 1660, and who played a significant part in Bunyan's trial and imprisonment.)

Bunyan did not let alone for long those former Puritans and Parliamentarians who had compromised or even profited by a change of allegiance at the restoration. Plyable, 'a turn-coat', is 'not true to his profession', and is despised even by God's enemies (68). 'One Temporary', whom Faithful had known 'about ten years ago', was 'a forward man in religion *then*' (my italics). He dwelt 'about two miles off of Honesty, . . . next door to one Turnback.' 'He was resolved to go on pilgrimage, . . . but all of a sudden he grew acquainted with one Save-self, and then he became a stranger

[44] Offor, iii. 664. He was quoting Ps. 73.
[45] MW iii. 169; Offor, ii. 54. See pp. 127 above and 332 below.

to me' (151–2). There is a pride here in the stalwartness of the godly, as well as contempt for Latitudinarians and other compromisers. There are many other covert references to the restoration. The Slough of Despond 'doth much spue out its filth ... against change of weather'; and then the 'good and substantial steps, placed even through the midst of the Slough, ... are hardly seen'. The steps, Bunyan's marginal note tells us, are 'the promises of forgiveness and acceptance to life by faith in Christ' (16).

There is indeed much to be read between the lines of *The Pilgrim's Progress* about the religious politics of the age. The inhabitants of Vanity are divided about the pilgrims, as men had been about Puritans in England before the civil war. In consequence, 'they fell to some blows, among themselves, and did harm one to another'. Christian and Hopeful are 'charged as being guilty of the late hubbub that had been in the Fair' (91). Their 'disloyal notions' were very like those with which Bunyan was charged in 1660–1 (93; cf. *GA*, 105–31). Hopeful also alludes to the restoration when he tells Christian 'that there were many more of the men in the fair that would take their time and follow after' Faithful (98).

Faithful was alleged to have said that Vanity's 'religion was naught, and such by which a man could by no means please God', as Bunyan was charged with thinking Anglicanism 'naught' (94–6; cf. *GA*, 113–19). In the third edition Bunyan added, apropos of Mr. By-ends, some more explicitly political passages, including a riotous caricature of fair-weather Puritans who turned their coats in 1660. ('The parson of our parish, Mr. Two-tongues' had been inserted in the second edition (99).) By-ends and his three friends produce good Latitudinarian divinity to justify becoming religious in order to get 'a good wife and good customers and a good gain', making 'religion a stalking horse to get and enjoy the world' (101–4). Sharrock compared both Mr. Worldly Wiseman and Ignorance (who ended up in hell) to the Latitudinarian and future bishop Edward Fowler. Sermons recorded by Pepys and Evelyn show that this was not too far-fetched a caricature. '"If you will go with us", Christian told By-ends, "you must go against wind and tide.... You must also own religion in his rags, as well as when in his silver slippers, and stand by him too, when bound in irons, as well as when he walketh the streets with applause"' (100; cf. 102). That made perfectly serious demands, relevant to everyday life in restoration England; we can all think of modern analogies.

The two lions outside the Palace Beautiful, which terrify Timorous and Mistrust, are said to represent civil and religious persecution, whose object is to prevent believers associating with the true church. When Christian approaches them he finds they are chained, which Sharrock thinks refers to the period of liberty under the Commonwealth. The lions were asleep when Faithful passed (43–5, 321, 71). In Part II the way past the lions 'had of late lain much unoccupied, and was almost all grown over with grass', because the lions are now backed by Giant Grim or Bloody-man. Grim still represents, Sharrock thinks, 'the civil power which puts into effect the penal laws against nonconformists' in 'the renewed outbreak of persecution' of 1681–4. But Grim had enclosed 'the King's highway' as 'mine own ground'. He must represent the power of landed JPs (218–19, 344).

In Part I, Giant Pope was 'grown so crazy and stiff in his joints' that Christian passes him 'without much danger' (65, 324). In Part II Giant Maul is less specifically the papacy than Giant Pope: he seems to represent persecution in general. He counters the charge—often laid against the Jesuits—that he 'did use to spoil young pilgrims with sophistry' by accusing Great-heart of gathering up women and children and carrying them 'into a strange country, to the weakening of my master's kingdom' (264, 347–8). England is dividing into two nations. We recall that the Latitudinarian Mr. Worldly Wiseman had been described in Part I as an alien (23; cf. 53: Christ 'turned to flight the armies of the aliens').

In Part I the Enchanted Ground 'represented a period of peace and toleration for the faithful.' Sharrock suggested that this referred to the years when the Declaration of Indulgence of 1672 briefly allowed dissenters to meet in public (136, 336). In Part II the Slough of Despond is 'rather worse than formerly'; for 'many that pretend to be the King's labourers and say they are for mending the King's highway . . . mar instead of mending' (187). Sharrock thinks this is directed against Baptists who disagreed with Bunyan on church membership. But the labourers have been at work 'for above this sixteen hundred years'; it seems more likely that it refers to clergy of the established church who offer 'their own carnal conclusions instead of the word of life' (15–16, 341).

The spring at the foot of the Hill Difficulty of which Christian

drank was now 'dirty with the feet of some that are not desirous
that pilgrims here should quench their thirst.' When Great-heart
explains this, Mercy reasonably asks, 'And why so envious tro?'
Great-heart prudently does not answer, leaving it to Bunyan's
marginal note to explain, ''Tis difficult getting of good doctrine in
erroneous times' (214–15). Offor noted a parallel passage in *The
Holy City* (1665) which attributed the muddying of the water to 'the
Romish beasts'.[46] We may suspect that Great-heart saw 'Romish
beasts' in the Church of England as well as further afield.

In general there is much more alarm in Part II about popery and
the dangers of persecution, in consequence of the Catholic leanings of Charles II and his brother and the menacing gestures of
French foreign policy. This fear is reflected in the town of Vanity,
where opinion is much more moderate than when Faithful was
burnt there. '*Then* the name of a professor was odious; *now* . . .
religion is counted honourable.' 'It was not now as in former
times.' But 'a monster out of the woods . . . slew many of the people
of the town. It would also carry away their children, and teach them
to suck its whelps.' The monster described is the Beast of Revelation, Antichrist. This may refer to persecution in general rather
than exclusively to the papacy. The idea of an international crusade
against the papal Antichrist, popular in the 1650s, no longer
seemed relevant. In the 1680s the threat of persecution came from
the Bedfordshire gentry and the Church of England.

But now protestantism is going over to the offensive. Great-
heart and other 'valiant worthies' among the pilgrims wounded the
monster and drove him off. He 'has not made that havoc of the
townsmen's children as formerly he hath done', and 'it is verily
believed by some that this Beast will die of his wounds.' In
consequence the pilgrims are held in great esteem by all but some
of 'the baser sort', so blind that they do not respect those who stand
up against the monster. (The reference here, Sharrock suggests, is
to the preachers of the 'Morning Exercises against Popery' in 1674
and later (277–8, 350). But it may be to protestant solidarity
reaffirmed during the Popish Plot. On certain issues the two
nations could reunite.)

Part II, whilst welcoming unity among protestants, urged
strongly the virtues of watchfulness and steadfastness. 'He that

---

[46] MW iii. 104.

lives in such a place as [Vanity] is, that has to do with such as we have, has need of an item to caution him to take heed, every moment of the day' (275, 277). It was said of Mr. Valiant-for-the-truth that 'no man could ever make him face about'; and of Mr. Fearing, 'a man that had the root of the matter in him' (173, 249–50) – a phrase Oliver Cromwell had used – 'he would not go back again, neither'. Vigilance is still necessary for pilgrims. 'They that get *slips*' going down the hill from the Palace Beautiful 'must look for *combats*' in the Valley of Humiliation' (236–7; cf. 217: dangers of resting places).

In the most helpful analysis of *The Pilgrim's Progress* I have read for a long time, James Turner describes Bunyan as 'a despised itinerant manual worker, excluded from landownership, exposed to the rigours of the open road as he travelled and the violence of property-owners if he deviated; yet he was a householder and artisan, descended from yeomen and small traders. . . . He dissociated himself indignantly from the homeless poor. . . . He saw place as property', something from which the landless were excluded. Giants who challenged trespassers on their property are common in Germanic folklore, Golder told us long ago.[47] But the issue had acquired a new sharpness in post-restoration England.

The giants in *The Pilgrim's Progress* ask, 'Why are you here on my ground?' (267). Christian, Turner continues, 'shoulders it with [his] adversary, saying "Give place to me, that I may dwell" – a text heavy with radical political implications.'[48] Apollyon 'tries to insist that Christian, having been born in his "dominions", must work for his wages.' '"Your service was hard", Christian replies, "and your wages such that a man could not live on."' Apollyon counters: 'There is no prince that will thus lightly lose his subjects' by letting them emigrate to mend themselves when they were unable to live on their wages (57).

Wages were fixed by JPs, drawn from the gentry. The landlord's

[47] Turner, 'Bunyan's Sense of Place', in Newey, 91–110. Unless otherwise stated, quotations in this and the following four paragraphs are from Turner's article; Golder, 'Bunyan's Giant Despair', 374.

[48] 'Ralph Austen, proposing radical land reforms in the light of the coming "gospel days" of 1653, used these very words to describe the poor clamouring for land (Preface to *A Treatise of Fruit Trees*, 1653)' – Turner's note (Newey, 109). Mr Turner is developing here a point made by Edward Thompson in *The Making of the English Working Class* (Penguin edn.), 35. Cf. *The House of the Forest of Lebanon* (posthumous), Offor, iii. 515.

'servants and labourers', declared a pamphlet of 1660, 'are in the nature of his vassals; his tenants indeed are free, but in the nature of subjects.'[49] JPs had a power of summary arrest. Mr. Great-heart asserts a right of way against Giant Grim, who has blocked up the King's highway by enclosure. This confrontation 'echoes the struggles against private enclosures which raged throughout England in the sixteen-fifties.' Giant Despair's complaint, 'You have this night trespassed on me by trampling and lying on my grounds', like vagabonds, leads on to 'and therefore you must go along with me' to his dungeon. After their escape the pilgrims did not feel safe until they were off Despair's property and out of his jurisdiction on the King's highway again (218–19, 113, 118; cf. 59). 'The whole Giant Despair episode', Turner suggests, 'is a vivid reconstruction of a country estate as it is experienced by those excluded from it. . . . Despair is less an abstract or existential inner state than the emotional response of the poor Christian to repression and social contempt.'[50]

By contrast, the Pilgrim seeks 'an inheritance', hopes to 'inhabit' a 'kingdom of great plenty', where he will be provided for by the 'owner of the place', 'the Lord, the Governor of the country'. Great-heart knows 'many labouring men that have got good estates' in the Valley of Humiliation (237–8). In Emanuel's Land, on the Delectable Mountains and in Beulah, lands and their produce are 'rent-free', 'common . . . for all the pilgrims' (55, 119, 155, 303). In the Celestial City, it is said, pilgrims have houses of their own. Access to the orchards and vineyards of the King is free. All material needs are met, and they are in continual and easy contact with the King (176, 187). In Part II Christiana and Mercy 'have all things in common', even though Mercy is a hired servant (185). So in Bunyan's *The Holy City* (1665) 'plums and figs and grapes and apples . . . will be open to every passenger, . . . in common and free for all.' It is all very reminiscent of the medieval peasant's Land of Cokayne, or of Fifth-Monarchist visions of a material heaven on earth.[51] Like the latter, it implies a sharp critical comment on contemporary landlord attacks on traditional customary rights.

[49] [Anon.], *The Gentry rule the nation.*
[50] Turner, in Newey, 99–100.
[51] MW iii. 185–6; cf. *A Discourse of the Building of the House of God* (1688), 'rent-free'.

Turner makes a valuable further point about Bunyan's symbolism, to which I return in chapter 26. Hills, heights, represent lordship, the great and powerful, the gigantic walls built 'of purpose to keep Israel out of his possession'. 'There were giants on the earth in those days' (Genesis, 6: 4) refers 'to the very dads and fathers of all that monstrous brood' of persecutors. 'By these giants and by these high walls, God's children to this day are sorely distressed.'[52] It was then a reasonable question to ask, 'Whose Delectable Mountains are these?' They could be expected to belong to an enemy. It is interesting evidence of what may be a softening in Bunyan's social attitudes that in Part II he contemplated the possibility that 'the spirit of grace shall spring up in *some* that are great and mighty, as well as in *many* that are poor and low' (231).

The social emphases of *The Pilgrim's Progress* have long been recognized; but perhaps they have been insufficiently stressed in accounting for the book's popularity. Its relative neglect by the polite literary world during the century and a half after Bunyan's death is explained in part by its 'low' style, but also by its contempt for the aristocracy and gentry, expressed with remorseless regularity and lethal accuracy in all his writings, especially in *The Pilgrim's Progress*. Hence its popularity during the same period with the middle and lower classes, and in America; hence its influence on the early working-class movement — so long as the aristocracy and gentry seemed the main enemy. Hence perhaps something of its international appeal. 'The symbolic landscape of the landless', Turner concludes, 'remained for two centuries one of the principal possessions of the dispossessed.'[53]

iv. Progress, Circular, Linear, and Psychological

Royalty used to go on progress round the kingdom: James I spent a night at Luton in Bedfordshire in 1605 on one of his progresses. But as government became more centralized, as revenues came in instead of having to be collected, so royal progresses became rarer. This coincided with a time when the lowest class of the population appears to have been most mobile. Was Bunyan's title, whose apt alliteration we take so entirely for granted, intended to suggest that

---

[52] *The Saints' Knowledge of Christ's Love* (posthumous), Offor, ii. 8.
[53] Newey, 109; cf. chapter 29 below.

his pilgrim was a king? 'Common beggars have their progresses as well as kings,' George Wither had written in his very popular *Brittans Remembrancer* of 1628. We recall the Ranter Abiezer Coppe's remark to the beggar whom he befriended: 'because I am a king I have done this.'[54] More prosaically, heads of Oxbridge colleges still went on progress round their manors in Bunyan's time, collecting rents.[55]

Bunyan's *The Pilgrim's Progress* was 'from this world to that which is to come', just as Jesus Christ walked 'through this world, from the cradle to his cross' on 'his progress'.[56] This use of the word in a linear sense, a journey from A to B, is rather unusual in the seventeenth century. James I and Warden Woodward went on circuit, returning to their starting-point. Spatially they made no progress at all. *OED* cites Bunyan's title under the rubric 'onward march, journeying, travelling, marching forwards or onwards'. The examples which it gives of 'progress' in this modern sense come mostly from a later period. Understanding of contemporary usage may help to explain what Stanley Fish saw as mystifying features of Bunyan's book. The events in it are not necessarily sequential, nor is there a steady advance across country. Drawing a map of the pilgrims' route, as eighteenth- and nineteenth-century illustrators tried to do, is as difficult and elusive as producing a time-chart for *Grace Abounding*. The pilgrims travel a long way before reaching Vanity Fair, though it turns out to be identical with the City of Destruction from which they had started; but now it is utterly alien to them. The 'progress' is psychological, not geographical; the landscape reflects the inner state of the pilgrims, who, though 'strangers in the world', 'were going to their own country' (90).[57] Envy and Pickthank knew Faithful, and the latter and Hopeful were well acquainted, though Hopeful was born in Vanity, whilst Faithful was a stranger, speaking a different

[54] D. and S. Lysons, *Magna Britannia* for Bedfordshire (1978), 110; Wither, *Brittans Remembrancer*, Spenser, Soc. (1880), i. 236; Coppe, *A Fiery Flying Roll* (1649), in N. Smith (ed.), *A Collection of Ranter Writings from the Seventeenth Century* (1983), 103.

[55] e.g. *Progress Notes of Warden Woodward for the Wiltshire Estates of New College, Oxford, 1659-1675*, ed. R. L. Rickard, Wiltshire Archaeological and Natural History Soc., Records Branch, 13 (1957), *passim*.

[56] *GA*, 37-8.

[57] W. M. Kaufmann, *The Pilgrim's Progress and Traditions of Puritan Meditation* (Yale UP, 1966), 112-16; S. Fish, *Self-Consuming Artifacts: The Experience of Seventeenth-Century Literature* (California UP, 1972), esp. 229-60; Turner, in Newey, 106-9; 114 (P. Edwards, 'The Journey in *The Pilgrim's Progress*').

language. In Part II time seems as elusive as space was in Part I. Christiana's children grow up from infancy to marriageable age; Christiana herself becomes 'an aged matron' (90–4, 140, 259).

v. Satire and Vanity Fair

Literary critics these days have discovered Bunyan the satirist.[58] He lived in an age of brilliant satirists – Butler, Marvell, Rochester, Dryden, following on from Overton and Walwyn and others whose pens had been liberated by the Revolution. But Bunyan's satire is of a particular kind. It is directed almost exclusively either against the aristocracy, the gentry and the rich generally, or against hypocritical turncoats and the self-satisfied godly.

Bunyan's success as a satirist comes from his realism. Unlike Dryden he does not pillory individuals, nor is he as savage as Butler or Rochester, or as he could be himself in theological polemic. Mr Worldly Wiseman has been compared to Edward Fowler, but I think he is rather a type composed from the characteristics of many real people whom Bunyan had encountered, so that he is recognizably individual, the personification of the social attitudes of Puritans who conformed at the restoration. Similarly Bunyan's aristocrats, so carefully and brilliantly named, are types but also have individual characters. Many such had been introduced into the freedom of Bedford corporation after 1660.

It is the wit of the satire that most strikes the reader – Captain Pope's scutcheon in *The Holy War* was 'the stake, the flame and the good man in it' (*HW*, 229), which deals simultaneous blows at popery, at all persecution, and at the aristocracy's heraldic foolery. Mr By-ends, whose great-grandfather, a waterman, got his money by 'looking one way, and rowing another', is the perfect emblem of those former Parliamentarians and Puritans who accepted the restoration (99). Bunyan's earlier remark that God's own, unlike gentlemen, 'cannot with Pontius Pilate speak Hebrew, Greek and Latin', had hit at the pretensions of those clergymen who despised unlearned preachers.[59]

---

[58] Earl Miner, 'The Restoration: Age of Faith, Age of Satire', in *Poetry and Drama, 1570–1700: Essays in Honour of Harold F. Brooks*, ed. A. Coleman and A. Hammond (1981), esp. 104–5; B. Hammond, '*The Pilgrim's Progress*: Satire and Social Comment', in Newey, 118–31; cf. Brown, 25–6; John Nicholson, *John Bunyan and the Visionary Search for an English Conscience* (1983), sect. 6.

[59] *A Few Sighs from Hell*, MW i. 304.

The satire is most obvious in Vanity Fair, where all is for sale, 'as houses, lands, trades, places, honours, preferments, titles, countries, kingdoms, lusts, pleasures, and delights of all sorts, as whores, bawds, wives, husbands, children, masters, servants, lives, blood, bodies, souls, silver, gold, pearls and precious stones and what not' (88). Part of the effect comes from the incongruous lumping together of so many incompatible things – kingdoms and lusts, whores and wives, servants and lives, souls and silver. But some of the items are worth dwelling on for a moment. They come out so fast that their individual significance is easily missed. Over all is the money power, reducing all aspects of life to the same level: the human and the political as well as the economic.

'Places', 'honours', and 'titles' are aimed at the court and its permeation by money: 'preferments' is a blow at the restored Anglican clergy, for many of whom – Fowler, for instance – conformacy had brought the possibility of high and lucrative office in the church. In *The Greatness of the Soul*, published between Parts I and II of *The Pilgrim's Progress*, Bunyan lists, among 'things far lower, more base, but much more easy to obtain', kingdoms, dukedoms, gold, and silver. This makes it the more likely that in 'countries' and 'kingdoms' there is an echo of the preacher who is said to have proclaimed before the face of General George Monck, Duke of Albemarle, 'some men will betray three kingdoms for filthy lucre's sake.'[60] But Bunyan would agree with the contemptuous sentiment and would admire the courage of the preacher who dropped his handkerchief at the Duke's feet as he said it – if indeed he did say it. 'Lusts, pleasures and delights of all sorts' must also refer to the court: 'wives', 'husbands', to the economic transactions which were upper-class marriages and which perhaps were spreading down into those of good bourgeois nonconformists. The list makes points which if spelt out at greater length would have been seditious; if the censor had read more carefully he might reasonably have taken umbrage. The speed of the calculated jumble enables Bunyan to get away with it, as well as adding to the black comedy.

In the trial of Faithful in Vanity Fair the three informers, Envy,

---

[60] MW ix. 236; cf. *Of Antichrist and his Ruin*, Offor, ii. 78: kingdoms, crowns, places, preferments, offices, put up to sale thanks to Antichristian covetousness. In Bernard's *The Isle of Man* the character Covetousness 'propoundeth offices to sale, and so maketh the buyers to sell their duties for profit to make their monies' (160).

Superstition, and Pickthank, reinforce the point about the truth
being on sale; and Envy is ironically made to denounce Faithful
who 'doth all that he can to possess all men with certain of his
disloyal notions, which he in the general calls principles of faith
and holiness.' He dared to affirm 'that Christianity and the custom
of our town of Vanity were diametrically opposed and could not be
reconciled.' That came near the knuckle again: Bunyan thought
that Fowler preferred the wisdom of this world to Christianity.
Pickthank returns to the charge of sedition: 'he hath railed on our
noble Prince Beelzebub, and hath spoken contemptuously of his
honourable friends', and the rest of the nobility. 'If all men were of
his mind, if possible, there is not one of these noblemen should
have any longer a being in this town' (93–5). Here the allegorical
meaning seems to blend with a directly political sense. Faithful was
punished 'according to their law' (97). This law and its courts, as
Mrs Bunyan knew, would not give the pilgrims justice.[61]

There has been some dispute as to whether Vanity Fair represents the Church of Rome or the money power. I do not see why
we have to choose: Bunyan could perfectly well have intended
both. ('The ware of Rome and her merchandise is greatly
promoted in this fair: only our English nation, with some others,
have taken a dislike thereat. . . . This Fair . . . is an ancient thing, of
long standing.') From Luther onwards part of the protestant case
against Rome had been its profitable trade in indulgences for sin.
But 'he that will go to the [Celestial] City, and yet not go through
this town, must needs go out of this world' (89). The fact that 'all
order was confounded' in the Fair (as in the Valley of the Shadow
of Death) would fit Bunyan's view of either Rome or the unacceptable face of capitalism (62–4, 90, 299–300). Milton in Book I of
Paradise Lost has a similar linkage of popery and the money power.
The fallen angels mined gold in hell, and built Pandemonium,
possibly on the model of St Peter's in Rome. The simple emblem
of the man with the muckrake, 'that could look no way but
downwards', recalls the downwards look of Milton's Mammon.[62]

A comparable satire on the all-pervasive corrupting influence of

---

[61] Cf. Winstanley, 'your laws' (*A New-years Gift for the Parliament and Army* (1650),
in *The Law of Freedom and Other Writings* (Cambridge UP, 1983), 168). Describing
Faithful's beliefs as 'notions' is no doubt intended to recall Ranter 'notionists'.

[62] *Paradise Lost*, i. 680–4, 690–2, 713–37; cf. Milton, *Poems* (1968), 503 n. I owe this
point to Bridget Hill.

the money power is *Gulliver's Travels*. Swift was an early admirer of Bunyan. It is perhaps significant that *Gulliver's Travels*, like *The Pilgrim's Progress*, became a children's book. Their attacks on the money power sliming over court and country were too pointed to be taken seriously. As adults came to terms with the market economy, they let their children enjoy *The Pilgrim's Progress* and *Gulliver's Travels* as fairy stories.[63] A third work from this half-century which also became a children's book was *Robinson Crusoe* — about a man walking alone, like Christian, far from the trammels of commercial society, but equipped with up-to-date tools and all the bourgeois virtues.

Already Bunyan is gunning for hypocrisy, a main target of his writings of the 1680s. Plyable, Faithful tells Christian, was 'a turncoat, he was not true to his profession'. He was despised by those he turned from and by those he turned to (68). Formalist and Hypocrisy do not enter at the wicket-gate but climb over the wall into the way (39). Men like Talkative, 'whose religion is only in word', make 'religion so stink in the nostrils of many as it doth' (85). The casuistical conversation of Mr. By-ends and his three cronies, showing that gain is godliness, first appears in the third edition (1679), the portrait of the Latitudinarian Mr. Worldly Wiseman in the second edition (1678). Sharrock conjectured that success may have given Bunyan courage to print them (p. xxxv). Or perhaps the censorship was lighter after 1678. 'O Man of God! / Art thou offended?' Bunyan had asked in 'The Author's Apology for his Book'. He had reason.

If we ask what is the common factor shared by the victims of Bunyan's satire — the rich and well-born, the time-servers and the hypocritical godly — it is manifestly their lack of any sense of sin: the deficiency which had linked Ranters, Quakers, and Latitudinarians in his earlier criticisms.

vi. *Christian's Wife and Children*

Bunyan's Pilgrim is walking in the fields, thinking of the imminent destruction of his city, when he cries out, 'What shall I do?' 'What shall I do to be saved?' He does not run because he did not know which way to go, until Evangelist shows him. Then Christian

---

[63] Kettle, *An Introduction to the English Novel*, i. (1951), 42–5.

began to run, putting his fingers in his ears so as not to hear the cries of his wife and children (8–9).

It is a dramatic opening. Allegorically it is very telling, based on the Biblical adjuration to leave one's family for Christ's sake. But taken literally it is horrifying. Abandoning his family to the mercies of the parish authorities was just about the most brutal act a man could commit. When Bunyan himself was imprisoned 'the many hardships, miseries and wants that my poor family was like to meet with ... would break my heart to pieces.' The story of a predestined saint starts off with a terrible jolt. It is unpleasantly true to the life of the poor in the seventeenth century. Many men fled from a poverty in which wife and children had become burdens. When God commanded, he had to be obeyed: but the consequences for dependants remained. 'Yet, thought I, I must do it, I must do it.' The Quakers James Nayler and Richard Hubberthorne deserted their families for the Lord in precisely similar circumstances. 'Escape for thy life', the millenarian John Mason warned his disciples around 1688.[64]

Bunyan's friends – perhaps especially his women friends – may have pointed out to him the unacceptability of this opening. He began to tinker with it from the second edition. The Pilgrim no longer simply walks out on his family. Bunyan added a passage making Christian return home and expostulate, vainly, with his wife and children; and he also introduced a long conversation between Christian and a character who speaks only in the second edition. Her name, appropriately, is Charity. In the first edition the pilgrim was cross-examined at the Palace Beautiful only by Prudence and Piety. In the second edition Charity asks about his wife and children: 'Why did you not bring them along with you?' Christian weeps, and justifies himself at great length (8–9, 47, 50–2; cf. Brown, 249–51). Also in the second edition Evangelist reminds Christian that he that 'hates not his father and mother and wife and children, ... he cannot be my disciple' (23). When Mercy in Part II leaves her parents to go on pilgrimage, her act of Biblically authorized disobedience has none of the economic consequences that the defection of the head of a household would have. Even so, she does it with 'a very heavy heart' (206).

---

[64] *GA*, 97–9; Lindsay, *Bunyan*, 192–3; Thomas Ward and Valentine Evans, *Two Witnesses to the Midnight Cry* (1691), 10.

In the posthumously published *The Heavenly Foot-man*, often thought to have been written about the same time as *The Pilgrim's Progress*, the subject seems to have been on Bunyan's mind. When he described how 'some run from father, mother, friends and companions . . . because they would not lose their souls', he omits wives. When Lot's wife was turned into a pillar of salt, 'let what would become of her, Lot would not so much as look behind him to see her. . . . His heart was indeed upon his journey, and well it might. . . . His life lay at stake, and he had lost it if he had but looked behind him. . . . Thy soul is thy own soul, that is either to be saved or lost; thou shalt not lose *my* soul by *thy* laziness.' Bunyan inserted a long passage about Lot's wife in the second edition of *The Pilgrim's Progress*. He was clearly on the defensive against readers' criticisms (108–10).

Bunyan was still nagging away at the same point in Part II. Christian 'was *forced* to go on his progress without them [his wife and children]' (174 – my italics). Mr. Sagacity, introducing Part II, says that Christiana and her sons 'all played the fool at first, and would by no means be persuaded by either the tears or entreaties of Christian' (176–7). Christiana, he adds, wondered 'whether her unbecoming behaviour towards her husband was not one cause that she saw him no more.' She recalled 'all her unkind, unnatural and ungodly carriages to her dear friend, which also clogged her conscience and did load her with guilt', remembering how she had 'hardened her heart against all [her husband's] entreaties and loving persuasions. . . . to go with him.' At one time recalling 'how like a churl I had carried it to him' she contemplated suicide (177).[65] Her interpretation of her guilt ('vile wretch that I was') was accepted by her children and confirmed not only by Mr. Sagacity but also by a heavenly visitant who tells her that God is ready to forgive her for 'the evil thou hast formerly done to thy husband in hardening thy heart against his way'; and he invites her to go on pilgrimage (177–82, 205, 212; cf. 194).

Throughout Part II Christiana and her band are continually being reminded that Christian has preceded them on their journey. Memorial stones recall his struggles and triumphs. There

---

[65] This seems to me a more likely interpretation of 'guilt . . . would have drawn me into the pond' than Sharrock's, who refers it to the Slough of Despond. The Slough was not a pond, and anyway Christiana had not yet encountered it (205, 343). Cf. Giant Despair's wife, who urged suicide for the imprisoned pilgrims (114–15).

have been changes in the route. The byways where Formality and Hypocrisy got lost have been blocked by posts, chains, and a ditch — though determined stragglers could still circumvent them (215). This has curious consequences for the allegory. Bunyan had told Fowler that it was not good enough to follow Christ as an example: only faith in his redeeming blood saves. Christian's example seems more acceptable: some of his victories seem to have been effective once for all. Great-heart and his shooting parties just finish off work which Christian had so well begun.

Bunyan is trying to justify himself in making Christiana grovel before the memory of her husband in the additions to Part I and in Part II. These revisions, made long after he had first told the story, suggest that he had originally failed to take account of the pilgrim as a human being. This in turn suggests a certain moral insensitiv-ity. The opening is explicable in terms of the allegory and of the Biblical injunction to forsake father, mother, wife, and children for Christ's sake. But the realism of the story — not least of this scene — makes it difficult for us to forget Mrs. Graceless and her children as living persons. I cannot accept the view that 'only by reading the opening of Part II can we appreciate what happened at the opening of Part I.'[66] That is to connive at Bunyan's rewriting of Part I. The revisions, and Part II, were written at least in part in order to give the husband the last word in this proxy matrimonial brawl. Part II is a modification of as well as a sequel to the original Part I.

When he published *The Pilgrim's Progress* Bunyan had been married to Elizabeth for nearly twenty years. For much of this period he had been separated from her, in prison, in hiding, and in pursuit of his two vocations, as tinker and as pastor. He must have known what hardships she suffered over these years. One wonders what she thought of the opening of Part I. We know very little about her. The one scene in Bunyan's life in which she figures prominently is when she is pleading to the judges for her husband's release. Forgetting womanly modesty, she beards them in public, contradicts them several times ('it is false'), makes the most of her recent miscarriage, and finally accuses the judges of social dis-crimination: 'Because he is a tinker, and a poor man, therefore he is despised, and cannot have justice.'[67] On the little evidence we have — supplied by Bunyan — she seems in no way inferior morally to her husband.

But in some respects Part II is more sympathetic to women than Part I. It deals specifically with the salvation of women — single women or widows, not dependent on men. The rules of the Palace Beautiful are drawn from those of Bunyan's own church. It is 'one of the virgins of the place' who introduces the pilgrims, as Bunyan himself had been introduced by the poor women whose conversation had first attracted him. But the women pilgrims had to be organized under male leadership and protection. Men gradually steal the centre of the stage — not only Mr. Great-heart and Old Honest but Mr. Feeble-mind, Mr. Fearing, and Christiana's boys as they grow up. They tend to monopolize the dialogue as well as the action. Part II is concerned with helping along those less strong in grace, whether male or female.[68] Some have seen in it 'a warmer Calvinism', paralleling *Come, and Welcome*, published in 1678.[69]

Bunyan never really recanted his view that my soul is mine and thine thine. He explained, expostulated, defended, rewrote; but his position remained hard. We may perhaps contrast him with Milton. Theologically Milton disapproved of Adam's human weakness when he — unlike Lot — decided to die with Eve rather than live without her 'in these wild woods forlorn' — the earthly Paradise without Eve. But the poetry in which Adam tells her of his decision shows that a large part of Milton's heart thought Adam was right, and not — as the narrator smugly comments — 'fondly overcome with female charm'. Bunyan reveals no such agreeable weakness. Absolute devotion to any human being was, for him, sinful servitude.[70]

---

[68] I owe this point to the unpublished Alberta D.Phil. thesis of Aileen Ross, 'Millenarianism in the Works of John Bunyan' (1986), 267.

[69] Sharrock, *Casebook*, 184; MW viii. 237.

[70] Cf. H. Gohaim, *Tradition and Paradise Lost* (Gauhati, Assam, 1977), 247.

19. *The Life and Death of Mr. Badman*

> To the best of my remembrance all the things that here I
> discourse of, I mean as to matter of fact, have been acted upon the
> stage of this world, even many times before mine eyes.
>
> BUNYAN[1]

BUNYAN intended *Mr. Badman* as a parallel piece to the very successful *The Pilgrim's Progress*. That had been about the life and struggles of one of the elect: *Mr. Badman* was about 'the life and death of the ungodly, and their travel from this world to hell' (Offor, iii. 590). *Mr. Badman* is less successful because in relating the life of a man predestined to eternal damnation there is no struggle, no conflict, no suspense. Mr. Badman's life is all of a piece, from his horrid childhood to his impenitent death. For a moment, when he was ill, he went through the motions of repentance; but once well again, the devil a saint was he.

The dialogue form in which *Mr. Badman* is written recalls Dent's *Plaine Mans Path-way to Heaven*.[2] But *The Pilgrim's Progress* had given Bunyan plenty of practice in the form. The scene is carefully set, involving ordinary people, the neighbours Wiseman and Attentive, who meet while *walking* in the early morning (Offor, iii. 595). The most lively and interesting parts of the book are the anecdotes, mostly drawn from Bunyan's personal experience. Alick West suggested that half of Bunyan went into Mr. Badman—his pleasure in the vigour of language, his intellectual daring, his desire to live to the full the highest life he can conceive of (like Marlowe, he was an overreacher), his robust defiance of what infringed his liberty (like the Ranters).[3] Mr. Badman has some things in common with Satan in *Paradise Lost*, into whom part of Milton went.

Bunyan is careful to tell us that he has personally observed 'all the things that here I discourse of' (590). Sometimes he gives names, as of 'H.S. once my companion', who asked, 'What would the devil do for company if it was not for such as I?' (607).[4] For us

---

[1] *Mr. B.*, The Author to the Reader, Offor, iii. 590. [2] As Sharrock suggests (p. 98).
[3] A. West, *The Mountain in the Sunlight* (1958), ch. 1.
[4] 'H.S.' was not named when Bunyan first used this anecdote in *GA*.

the most vivid passages are those dealing with Mr. Badman's courtships and marriages. His first wife was an orphan, godly but rich. 'He wanted money, and that must be got by a wife or no way.' To win her he had to appear godly himself. There is aesthetic satisfaction in observing the skill and thoroughness with which Mr. Badman outwits and wins her (618). There is a similar satisfaction in seeing him hoist with his own petard by his second wife, as wicked as he and rather cleverer. Their marriage seems to have ended in agreement to separate (655). The realistic action and dialogue here look forward to Defoe. But the whole is larded with what today seems far too much heavy moralizing. For Bunyan these passages were certainly the core of the book.

Children should not marry without the advice of their elders — of friends if they are orphans, or of a minister, or the church. Mrs. Badman should never have trusted 'her own poor, raw, womanish judgment' (622). 'It is too much the custom for young people now to think themselves wise enough to make their own choice' (619). On the other hand we can admire the first Mrs. Badman's defence of her right to go to religious meetings against her husband's wishes, though it leads on to a conventional discussion of the undesirability of marrying an unbeliever. Mr. Badman has Ranter views on marriage, quoting the proverbial 'Who would keep a cow of their own, that can have a quart of milk for a penny' (654).[5] It is Mr. Badman who tells the story, which I cited earlier, about the man 'in Oliver's days' who was tempting a maid 'to commit uncleanness with him'. If she became pregnant, he said, she should lay paternity on the Holy Ghost (613).

Mr. Badman is an atheist — 'if there be such a thing as an atheist in the world' (626). He delights in exposing the humbug and hypocrisy of his wife's co-religionists, in a way that often seems to the modern reader to strike home — as Bunyan intended. Badman's mockery of his wife's religion looks back to the Ranters, especially his daring speculations about the Bible. How do you know the Scriptures to be the Word of God? he asks. They are 'as a nose of wax, and a man may turn them whithersoever he lists.' They are

[5] J. Ray, *A Collection of Proverbs* (Cambridge UP, 1670), 74; M. P. Tilley, *A Dictionary of the Proverbs in England in the Sixteenth and Seventeenth Centuries* (Michigan UP, 1950), 126. I owe this reference to the kindness of Bernard Capp. Tilley gives two examples from 1659, one from 1670. Since Ray's *Collection* was published in the latter year, this may suggest an interregnum origin for the proverb — perhaps in the army.

self-contradictory and make mention of a thousand impossibilities. Because of their alleged sanctity, disputes arising from them 'are the cause of all dissensions and discords that are in the land'. That last phrase, whether Bunyan knew it or not, is a direct quotation from 'the King of the Ranters', Thomas Tany (Theareaujohn) (646).[6]

All this recalls Bunyan's own doubts, recorded in *Grace Abounding* and *A Few Sighs from Hell*. The Bible was not the Word of God, but a historical document, possibly deliberately concocted by politicians to hold 'poor ignorant people' in subjection. Andrew Wyke the Ranter had said that 'the Scripture to them was no more than a ballad'.[7] Such ideas go back to Ralegh's and Marlowe's circles, if not earlier.

Analogous perhaps is Bunyan's critique of the psychological explanation of religious melancholy, of which the Leveller William Walwyn and the Digger Gerrard Winstanley had been exponents, though more probably Bunyan heard it among Ranters, either in the army or in Bedford. Again this is an old tradition: Antilegon in *The Plaine Man's Path-way to Heaven* had recommended merry books as a remedy against melancholia induced by fear of hell. Bunyan offered *The Pilgrim's Progress* to 'divert ... from melancholy'.[8] Mr. Badman's doctor, with the irreligion traditionally attributed to the medical profession, explained away his patient's 'sick-bed fears', which had made him beg his wife to pray for him and had given her hopes of a great change in his life. They 'did arise from the height of his distemper', his doctor assured him, and from loss of sleep. 'So soon as you got sleep and betook yourself to rest, you quickly mended, and your head settled, and so these frenzies left you.' Sleep did indeed help, and so Mr. Badman 'never minded religion more' (650–1). It is remarkable that Bunyan should still be settling accounts with his Ranter enemies thirty years after he first encountered them.

Mr. Badman's habit of loading his talk with oaths and curses recalls Bunyan's own unregenerate days. Swearing is gentleman-like, men like Mr. Badman thought (601). As in *The Pilgrim's Progress* and *The Holy War* there is much social satire. The book

⁶ J. Reeve, *A Remonstrance from the Eternal God* (1653), 4–5. (I cite from the reprint of 1719.) For Tany see *WTUD*, 225–6.

⁷ MW i. 333, 343; cf. *Leyborne – Popham MSS* (Historical MSS Commission, 1899), 57.

⁸ Dent, 408; *PP*, 7.

begins with a long and ironical account of the pomp and ceremony of 'great men's funerals, those badges and escutcheons of their honour' (590–1). There are anecdotes of 'a very unclean person' who was 'a great man', of a lady who bears a bastard to 'a brave young gallant' in 'a stately home'. They murder the new-born child. Joseph was tempted in Egypt by 'a great miss, the wife of the captain of the guard'. When Mr. Wiseman overheard the conversation about attributing paternity to the Holy Ghost, he 'had a mind to have accused him for it before some magistrate; but he was a great man and I was poor and young, so I let it alone' (611–13). On the other hand, 'the poor, because they are poor, are not capable of sinning against God as the rich man does' (631). The theme of Dives and Lazarus, frequently used by Bunyan, recurs very early (592). The idleness of Mr. Badman as apprentice is contrasted with the virtuous industry of his master, whose trade was 'honest and commodious' (605–6). Unlike the hero of *The Pilgrim's Progress*, Mr. Badman was – significantly – not one of the very poor. His father (unlike Bunyan's) set him up in business with a handsome sum, to which he soon added the dowry of a rich wife. He had enough money to want to make more.

Sociologically, some of the most interesting pages of the book are those giving economic advice to shopkeepers and small traders, whose traditional standards had been upset by the perplexing advance of the capitalist economy. When in the 1640s congregations organized themselves under elected mechanic preachers, free from control by parson or squire, they naturally discussed, among other things, questions of economic casuistry. Correct economic behaviour was incumbent on believers; improper conduct reflected badly on the reputation of the church and therefore on God's cause. After 1660 persecution forced upon congregations the necessity of seeing that their members were above suspicion in business matters as well as in doctrine and private conduct. Congregations had to look after those of their members who had suffered poverty in consequence of persecution or for more humdrum reasons.[9]

Bunyan advised deacons to use poor relief to encourage industry and discourage idleness. Church members must see to it that their

---

[9] P. S. Seaver, *Wallington's World*, ch. 4; Tibbutt, *Minutes*, 24: a collection made for 'our several distressed friends'. This practice became institutionalized after 1660.

children were industrious. 'None that can work among us idle be.' It was necessary carefully to distinguish the faithful from the rest, excluding some, establishing and enforcing appropriate norms of conduct. This supervisory function has led to nonconformist congregations being called 'schools of capitalism'. Drunkenness, excessive sexual indulgence, were bad for the pocket as well as for health, and so were of economic as well as moral concern to the church. The point is hammered home in *Mr. Badman*. At about the same time the Fenstanton Baptists were reacting equally strongly against church members accused of idleness, of failure to pay debts 'to the great dishonour and scandal of religion', or of profiting from a monopoly.[10]

Gifford had instructed his deacons to 'have a constant stock by them to supply the necessities of those who are in want'; and he admonished the rich to give more generously. In *The Building of the House of God* (1688) Bunyan showed the church carefully checking up on the deacons who administered poor relief. In 1669 Richard Dean was cut off from the Bedford church, among other things for 'defrauding in his calling, selling to several persons deceivable goods, to the great dishonour of God and scandal of our profession.' Four years later the church was upset 'that some have run into debt more than they can satisfy', which was again 'to the great dishonour of God and scandal of religion.' Some days were set apart 'for humiliation with fasting and prayer'. In 1677 Edward Dent was expelled for his failure 'honestly and Christianly' to 'take care to pay his creditors in due time . . . though he had been often exhorted to it.'[11]

So *The Life and Death of Mr. Badman* was dealing with problems of immediate topicality in the Bedford church. Mr. Badman was a fraudulent bankrupt, 'breaking' two or three times to his own financial advantage (628–9). Bunyan devotes many pages to analysis and denunciation of this offence, to which professors seem to have been especially prone. He takes all bankruptcies as presumptive evidence of wickedness. Mr. Badman is also guilty of fraud in his business dealings, using deceitful weights and measures; and of

---

[10] *The Building of the House of God* (1688), *Poems*, 290, 301–2, 305–6; *Fenstanton Records*, *passim*.

[11] Tibbutt, *Minutes*, 20, 63, 76, 83; *Poems*, 290–1; cf. *Solomon's Temple Spiritualized* (1688), Offor, iii. 493; *The Jerusalem Sinner*, MW xi. 27–30: necessity of having a good reputation.

many other tricks. He is interested in maximizing his profits, not in selling at a fair price. He makes his customers pay twice over if he can, and takes every advantage of his neighbours' necessities. He would hoard until prices rose. He was a usurer (633–44).

Perkins had faced similar issues eighty years earlier. His Worldling asked, 'Is it not lawful for us to do with our own what we will?' He claimed to be only following the market. 'I do nought but that which everybody doth.' He had 'a good heart to God'.[12] Bunyan's Mr. Attentive repeated the plea almost verbatim. 'You seem to import that it is not lawful for a man to make the best of his own.' Mr. Wiseman replied, 'If by making the best you mean to sell for as much as by hook or crook he can get for his commodity, then I say it is not lawful.' 'A man, in trading, must not offer violence to the law of nature; . . . do unto all men even as ye would that they should do unto you, Matt. 12.' This led Mr. Wiseman to a lengthy discussion of how to know what to ask, 'since there is no settled price set by God upon any commodity.' Extortion, Wiseman observed, 'is most commonly committed by men of trade', but also, he added illuminatingly, 'sometimes by them in office, about fees, rewards and the like.' 'Those vile wretches called pawn-brokers' are also guilty, who profit by the poor's necessity (242–5).

How, in short, is traditional morality to be adapted to the impersonal capitalist market? Wiseman, who knows all the answers, said that each man must follow his own conscience, but always check it carefully against the Word of God. 'A professor should not owe any man anything but love. Charity seeks not her own, not her own only' (633–42). George Fox was similarly concerned with problems of the ethic of the just price in a world coming to be dominated by the free market.[13]

Bunyan stresses that religious duties are not the whole of religion. 'Thou mayest help thy faith and thy hope in the godly management of thy calling', in 'worldly duties'. In *Christian Behaviour* (1663) he had discussed the relations of parents and children, husbands and wives, masters and servants. There is much similar advice in *A Case of Conscience Resolved* (1683) and *A Holy Life* (1684). A tradesman should 'look well to his shop himself', not

---

[12] Perkins, *A Fruitful Dialogue concerning the end of the world, Works*, (1616–18), iii. 465–6, 471. This was Perkins's first published work. Note that considerations of commercial morality come into a discussion of the end of the world.

[13] George Fox, *Gospel-Truth Demonstrated in a Collection of Books* (1706), 74.

leave it to servants. He should keep strict accounts (610). Heads of households have a duty to educate their prentices, in the things of God as well as of their trade: they should use the Sabbath to indoctrinate them (606–7). It was bad that Mr. Badman swore, but worse that he calls upon his maker in business transactions. 'No buyer should lay out one farthing with him that is a common swearer in his calling', Mr. Wiseman advises (600–2).

One consequence of the necessity of relieving persecuted or poverty-stricken members was a certain ambivalence in attitudes towards well-to-do church members. Gifford had said they were to be given no privileges because of their wealth. But did a degree of complaisance steal in on the congregation, which had originally been composed of 'mean' men and women? Such considerations affected all the sects. They needed money to do good with, and therefore were reluctant to offend rich members. Bunyan was concerned with this problem in his continual harping on the sins of the godly rich — their pride, their covetousness, their hypocrisy — in his later writings. In his preface to *Mr. Badman* he wrote, 'Some men make a profession, I doubt, on purpose that they may twist themselves into a trade' (594).

Mr. Badman regards himself as morally superior to the hypocritical godly. Bunyan's own invective equals anything Mr. Badman produces. 'They are Mr. Badman's kindred. For they are a shame to religion, . . . these slithy, pick-pocket men.' 'Better never profess than to make profession a stalking horse to sin.' To plead custom, or the example of the godly, even of good ministers, is no excuse (632–6, 644–5). Such characters are no better than Mr. Badman when he pretends religion in order to trap his first wife. 'In all this his glorious pretence of religion, he was but a glorious painted hypocrite, and hypocrisy is the highest sin that a poor carnal wretch can attain unto' (619). Winstanley and Milton would have agreed.

'That professing men . . . shall be many of them base' was a 'prophecy of the last times'. Millenarianism is an unspoken background to *Mr. Badman*. 'Bad men make bad times', says Mr. Wiseman at the beginning of the book (594; cf. 627). The wickedness of this society horrified Bunyan, perhaps increasingly since he had spent more time in London. 'England shakes and totters already, by reason of the burden that Mr. Badman and his friends have wickedly laid upon it' (590). 'Wickedness, like a flood, . . .

begins already to be above the tops of the mountains'—i.e. to prevail among the highest classes. 'Without repentance, the men of God's wrath are about to deal with us, each having his "slaughtering weapon in his hand" (Ezek. IX. 1, 2).' 'I . . . shall pray that this flood may abate in England; and could I but see the tops of the mountains above it, I should think that these waters were abating' (592–3).

Bunyan's wrath with England's wickedness becomes tedious because it is indiscriminate: he collects stories of judgments on sinners from Samuel Clarke's *Mirrour for Sinners* (1646; another edition in 1672) and other such works. The best story came from *Mirabilis Annus* (1661), printed by Bunyan's printer Francis Smith for Bunyan's friends Henry Jessey and George Cokayne. The most vivid detail was an addition by Bunyan, that Dorothy Mately stole 2*d.* out of the pocket of a young iron worker who 'had laid his breeches by, and was at work in his drawers'. She came to an appropriately bad end (604).[14]

Bunyan's object is to convince his readers of sin. 'No man can be saved except he repents', and 'repentance cannot be produced where there is no sight and sense of sin.' At the day of judgment men shall 'be judged, not only for what they are but for what they would be.' As the will may be taken for the deed in those who earnestly seek salvation, so many have desires in their hearts for greater wickedness than they can actually attain to, as Bunyan knew from experience: here too the will shall be taken for the deed (652, 656, 661–2, 627; *GA*, 71).

Mr. Badman died in his bed, 'as quietly as a lamb', 'like a chrisom-child, quietly and without fear' (659, 664). This scene is very carefully prepared. 'I desire not to see another such man, while I live, die in such a sort as he did', said Mr. Wiseman early in the book. Mr. Attentive is all agog, thinking he is in for another improving story of a terrifying death as the fitting conclusion to a wicked life (595–6). The build-up and suspense are skilfully maintained. Mr. Badman's death was 'worse than was the death of the gallows', says Mr. Wiseman. 'Of his dying I will give you a relation anon.' Mr. Attentive keeps urging him to get to the point (601, 633, 642).

[14] M. Hussey, 'John Bunyan and the Book of God's Judgments: A Study of *The Life and Death of Mr. Badman*', *English*, 7 (1948–9), 165–6.

Bunyan was anxious to controvert the 'frivolous and vain' opinion 'among the ignorant' that a quiet death means a safe transfer to heaven. On the contrary, 'there is no surer sign of damnation than for a man to die quietly after a sinful life.' This follows from 'the necessity of repentance' (659–65). Why did Bunyan feel so strongly on this subject? Holy dying was a matter of considerable discussion in the seventeenth century. The courage and constancy of Foxe's martyrs had been used to justify the protestant faith. But that was a double-edged weapon. The brave death of the Arian heretic Bartholomew Legate in 1612 seemed to many to justify his beliefs. Charles I in 1649 and the regicides in 1661–2 also made good ends, to the advantage of their respective causes. So did the first Mrs. Badman (652). A passage in *A Few Sighs from Hell* (1658) suggests that Bunyan early had 'woeful and daily experience . . . when we go to visit them that are sick in the towns and places where we live' of the unjustified confidence of many hardened sinners who died easily and confidently. Perhaps, as is hinted in *Grace Abounding*, Bunyan was not sure that he would die well. Christian in *The Pilgrim's Progress* endured 'conflict at the hour of death'. Ignorance, ferried across the River of Death by Vain-hope, did not meet 'half the difficulty' — and went straight to hell. In fact Bunyan — like Milton — was to die as peacefully as Mr. Badman.[15]

[15] John Davies of Hereford, *Complete Works*, ed. A. B. Grosart (1878), ii. iv, 78; MW i. 269–70; *GA*, 99–100; *PP*, 157, 162, 338; Helen Darbishire, *Early Lives of Milton* (1932), 33. In the posthumous *Paul's Departure and Crown* Bunyan discusses the prospects of an easy death for the faithful (Offor, i. 741–2). Bob Owens kindly pointed out to me the relevance of the passage from *A Few Sighs*. He compares Dent's *Sermon of Repentance* (1582).

20. *The Holy War*

Mansoul it was the very seat of war.

Diabolus: 'If we get them a second time they shall be ours for
ever'.

BUNYAN[1]

i. *Allegory and Epic*

BUNYAN'S epic combines at least four allegories. The first is
the history of the universe from the fall of Diabolus/Satan and
the rebel angels. In diabolical conclave they resolve to avenge
themselves by seizing the town of Mansoul. Its inhabitants were
tricked as Adam and Eve had been in Eden. 'They looked, they
considered, they were taken with the forbidden fruit. . . . So they
opened the gates, Eargate and Eyegate' (10–17). But *The Holy War*
is also an allegory about the process of conversion within the
individual soul, brought about by a combination of internal and
external factors. Thirdly (part perhaps of the first allegory), the epic
alludes to the history of the English Revolution, from the Antichristian tyranny of Charles I and his bishops, through the all-too-
brief rule of the saints, to the return of Diabolus in 1660, and his
ultimate overthrow. Finally, it alludes to the history of Bedford
corporation from 1650 to 1682, the date of publication. Bunyan's
vast cosmic drama is rooted in the politics of a small town.

Mr Mullet suggests that *The Holy War* was 'a Puritan *Absalom
and Achitophel*'. It certainly was intended to have contemporary
relevance. Bunyan slyly hinted this when he said it would 'serve to
give a taste to them that love to hear tell of what is done beyond
their knowledge, afar off in other countries'. Tindall, who worked
out in detail the analogies between *The Holy War* and seventeenth-
century English politics, pointed out acutely that whereas Bunyan's marginal comments (which in his Preface he urged readers to
consult) usually refer to the allegory of conversion, his marginal
citation of texts bears on his political allegory.[2]

---

[1] *HW*, 4, 165.
[2] M. Mullet, 'The Internal Politics of Bedford, 1660–1688', P B H R S 59 (1980), 35;
Tindall, 156–9, 268.

Commentators have noted similarities between *The Holy War* and the history of Bedford corporation. But the events which Bunyan so vividly describes seem to anticipate purges which took place in Bedford between 1683 and 1687, after the book had been published. This is confusing, but there are several points to be made. First, references in *The Holy War* are not only to post-restoration Bedford: to understand them we have to go back to 1650, when Bunyan was first beginning to take an interest in politics. Secondly, by 1682 there had been purges in corporate towns near Bedford. Thirdly, as in *The Pilgrim's Progress*, the narrative unfolds psychologically, not chronologically: descriptions in the allegory of what appears to be the persecuting government of Charles I can perfectly well accommodate detail from Charles II's reign. What matters is the atmosphere of persecution, its effect on the persecuted, the sufferings of the godly, and their endurance, not precise chronological accuracy.[3]

Sharrock suggested that the metaphor of military campaigning is less effective than the metaphor of a journey. It reinforces Bunyan's tendency to reduce everything to black-and-white categories — as in *Mr. Badman*.[4] In *The Holy War* we get something like the racial theory of inheritance of salvation held by the Muggletonians. Only the inhabitants of Mansoul can be saved, as for Reeve and Muggleton it was only the descendants of Abel. Petitioners to Emanuel distinguished between natives and Diabolonians. Each Diabolonian whom Emanuel orders to be tried is described in the indictment as 'an intruder upon the town of Mansoul' (119–20). The Diabolonians 'came with the tyrant when he invaded' (161). Have we here an echo of the radical Parliamentarian theory of the Norman Yoke, that all the ills of England date from the invasion by the Norman tyrant who extinguished Anglo-Saxon liberties?[5] For Winstanley and many others the Normans were the gentry and nobility. The Diabolonians use an 'outlandish' speech (123; Norman French still survived in the law courts). El Shaddai's castle was originally built to protect Mansoul against 'the terror of strangers'; it is to be garrisoned only by men

[3] P. Salzman, *English Prose Fiction, 1558–1700: A Critical History* (Oxford UP, 1985), 263–4.

[4] Sharrock, 118. Does this make the *Odyssey* a better poem than the *Iliad*?

[5] For the Norman Yoke see my *Puritanism and Revolution* (Penguin edn.), 58–125; cf. Offor, ii. 270.

of the town (8). All the privileges which Emanuel grants to Mansoul are for 'the old natives and true inhabitants thereof' (138). 'All that were natives' must 'look to their watch' (149).

But as with the Normans and the Anglo-Saxons, the continuance of occupation made national distinctions increasingly difficult to draw. (The Bunyans were of Norman origin!) Miscegenation led to the need for tests to ascertain racial purity (150, 161). The character Atheism is 'a Diabolonian, the son of a Diabolonian' (120). Some of the natives are 'grown aliens to a better state' (105). Carnal-Security is a half-breed, but a 'Diabolonian by nature' (157). The Doubters and the Bloodmen, however, are clearly 'outlandish men' (237, etc.). The Doubters were to be totally extirpated: distinctions were drawn between different types of Bloodmen. The best and the worst of the leaders came to Mansoul from outside. Lord Mayor Understanding described Diabolus and Incredulity as 'foreigners' (60); so are Captain Credence and Mr. God's-peace (149). Diabolus is 'king of the blacks or negroes' (9).[6]

Bunyan loved a good fight, as witness the many duels in *The Pilgrim's Progress*. When the Interpreter showed Christian a man fighting his way into a stoutly defended palace, the pilgrim smiled and said he knew what it meant (33–4). All the other emblems had to be explained for him. Bunyan's description of military happenings in *The Holy War* must have taken him back to his own experience in the army. Emanuel's army, like the New Model, marches through many regions, 'not hurting or abusing any'. 'They also lived upon the King's cost in all the way they went' (38: 'King's cost' is the equivalent of public cost for Parliament's army). The sudden reversal by which a victorious charge was transformed into a rout recalls many of Cromwell's battles, including Naseby (200–1, 273). Bunyan must have been present when orders were given 'that all the trumpets in the camp should sound . . . and that the soldiers should shout for joy' to celebrate a victory. He must have seen 'military men' discovering 'their skill in feats of war' to the civilian population of a garrison. 'They marched, they countermarched, they opened to the right and left, they divided, and

---

[6] Mark Rutherford, *John Bunyan* (n.d., 1923?), 217; Cf. *PP*, 23: Mr Worldly Wiseman is an alien; 53: Christ 'turned to flight the armies of the aliens'; 244: England is the Pope's kingdom. Popery was often associated with the Norman Yoke in the myth. Cf. pp. 37–8, 135 above.

sub-divided, they closed, they wheeled, made good their front and rear with their right and left wings' (110–11).[7] Mansoul was 'fair as the sun, clear as the moon, and terrible as an army with banners' (146–7). Bunyan goes out of his way, indeed, to remind us of his own military experience:

> I saw the Prince's armed men come down
> By troops, by thousands, to besiege the town.
> I saw the captains, heard the trumpets sound,
> And how his forces covered all the ground.
> Yea, how they set themselves in battle-ray
> I shall remember to my dying day.
> I saw the colours waving in the wind . . .   (2)

Another echo of Bunyan's time at Newport Pagnell is that Mr. Prywell was commissioned Scout-Master-General 'for his diligent seeking of the welfare of this town', and because 'he was so naturally inclined to seek their good and also to undermine their foes'. This, Sharrock and Forrest tell us, was 'an appointment peculiar to the Parliamentary army' (183–4, 271). Sir Samuel Luke was Scout-Master to the Earl of Essex, Leonard Watson to the New Model Army, and George Downing to Cromwell's army in Ireland.[8]

So the army of the saints fighting against Babylon is always present in *The Holy War*. Preaching officers and soldiers had been symbols of the New Model's democracy. General Incredulity, at Diabolus's command, denounces the preaching captains of Emanuel's army as 'some vagabond runagate crew, . . . gotten together in tumultuous manner, . . . ranging from place to place, to see if', by flattery or threats, they could secure control of 'some silly town, city or country' (145–7, 158). It might be any royalist officer's sneer, or the complaint of a post-restoration J P.

Bunyan made many direct allusions to the events of the English Revolution. Diabolus warns that El Shaddai 'is raising of an army to come against you, to destroy you root and branch' (33). Puritans in the early 1640s had insisted on destroying episcopacy 'root and branch'. God's ministers in Mansoul are accused of turning the world upside down, as radical preachers had been during the Revolution (40). Diabolus, like Charles in 1642, like Satan in

---

[7] Cf. *The Doctrine of Law and Grace* (1659), MW ii. 141–2.
[8] C. H. Firth, *Cromwell's Army* (1902), 64–6.

Milton's War in Heaven, sets up his standard in the North. The Doubters came from the land 'furthest remote to the North' (189, 227; *Paradise Lost*, v. 685–93; cf. *MER*, 371–2. All derive from Isaiah 14: 13 or Zechariah 2: 6). The day of fasting which the inhabitants of Mansoul observed after repenting of their sins (158) recalls the fasts of the 1640s.

The phrase 'new-modelling', which originated with the New Model Army in 1645, had already been extended to Charles II's 'new-modelling' of corporations, and in this sense Bunyan applies it to Diabolus's and Emanuel's purges in Mansoul (18, 117, 256). The orations of Diabolus ('as if he had been a lamb') and Ill-pause at Ear-gate could recall Charles II's Declaration of Breda of April 1660, with its generous promises of reconciliation, its echoes of Parliamentarian phrases: 'You are not a free people', but in 'slavery' and 'bondage', from which Diabolus will set the town 'at liberty' (14–15, 21). Diabolus hastens to establish the myth that Mansoul had accepted him whole-heartedly and voluntarily— again like Charles II (35–6). General Incredulity, the foreigner whom Diabolus makes Lord Mayor of Mansoul, speaks for 'my prince, for his government and the quieting of the people', when he claims to be maintaining law and order against the 'mutiny' of Lord Understanding and the army preachers (59–61). When Mr. Hate-lies, witnessing against No-truth, declared, 'this was not done by stealth, or in a corner' (129), many must have heard an echo of Major-General Harrison's famous words when he was on trial as a regicide: it 'was not done in a corner'.[9]

As usual, Bunyan has a jibe at those who conformed at the restoration. Mr. Tradition, Mr. Human-wisdom, and Mr. Man's Invention had volunteered for El Shaddai. But after Diabolus's victory they decide that 'they did not so much live by religion as by the fates of fortune', and change sides (51–2). Here, say the Oxford University Press editors, 'is the mechanic preacher's jaundiced comment on ministers who had accepted the restoration church settlement, like Edward Fowler' (p. xxxvii). It could also refer to Hobbes and other *de facto* political theorists who facilitated acceptance of 1649 by royalists, of 1660 by Parliamentarians. Lord Willbewill, who took service under Diabolus, then switches to put his very considerable abilities at the disposal of Emanuel, followed

---

[9] [Anon.], *Trial of the Regicides* (1661), 55–6, printed by Simon Dover.

by his clerk, Mr. Mind. This is primarily an allusion to the important role of the will in the process of conversion. As Bunyan had written in *A Treatise of the Fear of God* a year or two earlier:

the heart is, as I may call it, the main FORT in the mystical world, man. . . . As the heart in general, so the will in special, that chief and great faculty of the soul, is the principal that is acted by this fear [of God]. The will, which way that goes, all goes.

The fear of God is placed 'in the will, that the man may thereby the better be kept from final and damnable apostasy.'[10] But Lord Willbewill may also suggest royalists who had come to distrust the King and his policies. One possibility would be Anthony Ashley-Cooper, Earl of Shaftesbury, who worked for the restoration and accepted ministerial office but became leader of the exclusionist Whigs in the crisis of 1678–81. In the fighting Willbewill 're-ceived a wound in his leg', in consequence of which he limped, like Shaftesbury (pp. xxxvi, 82). Shaftesbury was 'in a sense a living embodiment of the antipopery feeling of seventeenth-century Englishmen', writes Ashcraft, 'coupled with a sympathy for tolera-tion and the advancement of trade.' A pamphlet dedicated to Shaftesbury in 1679 told him that 'the work of your day is to pull down this cursed Antichrist . . . and set up our blessed Christ in his throne.'[11]

In *The Holy War* the Diabolonian rank-and-file supporters were vagabonds, the commanders peers; there is a long list of the latter (144–5, 161, 199, 202). Mr. Lustings was 'a great man indeed', 'a man of high birth, . . . used to pleasures and pastimes of greatness', accustomed 'to follow my will as if it were law' (121–2). The devils bow and scrape to one another in a most refined manner. When Mr. Loth-to-stoop comes as envoy he has to perform 'a Diabol-onian ceremony or two' before he can get down to delivering his message (78). 'The poor and beggarly art of complimenting',

---

[10] *A Treatise of the Fear of God* (1679), MW ix. 124–7.

[11] R. Ashcraft, *Revolutionary Politics and Locke's Two Treatises of Government* (Princeton UP, 1986), 176; Christopher Ness, *A Distinct Discourse and Discovery of the Person and Period of Antichrist*. I owe this reference to Dr W. R. Owens's thesis. If there is anything in my tentative surmise that Lord Willbewill may hint at Shaftesbury, then an obvious candidate for Mr. Mind would be John Locke. This would imply that Bunyan knew more about Shaftesbury's entourage than there is yet any reason to suppose. But Owen was in contact with this entourage (Ashcraft, op. cit. ch. 3, *passim*; 369). I am indebted to Professor Kenneth Haley for guidance on Shaftesbury.

Bunyan called it in the posthumous *Christ a Complete Saviour*: 'the more compliment, the less sincerity'.[12]

On the other side, Mr. Desires-awake, the man whom Mansoul sends as ambassador to seek assistance from Emanuel, lives in a very mean cottage; he takes with him Mr. Wet-eyes, 'a poor man'. Old Inquisitive, 'a mean man of estate', helps to interpret Emanuel's reply. Yet there are gentry who salute Emanuel on his arrival (95, 99, 103, 224, 226; cf. 156). The poor, as Richard Schlatter pointed out, continue to exist, and to need charity, even under the rule of Emanuel.[13]

Diabolus, like Charles II, had a proper appreciation of the value to any government of a state church and censorship. Mr. Filth, Diabolus's PR man, is generally taken to hint at Roger L'Estrange, Charles II's censor and author of scurrilous pamphlets against nonconformists (pp. 31, 257, xxxiii). In offering terms to Emanuel, Diabolus pledges himself 'that none of these things may fail, I myself at my own proper cost and charge will set up and maintain a sufficient ministry, besides lecturers, in Mansoul.' Emanuel rejects the offer; he relies on preaching officers like Captain Boanerges, of a type with which Bunyan must have been familiar at Newport Pagnell. One of the tasks of the preachers in Mansoul is to give the alarm to the town when a plot is discovered, to summon them together to hear a short exhortation to watchfulness (84, 158, 181).

Mansoul is policed by 'red-coats and black-coats', who 'walked the town by clusters' (205). In Bedford in 1670 soldiers were called on to distrain dissenters' goods for non-payment of fines; and no doubt on other occasions. 'Black-coats' was a traditional name for parsons; 'ignorant and unlettered' persons in Massachusetts despised 'black-coats that have been at the ninneversity'. Experience of the civil war reinforced the analogy with redcoats. *Light Shining in Buckinghamshire*, an anonymous near-Digger pamphlet of 1648, spoke of priests as 'the black guard of Satan'. The great sickness which weakened Mansoul looks like the Great Plague of 1665, which seriously hampered England's war effort against the Dutch (158, 171). Bunyan's readers would recall that plague was said to

[12] Offor, i. 213.
[13] R. B. Schlatter, *The Social Ideas of Religious Leaders, 1660–1688* (Oxford UP, 1940), 110.

occur only under the monarchy (1603, 1625), not under the Commonwealth.[14]

The Doubters, who serve in Diabolus's first and second armies, represent free-will men generally, from Ranters and Quakers to Latitudinarians (186–7). The Bloodmen, from whom Diabolus raises 15,000 men for his second army, signify persecution generally; and since persecution is Antichristian (275), Giant Pope is one of their captains (228–9, 275). But Bunyan was careful to point out that persecutors are of three types. 'One sort of them . . . did ignorantly what they did.' After defeat, those who ask for mercy are pardoned. 'Another sort . . . did superstitiously what they did.' They sound more like papists; the few who 'could be brought to see their evil . . . and asked mercy' receive it. 'The third sort . . . did what they did out of spite and implacableness.' They are bound over for trial, being incorrigible (233–4). The Diabolonian plot discovered by Mr. Prywell, about which the Subordinate Preacher gives the alarm to the town, 'is strongly reminiscent of the early statements of Protestant informers during the Popish Plot, even to the threat of invasion by a large foreign army' (181, 271 — editor's note). Cerberus, Hell's porter, swears 'by St. Mary' (171). The fact that 'the world are convinced by the well-ordered life of the godly' in Emanuel's army (39), may refer either to the Commonwealth dominated by Cromwell's army, or to the vigorous anti-papal preaching by nonconformist ministers in the 1670s, and early 1680s in which Bunyan participated.

Informers

> whose very name, and whose profession
> Throughout this land is foul and scandalous,

had long been unpopular. 'The reproach of the human race', an Anglican vicar called them in 1682. Even Mr. Worldly Wiseman thinks that 'only a man of very wicked life' would turn informer. 'Vile and base and reckoned among the worst of men' was Bunyan's verdict in 1685, 'odious and filthy' in the eyes of the people. In Faithful's trial in Vanity Fair, Envy, Superstition, and Pickthank

---

[14] Lyle Koehler, 'The Case of the American Jezebels: Anne Hutchinson and Female Agitation During the Years of the Antinomian Turmoil, 1636–40', *William and Mary Quarterly*, 3rd Ser. 31 (1974); Brown, 206–7; *The Works of Gerrard Winstanley* ed. G. H. Sabine (Cornell UP, 1941), 622; Hobbes, *English Works*, ed. Sir W. Molesworth (1839–45) iv. 235–6; *MCPW*, vi. 461.

are informers against him. In the absence of a police force, informers were extensively used by restoration governments. 'You can't build a ship without using crooked timber', Archbishop Sancroft said. Bernard Capp tells of a Fifth-Monarchy meeting at which five informers were present.[15] It was a profitable trade: the informer pocketed one-third of any fine imposed. He might do even better by blackmail. Mr. Badman threatens to inform against meetings of his wife's godly friends, and refrains only because 'he was a tradesman' who 'must live by his neighbours' — an interesting comment on how the effectiveness of persecution might be limited by neighbourly solidarity. Mr. Wiseman is led on to tell two stories of divine judgments visited on informers (624–5). In *The Holy War* a good character, Diligence, overhears some Doubters plotting and informs against them. In the evidence which Diligence gives at their trial Bunyan seems to be parodying the style and behaviour of informers against nonconformists.

I chanced to hear a muttering within this gentleman's house; then thought I, what's to do here? So I went up close, but very softly, to the side of the house to listen, thinking, as indeed it fell out, that there I might light upon some Diabolonian conventicle. So, as I said, I drew nearer and nearer, and when I was got up close to the wall, it was but a while before I perceived that there were outlandish men in the house. . . . Now hearing such language in such a tottering cottage as this old gentleman dwelt in, I clapped mine ear to a hole in the window, and there I heard them talk as followeth . . . (239).[16]

As Dr Rivers says, this is Bunyan at his witty and satirical best: the allegorical language of Canaan which the godly used was often misunderstood. 'Some Diabolonian conventicle' (239) employs the word which an informer would use to describe a dissenting meeting.

The Doubters are sentenced to death by crucifixion. The

[15] Francis Thynn, *The Debate between Pride and Lowliness*, 44–8; cf. 32–3; S. Bolde, *A Sermon against Persecution* (1682), 23; cf. [Anon.], *The Character of an Informer* (1675), *passim*, and F. Bate, *The Declaration of Indulgence: A Study in the Rise of Organized Dissent* (Liverpool UP, 1908), 32, 46, 49, 69, 131–4; *PP*, 93–5; *The Pharisee and the Publican* (1685), MW x. 118; G. R. Cragg, *Puritanism in the Period of the Great Persecution 1660–1688* (Cambridge UP, 1957), 60–3; B. S. Capp, *The Fifth Monarchy Men: A Study in Seventeenth-Century Millenarianism* (1972), 205; cf. 209–10, 243; R. L. Greaves, *Deliver Us from Evil* (Oxford UP, 1985), 14–16; C. E. Whiting, *Studies in English Puritanism, 1660–1688* (1937), 435–7.

[16] I owe this point to a personal communication which Dr Rivers was kind enough to send me.

allegorical sense is clear enough: one should look out for and destroy one's doubts. But did Bunyan also mean that in the godly society espionage and death sentences would be employed against unbelievers? Tindall's conjecture that Doubters represent Latitudinarians does nothing to reduce the possibility.[17]

The interplay of the four allegories had disastrous results for *The Holy War* considered as an epic. Bunyan took pains in writing it; he published nothing else between 1680 and 1682, possibly because he was concentrating on this work.[18] By that time *The Pilgrim's Progress* had won him a great reputation, and we may assume that he hoped to equal or even improve on it with *The Holy War*. But the theology got in the way. In *The Pilgrim's Progress* the multiple allegories focus on the person of Christian. But in *The Holy War* the battles are fought between allegorical puppets, not real human beings. When Diabolus encounters Emanuel, the outcome is certain. It is in between the fighting that Doubters and Bloodmen are able to enter Mansoul. Only a military solution is possible. Mansoul cannot save itself by its own efforts, but has to be taken by divine assault, since Christ's righteousness is imputed (262).

Mansoul is obedient to each occupying army in turn (18, 165). This may throw retrospective light on the willingness of so many of the godly to accept Army dictatorship in the 1650s—William Sedgwick, for instance—and perhaps even on the *de facto* political theorists of the years after 1649.[19] The *policies* of Emanuel and Diabolus (as opposed to the *content* of those policies) are identical. Emanuel purges and new-models, just as Diabolus did (117–19)—just as Oliver Cromwell and Charles II did. Emanuel and Diabolus nominate corporation officials (25, 257), as the Major-Generals and Charles II did. Both have their state churches. Both rely on military rule (113). El Shaddai's spokesmen threaten terror rather than offering love (44–7). Diabolus's apparent greater moderation is hypocritical. Both use spies and informers (236), both have show trials (237) in which informers of the same type denounce the accused (119). Both sentence to death those whose opinions they deem dangerous to their regime (241–2).

The slaughter of the Diabolonians has its analogy in Cromwell's massacre of Irish civilians at Drogheda and Wexford, and in Samson's massacre of the Philistine aristocracy and clergy: they

---

[17] Tindall, 53, 154, 239.   [18] Sharrock, 118.
[19] See my *The Experience of Defeat*, 97–106.

like Bunyan believed that it was a religious duty to hate the enemies of God. Bunyan leaves us in little doubt that the Diabolonians, though in one sense ideological abstractions, also correspond (like Milton's Philistines) to the royalist aristocracy and gentry in restoration England.[20] There are those who argue that Samson's use of violence against God's enemies in *Samson Agonistes* shows that Milton intended us to see him as a flawed hero. Would they say that Bunyan intended us to see Emanuel as similarly flawed in *The Holy War*? The difference between the punishments handed out by Emanuel and Diabolus, Bunyan would no doubt claim, is that Emanuel was right and Diabolus wrong. There may be a lack of imagination in Bunyan's inability to envisage a form of rule which should be different from and better than that which he had experienced in England; or perhaps it only shows how little importance he attached to political arrangements.

ii. Sources for the Epic

John Canne's *Emanuel* [sic] *or God with us*, celebrating Cromwell's victory over the Scots at Dunbar on 3 September 1650, reminds us that the name which Bunyan gives to Christ in *The Holy War* was traditionally used by Fifth Monarchists when they referred to Christ in his millennial capacity: we may compare Immanuel's Land in *The Pilgrim's Progress*, within sight of the Celestial City (119, 332). El Shaddai as a name for God the Father is less familiar. Lewis Bayly said that it meant Omnipotent, 'because he is perfectly able to defend his servants from all evil; to bless them with all spiritual and temporal blessings; and to perform all his promises which he hath made unto them for this life and that which is to come.' The name was exclusive to God the Father, and so is appropriate to distinguish him from Emanuel. Preston translated El Shaddai as 'all-sufficient', by contrast with the utter lack of sufficiency in human beings: 'if you will enter into covenant with him, ... he will be all-sufficient to you', even in 'the church's troubles'.[21]

---

[20] Jack Lindsay drew the parallel with *Samson Agonistes* (*John Bunyan*, 221–2); cf. *MER*, ch. 31.

[21] Bayly, 21; J. Preston, *The New Covenant* (5th edn., 1630), Sermons 1–5, *passim*, esp. 37–8, 98, 107. Richard Montagu counterposed El Shaddai and Emanuel in a sermon preached before James I (*Immediate Addresse unto God alone* (1624), 10). He is a most unlikely source for Bunyan.

Bunyan may have seen Richard Bernard's *The Bible-Battels* (1629), 'an history of the holy wars'. He is more likely to have read Bernard's *The Isle of Man*, in which he could have found hints for Lord Willbewill. In *The Isle of Man* the five doors of Sin's lodging are the five senses, like the five gates of Mansoul. Old Man, having been convicted of original sin, is sentenced to be crucified, like the Doubters in *The Holy War*. Sir William Denny may have been reading Bernard when he wrote of 'the camp of resolution': 'Five ports there are (and sentries to each gate)', the five gates being the five senses.[22]

In Arthur Dent's *The Plaine Mans Path-way to Heaven* a 'caviller' said, what you call 'covetousness, it is but good husbandry.' Vice also takes upon itself the name of virtue in *The Isle of Man*. 'Covetousness, under the name of Good-husbandry, . . . pride of apparel, under the name of decency and handsomeness', and many more.[23] Bunyan was thus drawing on a well-established tradition when he wrote in *The Holy War*: 'these Diabolonians love to counterfeit their names: Mr. Covetousness covers himself with the name of Good Husbandry, and the like. Mr. Pride can, when need is, call himself Mr. Neat, Mr. Handsome, or the like, and so all the rest of them.' 'The Lord Covetousness called himself by the name of Prudent-thrifty; the Lord Licentiousness called himself by the name of Harmless-mirth; and the Lord Anger called himself by the name of Good-zeal' (125–7, 130, 168, 216, 243).

Professor Sharrock points out that similar name-changing is to be found in Skelton's *Magnificence*. Crafty Conveyance became Surveyance, Counterfeit Countenance became Good Demeanour, Cloaked Collusion Sober Sadness. Bunyan is perhaps more likely to have read George Wither than Skelton:

> Some vices there I saw themselves disguise
> Like virtues, that their foes they might surprise. . . .
> Pride went for Comeliness, profuse Excess
> For Hospitality, base Drunkenness

---

[22] J. B. Wharey, *A Study of the Sources of Bunyan's Allegories* (Baltimore, 1904), 89–90; Tindall, 195, 200; Talon, 240–2; *The Isle of Man*, 74–5, 89–90, 133, and *passim*; Bernard, *The Bible-Battels: Or, The Sacred Art Military. For the rightly waging of warre according to Holy Writ* (1629), sig. §. 5; Sir William Denny, *Peleconicidium*, 171, 184. My attention was drawn to Denny by Turner, 'Bunyan's Sense of Place', in Newey, 102.

[23] Dent, 107; Bernard, *The Isle of Man*, 74.

> Was called Good fellowship; blunt Rashness came
> Attired like Valour: Sloth had got the name
> Of Quietness; accursed Avarice
> Was termed Good husbandry.[24]

Wither may well have drawn on *The Isle of Man*, then just published. But the idea was familiar.

Despite many good passages and striking phrases, *The Holy War* remains stiff and artificial by comparison with *The Pilgrim's Progress*. For this the allegorical form is partly to blame, but also Bunyan's inability to escape from old-fashioned fighting. The chief inhabitants of Mansoul, being abstractions, cannot be wounded or killed: only some 'of the inferior sort' (90, 198). There is little room in *The Holy War* for the compassion and tolerance shown in *The Pilgrim's Progress*. El Shaddai makes out-of-date feudal claims to his rights in Mansoul (74–5, 78), and they are enforced by hard and brutal terror rather than by love (56–7, 61–4). Part of Bunyan's problem is the obsolescence of the epic as a genre, of which Milton was aware. Gunpowder had taken the fun out of hand-to-hand fighting; military swashbuckling and *élan* gave place to 'the better fortitude / Of patience and heroic martyrdom'.[25] Bunyan was unaware of Milton's criticisms of epic; or, if he did know of them, he relied on allegory to get him round the problem. The trouble is that his realism is too effective for him to be able to address us only in allegorical terms. A particularly insensitive use of allegory comes with the crucifixion of captured Diabolonians—Biblically justified but unpleasant (134–5, 196).

Bunyan wrote his *Odyssey* first; his *Iliad* proved much more difficult. The gentle flow of *The Pilgrim's Progress* keeps wayfaring going; but warfaring needs a firmer structure. The politico-religious situation was more tense in 1681–2 than when Bunyan wrote *The Pilgrim's Progress*. The Whig defeat and fears of what was believed to be the alliance of Charles II and his brother with Louis XIV and international popery meant that the toothless and ineffective Giant Pope of the earlier allegory—much less danger-ous than Giant Maul (persecution) in Part II—was transformed in *The Holy War* into Captain Pope, an active combatant with a menacing scutcheon (229).

[24] See Sharrock, 137; Wither, *Brittans Remembrancer* (1628), Spenser Soc. (1880), i. 230–1.
[25] Milton, *Paradise Lost*, ix. 27–33; *Paradise Regained*, iii. 74–8.

The conclusion is unsatisfactory too. Emanuel never really completes his job. *Paradise Lost* can end with 'The world was all before them, where to choose', because that was the beginning of human history. But nothing has been finally settled by the end of *The Holy War*, just as nothing had been finally settled in the political crisis of 1679–81. The testing of the soul by evil, which Milton thought essential for virtue, will continue even after Mansoul has been liberated (277). Diabolonians are still lurking in the town (243–4), suffered by Emanuel 'to keep thee wakening, to try thy love'; its inhabitants are 'to watch, to fight, to pray' (249–50). 'The problem of evil' remains: God's ways are still mysterious. 'Hold fast till I come' is Emanuel's last word.

No doubt there are theological reasons for the survival of evil, which recall Bunyan's arguments with Ranters and Quakers in the 1650s. Atheism's remark, 'as good go to a whore-house as to hear a sermon' (121), echoes the Ranter Lawrence Clarkson;[26] Carnal-Security's remedy for what he chooses to regard as Godly-fear's religious melancholy recalls the doctor's advice to Mr. Badman: 'You want sleep, good Sir' (155). What Bunyan most disliked about Ranters and Quakers was their insistence that human perfection was possible on earth. For Bunyan, even in the millennium, even when the saints come to power, there will still be opponents of their rule; the godly themselves will not be immune from sin and backsliding, as he warned increasingly in his writings of the 1680s. The Doubters will still be there, just as the poor will still exist as objects of charity. Bunyan cannot share Milton's hope of 'a Paradise within you, happier far', to be attained on earth. Bunyan's conviction of sin is so strong that he cannot conceive of life on earth without it, without constant vigilance, constant trial. In *The Pilgrim's Progress* we get a brief glimpse of a different world, attained after the pilgrims cross the River of Death. But in *The Holy War* life during the millennium has to be lived on earth. How could that be without temptation, without struggle?

There are marvellous phrases in *The Holy War*. Love-flesh, whom Diabolus appointed Governor of a fortified post in Mansoul, 'could find more sweetness when he stood sucking of a lust, than he did in all the Paradise of God' (26). Mr. Wet-eyes could 'see dirt in mine own tears and filthiness in the bottom of my

---

[26] Clarkson, *The Lost sheep Found*, 28–9, 33.

prayers' (101). If the citizens of Mansoul had loved their Prince, 'then should their peace have been as a river, when their righteousness had been like the waves of the sea' (152). In one of the few personal interventions of the narrator after the opening paragraphs, Bunyan says, 'It made me laugh to see how old Mr. Prejudice was kicked and tumbled about in the dirt.' It made Lord Willbewill smile too. 'Therefore we dare not despair' is the message of the book, heartening to the beleaguered godly. *The Holy War* shows that millenarianism is still on Bunyan's agenda; but the citizens of Mansoul need help from outside if they are to win.

Bunyan laboured to write a popular epic in *The Holy War*, but he could not approach the one he had written in *The Pilgrim's Progress*. He may have pulled harder than in writing the earlier allegory; but what came was less spontaneous, less alive. So I cannot, with Tillyard, see *The Holy War* as a great epic. Bunyan came too late for 'positive hopes of a holy community in England, that had earlier held men's minds.' Milton, twenty years Bunyan's senior, was devastated by the Revolution's failure; but his participation in politics had given him a commitment that Bunyan lacked. Bunyan was 'forced to the irresponsibility of being in constant opposition'.[27] In politics, and religious politics, he was always reacting to events; the idea of a share in controlling them did not occur, could not occur.

iii. *The Holy War and Bedford Corporation*

In many English towns there were conflicts in the mid-seventeenth century between traditional ruling oligarchies and broader groups of freemen who aspired to a bigger share in government. In Bedford, as in most other towns on which we have information, conflict began to come to a head around 1646–7. By 1647 a great part of the armies had been demobilized; and 1647 was the year in which the New Model Army intervened in politics. Levellers were advocating democracy in London and for the country as a whole. Ideas of more representative government spread rapidly in a country which had enjoyed seven years of unprecedented freedom of discussion. Those who were most

---

[27] E. M. W. Tillyard, *The English Epic and its Background* (1954), 390–1.

prominent for the democratic cause in Bedford politics, its historian tells us, were associated with Independency and republicanism.[28]

We could guess that demobilized soldiers would play a part in the urban democratic struggles. For Bedford we can document it. In 1646 a petition to Parliament from 'certain well-affected persons' took the Leveller line that all just power derives from the people. Power in Bedford, the petitioners claimed, had been usurped by persons disaffected to Parliament and the present government, who had not been elected but claimed a right of hereditary succession to the chief offices of the town. They petitioned Parliament for a revised charter under which freemen would be entitled to vote for candidates chosen from among themselves, instead of voting on a list prepared beforehand by the oligarchy. This petition was countered, predictably, by the mayor and 'the better sort'. 'The chief sticklers against the present government' [of the town], the better sort complained, were John Eston and Samuel Gibbs: sons of freemen, both were young and unmarried; neither of them was a householder. Samuel Gibbs had been an apprentice in London and had then served in the Army. His brother Thomas was another leader of the popular party, who sponsored another petition to Parliament in 1649, signed among others by Samuel Gibbs and John Eston. Agitation around this led to significant constitutional changes in the more favourable atmosphere of 1649–50. Already in 1649 a compromise had been worked out by which office-holding was restricted to Bedford residents – a blow at the local gentry. Canvassing and bribery were prohibited.[29]

Until 1650 a two-class system had prevailed among the citizens of Bedford. The 'burgesses' were a privileged group who monopolized office and its spoils. In January 1650 Parliament approved what was in effect a constitutional revolution: the burgesses were stripped of their main privileges, and annual elections were instituted. Eight members of the new and enlarged Council of eighteen were known members or associates of the Bedford congregation. On 5 April 1650 what came to be called 'the Levelling Act'

[28] *The Minute Book of Bedford Corporation, 1647–1660*, ed. G. Parsloe, PBHRS 26 (1949), pp. viii, xxxii.
[29] Id., 'The Corporation of Bedford, 1647–60', *TRHS*, 4th Ser. 29 (1947), 154–7; id., *Minute Book*, pp. ix. 19–21, 28–9. We have met the names of Gibbs and Eston as members of the Bedford congregation.

abolished the distinction between burgesses and freemen. The burgessdom was opened to any apprentice who completed his service. The mayor was given an expense account, presumably to avoid having always to appoint a rich man. High Wycombe was the only other English town to achieve so democratic a constitution.[30]

In 1656–7 Major-General Boteler intervened rather high-handedly to purge the corporation; the voting system was made less democratic by restricting candidates to a list of twenty nominated by the mayor, aldermen, and bailiffs. Boteler himself was admitted as a freeman. In 1660 everything changed. The constitution established by the 'Levelling Act' of 1650 was abruptly scrapped. Equality between freemen and burgesses was abolished; henceforth representatives were to be chosen out of the burgesses only. 'Bedford corporation in 1664', its historian concludes, 'was legally less amenable to the wishes of the freemen than at any time after 1610'.[31]

The Long Parliament and the Major-Generals had set a precedent for purges. After 1660, in nearly all boroughs, commissioners, chosen from the local gentry who knew their enemies, conducted a ruthless purge. 'It was', Mr Hutton concludes, 'a partisan purge unprecedented in English municipal history, far exceeding anything during the wars and Revolution'.[32] Diabolus in *The Holy War* clearly had learnt from English experience in 1660–3. 'He now bethinks himself of new-modelling the town, . . . setting up one, putting down another at pleasure.' The Lord Mayor and Recorder were immediately sacked. 'All remains of the laws and statutes of Shaddai that could be found' were destroyed. A garrison was established in the town (18–26).

In Bedford John Eston, father of the freemen leaders of 1647–9, himself three times mayor, together with another alderman, was removed from office. Numerous nobles and gentlemen were admitted to the burgessdom—some of them, like Bunyan's particular enemy, Sir Henry Chester, former supporters of Parliament—just as Diabolus had admitted Lord Fornication, Lord

[30] Id., 'The Corporation of Bedford', 155, 158–60; id., *Minute Book*, p. xiii; Joyce Godber, *The Story of Bedford: An Outline History* (Luton, 1978), 68, 72; P. Clark and P. Slack, *English Towns in Transition, 1500–1700* (Oxford UP, 1976), 137.

[31] Parsloe, 'The Corporation of Bedford', 161, 164–5; id., *Minute Book*, pp. xxiii, 95–9.

[32] R. Hutton, *The Restoration: A Political and Religious History of England and Wales, 1658–1667* (Oxford UP, 1985), 159–61.

Murder, Mr. Idolatry, and many others, including 'that horrible villain, the old and dangerous Lord Covetousness' (144–5, 161). Among the five JPs who sent Bunyan to jail, four had been admitted as burgesses in 1661, including Kelyng and Chester. Those freemen who had been upgraded to burgessdom 'by colour of the Levelling Acts' were weeded out. Henceforth no one could claim to be a burgess by birthright, or attain it by serving apprenticeship. The opportunity state was left behind. The town electorate, widened in 1650, was reduced again. Wearing gowns, against which a successful protest had been made in 1651, was once more insisted on.[33]

So Bedford was restored to Diabolus's party. In *The Holy War* Tradition, Human-wisdom and Man's-invention, who had served in Shaddai's army, readily change sides when they are taken prisoner. So do some officials, like Lord Willbewill and his clerk, Mr. Mind (22, 27, 51–2). But in Bedford feuding continued throughout the 1660s and 1670s. Robert Audley, Deputy Recorder from 1675, was 'very indulgent to all dissenters'. In 1675 William Fenn, mayor, failed to swear the required oaths of office. Next year the political climate apparently encouraged the popular party, who got William Lord Russell admitted as burgess and in 1679 elected as the town's MP, replacing Lord Bruce, son of Charles II's agent for the town, the Earl of Aylesbury. In 1682 the Earl of Kent, an associate of Shaftesbury's, was added to the burgesses. Parliamentary elections in 1680–1 were 'disorderly'; bailiffs and mayor were accused of permitting unauthorized persons to vote. The government's reponse was an order in Council of April 1681, removing two town chamberlains, who were alleged to have favoured conventicles – including presumably Bunyan's congregation. Audley was accused before the Privy Council of being 'an enemy to the government and to the Church of England, and a great countenancer of conventicles and fanatics in the town of Bedford.' He was 'the head and pillar of the disaffected party', which was said to include many aldermen.[34]

By 1683 the Whigs had been defeated in national politics. In

---

[33] Parsloe, 'The Corporation of Bedford', 161; id., *Minute Book*, pp. ix, 147–9, 162–3, 174; Brown, 82–3, 102, 182; M. Mullet, 'The Internal Politics of Bedford, 1660–1688', PBHRS 59 (1980), 8–9.

[34] Mullet, 'The Internal Politics of Bedford, 1660–1688', 9–11, 13–14, 16–18; Brown, 295.

Bedford Paul Cobb, Bunyan's old adversary, was elected mayor, and Audley was removed from office. The corporation was swamped by the admission of seventy-six new burgesses, mostly local gentlemen and clergymen, including some of Bunyan's persecutors in 1661. Cobb had no doubt been reading *The Holy War*, in which Diabolus 'made several burgesses and aldermen in Mansoul: such as out of whom the town, when it needed, might choose their officers, governors and magistrates.' Diabolus himself chose replacements for the Lord Mayor and Recorder — as Charles II was to do when even Paul Cobb proved insufficiently complaisant. So did James II.[35]

In *The Holy War* Diabolus imposed a 'new oath and horrible covenant' which would have forbidden attempts to abolish any of his laws. This, Mr Mullet suggests, recalls Danby's proposed Tory-Anglican 'test' of 1675;[36] or it might refer to the oath rejecting the Solemn League and Covenant imposed after the restoration. Just as Shakespeare's *Richard II* 'foresaw' Charles I's personality and fate, so *The Holy War* 'foresaw', in a much shorter perspective, the events of 1683–8, when Bedford's charter was changed again and again. But Diabolus could have learned how to purge corporations from Major-Generals or from the experience of 1661–2; and Bunyan in 1680–2 must have been well informed both of the internal politics of Bedford and of what was happening in neighbouring towns. In Northampton in September 1681 the Earl of Peterborough brought down a new charter amid scenes which were repeated in Mansoul in Bunyan's book of 1682, and in Bedford in 1683. Bunyan would know that the Recorder and his deputy were key figures in the struggle for control of the corporation because of their role in elections. Mansoul's Recorder, Mr. Understanding, exemplified the role which Robert Audley played in Bedford in 1681. Mr. Lustings is perhaps a less fortunate personification of Audley's successor as Recorder, the Earl of Aylesbury (18–19). In 1683–4 he co-operated with Charles II in persuading the town to surrender its charter. In addition to the Recorder and Mayor, several aldermen and burgesses were replaced, just as Bunyan had described Diabolus doing in *The Holy War* (18–26).[37]

[35] Mullet, 'The Internal Politics of Bedford, 1660–1685', 21, 24; Brown, 330.
[36] Mullet, 'The Internal Politics of Bedford, 1660–1685', 38.
[37] Ibid. 20–5, 38; Brown, 311, 316–21.

'And now Diabolus thought himself safe. He had taken Mansoul; he had ingarrisoned himself therein ; he had put down the old officers and had set up new ones; he had defaced the image of Shaddai, and had set up his own; he had spoiled the old law books, and had promoted his own vain lies; he had made him new magistrates, and set up new aldermen; he had builded him new [strong-]holds, and had manned them for himself. (26–7)

But Diabolus was no safer than the Stuart kings were: so long as he ruled, principled opposition would remain.

The new charter of 1684 gave Bedford the right to hold two annual fairs. Again this was following Diabolus's lead. 'I have granted you external things, wherefore the privileges wherewith I have endowed you do call for at your hands return of loyalty.' 'Let them grow full and rich', Lucifer had advised (216). Under the new charter important decisions of Bedford Council were to be submitted to Aylesbury's inspection before being entered into the minute book. A new obligation of secrecy was imposed on Council members. The charter gave the King power to remove members of the corporation at his pleasure. Symbolically, Lord William Russell was executed on a charge of treason two days after the charter had been brought down to the town amid scenes of great pomp.

The Holy War suggests that control over municipal government was crucial if the godly were to survive. This may prepare us for the readiness of some in Bunyan's congregation (and possibly even Bunyan himself) to co-operate with James II in 1687–8 (see chapter 25 below). For our purposes one interesting aspect of the epic is the detailed knowledge it shows of the workings of urban government. Bunyan's dissent necessarily made him acquainted with politics.

21. *Music, Singing, and Poetry*

Peace . . . is expressed by singing, because the peace of God when
it is received into the soul by faith putteth the conscience into a
heavenly and melodious frame.

BUNYAN[1]

Who would true valour see
Let him come hither;
One here will constant be,
Come wind, come weather.
There's no discouragement
Shall make him once relent
His first avowed intent
To be a pilgrim.

Who so beset him round
With dismal stories
Do but themselves confound;
His strength the more is.
No lion can him fright,
He'll with a giant fight
But he will have a right
To be a pilgrim.

Hobgoblin nor foul fiend
Can daunt his spirit:
He knows he at the end
Shall life inherit.
Then fancies fly away,
He'll fear not what men say,
He'll labour night and day
To be a pilgrim.

BUNYAN[2]

i. Music

MUSIC was a controversial subject in the seventeenth century. Francis Osborne denounced the 'time and cost' wasted
on it. John Locke thought music 'wastes so much of a young man's
time, to give him but a moderate skill in it, and engages him in such
odd company.' Jeremy Collier said that music was 'almost as
dangerous as gunpowder, and it may be requires looking after no
less than the press or the Mint.'[3] For Locke and his like by the end

---

[1] *Light for them that sit in Darkness* (1675), MW viii. 130.
[2] *PP*, 295: Mr. Valiant-for-the-truth's song.
[3] F. Osborne, *Advice to a Son* (1656), in *Miscellaneous Works*, i. 12; Collier, *A Short
View of the Immorality and Profaneness of the Stage* (4th edn., 1699), 278; Locke, *Some
Thoughts Concerning Education* (1693), quoted in P. Scholes, *The Oxford Companion to
Music* (1939), 282.

of the seventeenth century music was something that should be left to professionals, of an inferior rank; for Bunyan it was still a living part of popular culture.

The idea that Puritans were opposed to music has, one would have hoped, been scotched for ever by Percy Scholes's *The Puritans and Music*. But myths have a way of living on long after they have been disproved. Some Puritans disliked certain types of music in church services, since they believed that polyphony or choral singing, for instance, or the playing of organs distracted the attention of auditors from the intellectual content of worship; but under Puritan rule in the 1640s 'music flourished as never before'. Bunyan, like John Owen, played the flute, and Bunyan is said to have made himself a flute out of a chair-leg to play in jail. There survive a metal violin and a cabinet decorated with musical instruments which are believed to have belonged to him. The very title of *Grace Abounding* may come from a book of madrigals.[4]

Hymn- and psalm-singing, St Augustine tells us, were first introduced under persecution, 'lest the people should wax faint through the tediousness of sorrow'. Congregational singing, as opposed to singing by choristers only, was regarded as a protestant innovation. Bishop Jewell in 1559 thought that the kingdom of 'the mass-priests and the devil . . . is weakened and shaken at almost every note' uttered by large crowds singing together after the sermon at Paul's Cross. At Exeter, in the same year, laymen singing metrical psalms invaded the cathedral choir, despite the clergy's attempts to keep them out. In Elizabeth's reign a Puritan village in Northamptonshire abandoned the prayer book and substituted communal psalm-singing plus a sermon. London congregations in 1640 sang psalms to drown the prayer book service. Popular songs were adapted by reformers for religious themes: the Geneva psalter relied heavily on ballad tunes.[5] Congregational singing became controversial.

    [4] Scholes, *The Puritans and Music* (Oxford UP, 1934), 5, 384–7; my *Antichrist in Seventeenth-Century England* (Oxford UP, 1971), 75; P. Toon, *God's Statesman: The Life and Work of John Owen* (Exeter, 1971), 6; see p. 63 above.
    [5] Augustine, *Confessions* (Everyman edn.), 186–7; Jewell, *Apology for the Church of England*, Parker Soc. (1848–50), ii. 1231 (1st pub. 1562); W. M. Southgate, *John Jewel and the Problem of Doctrinal Authority* (Harvard UP, 1962), 39–40; W. J. Sheils, *The Puritans in the Diocese of Peterborough, 1558–1610*, Publications of the Northamptonshire Record Soc., 30 (1979), 28; B. Manning, *The English People and the English Revolution, 1640–1649* (1976), 32.

Hymns, as opposed to metrical psalms, came to be associated with the more radical sects, Baptists in particular. No congregational singing was envisaged by the Book of Common Prayer. George Wither in 1622 published *Hymns and Songs of the Church*, but he failed in his efforts to get it printed with the prayer book. In 1641 his *Hallelujah* assumed that his readers would be familiar with the metrical psalms. The Long Parliament's Directory of 1644 enjoined the singing of metrical psalms only. It must have been these that Bunyan enjoyed singing in Elstow parish church.

Congregational hymn-singing flourished during the breakdown of ecclesiastical controls in the 1640s, when congregations could take their own decisions. John Goodwin's church in Coleman Street sang hymns to celebrate the victories of Dunbar and Worcester; John Rogers's Independent church in Dublin sang hymns in the 1650s. John Cotton's *Singing of Psalms a Gospel Ordinance* (1650) was followed in 1653 by Thomas Ford's *Singing of Psalms the Duty of Christians*. (Ford had been chaplain to the regiment of his cousin, Sir Samuel Luke, when Bunyan was stationed at Newport Pagnell. Since Ford's book derived from sermons, Bunyan may have heard him preach on the subject. Ford became a nonconformist after the restoration, and is believed to have been the author of a pamphlet which attacked the bishops as 'unprofitable drones', guilty of covetousness, extortion, and oppression of tenants.)[6] John Goodwin, Vavasor Powell, Thomas Lambe, Christopher Feake, and Anna Trapnel all composed hymns. George Fox thought that Christians 'might sing in hymns, psalms and spiritual songs', so long as they avoided 'David's psalms made metre by Hopkins and Sternhold after the manner of the priests'. But not all Quakers agreed. The Story-Wilkinson Quaker separatists objected to any congregational singing; disputes continued.[7]

In 1660 the restored Church of England made no concessions

---

[6] [Ford?], *Felo De Se: or the Bishops Condemned Out of Their Own Mouths* (1668), cited MW i. p. xliv; *Calamy Revised*, ed. A. G. Matthews (Oxford UP, 1934), 303. In my *Economic Problems of the Church* (Oxford UP, 1956) I wrongly referred to him as Edward Ford.

[7] M. R. Watts, *The Dissenters: From the Reformation to the French Revolution* (Oxford UP, 1978), 309; Scholes, *Puritans and Music*, 381; *The Short Journal and Itinerary Journals of George Fox*, ed. N. Penney (Cambridge UP, 1925), 214–15; J. Frank, *Hobbled Pegasus: A Descriptive Bibliography of Minor English Poetry, 1641–1660* (New Mexico UP, 1968), 268–9, 283: John Goodwin.

towards hymn-singing. 'Men triumphing in a House of Commons that sang psalms' to celebrate a Parliamentarian victory were still remembered with resentment in 1679. 'Hymns', says their historian, 'seem to be more congenial to the persecuted' — again especially Baptists. In 1664 Benjamin Keach issued a *Child's Instructor* with hymns; but it was seized and destroyed, and he was pilloried and imprisoned for his pains. The book nevertheless went through thirty editions during the next 100 years. Keach introduced regular hymn-singing into church services at his Southwark congregation; it led to a schism.[8] Under the Indulgence of 1672 Vavasor Powell's collected hymns appeared, followed by Abraham Cheare's; John Playford's *Psalms and Hymns* had been printed in 1671, but it was not until 1685–6 that W. Rogers published *A New and Easy Method to learn to sing by Book*.[9]

Hymn-singing then was regarded by the authorities as potentially dangerous. It was associated with the lower classes, with Baptists and Muggletonians. John Mason, rector of Water Stratford, published *Spiritual Songs* in 1683, which became very popular; but he was no orthodox Anglican. He became a millenarian, followed by large crowds; like Bunyan, he taught that the poor were to be saved, not the rich. He wrote a poem on *Dives and Lazarus*. He did not even bother to discuss his opinions with learned men, whom he regarded as hopeless. His following assembled at Water Stratford to await the millennium, sharing their property in common. The popularity of his hymns seems to have been with dissenters rather than Anglicans.[10]

Among Baptists too the subject led to disagreements. Singing hymns and psalms could be seen as equivalent to repeating set forms of prayer; and you could never be sure that all those with whom you joined in song were the elect of God. The Hexham church in 1653 thought that 'singing of psalms with the world, that is with the multitude where you meet', was something that they, like the church at Coleman Street, London, would shun. Knollys

---

[8] A. Fletcher, *Reform in the Provinces: The Government of Stuart England* (Yale UP, 1986), 340; *Biographical Dictionary of British Radicals in the Seventeenth-Century*, 'Keach'.

[9] I have drawn largely here and in the preceding paragraph on W. T. Whitley, *Congregational Hymn-Singing* (1933), esp. chs. 4–6. I have been unable to identify Rogers's book.

[10] My *Puritanism and Revolution* (Penguin edn.), ch. 12; Watts, *The Dissenters*, 308.

and Keach, who favoured congregational singing, got involved in controversies on the subject in London after 1688.[11]

There had been disputes over this in the Bedford church from its earliest days. Gifford warned against them in his deathbed letter, but they recurred from at least 1674 onwards. Hymn-singing was not formally accepted until October 1690, two years after Bunyan's death, by a majority of eighteen to two. Even then the church insisted that none should 'perform in it but such as can sing with grace in their hearts'. Those who did not feel free to sing might depart from that part of the service. The discussion had clearly been acrimonious, and it continued until at least 1700.[12] The Toleration Act of 1689 removed one obstacle to hymn-singing: congregations were no longer afraid to draw attention to their existence.

There can be no doubt about where Bunyan stood in these disputes. He loved music, and had no use for 'closed-communion' arguments. As early as 1659 he anticipated 'singing the Lord's songs' in the New Jerusalem. Several of his poems deal with music; two are printed with tunes, which have not been identified. Scholes suggested that these might be of Bunyan's own composition, but Midgley is doubtful. One tune 'has something of the character of a jig, and he may well have remembered it from his unregenerate dancing days.'[13]

Tindall suggested that the songs in *The Pilgrim's Progress* were intended as propaganda on behalf of church singing. They are preponderantly in the measures of Sternhold and Hopkins. The Interpreter 'did usually entertain those that lodged with him with music at meals, so the minstrels played' and someone sang. 'Music in the house, music in the heart, and music also in heaven for joy that we are here', cried Mercy in the Palace Beautiful. (The emphasis on women playing and singing is probably connected with Bunyan's view of women's domestic role, expressed in the

[11] *Fenstanton Records*, 339; B. R. White, *Hanserd Knollys and Radical Dissent in the Seventeenth Century* (Friends of Dr Williams's Library, 1977), 23. Knollys published an early defence of congregational hymn-singing in his preface to Katherine Sutton's *A Christian Womans Experiences* (Rotterdam, 1663), ibid. 28. For disagreements among Baptists about congregational singing, see Scholes, *The Oxford Companion to Music*, 74–5.

[12] Tibbutt, *Minutes*, 92–3, 100, 113, 122, 209.

[13] Ibid. 92–113; *Law and Grace*, MW ii. 124; *The Holy City*, MW iii. 121; *PP*, 234–5, 238, 242, 259, 277, 338; Scholes, *Puritans and Music*, 154; *Poems*, 337–8.

controversies about women's meetings going on at this time.) 'The church [is] to sing now new songs, with new hearts, for new mercies', wrote Bunyan in one of the last treatises he published; 'Sion-songs, temple-songs, must be sung by Sion's sons and temple-worshippers; . . . in the church, by the church.'[14]

Bunyan in his later writings continually insists on the acceptability of music, singing, and dancing. This emphasis stands out in Part II of *The Pilgrim's Progress* and in later additions to Part I. When Mr. Great-heart crosses the River of Death, 'the trumpets sounded for him on the other side', as they had done for Christ at his ascension. This may be a recollection of victory celebrations when Bunyan was in the army at Newport Pagnell. But instrumental music, singing, and dancing feature no less than martial music (*PP*, 160, 309).

Bunyan gave up his early addiction to bell-ringing—whether because he thought it sinful in itself, or only sinful on the Sabbath is not clear. (A Parliamentary ordinance of 4 April 1644 forbade, among other things, 'ringing of bells for pleasure or pastime' on Sundays.) Bell-ringing as such was far from being opposed by all Puritans. When a Russian ambassador came to England for the first time in 1645, after London had been under Puritan domination for four years, the merry pealing of church bells was one of the things he reported to the Tsar as having most impressed him. Others included the universal singing of psalms and the beautiful stained-glass windows in London churches—which, according to the legend, Puritans had by then destroyed, together with church bells.[15] Bunyan's delight in bell-ringing continued as long as he lived, and is expressed in *The Pilgrim's Progress* and *The Holy War*. In a poem called 'Upon a Ring of Bells' in *A Book for Boys and Girls* bell-ringing is mentioned with pleasure and no disapprobation: it shows knowledge of technical terms (231–2). Lewis Bayly had left £5 to his birthplace, Carmarthen, 'to buy a bell'.[16]

Bunyan stopped dancing as well as bell-ringing, though with more difficulty. But in *The Pilgrim's Progress* Christian and Hopeful dance when they escape from Giant Despair's prison. In Part II

[14] Tindall, 66–7, 243; *PP*, 204, 222, 341 – all in Part II; *Solomon's Temple Spiritualized* (1688), Offor, iii. 496; *Light for them that sit in Darkness* (1675), MW viii. 130.

[15] *GA*, 13–14; Scholes, *Puritans and Music*, 303–4; Z. N. Roginsky, *London, 1645–1646* (Yaroslavl, 1960), 11 (in Russian).

[16] Bailey, 'Bayly', 20.

there is dancing to the viol and lute as well as music on virginals, singing, and trumpets. In *The Holy War* every celebration calls for trumpets, and all the time there are singing-men and singing-women, music in every house, bells, pipes, and tabors, damsels playing on timbrels, dancing.[17] The vision of 'the elders of Mansoul . . . dancing before Emanuel' is particularly agreeable, and it is unlikely that Bunyan did not see its comic side. I suspect it relates to controversies over hymn-singing, in which Bunyan would hardly have failed to get his own way if he had not been opposed by elders.

Perhaps I am saying it at excessive length. But I think the point must be made that Bunyan, like most seventeenth-century Puritans, was no killjoy. He thought Quaker teetotallers were 'walking after their own lusts, and not after the spirit of God.' The pilgrims drink wines and spirits—the latter only in Part II. At the feasts which Emanuel gave to Mansoul there was 'brave entertainment', wines, and a succession of exotic dishes ('promise after promise').[18]

ii Poems

Anyone attempting to write about Bunyan's poems must depend heavily on Graham Midgley's excellent introduction to the Oxford University Press edition. This has established the case for regarding Bunyan not as a failed Herbert, Vaughan, Crashawe, or Herrick, but as 'the inheritor and refiner of a folk-tradition of verse', drawing on ballads, broadsides, chap-books, and metrical psalms. Midgley gives an intriguing list of possible influences on Bunyan from such sources, including *The Wofull Lamentation of Edward Smith, a poore penitent prisoner in the jayle of Bedford*, which was published some time before 1633; and *The Pensive Prisoner's Apology* (date uncertain) by a prisoner of conscience urging steadfastness and rejoicing in his suffering. Midgley reasonably suggests that Bunyan may have continued to read religious ballads and chap-books after his conversion: most of those which have survived were Puritan in tone (pp. xxvii–xxxvi). Indeed the echo of

[17] *GA*, 14; *PP*, 222, 233, 253, 283, 303, 309, 311; *HW*, 92, 105–16, 138, 149, 218, 223, 225, 275.

[18] *A Vindication* (1657), MW i. 185; *PP*, 52, 56, 60, 262 (wine—which is of course Biblical); 216–17, 234, 251, 262, 283 (spirits); *HW*, 113–16, 149, 200, and *passim*. Cf. acqua vitae in *The Holy City* (1665), MW iii. 179, and *The Water of Life* (1688), Offor, iii. 542.

Lovelace's 'To Althea, from Prison' in Bunyan's *Prison Meditations*:

> For though men keep my outward man
> Within their locks and bars,
> Yet by the faith of Christ I can
> Mount higher than the stars   (43),

may in fact come not from reading Lovelace's:

> Stone walls do not a prison make
> Nor iron bars a cage

but via *The Pensive Prisoner's Apology*:

> Yet though I am in prison cast
> My senses mounts on high,
> The wind that bloweth where it list
> Knows no such liberty   (xxxiii, 320)

Midgley points out that the stanza patterns in Bunyan's poems printed before 1684 — twenty-five types of them — all have their equivalent in Sternhold and Hopkins, but Bunyan was by now escaping from their 'metrical thud' and unvarying line lengths. This allowed him 'greater freedom and exuberance' (pp. xxiv–xxvi, xlvii). In addition to the popular ballad quatrain, adopted in and after 1665, he uses the pentameter couplet, not to be found in the metrical psalms, which he probably encountered in translations or imitations of Aesop's fables (by W.B. in a chap-book of 1639, by John Ogilby in 1651, and 'Anon.' in 1673), or from emblem books like Thomas Jenner's *The Soules Solace; or Thirtie and one Spirituall Emblems* (1626). The teaching of this popular work is in the central covenant tradition; 'the homely realism of the examples and the straightforward colloquial diction bring them very close to Bunyan's work in *A Book for Boys and Girls*' (pp. xxxix–xlii). The quatrain came to be regarded as vulgar, and its use dies out after Rochester until the Romantic revival — as emblems were to die, without resurrection.[19]

A Book for Boys and Girls is an emblem book. It is customary to derive English emblem books from the Counter-Reformation catholic tradition. But Bunyan was writing in a native protestant

---

[19] My *Writing and Revolution in Seventeenth-Century England* (Brighton, 1985), 4, 326.

tradition. Protestantism started from rejection of images as books for the simple, in favour of the Word, which the simple must be educated to appreciate. In protestant emblems the Word is illustrated not from complicated symbolic hieroglyphs, but from familiar natural objects. Not the image, but the Word and the Book of Nature are the message. The essential feature of the emblem books fashionable with intellectuals was the illustration, the wood-cut, which became increasingly complex, intricate and allusive; verses elaborated witty and ingenious conceits. Francis Quarles (*Emblemes*, 1635, and *Hieroglyphicks of the Life of Man*, 1638) successfully followed the protestant emblem tradition. For his pains he was described by Edward Phillips as 'the darling of our plebeian judgments'. George Wither (*A Collection of Emblemes*, 1635) wrote in a more popular style which Bunyan followed. Ben Jonson sneered at Wither as the idol of apprentices, journeymen, and fishwives. 'Vulgarly taken for a great poet', said Edward Phillips; 'a pitiful poet', Berkenhead agreed. Wither spent some months in prison on account of his satires, and his *Psalms of David* had to be published in the Netherlands in 1632 because of the censorship. Wither fought for Parliament in the civil war, and associated himself with radical sectaries. After the restoration he was in jail again.[20]

Bunyan's emblems take 'as their starting-point, not an intricately contrived problem picture which demands an interpreter, but common objects and actions from the real world of everyday life, which then . . . suggest moral or religious lessons.' His choice of subjects 'connects him most clearly with the parables of the Bible, . . . candles, lost sheep, coins, seeds, old wineskins and patched clothes', and with Aesop's fables. So here again Bunyan was doing something different. He was not at the degenerate dead end of a tradition. There had always been something childish about emblems: they appealed either to sophisticated grown-up children, or to more natural children. Bunyan wrote for the latter, for whom his type of emblem was in fact more appropriate. Wither and Bunyan may have given an extra lease of life to a tradition

[20] Barbara Lewalski, *Protestant Poetics and the Seventeenth-Century Religious Lyric* (Princetown UP, 1979), ch. 6, *passim*, esp. 192; Jonson, *Works*, ed. C. H. Herford and P. and E. Simpson (Oxford UP, 1925–52), vii. 659; Phillips, *Theatrum Poetarum* (1674), Pt. II, 56–7; P. W. Thomas, *Sir John Berkenhead, 1617–1679*, 182; A. Wood, *Athenae Oxonienses*, ed. P. Bliss (1817), iii. 684; my *Writing and Revolution*, ch. 6.

which was dying anyway, like the masque which in some respects it resembled (pp. xxxvi–xxxviii). Homely Biblical emblems first occur in the Interpreter's House in *The Pilgrim's Progress*.[21] Midgley suggests that *A Book for Boys and Girls* was a sort of overflow: it was published two years after Part II of *The Pilgrim's Progress* (p. xxxvii).

Unlike Vaughan and Traherne, who wrote much about childhood, Bunyan obviously liked the children for whom he wrote. There is little evidence that Vaughan or Traherne liked real children: it was the idea of childhood's innocence that appealed to them. Bunyan did not think children were innocent: they were the victims of original sin. But *A Book for Boys and Girls* nevertheless suggests that, despite his theories, he came closer to children than either Vaughan or Traherne. For Bunyan they are not figures in a rural landscape, still less symbols of a lost innocence, but people to be talked to and helped—and learnt from. Bunyan's theory was conventional Puritanism. Francis Cheynell, in a Fast Sermon of March 1646, emphasized to the House of Commons the importance of the correct education of children. 'The joys of heaven' should be represented to a child 'under the notion of a banquet, or a crown of gold'. 'Terrify him from sin by representing the torments of hell to him under the notion of fire and brimstone. . . . Children are excellent at the remembering of stories; relate the story of drowning the world, and the burning of Sodom to your children, such stories will work upon them.'[22] There is no mention of the love which led Jesus to say 'of such is the kingdom of heaven', in Bunyan any more than in Cheynell. Rather Bunyan draws attention to Christ's suffering: 'He shows me now his blessed hands and feet' (11; cf. 8, 15).

Bunyan repeatedly emphasized that children should be taught about hell, and that they are accursed. 'Upon the Disobedient Child' is written strictly from the parents' point of view. 'The rod of correction . . . is appointed by God for parents to use', Bunyan had written in *Mr. Badman*, 'that thereby they might keep their children from hell.' But flogging in this case was not successful. 'Since this young Badman would not be ruled at home', his father put him out as apprentice to a good man of his acquaintance. This familiar seventeenth-century practice did not work either.

---

[21] *PP*, 29–37, 199–203, 208–9.
[22] Francis Cheynell, *A Plot for the Good of Posterity* (1646), 25–8.

Bunyan's own eldest son, John, though apparently properly flogged in childhood, was by 1680 mixing with bad company (including another son of a member of Bunyan's church) and later took to 'drunkenness, card-playing, stoolball', and dancing round the maypole.[23]

Bunyan's preaching technique, which spills over into his prose writing, often involved emphatic repetition of a key phrase. The same effect was achieved in his verse by the use of slightly varied refrains: 'Unless we diligently watch and pray'; 'No man can travel here without a guide' (pp. lxi, 297–8, 118).

Bunyan's overwhelming horror of sin was accompanied by pity for the sinner. Milton seems to have felt little but contempt for the sinful irrationality of the masses. Bunyan again and again expresses pity and desire to help: his contempt is reserved for the hypocritical godly. Old men and women can be children, and need the same help that we give to boys and girls (190–2, 224).

A Book for Boys and Girls starts with some grim theology in 'The awakened Child's Lamentation' (197–202). But it relaxes as it proceeds. In Bunyan's 'emblem' poems the description of unexpectedly familiar natural objects is invariably far livelier and in better verse than is the moral drawn.

> A comely sight indeed it is to see
> A world of blossoms on an apple-tree.
> Yet far more comely would this tree appear,
> If all its dainty blooms young apples were   (229)

> If these ringers do the changes ring . . .
> My soul then (Lord) cannot but bounce and sing   (232)

> The frog by nature is both damp and cold,
> Her mouth is large, her belly much will hold:
> She sits somewhat ascending, loves to be
> Croaking in gardens, though unpleasantly   (240)

> There's one rides very sagely on the road,
> Showing that he affects the gravest mode.
> Another rides tantivy, or full trot,
> To show, much gravity he matters not . . .   (243)

[23] *I will Pray with the Spirit* (1662), MW ii. 268–9; *Mr. B.*, Offor, iii. 597, 605–6; *Christian Behaviour* (1663), MW iii. 30; Brown, 389; Patricia Bell, 'John Bunyan and Bedfordshire', in *The John Bunyan Lectures, 1978* (published by the Bedfordshire Education Service), 35–6.

So many birds, so many various things,
Tumbling i'th'element upon their wings.   (246)

'Upon a Penny Loaf':

The price one penny is, in time of plenty;
In famine doubled 'tis, from one to twenty   (247).

This watch my father did on me bestow,
A golden one it is, but 'twill not go   (248).

Some horses will, some can't endure the drum,
But snort and flounce, if it doth near them come   (252).

Or of a hen:

About the yard she cackling now doth go
To tell what 'twas she at her nest did do   (253).

'Upon the snail':

She goes but softly, but she goeth sure,
She stumbles not, as stronger creatures do:
Her journeys shorter, so she may endure,
Better than they which do much further go   (256).[24]

Spectacles are for sight, and not for show,
Necessity doth spectacles commend;
Was't not for need, there is but very few,
That would for wearing spectacles contend   (263).

Bunyan wrote several dialogue poems in which one of the spokesmen is a sinner—'Christ and the Sinner', 'Death and the Sinner' in *Profitable Meditations* (16–19, 21–4). The most interesting is 'The Sinner and the Spider' in *A Book for Boys and Girls* (214–21). Bunyan is imaginatively sympathetic to the Spider, which at first the Sinner treats with utter contempt: 'What black, what ugly crawling thing art thou?' He is won round by rational argument to see that there is much to be said for the lowly spider, who is perhaps the less undesirable creature of the two.

I spin, I weave, and all to let thee see
Thy best performances but cobwebs be....
I am a spider, yet I can possess
The palace of a king.

[24] Cf. *The Heavenly Foot-man* (posthumous): 'Some professors do not go on so fast in the way of God as a snail doth go on the wall' (MW v. 149).

The moral is theological, but something social comes through too.

Bunyan's arresting openings must have caught the attention of children, and there was really no need to listen to the long-drawn-out moral, since it is nearly always implicit in the opening. It was, says Midgley, 'a voice children would understand', distinguished by a gentleness unknown to other contemporary Baptist writers for children like Benjamin Keach (*Instructions for Children*, 1664), James Janeway (*A Token for Children*, 1671?; *A Token for Youth*, 1672?), Henry Jessey (*A Looking Glass for Children*, 1672) (pp. xliii–xivi). The genre was relatively new, and Bunyan was its most appealing practitioner. His poems are enjoyable because he himself obviously enjoyed observing and writing them. He wrote with gusto and wit.

> Well, Lady, well, God has been good to thee,
> Thou of an outcaste, now art made a Queen. . . .
> A beggar made thus high is seldom seen.

So Bunyan punningly apostrophizes the church, to teach the lesson of humility (257–9). The social point is pressed home in 'Of Physick':

> Let them be beggars, knights, lords, earls or dukes:
> You must not spare them, life doth lie at stake.   (262)

> Behold how huff, how big they look, how high
> They lift their heads, as if they'd touch the sky;

but they are only little boys swaggering on hobby horses (266). The beggar who:

> wants, he asks, he pleads his poverty;
> They within doors do him an alms deny.

turns out to:

> resemble them that pray
> To God for mercy and will take no nay.   (242)

Even when writing for boys and girls, Bunyan cannot resist a dig at inadequate professors. Unless they mortify their sin 'they are not worth a pin' (248: cf. 253–4 – 'Of the cackling of a hen'). And he uses 'The going down of the sun' to teach a sombre political lesson:

> Thou seemest angry, why dost on us frown? . . .
> Tell's, who hath thee offended? Turn again.

And he interprets:

> Our Gospel has had here a summer's day;
> But in its sunshine we, like fools, did play.
> Or else fall out, and with each other wrangle,
> And did instead of work not much but jangle.   (239)

Failure to reach agreement among the saints ruined the godly cause and led to the restoration: the children's generation must do better.

Almost equally remarkable, in its different way, is *Profitable Meditations*, published in 1661, when Bunyan was in Bedford jail. Bunyan is still fighting the spiritual battles soon to be recorded in *Grace Abounding*. There is the temptation to sell Christ (6, 9), which recurs even in *The Building of the House of God* (1688) (314). Despair threatens. Bunyan is still combating what he sees as the antinomian lack of a sense of sin, and the 'formalist's' reliance upon deathbed repentance. Yet he has to a remarkable extent freed himself from the intensity of self-questioning, and can now in a relaxed and almost flippant manner satirize the complacency of the godly hypocrite. The Sinner is speaking in a dialogue with Christ:

> Thy mercy, Lord, I do accept, as mine,
> Thy grace is free, and that thy Word doth say:
> And I will turn to thee another time,
> Hereafter, Lord, when 'tis my dying day. . . .
>
> I fear not but thy love I shall obtain,
> Though I with Sin be still in hearty love:
> I need not yet forsake my worldly gain,
> 'Tis grace, not works, that brings to Heaven above. . . .
>
> I have a mind to Heaven, I must confess,
> I fear to feel the sore revenging smart;
> Yet Sin give me, though Heaven I have the less;
> Take thou my mouth, but let sin have my heart. . . .
>
> This world is present, that world is to come,
> And I for my part am for present pay:
> Take thou all that, give me of this but some,
> I will not for thy wages make delay. . . .
>
> My work is great, my time is short also,
> My children's portions I have still to get:
> The world must be my friend and not my foe;
> I'll come hereafter, though I cannot come yet.   (17–19)

I cite only the Sinner's part of the dialogue: Christ's is less striking. (Often, I suspect, when Bunyan's verse seems to be bad, it is the religious platitudes which create this effect.) There is a lightness in Bunyan's wit in this dialogue which will not surprise readers of *The Pilgrim's Progress* or *Mr. Badman*, but which is often lacking in his theological works.

22. *Self-denial and Humility*

He hath put down the mighty from their seat: and hath exalted
the humble and meek. He hath filled the hungry with good
things: and the rich he hath sent empty away.[1]

i. Self-denial

IN *The Heavenly Foot-man* Bunyan listed six tests by which we
may know the cross—the doctrine of justification, mortifica-
tion, and perseverance; self-denial, patience, and communion with
poor saints. 'How hard are these things!' he commented. For Dent
self-denial was the fifth of eight signs of regeneration; for the
Puritan Lady Elizabeth Brooke, friend of Richard Sibbes, it was
'the foundation of religion'.[2]

Self-denial sounds a negative virtue; but as Bunyan saw it in the
world of the persecuted it was positive and testing. When Prince
Emanuel captures Mansoul he purges its officers and replaces
them with his own henchmen. The last whom he appoints is
Captain Self-denial, 'a young man, but stout'. When some of the
citizens are ready to wink at the behaviour of the Diabolonian
Self-love, Mr. Self-denial insists on his summary execution—to
the approval of Emanuel. Self-denial then is the opposite of
self-love and pride, sins to which even the elect citizens of Mansoul
remain prone. In *The Resurrection of the Dead* (1665?) Bunyan
asked, 'What act of self-denial hast thou done for the name of the
Lord Jesus . . . among the sons of men? . . . Art thou one of them
that wouldst not be won, neither by fears, frowns nor flatteries, to
forsake the ways of God or wrong thy conscience?' Here in the
immediate post-restoration years, self-denial clearly consisted for
the imprisoned Bunyan in refusing compromise, refusing to be
bought, refusing to allow self-love to live within the soul. 'One
Temporary' in *The Pilgrim's Progress* 'was resolved to go on
pilgrimage' until he 'grew acquainted with one Save-self'.[3]

---

[1] Luke 1: 46.
[2] *The Heavenly Foot-man*, MW v. 158–61; Dent, 33–4; Lady Brooke, quoted in J. T.
Cliffe, *The Puritan Gentry: The Great Puritan Families of Early Stuart England* (1984), 50.
[3] *The Resurrection of the Dead*, MW iii. 278–80; *PP*, 151–2; cf. *Christian Behaviour*,
MW iii, 44, 48–9.

In *The Jerusalem Sinner* (1688), self-denial, charity to my neighbour, and patient endurance of afflictions for Christ's name are the manifestations of practical love. In the posthumous *Christ a Complete Saviour* Bunyan praised 'the grace of humility' together with 'simplicity and godly sincerity'. Of the latter he added 'with how much dirt is it mixed in the best; especially among those of the saints that are rich, who have got the poor and beggarly art of complimenting.' 'God commands to self-denial', Bunyan wrote in his *Exposition on . . . Genesis*, 'but the world makes that a reason of their standing off from the very grace of God in the Gospel.' The fall of man resulted from Eve preferring 'the privileges of the flesh before the argument to self-denial'. In the posthumous *Paul's Departure and Crown* Bunyan criticized sermons 'where only grace is preached, and nothing of our duty as to works of self-denial' under Christ's yoke.[4]

In all these instances endurance and solidarity under persecution seem to be the keynote. Self-denial is a religious and almost a political virtue. The theme of *The Pharisee and the Publican* (1685) is the contrast between the 'proud self-conscious' rich man, who 'calls himself . . . one of God's white boys' and the 'vile and base publican'. Bunyan stresses that this parable is to be taken in conjunction with the parable of the unjust judge and the poor widow in the same chapter of Luke's Gospel, which was designed for 'the relief of those that are under the hand of cruel tyrants.' Self-denial is the virtue of Mr. Stand-fast, Mr. Valiant-for-the-truth, and those less stalwart characters in Part II of *The Pilgrim's Progress* who nevertheless refuse to turn back. 'Self-denial', Bunyan wrote in 1675, 'is one of the distinguishing characters by which true Christians are manifested from the feigned ones; for those that are feigned flatter God with their mouth, but their hearts seek themselves; but the sincere, for the love he hath to Christ, forsaketh all that he hath for his sake.' 'The Lord Jesus denied himself for thee; what sayest thou to that?'[5]

---

[4] *The Jerusalem Sinner*, MW xi. 80–1; *Christ a Complete Saviour*, Offor, i. 213; *Genesis*, Offor, ii. 430–1; Offor, i. 734; cf. *The Barren Fig-tree*, MW v. 25; *The Strait Gate* (1676), ibid. 91.

[5] *The Pharisee and the Publican*, MW x. 113–18, 196–7; *Instruction for the Ignorant*, MW viii. 38–43. Esau and Lot's wife are cited as characters lacking in self-denial.

ii. *Songs in* The Pilgrim's Progress

The songs of the Shepherd Boy and of Mr. Valiant-for-the-truth
in Part II are justly regarded as among Bunyan's best. It is
important to stress that they were *songs*. Bunyan must have had
tunes in his head when he composed them. In this they differ from
the poems in Part I, even those which are called songs. Controversies over hymn-singing were going on in the Bedford church
at the time of writing Part II: Bunyan may have intended these
songs for congregational singing.

They are still I believe sung in some churches, and are often
regarded as models of old-fashioned acceptance of an unequal
society. At first sight, the Shepherd Boy's song smacks of 'the
humble poor', of 'God bless the squire and his relations'.

> He that is down, needs fear no fall,
> He that is low, no pride;
> He that is humble ever shall
> Have God to be his guide.
>
> I am content with what I have,
> Little be it or much:
> And, Lord, contentment still I crave,
> Because thou savest such.
>
> Fullness to such a burden is
> That go on pilgrimage:
> Here little and hereafter bliss
> Is best from age to age.

By now I think we can see that Bunyan was not proclaiming a social
attitude. For him humility was a Christian virtue: to be humble
meant having a sense of your worthlessness in the eyes of God —
not of men. 'There was but one way with me', wrote Bunyan in
Grace Abounding; 'I must go to him and humble myself.' 'I never
heard a presumptuous man, in my life, say that he was afraid that he
presumed; but I have heard many an honest humble soul say that
they have been afraid that their faith had been presumptuous.' God
will look 'even to him that is poor and of a contrite spirit.' 'God
resisteth the proud', says Mr. Great-heart, 'but gives more, more
grace to the humble.' The Shepherd Boy's song follows.[6]

---

[6] *GA*, 54; *The Jerusalem Sinner*, MW xi. 69; *PP*, 237–8.

The seventeenth-century equivalent of 'God bless the squire and his relations' was *The Whole Duty of Man*, which urged the poor 'be often thinking of the joys laid up for thee in heaven and then, as a traveller expects not the same conveniences at an inn as he hath at home, so thou hast reason to be content with whatever entertainment thou findest here.'[7] One wonders how many poor men were entertained at inns on their journeys.

In 1665 or thereabouts Bunyan emphasized that humility was necessary to the attaining of grace:

> The promise is so open and so free
> In all respects, to those that humble be. . . .
>   A tender heart . . . may
> Obtained be of them that humbly pray.

Twenty-three years later he confirmed that we must be clothed with humility 'if we will . . . our Master's mind fulfil'.

> Christ bids us learn of him, humble to be.
> Profession's beauty is humility.

We must share each other's griefs and burdens, abandoning pride. 'Let each then count his brother as his better.'[8]

But there is a relationship between social position and Christian humility. The rich are exposed to temptations from which the poor are immune. The Shepherd Boy is singing in the Valley of Humiliation, which

was a traditional symbol of religious humility, conveniently conflated with low social status. . . . Discontent and Shame lurk in this valley, and remind Faithful of his 'lack of honour', of 'the scorn of the mighty, rich and wise' for religion. Yet 'many labouring men have got good estates in this Valley'.

Humiliation, as Turner puts it, 'is thus assimilated to class-hatred and opposition'. Humility was closely associated with self-denial in *The Strait Gate* (1676). It is the opposite of pride, as self-denial is the equivalent of contentment. Of false professors Bunyan wrote 'their pride saith, they have repented of their humility.'[9]

---

[7] *The Works of the . . . Author of The Whole Duty of Man* (1704), i, 62–3 (1st pub. 1658).

[8] *Ebal and Gerizzim* (1665?), in *Poems*, 114; *The Building of the House of God* (1688), ibid. 295–6.

[9] Turner, 'Bunyan's Sense of Place', in Newey, 98–9; *PP*, 237; *MW* v. 91; *The Barren Fig-tree* (1673), ibid. 25.

The Shepherd Boy's statements are factual. 'He that is down needs fear no fall.' 'He that is low' can easily avoid the sin of pride. 'Fullness to such a burden is / That go on pilgrimage' reiterated Bunyan's oft-repeated view that more poor than rich, more servants than masters, are likely to find their way to the kingdom of heaven. That is why the Shepherd Boy 'lives a merrier life, and wears more of the herb called hearts-ease in his bosom, than he that is clad in silk and velvet.'[10]

Again attention to seventeenth-century usage may help us. For John Downame and Thomas Taylor true humility was the virtue of Job and Jesus Christ. Andrew Marvell, writing about the same date as Bunyan, declared humility to be 'the lowliest but the highest of all Christian qualifications'. He had seen it exemplified in Lord Fairfax.[11] Sir William Denny, not one of the humble poor, described humility as

a voluntary inclination of the mind and declination of the haughtiness of the spirit, upon the inspection of ourselves and the beholding of the proper condition of our present state of being. . . . If thou desirest to be great in God's eyes, be little in thine own. As therefore thou lovest thine own salvation, be humble.

Mary Astell, not a very Bunyanesque character, nevertheless thought that 'a secure and humble seat' freed one from 'these necessary evils of the Great.'[12] Nothing we know about Bunyan suggests that he valued social humility. He thought himself, and was thought by his contemporaries, to be liable rather to the sin of pride. His Christian virtue of humility before God might include lack of humility in the presence of ungodly gentlemen.

In the light of Turner's account we may also see Mr. Valiant-for-the-truth's song a little differently. Giants and fiends have castles and dungeons as well as enclosures. They can force vagrants to work for them. The gentry were the form of persecuting power immediately known to ordinary people. Against them the pilgrim will 'have a right' to join the congregation of his choice, the one

---

[10] *PP*, 238; cf. *GA*, 27–8.
[11] Downame, *The Christian Warfare*, 267–8; T. Taylor, *Works* (1653), 410; Marvell, *Historical Essay on General Councils*, in *Works*, ed. A. B. Grosart (1868–75), iv. 142; *Upon Appleton House*, st. vi and viii.
[12] Sir William Denny, *Peleconicidium*, 95, 94 (should be 104); Bridget Hill (ed.), *The First English Feminist: Mary Astell's Reflections on Marriage and Other Writings* (1986), 188–9.

which he believes essential to his salvation ('My soul is my own soul'). His 'right to be a pilgrim' includes this right. 'His first proclaimed intent' to be a pilgrim refers either to joining a congregation or (less likely) to going public after the Declaration of Indulgence in 1672. Despite the power of his adversaries, 'there's no discouragement' that 'shall make him once relent' his decision: not 'dismal stories' of persecution and imprisonment, not social ostracism ('what men say'). Singing that song would strengthen the solidarity, self-confidence, and will to resist of a beleaguered congregation.

In *A Few Sighs from Hell* (1658) Bunyan had stressed the virtues of contentment even in poverty, as he was to do in The Shepherd Boy's song. But Bunyan knew too much to sentimentalize poverty. He knew about the 'many necessary inconveniences that attend him that is fallen into decay in this world. It is not a time now, will Satan say, to retain a tender conscience, to regard thy word or promise, to pay for what thou buyest, or to stick at pilfering. . . . How many in our day have, on these very accounts, brought religion to a very ill savour?'[13] The inconveniences were at least as much spiritual as social.

As we shall see in chapter 24, another matter much on Bunyan's mind when he wrote Part II of *The Pilgrim's Progress* was the backsliding and hypocrisy of godly members of his congregation. It may be that the stress on Christian humility, and on the perils and risks of being a pilgrim, were intended to shame them. If he thought of these songs as possible hymns for his congregation, this consideration would be even more relevant.

[13] MW i. 256–7; *The Saints' Privilege and Profit* (posthumous), Offor, i. 677.

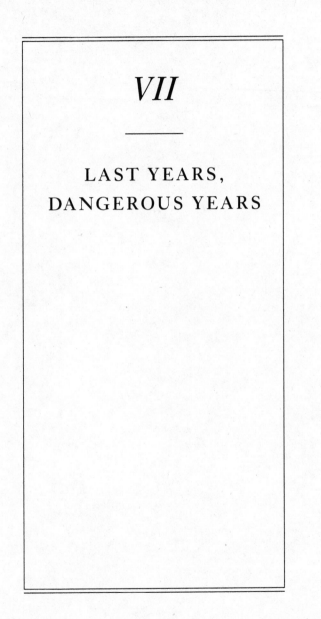

VII

LAST YEARS,
DANGEROUS YEARS

23. Bunyan's Printers

The prejudice the licensers were pleased to take against the
authors [Bunyan and one other] constrained my printing them
without licence.
                                       FRANCIS SMITH[1]

BUNYAN'S experience with printers is intriguing, and throws
more light on him than has perhaps been appreciated.[2] His
first book, *Some Gospel-truths Opened* (1656), was printed for John
Wright, to be sold by Matthias Cowley, Bookseller in Newport
Pagnell. *A Vindication of Some Gospel-truths* was also printed by
Wright for Cowley in 1657; *A Few Sighs from Hell* (1658) was
printed by Ralph Wood for M. Wright (widow of John Wright).
The Doctrine of Law and Grace Unfolded (1659) was variously
'printed for M. Wright', 'printed for M. Cowley'.

Bunyan may have come to know Cowley during his years in
Newport Pagnell: perhaps they served together. Cowley appears
to have been a Baptist. His first child is recorded as having been
buried in 1662, unbaptized. Bunyan's Bedford congregation had
associations with that of Newport Pagnell. In Edward VI's reign
local presses, banned by Henry VIII, had briefly flourished. From
1557 to 1640, and again after the restoration, printing outside
London, Oxford, and Cambridge was prohibited, in the interests
of government control.[3] Printing required very little capital equipment, and Cowley is a reminder that provincial printing might
have developed but for the repressive policy of post-restoration
governments, frustrating a burgeoning provincial cultural independence. It is not impossible that Bunyan positively wished to
encourage the local industry.

After 1660 there was a new situation, with fierce if erratically
enforced censorship. There was no return to the prerogative
control of the press which had existed before 1640. *Parliament*
passed the Licensing Act of 1662, providing that all books must be

---

[1] *An Account of the Injurious Proceedings of Sir George Jeffreys Knight . . . against Francis
Smith, Bookseller* (n.d., 1680?), 11.
[2] But see now J. Sears McGee in MW iii. 3–4, 199, 296–7.
[3] Brown, 123; J. N. King, *English Reformation Literature: The Tudor Origins of the
Protestant Tradition* (Princeton UP, 1979), 101.

licensed and entered in the Register of the Stationers' Company. This Act expired from time to time and was normally renewed except between 1679 and 1685. From 1681 to 1685 Charles failed to call a Parliament. But his judges nevertheless enforced censorship. It may have been less the expiry of the Licensing Act than the crisis of the Popish Plot that reduced the severity of the censorship after 1678. The Act was finally allowed to lapse in 1695, partly because of the difficulty of enforcing it, partly because of the opposition of booksellers to it.

Of Bunyan's major books only *The Pilgrim's Progress*, Part I, and *A Book for Boys and Girls* state on the title-page that they have been licensed as required by the Licensing Act of 1662. How did his printers manage to break the law successfully for twenty-eight years? And why did Ponder not license Part II of *The Pilgrim's Progress*? Francis Smith's remark cited as epigraph to this chapter reminds us that Richard Baxter was told by a licenser that they censored men rather than books. Bunyan was in prison from 1660 to 1672, and in 1669 his church was accused (wrongly) of having its hands in the blood of Charles I. There was undoubtedly 'prejudice' against him. But why were neither he nor his printers prosecuted for printing without licence? Francis Smith's account of his own experiences suggests that the system for enforcing the licensing laws was very haphazard; informers were often rival printers who 'could print and sell, and connive at printing and selling, the same book'. Most of them were bribable.[4]

It is difficult for us to grasp the problems of law-enforcement in a society without a police force or a significant bureaucracy. The attempts of Laudians and Presbyterians to introduce their very different disciplines are often seen as outrageous infringements of the liberty of the subject. They might equally well be seen as first steps towards reducing the chaos of London to some sort of order by enforcing norms of behaviour which after three centuries we have internalized. The impossibility of enforcing the Licensing Act without a large bureaucracy was indeed one of the reasons for allowing it to lapse after 1695.

⁴ Smith, *An Account*, 11, 20; *Reliquiae Baxterianae*, 123; F. S. Siebert, *Freedom of the Press in England*, 1476–1776 (Illinois UP, 1952), 253, 262. The sixth edition of *Come, and Welcome* (1688) was the only one declared to be 'licensed and entered according to order' (MW viii. 236).

Siebert estimated that probably not more than half the pamphlets and books published at this time were licensed. Very little effort, he suggested, was made to suppress opposition pamphlets in the early years of Charles II's reign, although control was tightened up in the crisis years of the 1680s. The Stationers' Company, mainly responsible for working the system, was reluctant to initiate prosecutions, partly because it did not want to deprive its poorer members of profits from 'risky' popular books, partly out of sympathy with opponents of the government. The censorship laws, like those against nonconformists, worked quite arbitrarily. Some printers broke them for twenty years with impunity: others were penalized to the utter disruption of their economic and family life. In 1664 John Twine, a London printer, suffered the gruesome penalties of high treason for printing a treatise justifying the right of peoples to call their governments to account — a Miltonic theme.[5] Printers were always potentially at risk from informers or jealous rivals.

The second edition of Bunyan's *I Will Pray with the Spirit* (1663) was printed in London 'for the author': no copy of the first edition survives. It was unlicensed. But Bunyan had already chosen another printer for his verse *Profitable Meditations* (1661–2?). This was Francis Smith, generally known as 'Elephant Smith' from his shop at the Elephant and Castle. Smith was a Baptist, 'teacher' of a congregation in Goswell Street. Bunyan may have known him, or known of him, before the restoration. In 1659 Smith printed a pamphlet attacking Quakers, which must have pleased Bunyan.[6] In the same year he printed the Leveller Captain William Bray's *Plea for the People's Good Old Cause*. In December 1659 Smith's house was frequently searched for arms. In March 1660 he signed *A Brief Confession*, with thirty-nine other Baptists. Later that year he published *Symptomes of Growth and Decay*, a treatise of his own writing, with prefaces by Henry Jessey and Henry Denne. In this and other writings Smith was as critical as Bunyan himself of 'the

---

[5] F. S. Siebert, *Freedom of the Press in England*, ch. 12, *passim*; [Anon.], *A Treatise of the execution of justice wherein it is clearly proved that the execution of judgment and justice is as well the people's as the magistrate's duty, and if the magistrate pervert judgment the people are bound by the law of God to execute judgment without them and upon them* (1663).

[6] J. G. Muddiman, *The King's Journalist, 1659–1689* (1923), 158. For Smith I have drawn on his own *Account of the Injurious Proceedings of Sir George Jeffreys . . . against Francis Smith* (1680?), and on the article by R. Zaller and H. T. Blethen in *Biographical Dictionary of British Radicals: The Seventeenth Century*, iii. (1984). Smith is not in *DNB*.

sins of professors', their 'running from one thing to another'. In 1669 Smith published the second edition of Bunyan's millenarian work, *The Holy City*; the first edition in 1665 had no printer's name.[7]

Smith is one of the many unsung heroes of the struggle for freedom of the press in England. Or, as Henry Muddiman put it in 1684, he was 'the prime dispenser of all sorts of the most lewd and seditious pamphlets.' It all depended on the point of view. Smith spent much of his life in and out of prison – three times in 1660. In 1661 his house was searched again when he was accused of participating in Venner's revolt: but Smith was rescued by trained bands. He was imprisoned later in the year for printing, in association with Giles Calvert and Livewell Chapman (famous radical printers of the revolutionary decades), *Mirabilis Annus*, a collection of post-1660 portents and calamities which were taken to show divine disapproval of the restored monarchy. It was a bestseller, and called forth many replies, including Dryden's *Annus Mirabilis*. In consequence of this last rallying gesture of the defeated revolutionaries, Smith lost his shop and his trade for two years. In 1666 his stock of books was seized; a number of them perished in the Great Fire – which may account for the rarity of many of Bunyan's early works. Smith was 'restrained' by King's messengers ten times between 1661 and 1680. One messenger, Smith observed, not without pride, 'said he had more trouble with me than with all the booksellers and printers in town besides.' Smith was, as he plausibly tells us, the victim of bullying and injustice from Judge Jeffreys. Eighty years before Wilkes, Smith was querying the legality of general search warrants. In 1680 he claimed – no doubt with some exaggeration – that since 1660 he had lost nearly £1,400 in fines, fees, and damages. Thomas Brewster, Giles Calvert, Livewell Chapman, and Simon Dover had suffered similar or worse fates.[8]

In 1666 Smith printed an account of the Great Fire, attributing it to papist incendiaries. An anonymous pamphlet of 1670 about persecution of nonconformists in Bedford seemed to that excellent judge John Brown likely to have been printed by Smith. In 1671 he

---

[7] MW viii. 3; Smith, *An Account*, 8; MW iii. 296–7; Brown, 168.

[8] Muddiman, *The King's Journalist*, 243; Smith, *Profitable Meditations* (1660); id., *An Account*, 8–9, 17–20, and *passim*; Brown, 172.

was charged with preaching in contravention of the Conventicle Act; in 1673, under the Indulgence, he was licensed to preach in Croydon. Next year he was arrested for illegally publishing the proceedings of Parliament.[9] (Six years later the House of Commons appointed him its official printer.) Between 1678 and 1681 Smith was many times charged with publishing seditious pamphlets, but sympathetic London juries returned ignoramus verdicts.

In 1679 Smith was accused of going 'up and down getting hands to petitions for sitting of the Parliament', and made his defence before Charles II himself. A year later he printed a speech attacking the King, which had been prepared by Shaftesbury but was never delivered. In March 1681 Smith presented each MP at Oxford with a copy of *Vox Populi* which he had printed. From February to April 1681–2 he published *Smith's Protestant Intelligence* – in close contact with Shaftesbury, it was said. Smith's autobiographical *An Account of the Injurious Proceedings of Sir George Jeffreys . . . against Francis Smith* was dedicated to Shaftesbury, 'I having in many cases experienced your Lordship's kindness', as well as sharing the indebtedness to him of all protestant Englishmen.[10]

Smith's apprentices included Edith and Stephen College. Smith printed *The Raree Show*, a ballad attacking the King and the Duke of York by the 'protestant joiner', Stephen College. ('What have such people to do to interfere with the business of government?' asked Jeffreys whilst sentencing College to death; J. G. Muddiman in the present century thought *The Raree Show* 'too offensive to quote'.) On 15 April 1681 Smith was committed to Newgate and charged with high treason; he was alleged to have declared 'he would never leave printing and writing till this kingdom was brought to a free state.' Next year he was reported as plotting with Titus Oates and Henry Danvers.[11]

Between 1661 and 1678 Smith printed nearly all Bunyan's books. In 1666 *Grace Abounding* was given to a twenty-four-year-

---

[9] Brown, 208; Smith, *An Account*, 11; Muddiman, *The King's Journalist*, 161.

[10] Smith, *An Account*, Dedication and p. 21; Muddiman, *The King's Journalist*, 211–14, 228, 246. The speech was reissued on 19 September 1681.

[11] D. F. McKenzie (ed.), *Stationers' Company Apprentices, 1641–1700*, Oxford Bibliographical Soc. (1974), 153; K. H. D. Haley, *The First Earl of Shaftesbury* (Oxford UP, 1968), 648; R. L. Greaves, 'The Tangled Careers of two Stuart Radicals: Henry and Robert Danvers', *Baptist Quarterly*, 29 (1981), 38; Muddiman, 236–7; R. Ashcraft, *Revolutionary Politics and Locke's Two Treatises of Government* (Princeton UP, 1986), 347.

old, George Larkin, probably because Smith's warehouse was liable to be raided. Bunyan may have been trying to help Larkin, also a printer of unlicensed pamphlets: in 1668 he was prosecuted for his connection with the notorious *Advice to a Painter*. In 1682 Larkin printed *The Impartial Protestant Intelligencer*, an Exclusionist newspaper.[12]

In 1665 Bunyan had given *The Holy City* to J. Dover to print. This was no doubt Joan Dover, widow and successor of Simon Dover; Bunyan may have been making a gesture of solidarity with a victim of political persecution. Simon Dover had printed the speeches of the regicides, and many other seditious books. He had been convicted of seditious libel, heavily fined, pilloried, and imprisoned. He died in jail shortly afterwards, and his widow ('a common printer for all scandalous pamphlets') seems soon to have gone out of business (or died). Bunyan reverted to Smith for the second edition of *The Holy City* in 1669 (the first appeared with no printer's name) and for the third edition of *Grace Abounding* (between 1672 and 1674): no copy of the second edition survives, but Smith may have published that too. Nathaniel Ponder took over the fifth and sixth editions (1680, 1688). In 1673 Jonathan Robinson printed the first edition of *The Barren Fig-tree*, and John Wilkins *Differences in Judgment about Water Baptism*.[13]

In 1678, with Smith in permanent trouble and occupied with politics, Bunyan switched to another radical, Benjamin Harris, who printed *Come, and Welcome*. Between July 1679 and January 1679–80 Harris printed the Whig Exclusionist *Domestick Intelligence, Or News both from Court and Country*, continued as *The Protestant (Domestick) Intelligence* until mid-April 1681. He also printed a number of political ballads, broadsheets, and pamphlets. Harris was in continual trouble with the authorities. He was accused by Jeffreys in 1679 of publishing a book 'only designed to rake up all sedition and rebellion'. Lord Chief Justice Scroggs agreed about the book; and added, 'there is scarce any but Smith

[12] F. M. Harrison, *A Bibliography of the Works of John Bunyan* (Oxford UP, for the Bibliographical Soc., 1932), xx; Greaves, *Deliver Us from Evil* (Oxford UP, 1986), 212, 215, 221–5, 267; Brown, 228. For Larkin, see Michael Treadwell, 'A New List of English Master Printers, c.1686, *The Library*, 6th Ser. 4 (1982), 60.

[13] L. H. Silver, 'Bunyan's *Barren Fig-tree*', *The Library*, 5th Ser. 5 (1951), 61; C. E. Whiting, *Studies in English Puritanism 1660–1688* (1937), 551; N. Penney (ed.), *Extracts from State Papers relating to Friends, 1654 to 1672* (1913), 229–30. Joan Dover printed Fifth-Monarchist and Quaker books.

that is so factious a seller of books as Harris.' Harris was pilloried and fined the vast sum of £500. The jury tried to get him off by returning him guilty only of selling the book, but Scroggs overruled them. Harris's Case gets into the textbooks of constitutional history since in 1680 Scroggs laid it down that any book which was 'scandalous to the government' might be seized; and that no man had a right to publish without permission any matter bearing on government. In 1681 Harris was pilloried again; after 1685 he emigrated, first to the Netherlands, then to New England, where he published the first American newspaper. He was back in England by 1695, printing various newspapers. John Harris, who in 1685 printed Bunyan's *A Discourse upon the Pharisee and the Publican*, may have been Benjamin's son. He is said to have written a poem on Lord William Russell.[14]

Bunyan's principal publisher after 1678 was Nathaniel Ponder (1640–99). Ponder printed Part I of *The Pilgrim's Progress, Mr. Badman* in 1680, and Part II of *The Pilgrim's Progress* in 1684. Ponder too was a political and religious radical. His father had been in trouble with the ecclesiastical authorities as long ago as 1634; twenty-two years later he was a founder and first elder of the Rothwell (Northants) Independent church. Nathaniel Ponder had Bedfordshire connections, and in 1672 helped nonconformist ministers to procure licences, John Whitman to preach at the house of Bunyan's friend George Cokayne, Cotton End, Bedfordshire, for instance, and many in Northamptonshire and adjoining counties. Ponder married a gentleman's daughter, whose father Robert Guy and his son in 1677 purchased land at Northill, Bedfordshire. Nathaniel Ponder was the publisher of John Owen, who may have introduced him to Bunyan. Ponder published many nonconformist books and was imprisoned for printing Andrew Marvell's anonymous *The Rehearsal Transpros'd* in 1672 – the classically witty defence of the nonconformist position. Owen had been involved in printing and proof-reading Marvell's book: it would be agreeable to think that he introduced the two great satirists to one another. In 1676 Ponder was imprisoned for printing a seditious pamphlet without licence: he was discharged

---

[14] Harrison, *A Bibliography*, pp. xxii, xxiv; [Anon.], *A Short but Just Account of the Tryal of Benjamin Harris* (1679), 2–7; MW viii. 231; Muddiman, *The King's Journalist*, 250; Whiting, *Studies in English Puritanism*, 570–1; MW x. 107.

after paying fees and entering into a bond for £500. In 1682 he published Bulstrode Whitelocke's *Memorials*.[15]

For Bunyan Ponder printed *A Treatise of the Fear of God* (1679), *A Caution to Stir Up* (1684), *The Seventh-Day Sabbath* (1685), *A Book for Boys and Girls* (1686) and *The Water of Life* (1688), the fifth and sixth editions of *Grace Abounding* (1680 and 1688), and the third editions of *Law and Grace* and *One Thing is Needful* in 1683.[16] But Bunyan did not have the same steady relationship with Ponder that he had had with Smith. Perhaps Ponder just could not cope with the flow of works coming from Bunyan's pen in the 1680s. In 1682 *The Holy War* went to Dorman Newman and Benjamin Alsop (second edition Newman only, who also printed *The Advocateship of Jesus Christ* in 1688). Alsop printed four others of Bunyan's works in 1683–4. He too was a radical ('a wild sort of a spark') who published a eulogy on Shaftesbury's career in 1683, and went off to be a captain in Monmouth's army two years later. After 1685 he seems to have lived in exile in the Netherlands.[17]

So Bunyan employed the two most notorious radical printers of his day, Smith and Harris, and George Larkin, also a radical. Bunyan seems to have tried to help Simon Dover's widow. After 1678 Bunyan employed the nonconformist Ponder, who had also been in jail, and Ponder's former apprentice Benjamin Alsop, a Monmouth supporter. Only in the last six years of Bunyan's life – dangerous years – did he employ a relatively inoffensive printer like Dorman Newman; and he too was a nonconformist.[18]

Some have suggested that Bunyan dropped Smith as printer because he disliked the political extremism which the latter showed after 1679. But Smith had been deeply involved in oppositionist politics before Bunyan employed him, and Bunyan switched to Benjamin Harris, second only to Smith in political involvement. Professor McGee suggests, more plausibly, that Bunyan may have come to resent Smith's printing tracts

[15] Harrison, 'Nathaniel Ponder: The Publisher of *The Pilgrim's Progress*', *The Library*, 4th Ser. 15 (1934), 257–63, 282, 286–90; Marvell, *The Rehearsal Transpros'd*, p. xxiv; Brown, 248–9.

[16] Harrison, 'Nathaniel Ponder', 289–92; *GA*, p. xxxvi.

[17] Harrison, *A Bibliography*, xxiii–xxiv.

[18] Siebert, *Freedom*, 269; Harrison, *A Bibliography*, *passim*; Muddiman, *The King's Journalist*, 242–3; McKenzie, *Stationers' Company Apprentices*, 142. Newman may have had connections with the Wright family of printers (see p. 283). Joseph Wright was apprenticed to Dorman Newman in 1669 (ibid. 120).

advocating universal grace, and attacks on Bunyan himself by Thomas Paul, Henry Danvers, and John Denne.[19]

The evidence presented in this chapter suggests to me that Bunyan chose his printers *because* of their radicalism. Any other explanation would necessitate postulating a remarkable series of coincidences. Evidence from Bunyan's posthumous works given in chapter 26 may throw further light on the difficult problem of his attitude towards politics. Bunyan became quite well-informed about the technicalities of printing: he was not uninvolved here either.[20]

[19] J. S. McGee, Introduction to *Christian Behaviour*, MW iii. 3–5. I am very grateful to Professor McGee for allowing me to read this in advance of publication.

[20] See e.g. MW ix. 162, 359 n.

24. *The Palace Beautiful*

He that will keep water in a sieve must use more than ordinary
diligence.   BUNYAN[1]

THE Palace Beautiful in *The Pilgrim's Progress* represents the
separatist congregation. I have tried to suggest how highly
Bunyan valued the fellowship and mutual support of the Bedford
church, which he saw as a garden growing well-tended flowers in
good order. But these high expectations were not always realized.
How important was the exact manner in which the flowers were
planted? In *Mr. Badman* and in minutes of the congregation there
is much evidence of unsatisfactory professors; and *A Case of
Conscience Resolved* (1683) arose from controversies over the demand from women of the congregation for separate meetings. In
this chapter I want to look at three specific ways in which reality
diverged from the ideal.

i. Baptism and the Church

Ranterist: 'You make such a deal of do about water baptism as so needful,
that there may be no church fellowship held without it; but for ought I see
yet 'tis a matter of no such weight.'[2]

After Quakers and Latitudinarians Bunyan's third major controversy was with fellow-Baptists. Was adult baptism essential
before a saint could be admitted to the church? Many leading
'closed-communion' Baptists thought so. In 1673 Bunyan published *Differences in Judgment about Water Baptism, no Bar to
Communion, in answer to a book written by the Baptists and published by
Mr T. P[aul] and W. K[iffin]*. Henry Danvers associated himself
with the views of Paul and Kiffin. So did John Denne (son of Henry
Denne), who claimed that in this respect Bunyan was no better
than a Quaker: and indeed Bunyan had said, 'I walk according to
my light with God, otherwise 'tis false.' But Henry Denne, Dell,

---

[1] *Israel's Hope Encouraged* (posthumous), Offor, i. 619.
[2] Samuel Fisher, *Baby Baptism meer Babism* (1653), 491. Fisher, later a Quaker, was
still a Baptist in 1653. In his dialogue a 'Baptist' opposes the views of the 'Ranterist'.

Vavasor Powell, John Simpson, and John Saltmarsh agreed with Bunyan, as did John Gibbs of Newport Pagnell. Bunyan also claimed the support of Henry Jessey, who had died in 1663.[3]

Bunyan's impatience with forms and ceremonies is in full accord with the legacy of John Gifford, who urged church members 'not to be found guilty of this great evil, . . . separation from the church about baptism . . . or any external.' Bunyan could also have learnt dislike of 'doubtful disputations' concerning 'any judgment or opinion about externals' from Hobson's sermon at Newport Pagnell in 1645. In 1658, under Burton, John Crane was admitted to the church 'though differing in judgment about some outward things'. Bunyan clearly found this attitude congenial. He insisted that he never meddled 'with things that were controverted amongst the saints, especially things of the lowest nature' which 'neither in doing nor in leaving undone did commend us to God to be his.' And he added, with deliberate disrespect, 'there is no stinted order prescribed' for posture in prayer, whether 'kneeling, or standing, or walking, or lying or sitting'.[4]

Bunyan himself rejected the label 'Baptist', no doubt in part because of his unhappiness about the rigidity of 'closed-communion' Baptists. In *The Heavenly Foot-man*, probably written about this time, Bunyan warned against keeping 'too much company with some Anabaptists, though I go under that name myself'. In *A Confession of my Faith* (1672) he went further, saying that 'those titles of Anabaptists, Independents, Presbyterians or the like' came 'from hell and Babylon, for they naturally tend to divisions'. When the Bedford church took out its licence in 1672 it was as 'congregational'; not 'Baptist'. Other churches which historians pigeon-hole as Baptist did the same. Sectarian lines were not

---

[3] Henry Danvers, *Treatise of Baptism* (2nd. edn., 1674); John Denne, *Truth Outweighing Error* (1673), both quoted in R. L. Greaves, *Saints and Rebels: Seven Nonconformists in Stuart England* (Mercer UP, 1985), 169–70. See also id., 'The Tangled Careers of two Stuart Radicals: Henry and Robert Danvers', *Baptist Quarterly*, 29 (1981), 32–43; Dell, *Several Sermons and Discourses* (1709), 440–58; *GA*, 163; Greaves, *John Bunyan* (Abingdon, 1969), 138; id., 'John Bunyan's *The Holy War*', *Baptist Quarterly*, 26 (1975), 164; M. F. Hewett, 'John Gibbs, 1627–1699', 320. For Henry Denne see *Dictionary of Seventeenth-Century Radicals*.

[4] Tibbutt, *Minutes*, 19, 26; *GA*, 87; *The Pharisee and the Publican*, MW x. 221–3. Hobson contrasted 'external ordinances' with 'God in his ordinances' (*A Garden Inclosed*, 17).

yet fully drawn. Many churches traditionally called 'congregationalist' sheltered under the name 'Presbyterian' in 1672. As late
as 1766 the Bedford church still thought of itself as 'Independent'.[5]

In Bunyan's *Confession of my Faith, and a Reason of my Practice* he
declared: 'I dare not have communion with those that profess not
faith and holiness', or with the openly profane; but he could
communicate with visible saints who differed from him in judgment about water baptism. It was wrong to think that 'because in
time past baptism was administered upon conversion, that therefore it is the initiating and entering ordinance into church communion, when by the Word no such thing is testified of it.' 'It is
love, not baptism, that discovereth us to the world to be Christ's
disciples.' Disagreement on such subjects, he added significantly,
'greatly prevailed to bring down these judgments which at present
we feel and groan under' — i.e. persecution. Men are too 'wedded
to their own opinions', he declared in 1683: Presbyterians,
Independents, Anabaptists.[6]

Bunyan was himself baptized on admission to the church in
1655, but as early as *The Doctrine of Law and Grace Unfolded* (1659)
he declared that it was the spirit of blasphemy to say that there was
no ground for assurance of grace, or for church membership,
unless one was rightly baptized. He was properly contemptuous of
'comparing water baptism to a gentleman's livery, by which his
name is known to be his.' (Bishop Aylmer in Elizabeth's reign had
compared the surplice to 'the Queen's livery'.) In Part I of *The
Pilgrim's Progress* Christian was not baptized when he entered the
church; among the many afterthoughts in Part II is a concession to
baptism: Christiana and her children enter 'the bath of sanctification' after professing their faith at the House of the Interpreter.
This is balanced by the fact that Mercy is admitted to the wicket-
gate by its Keeper, Christ, even though she had received no
invitation from the King but only from Christiana. The Keeper of
the Gate reassures her, saying, 'I pray for all them that believe on
me, by what means soever they come unto me.'[7]

[5] MW v. 191; Tibbutt, *Minutes*, 203; cf. T. Richards, *Wales under the Indulgence*
(1928), 195–6, 203, 207.
[6] Offor, ii. 602–15; *A Holy Life* (1683), MW ix. 326–8; cf. *The Heavenly Foot-man*,
MW v. 151–3; See also *The Saints' Knowledge of Christ's Love* (posthumous), Offor, ii.
32 — against disagreements about the extent of Christ's love.
[7] *GA*, 171; MW ii. 182; *Differences in Judgment*, Offor, ii. 626, 635; W. Pierce, *An
Historical Introduction to the Marprelate Tracts* (1908), 78; *PP*, 189–90.

Protestantism had reduced the sacraments from seven to two. Bunyan (like the Quakers) minimized the significance even of these two 'ordinances', though communion remained the more significant. Baptism without walking in newness of life is pointless. The Holy Ghost *may* accompany the baptized in the very act of administering baptism; but it and other ordinances acquire significance through the fellowship of the congregation.[8]

The controversy became heated on both sides, especially when Kiffin sneered at Bunyan's lowly origins and ignorance. (Kiffin had been apprenticed to John Lilburne, later the Leveller leader: but he was by now a wealthy man. The story is told that he thought it cheaper to give Charles II £10,000 than to lend him the £40,000 for which the King had asked.) Bunyan retorted in kind. But it was really no time for internecine war among the saints; in the posthumous *House of the Forest of Lebanon* Bunyan insisted that recent contests in print among the godly, though to be deplored, were not about fundamentals. The Antichristian darkness had not so prevailed as to sever the saints from their head.[9]

We are dealing here partly with traditional protestant hostility to ceremonies: what matters is the motive of the heart, not the outward activity. But Gifford and Bunyan were stressing another point of principle, the right of the congregation to decide for itself who were qualified to join it, irrespective of any external circumstances whatsoever. 'The Lord's Supper, and not baptism, is for the church as a church.'[10] Baptism concerns the individual, not the church; participation in the Lord's supper is a duty of individuals to the church as a whole, part of the process by which flowers help one another to grow in the well-tended garden.

Although Bunyan never had any doubt about where he stood, the controversy pained him, especially the social sneers to which Kiffin resorted. It was further evidence of that inadequacy even of professors at which we shall be looking in section iii of this chapter.

---

[8] *A Holy Life* (1683), MW ix. 258–9; *The Desire of the Righteous Granted* (posthumous), Offor, i. 757; Greaves, *John Bunyan*, 137–43; Offor, ii. 524.

[9] Offor, iii. 244–5.

[10] My *Change and Continuity in Seventeenth-Century England* (1975), ch. 3; Offor, ii. 629–30; W. Urwick, *Bible Truth and Church Errors* (1888), ch. 5: 'John Bunyan not a Baptist', *passim* — the best treatment of this question.

ii. Bunyan and the Woman Question

Doubtless the woman was, in her first creation, made subordinate to her husband. Women therefore, when they would perk it and lord it over their husbands, ought to remember that both by creation and by transgression they are made to be in subjection to their husbands.[11]

Controversies over the opening of *The Pilgrim's Progress* must have brought home to Bunyan the existence of the woman question. But he cannot have been unaware of it previously. One of the most remarkable features of the 1640s had been the establishment of countless congregations outside the state church which controlled their own affairs democratically. In the more radical of these women played a part in church government. Some allowed women to speak in church, even to preach. Many women took upon themselves to prophesy, whether anyone authorized them or not. Women like Mary Cary and Anna Trapnel published on religious matters themselves: so did an eccentric like Lady Eleanor Davies.

Quakers were conspicuous in this area. Quaker women missionaries went on preaching tours in England, Europe, and America. St Paul's prohibition of women speaking in church presented problems. Ranters, Fox tells us, laughed it off by saying that Paul was referring to the Whore of Babylon, not to women in general. The Quakers' approach was subtler. Under the Law, women were not to usurp the authority of men. 'But Christ [is] in the male as in the female, who redeems from under the Law. . . . Christ in the male and female, who are in the spirit of God, are not under the Law.'[12] In the 1670s Quaker women's meetings were being organized all over England.

Baptist churches developed something of the same tolerant attitude. Even when women were not calling for the right to preach or to participate in the government of congregations, they were discussing religious matters in an unprecedented way. Bunyan's own introduction to the Bedford congregation came from hearing three or four poor women talking about the things of God; it was they who introduced him to Gifford. When in *The Pilgrim's Progress* the travellers come to the House Beautiful,

[11] Bunyan, *Genesis*, Offor, ii. 438.
[12] G.F., *The Great Mistery of the Great Whore Unfolded* (1659), 286. The point had been made by Mary Cole and Priscilla Cotton in 1655, apparently before Fox. I owe this information to the kindness of Valerie Drake.

virgins meet them and decide whether they may be admitted. In Bunyan's many changes in and rewriting of the reasons for the Pilgrim's precipitate departure from his family we may perhaps see evidence of pressure from, among others, women of the Bedford congregation.

Gifford's congregation started with 'twelve of the holy brethren and sisters' – two married couples, two men, and six single ladies. A list of early members gives ninety-five women out of a total of 142 – again a ratio of two to one. This preponderance of women seems to have continued, as it did in most separatist congregations. (As with Roman Catholic recusants, women may have acted for their menfolk, whose sympathy might not run to risking heavy fines.) When Quakers held a meeting at John Crook's house, Beckrings Park, in May 1659, they were opposed by 'one woman of Bunyan his congregation'.[13]

In 1663 Bunyan had quoted St Paul, 'I suffer not a woman to teach'. 'It is an unseemly thing', Bunyan commented, 'to see a woman as much as once in all her lifetime to offer to overtop her husband; she ought in everything to be in subjection to him.' He denied intending that 'women should be their husbands' slaves': 'the wife is master next her husband, and is to rule all in his absence.' This was the accepted view of the equality in subordination of the wife in the household economy. But in Bunyan's tract the duties of wives occupied twice as many pages as the duties of husbands. In a passage added to the second edition of *The Pilgrim's Progress*, Giant Despair is shown getting into difficulties because he failed to exercise male supremacy and actually listened to his wife's bad advice.[14]

Widows were in a more favourable position. They might be economically independent; if so they could escape from male tutelage until they remarried. In *A Discourse of the Building of the House of God* (1688) Bunyan gave an account of the church and its officers. After describing pastors, elders, and deacons, he mentions widows:

[13] *PP*, 349 n; Greaves, 'John Bunyan and Nonconformity in the Midlands and East Anglia', *Journal of the United Reformed Church History Soc.*, 1 (1976), 189–90; Patricia Bell, 'John Bunyan and Bedfordshire', in *The John Bunyan Lectures, 1978* (published by the Bedfordshire Education Service), 38–9; Tibbutt, *Minutes*, 84; id., 'John Crook', 115–16. See also K. V. Thomas's pioneering article, 'Women and the Civil War Sects', *P. and P.* 13 (1958).

[14] *Christian Behaviour* (1663), MW iii. 32–6, 26–8; *PP* 114–17.

> I dare not say they are in office, though
> A service here they are appointed to.

Their duty was 'to teach the younger women what / Is proper to their sex and state, what not', for which purpose 'they must be very aged'. 'Proper' meant:

> To be discreet, keepers at home, and chaste;
> To love their husbands, to be good, shame-faced;
> Children to bear, to love them.

Widows also looked after the sick.[15] Other separatist churches allotted similar 'services' to widows, sometimes less grudgingly than Bunyan.

A crisis seems to have occurred in the Bedford congregation in the early 1680s. The women of the congregation had apparently been holding separate meetings, we do not know for how long, until Bunyan came to think that such meetings 'lacked a bottom in the Word', and called them in question. He gave his reasons, backed by Scriptural authority ('as was but reason'); and 'so subject to the Word were our women', he tells us, that they gave up what could not be proved to be a duty. But in London a Mr K drew up a series of arguments justifying separate women's meetings, 'the rule for praying being so general to all'. This paper appears to have been distributed in Bedford among members of Bunyan's congregation: perhaps not all the women in it were 'subject to the Word' as defined by Bunyan.[16]

Bunyan was displeased with this interference in the affairs of his congregation, and in 1683 he published in answer to Mr K, *A Case of Conscience Resolved*, which he tactfully dedicated 'to those godly women concerned in the following treatise'. Bunyan protested that he accepted the spiritual equality of women with men. But he accused Mr K of 'flattery, in soothing up persons in a way of their own, by making of them the judges in their own cause'. Bunyan restated the question by asking whether, in a settled church, 'it is the duty of the women of that congregation, ordinarily and by appointment, to separate themselves from their brethren, and so to assemble together to perform some part of divine worship', such as prayer, 'without their men'.[17]

---

[15] *Poems*, 291.   [16] *A Case of Conscience Resolved* (1683), Offor, ii. 660–1.
[17] Ibid. 659, 661–2.

Initially Bunyan argued from Biblical texts, which gave him a good case. But then he generalized. 'To appoint meetings for divine worship either in the whole church or in parts of it, is an act of power.' This power belongs either to the elders (who were men) or to the whole church, not to the women separately. 'I do not believe they [women] should minister to God in prayer before the whole church, for then I should be a Ranter or a Quaker.' Even men are not allowed to do this until their qualifications have been approved by 'the elders or principal brethren'; much less women, 'of whom it must be supposed that they have received no such gifts that they should use this power.' 'Nor do I believe they should do it in their own womanish assembly.' Women 'are forbidden to teach, yea to speak in the church of God,' because of their inability to manage such worship. 'They are not the image and glory of God, as the men are (I Cor. XI. 7). They are placed beneath.' When Eve tried, 'she utterly failed in the performance, though she briskly attempted the thing.' Satan knew what he was doing when he assaulted Eve rather than Adam. 'The man was made the head in worship, and the keeper of the garden of God.' To hold meetings from which men are excluded 'is an usurping of authority over them': more so if the elders are excluded.[18] Whether Bunyan knew it or not, the 'disorderly' women's meetings organized by Mrs Anne Hutchinson in Boston in the 1630s had led to a crisis of power which rocked the colony.

Bunyan's is a remarkably explicit assertion of male ascendancy, which had been challenged in New England and during the revolutionary decades in England. In the conservative atmosphere of the later seventeenth century such challenges were slowly overcome: Bunyan was swimming with the tide. Even Quaker women, who succeeded where those of Bunyan's congregation failed, found that women's meetings came to be left with social and charitable functions, but with none of the 'power' that Bunyan had feared.

Nevertheless the problem was still bothering him in his post-humous *Exposition on . . . Genesis*, where he speaks of women as 'that simple and weak sex'. 'The man that suffereth his wife to take his place, hath already transgressed the order of God.' 'Such a thing may happen, so that the woman, not the man, may be in the

[18] Ibid. 659–66.

right (I mean, when both are godly), but ordinarily it is otherwise.'
Preaching has to do with men; prayer has to do with men and with
God. 'We put not the weak upon this service'; some men even may
be too weak for it. 'Modesty and shame-facedness becomes women
at all times, especially in time of public worship.' Why women
more than men? 'In remembrance of the fall of Eve.' Separate
women's meetings 'manifest the unruliness of such women', and
are 'a shame and blemish to those churches which permit them.'
'Women are not to be blamed for that they are forward to pray to
God,' Bunyan conceded: 'I wish that idleness in men be not the
cause of their putting their good women upon this work.' The
explanation had been anticipated by a critic of women preachers in
1641: they preached only because 'there was a deficiency.'[19]

Bunyan realized that by taking this attitude he was 'like enough
to run the gauntlet among [women] and to partake most smartly of
the scourge of the tongues of some.' Perhaps his most dismissive
remark came in *The Advocateship* (1688). Here he says that under
'little children, fathers and young men' are comprehended 'all
men' (1 John ii. 12–14). He is discussing 'the children of God', and
appears to include both sexes.[20]

Professor McGee suggests that William Gouge, like Bunyan,
came under criticism from women for over-emphasizing the
obedience they owed to husbands. This was in his *Of Domesticall
Duties* (1622). The 1626 edition added the duties of husbands to
those of wives.[21]

There are echoes of this controversy in Part II of *The Pilgrim's
Progress*. Here Bunyan makes some amends. Women are the
leading characters in the book, their salvation is the issue. Gaius, in
an elaborate speech 'on the behalf of women', insists that 'as death
came into the world by a woman, so also did life and health.'
Almost all the women sing and play musical instruments. But they
are not equal to men. Only men, apparently, have burdens; only
women, it appears, have to wash at the Interpreter's House—
though this innovation may be a by-product of controversies on
the necessity of baptism for church members. The Interpreter
takes the women into a room where they can see living emblems

---

[19] *Genesis*, Offor, ii. 431, 438–9; *A Case of Conscience*, ibid. ii. 665, 673–4;
[Anon.], *A Discovery of Six Women Preachers* (1641), 1–5. I owe this reference to
Valerie Drake.

[20] Offor, ii. 660; MW xi. 145–6.   [21] MW iii. xxix.

like a hen and chickens. 'You are women, and they are easy for you.' The qualities of Mercy and Christiana are extolled. Yet they have to be rescued from perils by a Reliever, who is surprised that they did not petition the Lord for a male conductor through the dangers of the way. This (as Sharrock suggests) is a broad hint that they have overestimated their powers, perhaps as the women of the Bedford congregation had done in 1682–3. They need a man. Men in fact come to monopolize the action as well as the conversations. Women belong to men. Before his set-piece eulogy on women, Gaius had asked, 'Whose wife is this aged matron? and whose daughter is this young damsel?' The question is directed to the man, who is held responsible for the women who accompany him. Women are identified by their male owners and protectors. It is Gaius who takes the initiative in the series of precipitate marriages of Christiana's sons which follows. To challenge this hierarchy would raise, as Bunyan rightly saw, questions of *power*—an unusually frank recognition of the realities of sexual conflict.[22]

The point was made in the case of Agnes Beaumont in 1674. Bunyan's name was associated with hers in local gossip, apparently without any cause, at least on his side. Agnes may have had a crush on her pastor. She offended against the stern requirements of female subordination by going to hear Bunyan preach, with only the most grudging permission from her father. When her arrangements for getting to the meeting broke down, Bunyan refused to give her a lift on his horse until her brother had mediated strongly on her behalf. Bunyan no doubt knew of the father's attitude, but in his absence the brother was the man responsible for her. Agnes Beaumont's father was furious, but was too late to stop her. He shut her out of the house when she came home late at night. Four days later he inconveniently died, and Agnes was accused of murdering him. It seemed a natural consequence of her insubordination; she was lucky to be acquitted.[23]

Interesting is Bunyan's immediate assumption that only Quakers and Ranters allowed women to lead prayers before the whole church. How much did such subversion of degree and male supremacy have to do with his deep-seated hostility to Ranters and

[22] *PP*, 196, 202, 207, 212, 259–61, 313–14; cf. 220, and Sharrock, *Casebook*, 180.
[23] G. B. Harrison (ed.), *The Narrative of the Persecution of Agnes Beaumont in 1674* (n.d.), *passim*.

Quakers? As late as 1696 Sister Bar of Blunham was claiming 'a
spirit of prophecy', though after persuasion by the congregation
she abandoned it.[24] There was still something to alarm men.

Women play a very small part in Bunyan's voluminous writings.
In *The Holy War* no women come alive as characters. They exist
only to be ravished (204, 209), to sing and play tabors and timbrels
(109, 149, 223), or in order to establish the pedigree of Diabolonians (242–3). Yet Bunyan can reproduce a mother's baby-talk
with what sounds like accuracy (127). But we should not sentimentalize: the baby she was dandling, Falsepeace, became an evil
character. *The Holy War* is often associated with the chivalric
romances, but the love interest which is an essential part of their
tradition is completely missing.

In Part I of *The Pilgrim's Progress* Christiana exists only to be
deserted, Giant Despair's wife only to give bad advice to her
husband, who wrongly defers to her. Some female allegorical
personifications – Prudence and the like – minister to the male
pilgrims. Bunyan has much to say about marriage in *Mr. Badman*,
most of it pretty conventional. No one should marry an unbeliever – i.e. someone outside the sect. Children should not
marry without the advice of their elders, and girls should certainly
not trust their 'own poor, raw, womanish judgment'.[25] Mr. Badman's two marriages are purely economic transactions. In Part II
of *The Pilgrim's Progress* the marriages which Gaius rather perfunc-
torily arranges were no more love matches than those in *Mr.
Badman*. Their object was 'to preserve . . . a posterity in the earth'
to Christiana, and 'for the increase of the church' (260–1, 311).

Women fared no better in *Grace Abounding*. Bunyan's first wife
is mentioned, though briefly, and the three or four poor women in
the sun play an important though asexual role. Bunyan's account of
his second wife's intervention on his behalf with the judges is the
only positive role given to a woman in all his writings. That comes
in *A Relation of my Imprisonment*, which he never published. Here
he contrasts sharply with Milton. We think of the Lady who is the
heroine of *Comus*, of Eve and Dalilah. There are curious passages
in Bunyan's *Come, and Welcome, to Jesus Christ* (1678), where
Bunyan compares the love of Christ to love for a girl. In the
posthumous *The House of the Forest of Lebanon* he asked, 'Who that

shall meet . . . a comely and delicate woman . . . in a wood, unless he feared God, but would seek to ravish and defile her?'[26]

Bunyan seems never to have been wholly at ease with women. He replied angrily, and with considerable agitation, to accusations of promiscuity. (Paragraphs 301–17 of *Grace Abounding* were inserted in the third edition, probably after and because of rumours about Bunyan and Agnes Beaumont.) God had made him 'shy of women' from his 'first conversion until now'. (We can read what significance we please into that chronological reservation.) He hotly denied 'having carnally to do with any woman save my wife', though earlier he had claimed to be 'the very ringleader of all the youth . . . in all manner of vice and ungodliness . . . until I came to the state of marriage.' 'It is a rare thing to see me carry it pleasant towards a woman. . . . Their company alone, I cannot away with'. Bunyan no doubt protests too much, but he does seem to have been more at home with the male comradeship of the open road, or with the elders of the church. This would account for his 'roughness' and apparent insensitivity towards Agnes Beaumont. Or perhaps he was not in general very sociable. In *Grace Abounding* he speaks of God as a remedy against loneliness. The essence of conversion was that it separated the saint off from other men. Bunyan had specifically to insist in *The Jerusalem Sinner* (posthumous) that ministers should mix socially with worldlings, to the advantage of the latter.[27]

Robert Burton had anticipated Bunyan in finding the clothes women wore more provocative than nakedness would have been. Mr. Wiseman's denunciation of contemporary fashions of dress in *Mr. Badman* is also not original, though vividly expressed: 'their naked shoulders, and paps hanging out like a cow's bag.' The rhyme 'giggle . . . wriggle' in relation to 'the way of wantons with a maid' is perhaps revealing. On the other hand Bunyan seems to have done his best to help a woman who came to ask his advice when he was in Bedford jail.[28]

---

[26] *Come, and Welcome*, MW viii. 345–6, 349–50; Offor, iii. 522–3; cf. *The Desire of the Righteous Granted* (posthumous), Offor, i. 757.

[27] *GA*, 7, 90–7; MW xi. 81.

[28] Burton, *Anatomy of Melancholy* (Everyman edn.), iii. 8–9; *A Book for Boys and Girls, Poems*, 213–14; *Mr. B.*, Offor, iii. 645, 610. See pp. 121–2 above.

iii. 'Prayerless Professors'

You shall not by all your skill drive this love farther than the mouth. For with their mouth they show much love, but their heart goeth after their covetousness.[29]

In the controversies over open or closed communion (i. above), Bunyan and his church insisted on the right of the congregation to satisfy itself that an applicant for admission was in a state of grace: outward circumstances like baptism were of minor significance. Christ came to save sinners, not the merely morally righteous. But the congregation could err in its estimate of visible saints: in 1665 Bunyan was emphasizing the difficulty of discriminating between the elect and hypocrites. So members had to be kept continually up to the high standards demanded. Bunyan's criticisms of the worldliness and hypocrisy of the godly became increasingly harsh. As early as 1656 he observed that the foolishness of most professors must be a sign of the last times. Next year, recognizing that 'the pride, covetousness and impiety of hypocrites and carnal professors are great stumbling blocks to the poor world,' he had castigated disagreements among the saints about 'smaller matters'. *The Barren Fig-tree* (1673) is subtitled 'The Doom and Downfall of the Fruitless Professor'. Such professors are guilty of 'pride, ambition, gluttony', and many other sins. They 'make religion their cloak and Christ their stalking-horse'. Their prosperity is no sign of God's favour.[30]

Brown suggested that Mr. Badman recalls John Wildman, who joined the Bedford church in 1669 and was in continual trouble for lying and slandering. Expelled in 1683, he was still trying to get readmitted seventeen years later. But he was by no means the only backslider. Other church members were guilty — of selling 'deceivable goods', failing to pay debts, being 'drunk above the ordinary rate of drunkenness', brawling with neighbours, wife-beating ('often for very light matters'), fornication, scandal-mongering; women were reprehended for various forms of immodest sexual behaviour.[31] I gave examples in chapter 19.

In *Christian Behaviour* (1663) Bunyan reported having 'heard

---

[29] Bunyan, *A Holy Life* (1683), MW ix. 258.
[30] *A Vindication*, MW i. 126–7; *Some Gospel-truths*, MW i. 85; v. 9, 20, 30, 50, 62–3, and *passim*; cf. *Paul's Departure and Crown* (posthumous), Offor, i. 733.
[31] Brown, 193, 304–6; Tibbutt, *Minutes*, 17, 40, 63–86, 88–90, 121–2.

some poor servants say that in some carnal families they have had more liberty to God's things, and more fairness of dealing, than among professors. But this stinketh!' The sins of professors include 'a headstrong and stiff-necked spirit that will have its own way', more talk about religion than action; covetousness, pride, and licentiousness. Thirteen years later *The Strait Gate* was directed especially against professors, their formalism, their hypocrisy, their increasing willingness to compromise with the world around them. 'But few of them that profess have been saved,' Bunyan thought. He denounced 'the swarms of our prayerless professors', who wear 'religion only for a holiday suit . . . when they come among suitable company'. They 'hang it on the wall all the week, and put it on on Sunday'. The sin against the Holy Ghost 'feedeth upon professors'.[32]

In *The Heavenly Foot-man* Bunyan asked, 'Do you think every heavy-heeled professor will have heaven? . . . That scarce runneth so fast heavenwards as a snail creepeth on the ground?' 'Would you not say that such a man would be in danger of losing, though he run, if he fill his pockets with stones, hang heavy garments on his shoulders, and great lumpish shoes on his feet?' 'How froward, how hasty, how peevish and self-resolved are the generality of the professors at this day?'[33] Bunyan's later writings dwell ever more insistently on the dangers of prosperity for professors. 'Who is prouder than you professors?' a scoffer asked in *Mr. Badman*; and Mr. Wiseman admitted the justice of the implication. 'Let them grow full and rich' was Lucifer's counsel for ending Mansoul's resistance. Many in the town were allied to Self-love, and 'some . . . muttered' when Mr. Self-denial insisted on his summary execution.[34]

In *Come, and Welcome* (1678) Bunyan warned against a stereotype of conversion and *A Treatise of the Fear of God* (1680) concludes with 'A Word to Hypocrites'. Mr. Badman taunted his first wife with the pride of her religious companions, 'these slithy, rob-shop, pick-pocket men', who 'make profession a stalking-

---

[32] MW iii. 32, 44–6; MW v. 82, 84, 89, 99; cf. 69, 78, 83, 85, 90, 92–4, 103, 111–12, 119, 124, 127. On p. 89 'saint' should read 'suit'. Milton had made a similar jibe in *Areopagitica* thirty years earlier (*MCPW*, ii. 544–5).

[33] MW v. 149, 154–5, 161.

[34] *Mr. B.*, Offor, iii. 644; cf. *A Treatise of the Fear of God* (1680), MW ix. 27; *HW* 216–17, 244, 112.

horse to sin'. 'What are professors more than other men?' Bunyan asked in *A Book for Boys and Girls*; and he replied 'Nothing at all'. They cackle like a hen that has laid an egg.[35]

Bunyan's most prolonged indictment is in *A Holy Life* (1683). 'A great many professors have nothing to distinguish themselves from the worst of men except praying, reading, hearing sermons, baptism and communion.' 'They pinch the poor and nip from them their due', in order to maintain their own pride and vanity. 'But, says one, would you have us singular? and says another, would you have us make ourselves ridiculous?' 'What care I for my servant? I took him to do my work, not to train him up in religion'. God, Bunyan continued, is angry with England because of the sins of 'the swarms of professors . . . in every corner of the land', who are infected by the iniquity of the last times, 'horribly tainted with pride and covetousness (I exclude not the ministers, nor their families). Better open profane than a hypocritical naming of the name of Christ.' The emblems shown to the pilgrims in the Interpreter's House mostly deal with sins of this kind. The subject was on Bunyan's mind. In *Advice to Sufferers* (1684) Bunyan noted acutely that 'many, in a time of trouble for their profession, will study more to deceive themselves by a change of notions . . . than they will to make straight steps for their feet.' They care more about their property than about eternal life.[36]

'Even prayers may be performed with great hypocrisy', Bunyan insisted in *The Pharisee and the Publican* (1685). Nor were these just the failings of individuals: there had been a national degeneracy from the achievements and hopes of the past. Bunyan looked back nostalgically to the Puritans and the Marian martyrs. Jerusalem, once 'the place and seat of God's worship', was 'now . . . degenerated and apostatized'. It had become 'the shambles, the very slaughter-shop for saints', in which 'the prophets, Christ and his people, were most horribly persecuted and murdered'. Persecution may be caused by professors having forsaken the covenant, sinning against the light. 'Alas! We are a company of worn-out Christians.' 'Grace in the most of us is decayed.' The

[35] MW viii. 354–5; ix. 130–2; Offor, iii. 632; *Poems*, 248, 253–4.

[36] MW ix. 254–60, 281, 283, 290, 296–7, 307–8, 317–18, 323, 329, 342; MW x. 14–15; cf. 6, 58, 101; cf. also *Solomon's Temple Spiritualized* (1688), Offor, iii. 484, 489, and *Christ a Complete Saviour* (posthumous), Offor, i. 238. Note the word 'notions' again: ungrounded opinions.

young in particular are 'debauched' and 'profane to amazement'. This was perhaps a sign that the Second Coming was approaching. 'This twenty years', he wrote in *Of Antichrist and his Ruin*, 'we have been degenerating, both as to principles and as to practice; and have grown at last into an amazing likeness to the world, both as to religion and civil demeanour.' For this we cannot blame kings and governors, but only ourselves.[37]

In the treatises which Bunyan left unfinished at his death, criticism of the inadequacies of the formal godly intensified. 'As the empty barrel maketh the biggest noise', so 'great flocks of such professors . . . are full of air, full of emptiness, and that is all.'[38] 'The cold formal professor' was denounced in *The Desire of the Righteous Granted*, professors 'with itching ears' in *Paul's Departure and Crown*. 'Wicked men learn to be wicked of professors.' This last point was repeated in *The Saints' Knowledge of Christ* ('the profane do learn to be vile of those that profess') and in *Christ a Complete Saviour* ('sleeping professors' pay more attention to 'a twopenny customer' than to God). *Israel's Hope Encouraged* also remarked on 'the offensive lives and conversations of some that are professors.' 'Presumptuous professors' are guilty of pride, hypocrisy, pretences, 'self-seekings of commendations and applause'. They 'take care to shift for themselves . . . when they see the storm a-coming.'[39] It is the combination of persecution with the possibilities of worldly enrichment that caused the damage.

Some dissenters even ape aristocratic manners. 'Saints that are rich', Bunyan noted in the posthumous *Christ a Complete Saviour*, 'have got the poor and beggarly art of complimenting.' Some professors even 'take a great pet against that foundation of salvation', the doctrine of predestination. Many a professor, 'whose heart was never truly broken', was not 'so easily convinced that his righteousness is to God abominable as he is that his debauchery and profaneness is.' 'Professors cause the enemies of God to

[37] MW x. 128–34; cf. 205–6; *A Holy Life*, MW ix. 260, 290, 345; cf. *Israel's Hope Encouraged* (posthumous), Offor, i. 588; *The Jerusalem Sinner* (1688), MW xi. 14–15, 26, 47–8; *The Advocateship of Jesus Christ* (1688), MW xi. 99; *Of Antichrist and his Ruin* (posthumous), Offor, ii. 45. 'Twenty years' would suggest that *Of Antichrist* was written in the early '80s.

[38] MW v. 149, 161; *The Acceptable Sacrifice*, Offor, i. 718–19; ibid. i. 765–6, 722–3, 739–40.

[39] Offor, ii. 38; i. 214, 238, 587–8, 619–20; cf. 617, and *The House in the Forest of Lebanon*, Offor, iii. 535.

blaspheme.' 'They are as an open sepulchre, as full of dead men's bones. Their minds and consciences are defiled; how then can sweet and good proceed from thence? Their throat is filled with this stink; all their vocal duties therefore smell thereof . . .'[40]

This gloomy conclusion may be the consequence of Bunyan's closer acquaintance with London in the later years of his life, at a time when some dissenters (like William Kiffin) were indeed prospering to such an extent that they were becoming financially indispensable to governments. Persecution ceased less from principle than from interest.[41] Mr. Worldly Wiseman was added to the second edition of *The Pilgrim's Progress*.

But there were no doubt similar tendencies among the members of Bunyan's Bedford congregation. What Bunyan is describing worried all nonconformist sects. His jeremiad, like that of contemporary New England clergy, looked back sadly to an age which had looked forward with hope and confidence. As the millennium receded, the intense pressure of the quest for salvation eased off: pacifism succeeded militancy. Jerusalem's heroic days were over. As persecution nevertheless intensified, the congregations had to concentrate on survival. They could not afford to offend too many of their members who found it necessary to attend to worldly affairs. So for two quite different reasons the light of common day closed in upon them. The religion of the second generation was inevitably more formal, more concerned with conduct, with external appearances. John Goodwin, poles apart from Bunyan in theology, nevertheless echoed him when he spoke of 'the usual drowsiness, dullness or formality of old professors.'[42] The sting is in the word 'usual'. Dissent, it has been said, found victory in defeat after 1660, and defeat in victory after 1689, when there was no longer even persecution.

So the congregation did not entirely fulfil Bunyan's hopes for a

---

[40] Offor, i. 213; *Israel's Hope Encouraged*, ibid. i. 600; cf. 619–20; *The Acceptable Sacrifice* (posthumous), ibid. i. 718–19; *Paul's Departure and Crown* (posthumous), ibid. i. 439–40; *Justification by an Imputed Righteousness* (posthumous), ibid. i. 308; cf. *The Saints' Knowledge of Christ's Love* (posthumous), ibid. ii. 38.

[41] G. S. de Krey, *A Fractured Society: The Politics of London in the First Age of Party, 1688–1715* (Oxford UP, 1985), esp. 106–12.

[42] Goodwin, *A Being Filled with the Spirit*, 103 (1st pub. (posthumously) 1670). I quote from the reprint of 1867. Cf. Cragg, *Puritanism in the Period of the Great Persecution, 1660–1688* (Cambridge UP, 1957), 256–8.

garden of self-nourishing flowers. But although 'the Antichristian darkness' caused contentions among the godly, 'Antichrist could never divide them' about major matters.[43] Similarly the aspirations of women could be slapped down, because the whole drift of social development was unfavourable to them. But if the salt of the earth lost its savour? The moral laxity of the godly was contrasted with the achievements of the saints during the revolutionary decades, magnified no doubt in retrospect. Bunyan had devoted his life to awakening the godly, preparing for the rule of the saints; and now the saints were revealed as unfit to rule. The effects of this failure must have been devastating for him. The most poignant moment in *The Holy War* comes when the petitioners from Mansoul urge Emanuel to 'put no trust in his saints'.[44] It is difficult for us to conceive what it must have cost Bunyan to write those words. Wesley's observation that godliness begets industry and industry begets wealth which begets ungodliness has become a commonplace. Wesley learnt it the hard way. But for Bunyan, three generations earlier, it was a shattering reversal of his profoundest hopes. We must bear in mind his despair at the failure of professors when we come to consider his attitude towards James II. Desperate situations might call for desperate remedies.

[43] *The House of the Forest of Lebanon* (posthumous), Offor, iii. 524–5.
[44] *HW*, 112.

25. *Kings and Antichrist: Seeming Delays*

> The spirit of grace shall spring up in *some* that are great and mighty
> as well as in *many* that are poor and low.   BUNYAN[1]
>
> The leading men thought they were sure of the nation so long as
> popery was in view.   G. BURNET[2]
>
> Let the good Christian . . . not fret at seeming delays.
>   BUNYAN[3]

IT has been suggested that Bunyan from 1678 or thereabouts was mellowing, becoming more tolerant. He was certainly anxious to minimize disputes among the godly, and to establish broader unity among protestants; but this must be seen in the perspective of his growing fears of persecution, whether by papists or by the Anglican establishment and the Bedfordshire gentry. The international situation was becoming increasingly ominous. James's accession in February 1685 was followed in June by the passing of the Palatinate to a Roman Catholic family. The Elector Palatine and his wife, James I's daughter, had symbolized international protestantism in Bunyan's youth. In October 1685 Louis XIV revoked the Edict of Nantes, and Huguenot refugees flocked into England. Two months later the Duke of Savoy withdrew toleration from the Vaudois, who had been the focus of protestant sympathy in the mid-1650s, when Milton wrote his sonnet on those who kept the truth so pure of old, 'when all our fathers worshipped stocks and stones'. All the time Habsburg persecution of Hungarian protestants was continuing.

Bunyan showed his awareness of the threat to European protestantism in *Advice to Sufferers* (1684) and *The Pharisee and the Publican* (1685). But he had never seen Antichrist specifically in foreign policy terms, as for instance Fifth Monarchists and George Fox had done in the 1650s. A change had come with the Popish Plot of 1678. 'Then we began to fear cutting of throats,' Bunyan wrote, 'of being burned in our beds, and of seeing our children

---

[1] *PP*, Pt. II, 231. Italics in the original.
[2] *The History of My Own Time*, ed. O. Airy (Oxford UP, 1897), i. 266: discussing 1680.
[3] *The Pharisee and the Publican* (1685), MW x. 114.

dashed in pieces before our faces.' Yet he was reassured (so he said) to find that 'we had a gracious King, brave Parliaments, a stout City, good Lord Mayors, honest sheriffs, substantial laws against them.' The graciousness of the King was due to the 'brave Parliaments' and to the Lord Mayors and sheriffs elected after 1679. But the demonstration of protestant sentiment was impressive. The Bedford church started to hold regular meetings again in 1681–3. In December 1681 they decided that they would keep the first Thursday of every month to beg (among other things) 'the mercy and blessing of God upon the King and governors'.[4]

Bunyan probably sympathized with the Whig attempt to exclude the papist Duke of York from the succession. After its failure the Duke of Monmouth, the rival claimant, took temporary refuge from politics in his mistress's Bedfordshire house. In the absence of Parliaments Charles II initiated a purge of Whigs and nonconformists from local government, which left the Tory gentry in control. Hardly any meetings of the Bedford congregation are recorded between August 1684 and December 1686. Since for Bunyan all persecution was Antichristian, the ecclesiastical authorities and some at least of the gentry must have seemed to him to be acting as Antichrist's agents.[5] In Part II of *The Pilgrim's Progress* Giant Maul (persecution) is far more dangerous than Giant Pope in Part I.

After 1681 there were no more 'brave Parliaments', and the 'stout City' no longer had 'honest sheriffs', as Shaftesbury found to his cost. It was impossible for nonconformists not to have views about politics at this period. Recent research by Richard Greaves and Richard Ashcraft has shown that plots against the regimes of Charles II and James II were far more continuous than used to be thought, and that far more nonconformists were involved in them.[6]

Ashcraft suggests that Charles II pursued a consistent and persistent policy, from at least the Secret Treaty of Dover in 1670. Here he undertook to proclaim himself a Catholic, which 'would

---

[4] Offor, ii. 702, 220–1; *Israel's Hope Encouraged* (posthumous), Offor, i. 585; Tibbutt, *Minutes*, 85–8.

[5] MW ix. xxiv; Brown, 330; *HW*, 275; *PP*, 244–5.

[6] R. L. Greaves, *Deliver Us from Evil* (Oxford UP, 1986), *passim*; R. Ashcraft, *Revolutionary Politics and Locke's Two Treatises of Government* (Princeton UP, 1986), *passim*.

provide the ideological foundation for the English monarchy as an absolutist institution'. War against the Netherlands, in alliance with France, would promote England's colonial trade, and give Charles the opportunity to build up an army and extend his control over the militia. The King used the royal prerogative to enforce the Stop of the Exchequer, in order to provide funds for this war, and to grant indulgence to Roman Catholic and protestant dissenters. All of these actions could be seen as setting England on course towards absolutism and arbitrary rule.[7]

Dissenters were doubly involved in these plans. 'Only a very considerable expansion in trade could improve the government's revenues to the point where it might escape . . . indebtedness.' But, as a House of Lords committee on trade reported in 1669, 'some ease and relaxation in ecclesiastical matters will be a means of improving the trade of this kingdom' – a view supported by Locke. Shaftesbury thought that protestantism in England would be safe only if protestant dissenters were tolerated.[8] James II had other plans. Toleration would help to increase trade; rising customs and excise revenue would make the government financially independent and so in a position to promote Catholicism as a basis for absolute rule.

Dissenters were thus faced with choices. Acceptance of toleration by prerogative, against the wishes of Parliament, would give instant relief but might in the long run lead to Roman Catholic absolutism by splitting the protestants. In 1662 and 1672 dissenters had accepted Charles II's Declarations of Indulgence. But fears of a Popish successor led to the Popish Plot, the Rye House Plot, Argyll's and Monmouth's invasions: many dissenters supported Shaftesbury in 1678–82, some rallied to Monmouth in 1685. Others feared the prospects of a new civil war and revolution. The hard core of plotters, in exile in the Netherlands, included former Levellers like John Wildman as well as nonconformists; their objectives were political as well as religious. In the 1680s Anglicans and many dissenters in England preached nonresistance. 'Private men must keep within their own bounds, and follow their own employments,' declared a preacher before the Lord Mayor of London in October 1682. Bunyan came near to

[7] Ashcraft, Revolutionary Politics, 37–8; cf. 28–9.
[8] Ibid. 31, 34, 104, 119–20; cf. 230.

echoing those sentiments.[9] By 1687 James's policy had split and confused the dissenters.

Ashcraft suggests that Bunyan's friend John Owen, whose City congregation consisted largely of traders and merchants, was more closely involved with radical Whig conspiracy than had previously been thought. In the 1670s his assistant preacher and intimate friend was Robert Ferguson, 'the Plotter'. Ferguson had been arrested in 1663, and subsequently conspired successively with Shaftesbury and the Exclusionists, the Rye House plotters, and the Duke of Monmouth. Ferguson referred to Owen as a 'great and incomparable man'. Probably through Ferguson and the Duke of Buckingham (one of Owen's patrons) Owen became known to Shaftesbury and other Whig leaders. He kept up a correspondence with Ferguson in 1682–3 when the latter was in exile with Shaftesbury in the Netherlands. Owen was alleged later to have known of and supported the Rye House Plot.[10]

Another conspirator was Matthew Meade, a Bedfordshire man from Leighton Buzzard who was ordained by John Owen. Bunyan almost certainly preached at his Stepney church: the Bedford congregation had close relations with Meade's. Meade had been under surveillance in 1661 as one of the 'chief ringleaders' of dissatisfaction among London dissenters. He soon fled to exile in the Netherlands. He was back by 1669, and in 1683 – whilst trying to escape from England – he was arrested on suspicion of complicity in the Rye House Plot. Two years later Monmouth expected Meade to raise dissenters in London and Wapping; after the defeat of Monmouth's rising Meade fled to the Netherlands again.[11]

It is then hard to distinguish between those who were and were not involved in plots, as witness the career of George Cokayne (pp. 96–8 above); and it was difficult for any dissenter to avoid connections with men directly implicated in revolutionary politics, as we saw when we considered Bunyan's printers. Henry

---

[9] Samuel Freeman, *A Sermon*, 20–3; Ashcraft, *Revolutionary Politics* 292. For Bunyan see pp. 328–9 below.

[10] Ashcraft, *Revolutionary Politics*, 55, 74, 112–13, 369; D. D. Wallace, *Puritans and Predestination: Grace in English Protestant Theology, 1525–1695* (N. Carolina UP, 1982), 168.

[11] Charles Doe, 'The Struggler', Offor, iii. 766–7; Tindall, 211; Tibbutt, *Minutes*, 92; P. Earle, *Monmouth the Rebel: The Road to Sedgmoor, 1685* (1977), 65; Ashcraft, *Revolutionary Politics*, 366, 369, 436, 471.

Newcome, a Presbyterian divine, far more conservative than Owen or Bunyan, sheltered and helped Robert Ferguson in 1683, when he was on the run after the Rye House Plot. On the other side, republicans may have read Bunyan. Henry Neville in 1681 said, 'not the Giant Popery itself shall ever be able to stand before a Parliament.'[12] At that date the reference is likely to have been to *The Pilgrim's Progress*. There is no evidence to connect Bunyan with any revolutionaries. But it is not easy to be certain exactly where he stood, if he ever had a clearly defined position. Circumstances changed rapidly, and ideas had perforce to follow.

Bunyan may indeed have considered co-operation with James II. Tindall thought that Bunyan's reference to the role of kings in *Of Antichrist and his Ruin* was 'merely politic'. But I think it was more complicated than that. Bunyan stated traditional protestant doctrine. Martin Bucer had seen Edward VI, Henry Barrow had seen Elizabeth, as the ruler who would destroy Antichrist. Napier, Helwys, and Bussher allotted the role to James I; Henry Burton, even less plausibly, to his son. Arthur Dent had announced in 1603 that 'the kings of Europe shall overthrow Rome' — though perhaps the Turks might help.[13] Bunyan's writings of the 1650s, and the pronouncements of the Bedford congregation at that time, make it clear that he started with no prepossessions in favour of monarchy. But the overwhelming providence of 1660 had to be accepted as God's will. The sensational events of 1649 had similarly converted William Sedgwick into an enthusiastic supporter of the Army as God's instrument.[14] It was not only Puritans who accepted a providential view of history. A group of theorists, including John Dury, Anthony Ascham, and Marchamont Nedham, argued in 1649–51 that a government securely in power *de facto* must be accepted as ordained of God. Hobbes's version was more secular: the only thing that matters about a government is its ability to protect its subjects: questions of legitimacy or divine right are irrelevant to this overriding consideration. Such arguments induced many royalists to recognize the Commonwealth and Protectorate; after 1660 they helped former supporters of the republic to accept the strange dispensation of the restoration.

[12] Newcome, *Autobiography*, ed. R. Parkinson (Chetham Soc., 1852), 249–50; Neville, *Plato Redivivus*, in *Two English Republican Tracts*, ed. C. Robbins (Cambridge UP, 1969), 132.

[13] Tindall, 271; Dent, *The Ruine of Rome*, 259; Burton, *The Seven Vials* (1628), 102.

[14] See my *The Experience of Defeat*, ch. 4.

In December 1659 the Quaker Richard Hubberthorne had rebuked Baptists for declaring that they would be obedient in civil matters to any government which was or might be established. 'If Charles Stuart come', Hubberthorne growled, 'and establish popery and govern by tyranny, you have begged pardon by promising willingly to submit.'[15] But Baptists may merely have been less frank than Quakers. Henry Danvers, for instance, a consistent plotter against the restored monarchy, nevertheless insisted that the saints must pray for Charles II even whilst openly and secretly resisting as Providence permitted.[16] It sounds hypocritical, but, given the assumption that God for his own reasons has permitted the restoration of monarchy in England, this must be accepted so long as God appears to condone it. But it cannot be part of God's long-term purpose to perpetuate an Antichristian regime. We must expect that an opportunity will be given to his servants to make a change though they must not try to force God's hand by premature revolt.

After 1660 Quakers and others decided that Christ's kingdom was not of this world. The powers that be must be obeyed unless their demands conflict with God's, in which case resistance must be only passive. Bunyan differentiated himself from Quakers in theology; and he seems to have been closer to Danvers than to Quakers in his ideas after 1660. He protested his loyalty to the King whilst refusing to obey some of the government's orders. As early as 1665, in *The Holy City*, Bunyan had anticipated that 'in the latter day . . . God will take hold of kings'. 'Some of them will lay their hand to help forward the work of this city.'[17] So on Biblical and traditional protestant grounds he accepted that kings would cast down Antichrist. But it was not revealed which kings, or when.

Meanwhile Bunyan employed the well-established Parliamentarian distinction between the King and his evil advisers, some of whom, Bunyan thought, served Antichrist. In times of intensified persecution—the late 1660s, the mid-1670s, the early

[15] Edward Burrough and Richard Hubberthorne, *An Answer to a Declaration put forth by the People called Anabaptists in and about the City of London*, 4.
[16] Danvers, *The Mystery of Magistracy Unveiled* (1663), quoted in Greaves; 'The Tangled Careers of two Stuart Radicals: Henry and Robert Danvers', *Baptist Quarterly*, 29 (1981), 35.
[17] *The Holy City*, MW iii. 165–9.

1680s — the contrast between the King, whom perhaps God would one day enlighten, and local persecutors, who were 'beyond the reach of God's mercy',[18] must have supplied the only ray of hope in a gloomy world. Bunyan's position was based on religious conviction; but it also made good sense tactically. He could protest his loyalty and adjure his readers to obey and suffer. God's cause will prevail, even if not on earth in our time.

Bunyan's writings make it clear how right Hobbes was to wish to discourage belief in rewards and punishments in the afterlife. For him this belief is almost a definition of sedition. For Bunyan — and for innumerable other dissenters — it was the strongest reason for refusing to compromise with the Antichristian state church.

The failure of the Rye House Plot in 1683 forced nonconformists to rethink their positions, just as the defeat of Venner's rising had done in 1661. In *Advice to Sufferers* Bunyan gave 'seasonable counsel' to his co-religionists. He assumed that even severer persecution might unexpectedly strike, instancing the sudden execution of John the·Baptist. Bunyan recommended extreme wariness 'under the eyes of men': do not 'suffer thyself to be entangled in those snares that God hath suffered to be laid in the world for some'. 'I am not for running myself into suffering. . . . Suffering for a truth ought to be cautiously took in hand, and as warily performed.' But there are times when it may be necessary. 'Oppression', Bunyan agreed, 'makes a wise man mad'; but the saints must beware of being drawn into conspiracies, whatever the provocation. 'Let us mind our own business, and leave the magistrate to his work.' When governors lay a yoke upon our necks, we must not murmur, wince, shrink, or complain; our own sins are no doubt to blame. 'Discontent in the mind sometimes puts discontent into the mouth.' There should be no talking against the government, no mocking of 'men in place and power', no 'striving to deliver ourselves from the affliction': the magistrate is God's ordinance. To 'fear God and honour the King . . . is the way to make the work of thy enemies hard.'

Bunyan's concern is clear. Even if inferior magistrates 'act beyond measure cruelly . . . I will . . . love them, . . . pray for them'; the magistrate may be 'working out his own damnation by doing of thee good'. You cannot 'cause that no more wicked men should anywhere be in power'. It is not much use appealing to 'Kings and Parliaments and men in authority'. 'None of these things can save thee from being devoured by the mouth of the sons of Belial.' At all costs, a professor should not seek to be

> revenged of him, that doth him ill. (You know the subject I am upon). . . . Men that are unquiet and discontented, and that seek revenge upon them that persecute them for their profession, . . . put themselves upon the brink of those ruins that others are further from.

The advice to discontented professors is to turn a Christian other cheek; but it is supported by prudential considerations. Bunyan added, very self-consciously:

> I speak not these things, as knowing any that are disaffected to the government. . . . But because I appear thus in public, and know not into whose hands these lines may come, therefore thus I write. I speak it also to show my loyalty to the King . . . and my desire that all Christians should walk in ways of peace and truth.[19]

Although he professed to be talking about other countries when he said 'Antichrist is yet alive', Bunyan's references to the Church of England are clear. 'The government in all kingdoms is not yet managed with such light . . . as to let the saints serve God as he has said.' And Bunyan discussed very seriously, like Milton in the *De Doctrina Christiana*, whether flight from persecution was ever justified, or whether one should always stand and face the worst. His advice was sensible:

> If it is in thy heart to fly, fly: if it be in thy heart to stand, stand. Anything but a denial of the truth. He that flies . . . and he that stands has warrant to do so. . . . The man himself is best able to judge concerning his present strength.

Flight did not necessarily mean giving up: many protestants in the 1680s emigrated to the Netherlands and continued to plot from there against the English government. Those against whom Bunyan was severe were professors who made shameful concessions in face of persecution. In *The Pharisee and the Publican* (1685), after comparing publicans with 'our informers and bum bailiffs', Bunyan went on to ask, 'what shall we think of compliance

[19] MW x. 5, 8, 32–41, 45–9, 59, 99–103.

with a foreign prince to rob the church of God?'[20] This last passage was omitted from editions published after 1688, presumably because it might be thought to refer to William III. But in 1685 could no one imagine Charles II or James II 'complying with a foreign prince' against the church of God?

In January 1685 the Bedfordshire JPs in general sessions ordered that the laws against nonconformists should forthwith be put into vigorous operation. This decision was printed as a broadside to give it the maximum publicity. Bishop Barlow, hitherto suspected of softness towards dissenters, publicly associated himself with the new policy. Then followed Monmouth's rebellion in the summer of 1685, the last hopeless rising of the defenders of the Good Old Cause. On 23 December of that year Bunyan conveyed all his property to his wife, clearly as a safeguard against the possibility of being arrested or having to go underground. This action, and Bunyan's worries about the ethics of fleeing from persecution, may have arisen from the accession of a popish King; but it relates also to the pugnacity of the local gentry and clergy. James was soon to offer himself as an ally against this personification of Antichrist.[21]

Charles II had been able to rule without Parliament for four years, thanks to the co-operation of the Tory gentry. But it was no longer possible to govern in that way indefinitely. That James II did not try to emulate his father's personal rule of 1629–40 is evidence of the strength of Parliament. Since it could not be ignored, James tried to manipulate it, reversing the policy which his brother had so carefully evolved. Diabolus in *The Holy War*, 'not thinking himself yet secure enough', started 'new-modelling the town'. In 1687 James, hoping to tame the Parliamentary electorate and so get Roman Catholics admitted to political and military offices, repurged corporations, this time replacing Anglicans with dissenters and others prepared to support repeal of the Test Act. Nearly half the JPs of England were displaced. In many counties between 75 and 90 per cent of JPs who had been in

[20] MW x. 45–9, 73–5; *A Holy Life*, MW ix. 260, 290; cf. *Israel's Hope Encouraged* and *Paul's Departure and Crown* (both posthumous), Offor, i. 606, 726–7; ii. 219, 221; *MCPW*, vi. 605.

[21] Brown, 323, and ch. 15, *passim*; Mullet, 31; *HW*, 18–27. In 1662 one of Bunyan's fellow-prisoners had assigned all his property to his son (Joyce Godber, *History of Bedfordshire, 1066–1888* (Bedfordshire County Council, 1969), 234–5).

the commission since 1685 had been dismissed by 1688. These were 'the prime of the gentry'; they were replaced by 'ordinary persons both as to quality and estate (most of them dissenters).' Early in 1688 fourteen men were dismissed from Bedford cor- poration, including Paul Cobb. Six or seven of the replacements were members of Bunyan's congregation. The new Council set about a programme of reform, recovering from previous mayors moneys which had been diverted to the use of the oligarchy. It was as though the days of the Major-Generals had come again. This betrayal proved decisive in alienating even the most loyal Tories from the King. 'Some would think one kick of the breach enough for a gentleman', said Sir John Bramston, refusing to co-operate when James tried to reverse his policy again in October 1688.[22]

John Eston, son of a member of Bunyan's church but himself a conforming Anglican, was prominent in these changes. His name was put forward as a potential MP for the town who would support repeal of the Test Act—together, ironically, with the name of Robert Audley, recently turned out of office. But Audley did not prove sufficiently compliant, and he was replaced by one of Bunyan's former persecutors, William Foster, 'ever . . . a close opposer of the ways of God', and ready now to swallow his Anglican principles and do whatever the King wished. Bunyan— together with a former officer in the Parliamentarian army—was approached by a royal agent, we are told, who discussed with them the election of suitable MPs for Bedford. As in 1672, Bunyan would no doubt have welcomed toleration, even from a Roman Catholic king; he was unlikely not to favour repeal of the Test Act. He may have been momentarily seduced into considering the possibilities of active co-operation. Passive co-operation would have been in complete accordance with his proclaimed principles. William Penn seems to have had some such reasons for his active co-operation with James.[23]

[22] Brown, 350–4; Mullet, 'The Internal Politics of Bedford, 1660–1688', PBHRS 59 (1980), 26–31; Fletcher, *Reform in the Provinces: The Government of Stuart England* (Yale UP, 1986), 25; *Memoirs of Sir John Reresby*, ed. A. Browning (Glasgow UP, 1936), 494; *Autobiography of Sir John Bramston*, Camden Soc. (1845), 326.
[23] Brown, 348–54; Mullet, 'The Internal Politics of Bedford, 1660–1688', 26–7, 31; *GA*, 109; *HW*, 18–27; *A Confession of my Faith* (1672), Offor, ii. 601; i. 63. Foster, who had been active against Bunyan in 1661 and 1676, was one of Bedford's richer citizens (Godber, *History of Bedfordshire*, 238; ead., *The Story of Bedford: An Outline History* (Luton, 1978), 81).

How much further Bunyan would have gone we can only speculate. The record was muddied by his first biographers. Once the Glorious Revolution had happened it was impossible for them to admit that Bunyan could have been on the wrong side. 'His piercing wit penetrated the veil', wrote the Continuator of Bunyan's life (Cokayne?). 'He moved with caution and a holy fear', but he 'expressed his zeal with some weariness [wariness?]' against James's purges of corporations, 'as foreseeing the bad consequence that would attend it'. And when 'a great man . . . sent for him, as it is supposed, to give him a place of public trust, he would by no means come at him, but sent his excuse.'[24] We may be sure of his 'caution and holy fear'. But the Earl of Aylesbury (almost certainly the 'great man') was keeping James well-enough informed of Bedford politics for it to be unlikely that the offer of a job (if indeed there was such an offer) would be made without considerable thought and investigation. Many members of Bunyan's congregation did in fact co-operate. But after Bunyan's death and the landing of William the Liberator on the eighty-third anniversary of Guy Fawkes's Day, Bunyan's admirers would naturally credit him with having foreseen all.

The effect of James's actions had been to introduce a large number of dissenters from a socially lower class into local government. The Earl of Aylesbury was appalled by what he had to do. He spoke with some distaste of the Deputy-Lieutenants whom he was ordered to create in Bedfordshire: 'no one of the new ones had ever set foot in my house', and he had no intention of inviting them now.[25] In Bedford itself power had previously been shared between Anglicans and a nonconformist patriciate. James offended the dissenting establishment as well as the Anglican. Bunyan's church was divided. Mr Mullet speculates that many dissenters had shed their political radicalism as they prospered under the Stuart monarchy. James was subverting 'a fairly viable power-sharing system' by an unprecedented degree of government intervention. Who could be sure it would be a once-only exercise of royal power?[26]

It is in this light that we should consider the revival of millen-

[24] *A Continuation of Mr Bunyan's Life*, in *GA*, 169–70.

[25] Aylesbury, *Memoirs*, i. 167, 175, 181; Godber, *History of Bedfordshire*, 256. The Bruce family, of Scottish origin, had never been popular in the county.

[26] Mullet, 'The Internal Politics of Bedford, 1660–1688', 34–5.

arianism in the late 1670s and 1680s which Barrie White has seen in Hanserd Knollys and some have seen in Bunyan. Millenarianism was a permanent background to Bunyan's thought. In the 1650s he had believed the Second Coming to be imminent. But he came to recognize the folly of over-enthusiastic attempts to identify dates leading up to Christ's return: all one could do was to study the signs. These he increasingly thought he could identify in the England of the 1680s. The Preface to *Mr. Badman* is almost hysterical about the flood of wickedness which 'is like to drown our English world', including some who 'make a profession . . . on purpose that they may twist themselves into a trade', and so enrich themselves 'by the ruins of their neighbour'. He hinted at 'the last times', one of whose signs was 'that professing men . . . shall be many of them base'. *A Holy Life* (1684) refers to 'the dangerousness of the latter times'. There is much more evil in England now than there was under the rule of the Puritans. In *The Jerusalem Sinner* Bunyan reflected on the debauchery of youth, the decay of grace, and concluded: 'Just before Jesus Christ came in the flesh, the world was degenerated as it is now.'[27]

So Bunyan must have become increasingly worried in the 1680s. The godly were always, by definition, a minority. The visible elect had, with great difficulty, organized themselves in congregations; yet these congregations bickered among themselves, and many of their members showed signs of backsliding and compromise with the world. Bunyan's criticism of the defects of the visible elect extended even to ministers. So who is left to forward God's cause? The failure of many of the godly may be a sign of the last times, but the Second Coming will have to be an extraneous act of divine power like Emanuel's conquest of Mansoul, or Samson's divinely inspired destruction of the Philistine aristocracy and clergy. The failure of Monmouth's rebellion might suggest that Antichrist is not going to be overthrown by human effort alone: a miracle will be needed.[28]

In *The Building of the House of God* (1688) Bunyan repeated the cautions of *Advice to Sufferers*:

[27] B. R. White, *Hanserd Knollys and Radical Dissent in the Seventeenth Century*, 28–9; *Mr. B.*, Offor, iii. 592–4; MW ix. 334, 340, 345–6; xi. 47–8. Isaac Newton too 'seems to have been particularly preoccupied' in the 1680s with millenarian studies (M. C. Jacob, *The Cultural Meaning of the Scientific Revolution*, 91, 94).

[28] *The House of the Forest of Lebanon* (posthumous), Offor, iii. 536.

He makes us in this world discreet,
Prudent and wise . . .
That there may be no scandal in our ways. . . .

The godly are to be patient under persecution, not to resist. They
must hold out, abide with the truth:

Then may we look for that reward
Promised at the coming of the Lord.[29]

In 1687–8 Bunyan might have envisaged the possibility of a
permanent alliance between James II, English papists, and protestant dissenters which would have relieved the latter from persecution. The Popish Plot had suggested that there was little
danger from English Catholics. Such an alliance seems with our
hindsight a ridiculous prospect, but it might not have seemed so at
the time. The gentry and the clergy rather than the monarchy had
become for Bunyan the symbols of Antichrist. Such toleration as
dissenters received after 1660 seemed to be owed to kings rather
than to Parliament: the Popish Plot after all was believed to have
been directed against the King. In these circumstances the traditional idea that kings of the earth would overthrow Antichrist
might well revive. ''Tis a great encouragement to a man to hold up
his head in the country', Bunyan wrote in a work published in
1688, 'when he has a special friend at the Court.'[30]

Alternatively, Bunyan was in close touch with dissenting leaders
in London, and may have had some inkling of what was going on in
the Netherlands. The question must remain open. Either way, it
must have been clear to him that the godly alone could not
overcome Antichrist. If persecution was to be ended, it must be by
means of the power of the English state;[31] and to that nonconformists could contribute, but by no manner of means decisively.
So Bunyan's tactics were from any point of view sensible: non-
resistance, adherence to the truth, avoidance of scandal, readiness
to co-operate with any state authority which would grant
toleration.

[29] *Poems*, 284, 289–90, 292–5, 302–3. Cf. the similar approach in *The Holy City*
(1665), MW iii. 96–8; *Advice to Sufferers* (1684), Offor, ii. 705–6; *Of Antichrist and his
Ruin* (posthumous), Offor, ii. 45; *The House of the Forest of Lebanon* (posthumous), Offor,
iii. 526–7.
[30] *The Advocateship of Jesus Christ*, MW xi. 196.
[31] *Of Antichrist and his Ruin*, Offor, ii. 74: still unpublished when Bunyan died. See
next chapter for further evidence from Bunyan's posthumous writings.

26. Posthumous Writings:
'Who bid the boar come here?'

> It is the duty and wisdom of those that fear God so to manage
> their time and work that he hath allotted unto them, that they
> may not have part of their work to do when they should be
> departing the world.   BUNYAN[1]

> If you would understand the Scriptures you shall read it calleth
> rich wicked men mountains, and poor believing men valleys.
>
>   CLARKSON[2]

BUNYAN left a dozen treatises unpublished at his death. Of
these, we are told, most were prepared for the press, and he was
still working on *Exposition on . . . Genesis*. It seems pertinent to ask
why Bunyan left so much material unpublished which was ready
for printing. Censorship clearly had something to do with it. In
1685 so relatively harmless a man as Richard Baxter was jailed for
publishing a *Paraphrase on the New Testament*. In the four months
between the Declaration of Indulgence of April 1688 and his
death, Bunyan published five books and had passed proofs of a
sixth. It looks as though he was working rapidly through a backlog
of hitherto unpublishable material but had not got very far.

Let us look first at the incomplete *Exposition on . . . Genesis*.
Tindall described this as an 'exercise in veiled sedition'.[3] This may
seem to be putting it rather strongly; but the treatise is certainly
designed to convey points to which the censor might have objected
if put directly. Seventeenth-century use of Biblical commentaries
to make covert political suggestions has never, I believe, been
properly studied. It could be a way of discussing the undiscussable.
Thus William Sedgwick, son of a Bedfordshire gentleman, in his
Inquest for the Blood of our late Soveraign (1660), used Genesis to
criticize the Parliamentarian politicians who had enjoyed his
support until Providence decided against them.[4]

---

[1] *Paul's Departure and Crown* (posthumous), Offor, i. 728–9.
[2] *The Right Devil Discovered* (1659), 73–4.
[3] Tindall, 134.
[4] Sedgwick, op. cit. 1–146, *passim*. I have discussed this work briefly in my *The
Experience of Defeat*, 109–11.

Bunyan's *Exposition on* . . . *Genesis* depicts the struggle of good and evil from the week of creation: light against darkness, the waters above the firmament against those below. This struggle thus antedates Cain and Abel. But the murder of Abel involves all humanity and the social order. When Cain 'left off to fear the Lord, and had bloodily butchered his holy brother, Abel, then he seeks to be a head or monarch.' 'Abel was set in the lower rank', like Isaac and Jacob; but 'the blessing of God is not led by outward order.' 'Cain's brood' are 'lords and rulers first, while Abel and his generation have their necks under persecution.' Cain endeavoured 'the extirpating of all true religion out of the world.' 'Tyrants matter nothing . . . how much they destroy.' 'This is the word of the Lord against all those that are for the practice of Cain' — i.e. persecution. 'As I live, saith the Lord, I will prepare thee unto blood and blood shall pursue thee.' 'The proper voice of all the blood of the godly is to call for vengeance on the persecutors, even for the blood of Abel.' This moral had been drawn from the story of Cain and Abel by Winstanley and other Diggers. 'Cain is still alive in all great landlords', said a Digger pamphlet of 1650. William Erbery, John Canne, Baptists and Fifth Monarchists, the Ranters Abiezer Coppe, Lawrence Clarkson, and Jacob Bauthumley, William Sedgwick, Sir Henry Vane and George Fox had also used the myth.[5] But Bunyan could hardly be more specific in associating Cain, the first murderer, with monarchy and persecution.

Bunyan depicted Noah's as the first gathered church. It should 'maintain a separation from the cursed children of Cain'. (The locusts of Egypt were a type of 'our graceless clergy' of the Church of England.) Noah's separation 'should teach us not to fear the faces of men, no not the faces of the mighty.' So Bunyan brought Genesis immediately home to England and the state church's persecution. 'We are hated because we are religious, because we stand to maintain the truth of God.' 'To maintain God's truth . . . cannot be done but with great hazard so long as Cain or his offspring remain.' Bunyan even questioned 'whether it be lawful for a man to urge . . . the promise of grace and forgiveness' to persecutors. They fall 'beyond the reach of God's mercy'.[6]

---

[5] *Exposition on* . . . *Genesis*, Offor, ii. 447; Keith Thomas, 'Another Digger Broadside', *P. and P.*, 42 (1969), 61; *WTUD*, 146; Tindall, 111, 141, 266; Bauthumley, *The Light and Dark Sides of God* (1650), 81–2.   [6] Offor, ii. 449–51, 460, 475.

'All persecutors are not brutal alike; some are in words as smooth as oil; others can show a semblance of *reason of state*' (my italics). Persecutors are afraid of godly men and godliness, insignificant though the godly are in human terms. 'Let us learn therefore to be quiet and patient under the hand of wicked and blood-thirsty men. . . . When we are dead, our blood will cry from the ground against them.' 'Let Cain and God alone, and do you mind faith and patience.' Enos, 'a man that was miserable in this world for the sake and cause of God' nevertheless held out and made head against Cain and his offspring. The giants of Genesis, as of *The Pilgrim's Progress*, were persecutors.[7]

The waters of the Flood represent the great and mighty of the world; 'the flowing of them, their rage'. Here Bunyan apostrophized: 'thou church of God in England, which art now upon the waves of affliction and *temptation*' (my italics). Referring perhaps to James II's overtures to protestant dissenters, he added:

When the great ones of this world begin to discover themselves to the church by way of encouragement, it is a sign that the waters are now decreasing. . . . This should teach us while we are in affliction to look this way and that, if it may be the tops of the mountains may be seen. . . . Though men may be borne with, if they lie in their holes at the height of the tempest: but to do it when the tops of the mountains were seen, if then they shall forbear to open their windows, they are worthy of blame indeed.[8]

Could Bunyan be opening a window, to see if James would help to overthrow Antichrist? An alternative explanation would be that Bunyan knew that aristocratic support for William of Orange was growing in England.

The symbolism of mountains and valleys runs through Bunyan's writings, as it had through those of the Diggers, Clarkson, and other radicals: we should always be on the look out for it. Heights may be giants or walls. 'The grace of God is compared to water', Bunyan declared in *The Water of Life* (1688). 'The element of water naturally descends and abides in low places, in valleys and places which are undermost.' It passes by the established church. It does not flow over 'steeples and hills', and consequently is in 'low esteem . . . with the rich and the full'. 'It is therefore for the poor

---

7 Ibid. 450, 454–5, 461, 478, 487–9.
8 Ibid. 467–8, 477–8, 483.

and needy.' A similar point had been made in *The Holy City* (1665); in the new heaven and the new earth 'there shall be a smooth face upon the whole earth, all snugs and hubs and hills and holes shall now be took away.'[9]

We must not set times for God's salvation; but Bunyan foresaw some of the godly 'feeding upon . . . the kingdoms and estates of the Antichristian party.' There will be a time 'when thou comest out of the furnace'. 'It is counted a heinous crime for a man to run his sword at the picture of a king; how much more to shed the blood of the image of God?'[10] Noah, Daniel, Jeremiah, and Paul, Bunyan said, were excused of the treason of rebellion, since 'a man is not to be counted an offender, how contrary soever he lieth, either in doctrine or practice to men, etc., if both have the command of God and are surely grounded upon the words of his mouth.' The ultimate consoling thought was that 'the world is in our hand, and disposed by our doctrine, by our faith and prayers, although they think far otherwise and shall one day feel their judgments are according.'[11]

The Biblical description of Nimrod as 'a mighty hunter' means that he was a great persecutor. 'I am apt to think', Bunyan added:

that he was the first that in this new [post-diluvian] world sought after absolute monarchy. . . . He therefore would needs be the author and master of what religion he pleased, and would also subject the rest of his brethren thereto, by what ways his lusts thought best. Wherefore here began a fresh persecution . . . to lord it over the sons of God and to enforce idolatry and superstition upon them.

Some sons of the godly 'went away with Nimrod and the rest of that company into idolatry, tyranny and other profaneness.' 'Apostatizing from the Word, and desiring mastership over their brethren, they, as lords, fomented their own conceptions and then enjoined the people to build . . . mystical Babel.'[12] Nimrod was a

---

[9] *The Works of Gerrard Winstanley*, ed. G. H. Sabine (Cornell UP, 1941), 659; *The Saints' Knowledge of Christ's Love* (posthumous), Offor, ii. 8; *The Water of Life*, Offor, iii. 541–5; *The Holy City*, MW iii. 118, 304; cf. *Mr. B.*, Offor, iii. 590–4.

[10] It is difficult to think of Bunyan having read or seen Henry Glapthorne's heroic drama, *The Lady's Privilege* (1640), which contains a similar image (IV. ii). It must have been in common use.

[11] Offor, ii. 465–6, 477–8, 480, 483, 495–6.

[12] Ibid. 497–8.

traditional code word for monarchy, used by Milton, Erbery, and the Fifth-Monarchists John Rogers and Christopher Feake.[13] Nimrod was 'the usual symbol for Charles II among the Baptists.' Cain and Nimrod were captains of Bloodmen in *The Holy War*.[14] Bunyan treats tyranny, idolatry, and persecution as almost interchangeable. The relevance of this to post-restoration England is obvious. Also noteworthy is that he seems to have thought all men were brethren, and presumably equal, before monarchy was established.

Tindall was after all not so far from the mark. Did Bunyan ever hope to publish his *Exposition on . . . Genesis*? The other unpublished works are less openly 'seditious', and we must assume that Bunyan at one time or another had hoped they might be printed. They are difficult to date, but *The Heavenly Foot-man* is generally assigned to the late 1660s or early 1670s. Despite this early date it does not seem to have been one of those which Bunyan had prepared for the press before his death. Most of the volumes which Bunyan did prepare were probably written later. Why did he refrain from publishing, especially in view of the remark quoted as epigraph to this chapter? *The Heavenly Foot-man* condemns persecution as Antichristian, and threatens divine vengeance against it.[15] When repression tightened after the interlude of relative freedom in 1678–82, Bunyan may have decided that the times were not propitious for publishing such views except in the form of allegory. Like Locke, he prepared some treatises carefully for the press, keeping them ready in the hope of another relaxation, such as in fact occurred after his death.

This is mere speculation, but I have seen no better explanation, and it fits in with what we know of Bunyan's determination to say his say whenever possible. It will not explain failure to publish *The Desire of the Righteous Granted*, which Charles Doe heard Bunyan preach in 1685 or 1686. This seems wholly innocuous from the censor's point of view. Equally harmless is *Justification by an Imputed Righteousness*, which manages to discuss Cain and Abel with no social or political overtones. The same is true of *The*

[13] *Paradise Lost*, xii. 24–37; W. Erbery, *Testimony* (1658), 207; Rogers, *Jegar-Sahadotha: An Oiled Pillar Set up for Posterity* (n.d., 1657–8?), 68; Feake, Preface to *Mr. Tillinghast's Eight Last Sermons* (1655), sig. A 2v.
[14] Tindall, 266; *HW*, 228–9. Tindall gives other examples.
[15] MW v. 133–4; cf. 153, 178.

Acceptable Sacrifice: this, Cokayne tells us, had actually been 'put into the press by the author himself'.[16] All the other unpublished works contain passages to which the censor might well have objected. Bunyan may have turned to *Exposition on . . . Genesis* with a sense of desperation.

Of Antichrist and his Ruin, one of those prepared but not published, appears to date from the very early 1680s. ('This twenty years we have been degenerating', Bunyan said.) W. R. Owens suggests that the repeated protestations of loyalty which Bunyan makes in this tract, his rejection of revolution, may indicate a hope of publishing. We should not blame our governors for persecuting us, Bunyan says: they are misinformed by their servants. Kings (and no others) shall pull down Antichrist, but 'in God's good time', when they come to be enlightened. The ruin of Antichrist will be gradual. The King's tardiness may be the fault of the godly: 'be up and doing. . . . Pray that God would make him [the King] able to drive away all evil men from his presence, that he may be a greater countenancer than ever of them that are holy and good.' If that was written under Charles II, as is suggested by a reference to plots and conspiracies against the King's person and government, 'evil men' might well refer discreetly to the King's brother James.[17]

Owens adds that the expiry of the Licensing Act in May 1679 may have made it easier for a brief period to print speculations about the identity and fate of Antichrist. The reaction after 1681 may explain Bunyan's failure to publish. 'I do confess myself', Bunyan remarked, 'one of the old-fashion professors, that covet to fear God and honour the King. I also am for blessing them that curse me . . . and for praying for them that persecute me.' And he added, even more ambiguously, 'I only drop this because I would show my brethren that I also am one of them; and to set them right that have wrong thoughts of me.'[18]

Hence Bunyan was able, in *Of Antichrist and his Ruin*, simultaneously to call for the pulling down of Antichrist and to urge the godly to fear God and honour the king. Similarly in *The House of the Forest of Lebanon* (posthumous) he argued that 'the war that the church makes with Antichrist is rather defensive than offensive.'

---

[16] MW xi. xx; Offor, i. 311, 330, 333, 688.
[17] Offor, ii. 45, 50, 54–5, 58, 61–2, 72–4; cf. 68 – bad news from foreign parts.
[18] Ibid. 74.

'Let not therefore kings and princes be afraid: they will not be assaulted by temporal weapons.'[19]

Of Antichrist and his Ruin contains severe criticisms of the government in church and state. References to England and especially to the established church, are covert but clear. 'Civil laws that enforce ... matters of worship ... as in the Spanish Inquisition, ... as long as there is life in them, ... the spirit of the Man of Sin yet remaineth in them.' It will be some time before kings and princes come to be enlightened about the evils that are in such 'wicked Antichristian penal laws' and 'the abominable filthiness of that which is Antichristian-worship' in the Church. All that Bunyan asked for was toleration by the law of God and the law of the King. But now Antichristian names 'are worn by men of spiritual employ' — i.e. bishops. 'God has a quarrel with the names as well as with the persons.' 'There are men that are idols as well as things.' 'God honours no high priest but one.'[20]

The Whore 'hath turned the sword of the magistrate against those that keep God's law.' But her 'church-state ... must of necessity tumble.' Allusion to the Church of England is made clear by Bunyan's use of the word 'convocations'. 'Money, money, as the pedlar cries, ... is the sinews of their religion', 'the object of their offices and government'. That might apply equally to the Roman or the Anglican church. None are so insatiably covetous as the Antichristians. They have kingdoms and crowns, places, preferments, sacraments, etc. — all to get money. But 'a time is coming wherein there shall be no Antichrist to afflict Christ's church any more.' The saints 'shall take them captive whose captives they were; they shall rule over their oppressors (Isaiah 14.2).' And the conclusion is that 'Antichrist must be pulled down, down, stick and stone.' 'When men intend to build a new house, ... they first pull down the old one, raze the foundations, and then they begin their new.' The implications are clear. For all his calculated expressions of loyalty to the monarchy, Bunyan was careful to single out for specific praise 'the noble King, King Henry VIII' and 'the good King Edward, his son', as well as 'the brave Queen' Elizabeth. The Stuart kings were conspicuous by their absence.[21]

---

[19] Ibid. iii. 516, 526–7, 536.   [20] Ibid. ii. 43–4, 50–2, 74–9.

[21] Ibid. ii. 50, 78–82. For the antichristianity of the Church of England and its prayer book see also *I will pray with the Spirit* (1662), MW ii. 285; *A Reason of my Practice in Worship* (1672), Offor, ii. 615–16.

Bunyan reveals a deeper pessimism in this treatise than anywhere else. The worst is yet to come: the witnesses will be slain. When 'plots and conspiracies are laid against God's church all the world over, and . . . none of the kings, princes, or mighty states of the world will open their doors, then is the ruin of Antichrist at hand.' That would suggest that Bunyan was writing in the last years of Charles II or the first years of his successor. In the last days 'the basest of all sorts, sects, professions and degrees shall take shelter in Babylon . . . to devour and eat up the poor and needy, and to blow out the light of the Gospel.' 'There shall, for a time, be no living visible church of Christ in the world . . . A church, but no *living* church, as to church-state: a church in ruins.' These may be signs of the last times.[22]

A Discourse of the House of the Forest of Lebanon cannot be dated, but may come from the same period. Like *Solomon's Temple Spiritualized*, it is largely allegorical and typological, dealing with the mystery rather than the history. But it also discusses the tactics which the godly should pursue in time of persecution, when they are on the defensive, and how the church 'at last shall recover herself from the yoke and tyranny of Antichrist.' Faithful men will 'bear up the truth above water all the time of Antichrist's reign and rage.' A long quotation from 'Pomponius Algerius, an Italian martyr', taken from Foxe, stresses fortitude under torment and persecution. Its enemies allege that the church is 'for destroying kings, for subverting kingdoms and for bringing all to desolation.' But kings, princes, and potentates have nothing to fear. The church 'moveth no sedition'. 'The saints . . . know their places'; and Bunyan specifically rejected the 'extravagant opinions' of those [Fifth Monarchists] who think the kingdom of Christ will be won by 'carnal weapons'. 'Let but faith and holiness walk the streets, without control, and you may be as happy as the world can make you' — rather a large demand perhaps, if we consider how Bunyan would be likely to interpret 'walk the streets without control'. Yet earlier he had written 'and suppose they were the truly godly that made the first assault, can they be blamed? For who can endure a boar in a vineyard?' That surely lets a rather large cat out of the bag. God will 'return the evil that the enemies do to his church . . . when his time is come', 'even in this world'. 'The

Medes and Persians helped to deliver the church from the clutches
... of the King of Babylon.' 'Let this then encourage the saints to
hope, ... notwithstanding present tribulations. .... I have a bad
master, but I have but a year to serve under him, and that makes me
serve him with patience'.[23] (Whether men looked to the Duke of
Monmouth or to William of Orange to succeed the 'bad master',
such calculations must have influenced many in the 1680s).

Of *Paul's Departure and Crown* Offor says: 'it bears the marks of
having been composed ... towards the end of his pilgrimage.' It is
another call for courage under persecution. Notwithstanding 'the
murders and outrages that our brethren suffer at the hands of
wicked men ... through the violence of the enemies of God', there
must be 'a full and faithful performance of [the saints'] duty to God
and man, whatever may be the consequences thereof.' 'We seem to
lie under a contempt, and to be in a disgraceful condition.' But
Bunyan is severe against those who 'throw up their open profession
of his name for fear of those that hate him' and turn their coats as
'chief ringleaders of this cowardliness'.[24]

In all these unpublished treatises the themes of the godly under
persecution, and of God's ultimate revenge, loom large. Terror or
corruption are equally dangerous for the saints. But the day is
coming 'of breaking up of closet-councils, cabinet-councils, secret
purposes, hidden thoughts' of those that have been 'bold and
audacious in their vile and beastly ways'. That was from *Christ a
Complete Saviour*. In *Israel's Hope Encouraged* Bunyan assumed that
'we are sure to be concerned' in 'that common evil of persecution'.
A persecutor is 'but the devil's scarecrow, the old one himself lies
quat.' But that confident statement came after a grim vignette of 'a
man at the foot of the ladder, now ready in will and mind to die for
his profession.' 'Antichrist as yet is stronger than we.'[25] *The Saints'
Knowledge of Christ's Love* similarly attacked persecution by
'wicked spirits in high places', 'the rulers of the darkness of this
world'.[26]

The unpublished writings may help us to a better understanding
of Bunyan's thinking about politics. It changed over time, and it

[23] Ibid. iii. 513–36. Cf. MW i. 258, quoted on p. 89 above for 'walking the
streets without control'.
[24] Offor, i. 721, 723, 725, 727.
[25] Ibid. i. 219, 222–3; cf. 236; i. 581–2, 585, 602, 606; cf. *The House of the Forest of
Lebanon*, Offor, iii. 533.
[26] Offor, ii. 8–9, 13, 22.

contained apparent contradictions. We must relate the post-humous material to what Bunyan said in his published writings, where he was above all anxious to make it clear that God's people were wrongly 'looked upon to be a turbulent, seditious and factious people.' Nothing in his doctrines, he insisted in *A Confession of my Faith*, written towards the end of his first imprisonment, 'savoured either of heresy or rebellion', or justified twelve years in jail. Magistracy is God's ordinance.[27] In *The Holy City* (1665), he had reassured 'the governors of this world' 'that they need not at all . . . fear a disturbance' from that city. 'It is true, that kings and nations of this world shall one day bring their glory and honour to this city; but yet not by outward force or compulsion.' 'In the first day of the gospel, the poor, the halt, the lame and the blind are chief in the embracing of the tenders of grace. Yet in the latter day thereof, God will take hold of kings.' 'All the injuries that the kings and great ones of the earth have done to the church and spouse of Christ in these days of the New Testament, it hath been through the instigation and witchcraft of this mistress of iniquity. . . . This gentlewoman being laid in her grave, . . . these kings will change their mind . . .' – apparently after Antichrist's overthrow rather than taking a lead in the process.[28]

But Bunyan's advocacy of non-resistance was not as absolute as it appears; the unpublished writings make this clear. God will one day take revenge on persecutors. But persecution can be ended only by the exercise of state power. 'By magistrates and powers we shall be delivered from Antichrist.' Short of popular rebellion, who but kings could wield the necessary power? ('You have power in your hand', wrote Winstanley in his last desperate appeal to Oliver Cromwell; 'I have no power'.) This surely explains Bunyan's greater emphasis on the role of kings in the 1680s. What did he really hope for from the monarchy of Charles II and James II? Did he see Antichrist *principally* as the administrative power of the church and of the gentry, who do the persecuting; and did he really think that the monarchy would turn against them – as James briefly did in 1687–8? We recall that in *The Holy War* Antichrist was a gentleman. After his overthrow, those 'that are the slaves of Antichrist now . . . will have none to put them upon persecuting of

[27] *I Will Pray with the Spirit* (1662?), MW ii. 253; cf. 284; Offor, ii. 593, 601.
[28] Offor, iii. 404, 410, 430, 444, 446.

the saints. Now they shall not be made, as before, guilty of the blood of those against whom this gentleman shall take a pet.'[29] Or were Bunyan's eyes on a successor to Charles and James?

It is likely that Bunyan revealed more of his mind in his posthumous treatises than in those which he published himself. But we cannot be certain that even the former represent his uncensored thoughts: he presumably intended them to be published one day. Moreover, his ideas must have been changing rapidly in reaction to the changing policies of James II and the changing news from the Netherlands. Bunyan's providential view of history would incline him to keep his options open, to leave the godly room for manœuvre in an uncertain world for which God's immediate intentions were unclear. About God's ultimate intentions there could be no doubt; but during the forty years of Bunyan's adult life he had moved in ways mysterious to his faithful, and it was not for them to commit him or themselves in advance.

We know that the downfall of Antichrist was not imminent, and that the expulsion of James II was. But Bunyan was still uncertain whether he was living in the last times or not. In the Old Testament treason and rebellion are justified when the rebels acted on God's command. 'And suppose they were the truly godly that made the first assault, can they be blamed? . . . Who bid the boar come here?' The aggressors are the Antichristian persecutors. When God's time is come, some professors will feed upon 'the kingdoms and estates of the Antichristian party'.[30]

Bunyan was here interpreting the Biblical account of the raven and the dove which Noah sent out from the ark, and combining it with the avenging angels of Revelation 15. His attitude was ambivalent. He found this 'sort of professors in his church' rather distasteful; 'all the saints are not for such work as the raven.' But they will be acting on God's command 'and shall be tolerated'. So no doubt the sixteenth-century godly had squared their consciences when seeking alliances with land-grabbers like the Duke of Northumberland, the Earls of Leicester and Essex. The raven, 'though he was in the ark [i.e. in the church] was not a type of the

---

[29] Winstanley, *The Law of Freedom in a Platform* (1652), in *The Law of Freedom and Other Writings* (Cambridge UP, 1983), 285; *Of Antichrist and his Ruin*, Offor, ii. 54. Bunyan had used the word 'pet' about local gentry persecutors (p. 127 above).

[30] See p. 326 above. Contrast the assurance in *The Holy City* that the church was not destructive to kings or their revenues (MW v. 96).

most spiritual Christian; nay rather, I think of the worldly professor, who gets into the church in the time of her affliction.' The
rest of the saints will 'bend their spirits to a more spiritual and
retired work.'[31] If I interpret this aright, Bunyan is not excluding
all possibility of revolution: the truly godly could not be blamed if
they were provoked into making the first assault. But he might
rightly wonder whether the radicals who supported Argyll and
Monmouth, and some of whom were to support William of
Orange, were truly godly. Meanwhile James II's offers of toleration must not be spurned: toleration was more important for the
saints than constitutional issues. So Bunyan tried hard to combine
faithfulness to the Bible (as he interpreted it) with political realism.
The overthrow of Antichrist, necessary and glorious though it is,
will involve dirty work for somebody. Perhaps there is a role here
for 'prayerless professors'?

We cannot be sure what Bunyan was actually thinking about
contemporary politics in relation to the millennium. The evidence
is incomplete, unclear, perhaps contradictory. But I think this is
less a matter of caution and reticence in face of censorship than of
uncertainty and open-mindedness in Bunyan's own position. The
ends were clear and certain: the means might vary from month to
month, as James's increasingly desperate manœuvres slowly con-
solidated opposition to him among those who were not godly at all
but who might act as God's instruments. The truly godly, alas,
could not themselves control events: Mansoul could not be saved
by the unaided efforts of its citizens. As it turned out, 'The Medes
and Persians helped to deliver the church from ... the King of
Babylon.'[32] William of Orange was not Prince Emanuel, nor was
meant to be. The victory of 1688 was glorious and bloodless; but
nobody expected it to usher in the millennium.

---

[31] Offor, ii. 478–9.
[32] See pp. 330–1 above.

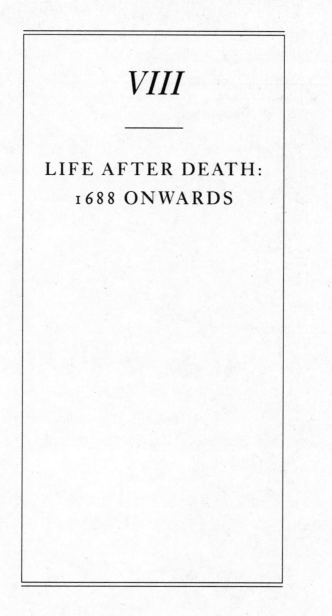

VIII

LIFE AFTER DEATH:
1688 ONWARDS

27. *Bunyan and Dissent*

> As for those titles of Anabaptists, Independents, Presbyterians,
> or the like, I conclude that they came neither from Jerusalem
> nor from Antioch, but rather from hell and Babylon, for they
> naturally tend to division.   BUNYAN[1]

DISSENT is a creation of the restoration. There had been
opposition to the state church long before 1640. The title of
Bruce McFarlane's book, *John Wycliffe and the Beginnings of English
Nonconformity*,[2] indicates some real continuity from the Lollards
to the nonconformist churches. The crucial distinction between
'the Church' and 'the churches' arose at the Reformation, when
the Bible was put into English. There were fierce controversies
over whether *ecclesia* should be translated 'the Church' or 'the
congregation'. The sects asserted for their congregations the
democratic rights that the traditional village community was
losing.

What was new about dissent after 1660 was its self-
consciousness and its national organization. Before 1640 there had
been underground separatist congregations, living precariously
and illegally; and 'Puritan' groups within the state church. During
the 1650s many who were to be extruded from the church in
1660–2 remained contentedly within it, including the Bedford
congregation. Quakers were most decisively opposed on principle
to any state church. But after the restoration those who could not
accept membership of the restored episcopal church, and those
who were expelled from it, had gradually to come to terms with a
new situation. It faced the clergy first, but as the Clarendon Code
directed persecution against all those who attended 'conventicles',
the laity too had to take decisions.

During the freedom of organization and speculation which had
prevailed in the revolutionary decades, groups of men and women
had rejected the idea that there should be in each parish an

[1] *A Confession of my Faith* (1672), MW v. 191.
[2] McFarlane (1952); now brilliantly supported by Maurice Keen in 'The Influence of
Wyclif', in *Wyclif in his Times*, ed. A. Kenny (Oxford UP, 1986), 127–45.

authorized (ordained) interpreter of the Scriptures, appointed from above, and preferably educated at Oxford or Cambridge. Instead they favoured spontaneously organized discussion groups, each congregation electing its own preacher. Discussion was encouraged, and such organization as there may have been was democratic. Winstanley went further than most when he proposed that in his ideal community one of the few offences liable to the death sentence should be preaching for hire. Very slowly this changed as congregations stabilized under a single charismatic preacher. But still he was expected to work to earn his living six days a week and/or to depend on the voluntary contributions of his flock.

Further changes came with persecution and illegality after 1660. For all dissenting congregations discipline, definition of church membership, excommunication of unsatisfactory members, became necessary. Even Quakers began to acquire the characteristics of an organized church, to the fury of some of their original adherents. For a brief period after 1672 nonconformist congregations were legalized, but only under the aegis of a state-licensed minister. After 1689 this system became permanent. The free, fluid groups of the revolutionary decades had turned into permanent congregations linked together in sects. How did a learned dissenting minister, educated at a dissenting academy, differ from the university-educated parson of the parish? There was loss as well as gain in this transformation, a reversion to some of the characteristics of the old parish churches. Goodman Bunyan, the very type of mechanic preacher, became 'Bishop Bunyan'.

There were political changes too. In the 1640s and 1650s many of the middling sort, previously excluded from politics, had been active both in county committees and in running their congregations. At the restoration many former Puritan clergy—including those who became 'Latitudinarians'—chose to be incorporated in the state church. Since exclusion from the church meant for laymen exclusion from central and local government, dissent soon lost its gentry adherents; they could carry out the social and political functions traditionally expected of them only if they were members of the state church. Some gentlemen continued to patronize dissenters after 1660, but only for one generation. Their heirs had to conform if they were not to become social pariahs. Dissent was a manifestation of the increasing polarization of society in the later seventeenth century.[3] This must have fortified Bunyan's awareness of class distinctions. His is the realism of the defeated. The saints could no longer hope, as they had done since the Reformation, that godly rule might be introduced by Parliament. Like Bunyan's conversion, Emanuel's victory had to come from outside.

After 1660 the reunited gentry recovered and reinforced their political power through the church. JPs tightened their control over the appointment of lower officials like constables. Successive conventicle acts harassed laymen of the middling sort as well as ministers. Informers — necessary in the absence of a police force or an effective local bureaucracy — were used to circumvent sympathy with the victims of persecution.

But this was not a restoration of the Laudian church. Indeed, taking the long view, one of the most significant consequences of the English Revolution was the failure to reconstruct the totalitarian state-ecclesiastical which had collapsed in 1640, when religious toleration established itself *de facto*. The early Baptists John Smyth and Thomas Helwys had insisted that all men had a right to choose how they would worship. The Leveller draft constitution, the Agreement of the People, made this one of five inalienable rights of citizens, with which not even the sovereign Parliament could interfere. Oliver Cromwell in 1654 was I think the first spokesman for an English government to assert that 'liberty of conscience is a natural right', fundamental to the constitution of the Protectorate. Monmouth's Declaration in 1685 promised this liberty to all protestant Englishmen.[4]

The effective establishment of this right in the 1640s involved a profound change in the nature of the English state. The church's attempt after 1660 to recapture its monopoly position failed. Nonconformists were too numerous; some became so rich that it was politically unwise to provoke them too far. The Church of England itself had to adapt to an increasingly commercial society.

[3] I owe this point, and much of the following paragraph, to P. W. Jackson's unpublished Exeter D.Phil. thesis, *Nonconformists and Society in Devon, 1660–1689* (1986), esp. 127, 134, 151, 192, 243, 336–40, 351. Dr Jackson points out that any surviving information about the social composition of nonconformist congregations is liable to overemphasize those of higher social status (313).

[4] Abbott, *Writings and Speeches of Oliver Cromwell*, ed. W. C. Abbott (Harvard UP, 1937–47), iii. 459. Neither Cromwell nor Monmouth would have extended this right to Catholics.

Church courts no longer prosecuted those who traded on holy days; the end of the oath ex officio meant that church courts had to depend on the voluntary confessions of offenders, and so lost much of their power. Excommunication ceased to be a serious sentence. Failure to restore the High Commission Court ensured that ecclesiastical censures could be enforced only with the co-operation of JPs. The secularism to which the Revolution had given free rein reinforced the long-standing erastianism of the Parliamentarian gentry, which had defeated Laudians and Presbyterians alike.

The church no longer looked to the monarchy as its staunchest defender. The Laudians had enjoyed the personal support of Charles I, and were in return the most devoted servants of royal policy; in 1688 the Seven Bishops were the first to take an open stand against James II. Power had moved from crown to Parliament, and the church's loyalty moved with it. The final adjustment after 1688 was slow and painful for many churchmen, but the Non-Jurors were as ephemeral as the dissenting gentry had been after 1660. The grudging Toleration Act of 1689 avoided statements of principle and refused political rights to nonconformists whilst conceding the right to worship on pragmatic grounds. But Locke, on the basis of Leveller ideas, produced a theoretical defence of religious toleration as a natural right.

The change from monopoly to pluralism in religion was made necessary by the dogged resistance of Quakers and men like Bunyan to enforced conformity. They drew their own lines between good and evil, what their consciences could and could not accept; and they succeeded in denying the state the right to decide for them. Dissenters did not speak of 'the state'; they saw local gentlemen and local ecclesiastical officials telling them what to think and how to behave. If they theorized at all, they saw the institutionalized power of evil, of Antichrist. But by their success in preventing the re-establishment of a single persecuting church they transformed the nature of the state. The Church of England remained a highly privileged institution; but its clergy lost their power to monopolize the interpretation of God's Word, as well as effective control of the censorship.

Unlike Levellers, Cromwell, and Locke, Bunyan contributed nothing to the theory of toleration, proclaimed no principles of natural right. But Mr. Valiant-for-the-truth's 'right / To be a pilgrim' amounted to claiming a right to join the congregation of his choice. For Bunyan there was only one true church, and its members had the divine right to worship as they believed God wished, a right which overrode any other considerations. Bunyan was not interested in the rights of any but the members of this true church, who must always be a minority until Christ's reign begins. Dissenters could agree only on dissent. But the obstinate determination of Bunyan and thousands of other English men and women, with many of whom Bunyan profoundly disagreed, made the traditional monopoly state church unworkable. In *The Pilgrim's Progress* entering a church is shown as a matter of choice; and persecution as the weapon of Antichrist.

There was nothing inevitable about the solution of 1689. For some time after 1660 many dissenters had waited in hope of a change for the better. Fortune's wheel had spun many times during the preceding twenty years. Some clergy who conformed — like Ralph Josselin — still refused to accept many ceremonies: lay men and women no doubt had similar reservations. Some looked hopefully to the more tolerant Charles II, then perhaps more nervously to James II. Their attitudes were affected by the fading of millenarian expectations. In the 1640s and 1650s most congregations had seen their religious duties as including reform of the state as well as of the church; the leading spokesmen for radical ideas had been sectaries, associated first with Levellers, then with republicans and Fifth Monarchists. The organized Quakers put forward radical programmes in the 1650s, calling for 'a new earth as well as for a new heaven'.[5]

The idea that religion could be separated from politics was novel in 1660. After that date sectaries became dissenters, half in and half out of the English state: political decisions were forced on them rather than sought after. But the absence of King Jesus and the presence of King Charles (and still more of the Cavalier Parliament) forced a considerable rethinking. Dissenters had to organize themselves in separatist congregations, and to link up nationally in ways hitherto unprecedented, accepting that they were no part of the national church and that they were often compelled to meet in conditions of illegality. It was impossible for dissenters as such to take part in the legal political activity to which they had

---

[5] E. Burrough, *To The Parliament and Commonwealth of England* (1659), 3.

become accustomed. Even after 1689 they remained second-class citizens.

This transformed the nature of congregations. In the 1640s and early 1650s sectarian organization rarely extended beyond the individual church: links between congregations were unstable and not institutionalized. When historians speak of 'Baptists' and 'Quakers' as though there were such entities, they are imposing retrospectively an order which did not exist. Baptists disagreed on sprinkling as against total immersion, on open or closed communion, on the acceptability or not of tithes. Among Quakers there was only rudimentary organization before the restoration. Nayler went his own way in defiance of Fox, Burrough pursued policies of which Fox disapproved. Before 1661 there were some pacifist Quakers, but they did not include Fox or Burrough: the peace principle was novel in 1661, and was certainly not immediately accepted by all Friends. Ranters had even less organization: there was a 'Ranter milieu' and some loose Ranter discussion and drinking groups. But there was no Ranter sect, and the groups dissolved and re-formed. This is the source of the view that the Ranters did not exist, which Professor J. C. Davis has endeavoured to prove.[6]

After 1660 tighter organization and discipline were forced on the congregations in order to survive. There were struggles within and between sects over conditions for church membership. Time and energy were consumed in discussing the conduct befitting a church member, in visiting and correcting backsliders, etc. Congregations necessarily became increasingly inturned. They ceased to make statements on politics, ceased to electioneer. Political activity could only take the form of illegal plotting: Greaves has shown how much of this there was in the years 1660–3, involving Presbyterians and Congregationalists as well as Baptists and Quakers.[7] But gradually stabilization of the regime reduced even millenarians to reliance on a miracle of divine intervention. Either Christ's kingdom was not of this world; or, if it was to come on earth, it would come when God willed it and created the necessary conditions, not when the saints willed it. The latter could only stand fast, maintain the faith, hold together God's servants as they

---

[6] See Appendix.
[7] R. L. Greaves, *Deliver Us from Evil* (Oxford UP, 1986), *passim*.

waited and prayed and hoped—as Samson did in Milton's play. Bunyan, like Milton, preserved a passive millenarianism. Some Anglicans, including bishops and Isaac Newton, retained an academic interest in dating the Second Coming; but as a fighting creed millenarianism died when Venner's failures in 1657 and 1661 were followed by the year 1666, which produced national catastrophes but not the end of the world.

As Ashcraft has shown, revolutionary politics survived the defeat of millenarian expectations. It was now a more secular campaign, turning on bills to exclude James Duke of York from the throne, on plots to assassinate Charles II and his brother, and culminating in Monmouth's invasion. But all these activities started from fear of and hostility towards Catholicism, which was held to be the inevitable precursor of absolutism in the state; and this anti-catholicism drew on deep popular feelings which were not held only by dissenters. So in the 1680s dissenters could not abandon politics, however much they might wish to. Charles and James politicized the issue of religious toleration, inevitably the first demand of all nonconformists. Many of Bunyan's friends and associates were to some degree aware of and favourable towards the revolutionary underground and the *émigrés* in the Netherlands. In 1687 dissenters were forced to take political decisions: to accept toleration for themselves was one thing, but they soon found that the price demanded was support for repeal of the Test Act, which might open the way to the establishment of Catholic absolutism. It was impossible to ignore James's policies, which were blatant where Charles's had been ambiguous: inaction now would have political consequences no less than action.

Nineteenth-century denominational historians (and even some modern historians) have read back into the years before 1689 the ideas and practices of eighteenth-century dissent. Continuity can indeed be traced between some of the religious groups of the revolutionary decades and later dissenting sects. It is perhaps clearest in the case of the Muggletonians, who abjured political activity from the start, and the Quakers. But those 'Congregationalist' and 'Baptist' groups which can be regarded as ancestors of the later sects had more in common with one another, and perhaps with Ranters, particularly in their radical politics, than they had with the sects which later looked back to them. Throughout the years 1660–89 the sects remained ambivalent towards politics. Only after 1689, after the defeat of the radical Whig programme, did dissent create for itself an identity that accepted political and social inferiority as a condition of spiritual purity. The congregations, now mostly abandoned by the gentry, were domesticated as they fitted into the revised version of the old world. In the process both the congregations and the old world underwent significant changes. Religious pluralism, consumers' choice, replaced monopoly; but the range of choice was far more restricted than it had been in the 1640s and 1650s.

The later seventeenth century sees the end of predestinarian theology as the major intellectual force it had been for the preceding century and a half. In the late sixteenth and early seventeenth centuries there had been controversies about grace, about predestination and free will, all over Europe, in Roman Catholic countries no less than in protestant.[8] By the end of the century these had ceased to be matters of urgent intellectual concern, not because solutions had been found but because they no longer seemed so immediately relevant. Why not? And why did predestinarian theology still attract the middling and lower sort who came to form the strength of dissent?

If the association of theories of predestination with social and economic insecurity has any validity,[9] then we note that the lines of social division had come to be drawn differently in England by the later seventeenth century. The great economic divide had left some of the middling sort, and its intellectuals, more prosperous, more secure, safely incorporated within the post-restoration establishment in church and state. The tensions and anxieties now affected a more articulate middling and lower middling sort on the margin, together with those below them: the 'meaner sort' were everywhere reported to form the strength of dissenting congregations. For such people the Calvinist discipline and self-discipline retained its attractions, and the eternal decrees still offered gratifying consolations for those able to see themselves as the elect and their rulers and worldly betters as the reprobate. It was Presbyterians, largely drawn from a higher social group, who were to abandon Calvinism in the eighteenth century.

[8] H. C. Porter, *Reformation and Reaction in Tudor Cambridge* (Cambridge UP, 1958), 282-3, 386-9; R. Tuck, *Natural Rights Theories: Their Origin and Development* (Cambridge UP, 1979), 52, 64.   [9] See pp. 20, 68 above.

The predestinarian theology had appealed especially to those excluded from active participation in politics. But the gathered churches were always a minority. Over time the failure of the visible elect to live up to expectations must have done a great deal to undermine theories of predestination. If the godly could not fall from grace, they must be even fewer than men like Bunyan had expected. The way was opened to a world in which the protestant ethic, with its emphasis on effort and will-power, survived without the predestinarian theology which had originally accompanied it. *The Pilgrim's Progress* may have helped in this transition, since its predestinarianism can be ignored.

We should therefore distinguish sharply between the heroic Puritanism of the mid-seventeenth century, on the one hand, and eighteenth-century dissent. The latter had its own virtues, but they are no longer heroic. Donald Davie has criticized me, no doubt rightly, for speaking uncharitably of 'sterile controversies' and 'spiritual desolation' in early eighteenth-century nonconformity. But there is a descent from *Paradise Lost* and *The Pilgrim's Progress* to the literature of eighteenth-century dissent. Davie praises the poems of Isaac Watts, which have indeed been seriously underestimated. But not even Watts can compare with Milton and Bunyan. There is nothing like them until Blake; and Blake was influenced not by mainline dissent but by Milton and by surviving Ranter and Muggletonian groups. 'What they express is socio-political resentment and aspiration thinly cloaked in religious terminology,' says Donald Davie of Ranters and Muggletonians; 'their ideas are beneath contempt.'[10] That seems to me as 'uncharitable' as anything I say about eighteenth-century dissent; and also to underestimate the 'socio-political resentment and aspiration' in Milton and Bunyan, though I would use less pejorative words to describe it.

In his prefatory note to the reader of *Mr. Badman*, Bunyan had seen as a 'prophecy of the last times' that 'professing men . . . shall be many of them base.' The last times did not come, and the godly had to adapt to a society where careers were open to the talents, and so where there could be no safeguards against the sinfulness of the majority of mankind. The godly became capitalists no less than reprobates, Mr. Badman pointed out. The real tragedy of post-

---

[10] Donald Davie, *A Gathered Church: The Literature of the English Dissenting Interest, 1700–1930*, esp. 15–17, 27, 52, and Lecture 2, *passim*.

revolutionary dissent was that Emanuel could put no trust in his saints. Bunyan and Milton were among the last to cherish the millenarian hope, against hope. It revived with Blake, who looked back to Milton and compared himself to Bunyan.[11]

In the period before 1640, historians have tended to assume, the thinking of the gentry, of the 'county community', is what matters. But in the revolutionary decades the social context widened. *Light Shining in Buckinghamshire* and *The Humble Representation of the Desires of the Soldiers and Officers in the Regiment of Horse for the County of Northumberland*, published in December 1648, foreshadowed the activities of the Diggers in Surrey in 1649. Local theological controversies got into print.[12] As we have seen, Bunyan's *The Holy War* is closely involved with the politics of Bedford corporation.

Bunyan is the first major English writer who was neither London based nor university educated. A Shakespeare, a Marvell, a Traherne, drew on his experience in the countryside of Warwickshire, Yorkshire, and Herefordshire; but they wrote for London and mainly in London. George Herbert had been Public Orator at Cambridge and a courtier before retiring to Bemerton; Vaughan, Herrick, Sir Thomas Browne, often thought of as regional writers, had all been educated at a university. Gerrard Winstanley perhaps comes nearest to anticipating Bunyan, with whom his prose bears comparison; but he cannot approach him in imaginative scope. Langland was London based. Bunyan the itinerant had linked town and country, Bedford and Elstow. In his later years, after *The Pilgrim's Progress*, he visited London frequently as a preacher in demand. But Bedford remained his home; the army had been his school, and prison his university.

Sectaries were meanwhile organizing themselves nationally. Excluded from politics and the universities, they nevertheless gained an identity as sects, and a greater identity as dissent. Their academies lacked social cachet, but they came to give a better, more modern, education than Oxford or Cambridge. Finally abandoning revolutionary politics, dissent nevertheless remained a

---

[11] Offor, iii. 594, 632–3, 644; Blake to William Hayley, 4 Dec. 1804, in *The Letters of William Blake*, ed. G. Keynes (1968), 108. I am indebted for this reference to Dr Michael Tolley of the University of Adelaide.

[12] For an example from Wiltshire see my *Religion and Politics in Seventeenth-Century England* (Brighton, 1986), 151–3, 176. Many more could be given e.g. chap. 8 (i) above.

force, albeit a minor one, in politics. Bunyan endowed it with a literature, which remained constantly in demand. In the more peaceful and comfortable eighteenth-century world, where the values of the Latitudinarians seemed to have triumphed, Bunyan's Pilgrim testified to the dissenting inheritance of compassion, of moral integrity, of struggle.[13]

Bunyan then succeeded to a radical tradition going back to the Lollards, which had no use for clericalism or ceremonial: it doesn't matter whether we pray sitting or lying or walking. The beauty of holiness consists not in incense or stained glass or deferential bowing, but in flowers helping one another to grow: and all flowers in the garden are equal. Bunyan also inherited the protestant conviction that our works cannot save us. We have sold our birthright, we can see dirt in our own tears and filthiness in the bottom of our prayers. But we dare not despair. Grace extended to such muck-heaps of sin as we are entails an overwhelming moral obligation to self-denial, to doing what good we can in however small a way. Bunyan was to die prematurely in consequence of getting soaked in a forty-mile journey on horse-back to reconcile a believer and his father: for 'the soul of religion is in the practic part'. Ultimately the monolithic church-state yielded place to religious pluralism; the sphere of religion was separated from day-to-day politics, became private. When public issues arose which called out moral imperatives — factory reform, slavery — we speak of the nonconformist conscience.

[13] The words are E. P. Thompson's: *The Making of the English Working Class* (Penguin edn.), 36. See also Alick West, '"The Holy War" and "The Pilgrim's Progress"', *Modern Quarterly*, NS 8 (1953), 169–82.

28. Bunyan and Popular Culture

John Bunyan, author of *The Pilgrim's Progress*, and several other little books of an antinomian spirit, too frequently to be met with in the hands of the common people, was, if we mistake not, a brazier of Bedford.

THE REVD THOMAS COX[1]

Whoever would assert an equality of genius between . . . Bunyan and Addison would be thought to defend no less an extravagance than if he had maintained a mole-hill to be as high as Teneriffe or a pond as extensive as the ocean.

DAVID HUME[2]

Samuel Johnson: [The Pilgrim's Progress] has had the best evidence of its merit, the general and continued approbation of mankind.

JAMES BOSWELL[3]

i. Between Two Cultures

SOMETHING is happening to popular culture all over Europe in the sixteenth and seventeenth centuries. The transformation takes different forms in Counter-Reformation countries, in Lutheran towns in Germany, in Sweden, in the England and New England of the covenant theology, and in Presbyterian Scotland. But something happened which we have not yet properly defined. T. S. Eliot got the question right, but 'dissociation of sensibility' is an inadequate answer. Phrases like 'the rise of individualism', 'of capitalism' are groping towards an answer, but a merely economic definition is too narrow. For England our answer must include — among many other things — an explanation of the decline of magic, of hell, of Calvinism as a dominant intellectual system, of millenarianism as a fighting revolutionary creed.[4]

---

[1] *Magna Britannia et Hibernia*, i. (1720), 153. Cox listed Bunyan among six Bedfordshire authors, one of whom was William Sedgwick.

[2] 'Of the standard of Taste', *Essays: Moral, Political and Literary* (1741–2). I cite from the World's Classics edition, p. 235.

[3] *Life of Dr Johnson* (Everyman edn.), i. 470–1.

[4] Keith Thomas, *Religion and the Decline of Magic* (1971); D. P. Walker, *The Decline of Hell* (Chicago UP, 1964). See now M. McKeon, 'Politics of Discourse and the Rise of the Aesthetic in Seventeenth-Century England', in *Politics of Discourse: The Literature and History of Seventeenth-Century England*, ed. K. Sharpe and S. N. Zwicker (California UP, 1987), esp. 50–1.

Bacon saw the inventions of printing, gunpowder, and the mariner's compass as the key to the modern age—though they were imported from China rather than invented in Europe. The compass and gunpowder made possible the opening up of Asia, Africa, and America to European trade and plunder. By 1800 an Industrial Revolution was under way in England and was beginning in other European countries. Printing, the Renaissance, the Reformation, the Revolt of the Netherlands, the English Revolution, and the scientific revolution were all parts of the process. As Peter Burke noted, 'the spread of literacy and the decline of the epic occurred together in Western Europe, while illiteracy and the epic survived together in Sicily, Bosnia, Russia.'[5] Printing gave ballads wider audiences; but fixing a single text discouraged the improvisations of the traditional singers. The spread of literacy widened the gap between upper-class and popular cultures. Bible-reading created a minority religious culture which to some extent cut across classes. Their dedication to this culture of the Bible and godly books left professors blind and indeed hostile to the attractions both of traditional popular culture and of the new science.[6]

In 1500 the European economy was preponderantly agricultural, social relations were preponderantly 'feudal', towns existed in the interstices of society by the grace of king or lords. Life followed agricultural rhythms, time was marked out by the seasons. Men and women worked feverishly when the season or the weather commanded it, and relaxed betweenwhiles, fasting in Lent when food was in shortest supply, celebrating harvest home and the midwinter feast when livestock for which fodder was not available were consumed. Gradually this culture yielded place to the regular rhythms of industrial production, in which the demands of labour discipline called for totally different attitudes. Machinery which is not regularly used is wasted; the market calls for regular production (modified by crises when over-production leads to unemployment). In the medieval culture the agricultural year was marked out by saints' days, most of them taking over traditional pagan seasonal festivals; in the modern world there are

---

[5] Burke, *Popular Culture in Early Modern Europe* (1978), 255–6; cf. 161, and chs. 8 and 9, *passim*.
[6] Seaver, *Wallington's World*, pp. viii, 190–2, 251.

six days of weekly labour (or five if you are lucky) punctuated by occasional holidays on which banks are closed. Peasant attitudes to time differ from industrial attitudes, even for part-time craftsmen with agricultural holdings: non-agricultural work ceases at harvest. Seventeenth-century English economists could not conceal their anger that men worked less when food was cheap. Something of the old low-level moral economy and 'social security' went; hospitality and *noblesse oblige* declined; something of Weber's capitalist rationality came in, as well as an attitude of devil take the hindmost. Dent and Bernard before Bunyan had summed up by saying Covetousness now called himself Good Husbandry.

So upper-class culture differentiated itself from popular culture. Puritanism was in an ambiguous position. Protestant hostility to saints' days and Puritan Sabbatarianism were not mere Bibliolatry. In the old calendar, as protestant propagandists pointed out, up to 100 working days a year were wasted in church-going and drinking. The great festivals led to over-consumption of assets which society could ill afford. The 'protestant ethic' of thrift, labour in one's calling to the glory of God, 'time is money', hatred of waste and idleness, fitted the needs of the new economy. The attack on church courts, which penalized labour on saints' days as well as imposing sexual norms, was part of the same campaign. Sabbatarianism was enforced by London and other towns, by JPs in the industrial counties, and by the House of Commons. The City Fathers disliked theatres on law-and-order grounds, and they were closed in 1642. Two years later Parliament ordered the destruction of all maypoles: they returned in 1660 as the appropriately phallic symbol of Charles II, together with theatres now more tightly controlled from above.

To some extent then Puritanism aided the newly evolving culture. But it appealed to more than one social group. Abolition of saints' days was to the advantage not only of employers but also of small householders working for themselves, and of labourers working on short-term contracts, though not for peasant proprietors or for labourers on yearly contracts. Puritanism, it has often been argued, appealed especially to emerging village élites, to those who prospered during the great divide.

Puritans were censorious of some aspects of the popular culture, for non-economic reasons. Philip Stubbes and Perkins disapproved of bull- and bear-baiting, of cock-fighting, both because they disliked cruelty and because of the pleasure which such activities gave to spectators. Despite Macaulay, the latter seems to me no worse a motive than dislike of cruelty. Violence was endemic in the society. The Dutch were shocked by English merchants' habit of beating their wives. Rough music and witch-rabbling were means of social control, of maintaining accepted norms: the victims might be wives who refused to accept their inferior status, or unhappy old women whom the community resented having to support. Despite social mobility, it was an intensely local society, hostile to strangers, especially those likely to become a burden on the rates. Executions were public holidays. Bunyan in jail tried to assess the chances of his having a good audience if he were hanged. And there were other considerations. Before 1640 cock-fighting and bear-baiting took place in several Bedfordshire parish churches. There might be religious as well as killjoy reasons for objecting to this, or to a Bedfordshire rector acting as a Christmas Lord of Misrule.[7]

It is not just a matter of conscious religious zeal or of conscious adherence to the good old ways. The Major-Generals in the 1650s were no doubt activated by godly zeal when they stopped bull- and bear-baiting; but they also encouraged local oligarchies to dis-gorge embezzled funds which should have been allocated to poor relief; and their prohibition of some horse-racing was motivated by fear of royalist uprisings. Such manifestations of 'Puritanism', together with the radicalism and 'enthusiasm' of sectaries, helped to drive many gentlemen to support the restoration of monarchy and episcopacy; and after 1660 Puritan gentlemen found dissent socially embarrassing. Dissenters were effectively excluded from national and local politics, from the universities and so from high culture. Some gentlemen patronized aspects of the popular cul-ture, cakes and church ales, maypoles and morris-dancing, bear- and bull-baiting, cock-fighting, the charivari. They maintained 'good neighbourhood' by imposing their own patterns of defer-ence on selected activities; others they ignored or despised and tried to suppress. Witch persecution ceased when the upper classes no longer believed in witchcraft. As David Underdown puts it, 'the old festive culture was being manipulated to reinforce the

[7] Brown, 5; J. S. Purvis (ed.), *Tudor Parish Documents of the Diocese of York* (Cambridge UP, 1948), 160–1; Joyce Godber, *History of Bedfordshire, 1066–1888* (Bedfordshire County Council, 1969), 292.

messages of obedience being transmitted in other ways by the church and the law.'[8]

So we get a threefold division. 'High' culture, that of Augustan literature, Latin-based; plebeian culture, traditional, magical, full of song and dance but virtually unlettered; and the dissenting culture of the Book, which rejected many aspects of the old rural culture but was excluded from 'high' culture. Simultaneously men were becoming more conscious of divisions between 'the people' and 'the poor'.[9] In the sixteenth and seventeenth centuries many yeomen and artisans came to share economic interests with the landed upper class, and looked down on those who had not been able to afford education. So the popular culture became 'vulgar': the word itself changes meaning; rejection of the popular and of the dissenting culture became necessary for the social climber. The word 'superstition', Peter Burke reminds us, undergoes a similar change, not only in English, from the 1650s. The traditional sense of 'false religion' gives way to 'irrational fears' — those of the lower classes.[10]

Many factors then contributed to the divergence of cultures. Paul Slack has convincingly shown that the impact of plague on large towns had serious consequences for traditional popular *mores*. Plague hit especially the poor. The attempts of governments and the rich to control it came up against ingrained social habits and perceived moral obligations. Shutting plague victims up in their houses, or in pest-houses in the fields, prohibiting crowded funerals — all these infringed 'neighbourliness' in the interests of 'order' — an order which was seen as benefiting the rich. The preachers' association of plague with 'sin' led them and magistrates to attack the sins of the poor — idle vagrants, ale-houses, drunkards, plays, as well as popular sports.[11] In 1665–6 the government feared that the discontented might take advantage of the plague to rebel. 'Now is the time if we will stir', said a Yorkshireman, 'for the Anabaptists and Quakers are not afraid of plague.'[12]

---

[8] Underdown, *Revel, Riot and Rebellion*, 63–4, 275–84; Thompson, 'Patrician Society, Plebeian Culture', *Journal of Social History*, 7 (1974), *passim*.

[9] See my *People and Ideas in Seventeenth-Century England* (Brighton, 1986), ch. 12; Walzer, *The Revolution of the Saints*, 134.   [10] Burke, *Popular Culture*, 241.

[11] For the especial appeal of plays to the poor see Underdown, *Revel, Riot and Rebellion*, pp. 50, 57–8, 69.

[12] Slack, *The Impact of Plague in Tudor and Stuart England* (1985), 231–40, 250–2, 298–309. The quotation is from p. 302.

'Neighbourliness' could mean very different things, though everyone agreed that it was a virtue. William Grant, chaplain to Bishop Goodman of Gloucester and pre-1640 vicar of Isleworth, lamented that 'all good fellowship was laid aside in the parish'. He promised to bring it in again, offering 'wine and tobacco to all that would come to the vicarage house on Sundays after prayers.' He was alleged to sit up till 2 or 3 in the morning playing cards. 'Good neighbourhood' was equally strongly advocated by Bunyan in *Christian Behaviour* (1663), but his conception of it was different both from Grant's and from that of the opponents of pest-houses. For Bunyan neighbourliness started from cultivation of the Christian virtues. In this light the Book of Sports had been socially divisive: it set the values of the middling sort against those of the populace, supported sometimes by gentlemen and parsons. David Underdown thinks that the divisions of 1642 were as much cultural as religious or political.[13]

The Reformation had posed as alternatives salvation through the sacraments and ceremonies of the church, and salvation through direct individual relationship to God. Two consequences followed: first, tension between individual consciences and any national ecclesiastical authority—Pope, king, bishops, presbyterian synods; and second a search to end the *isolation* of the individual that protestantism tended to create.[14] The widening rift between rich and poor undermined village unity. The increasingly oligarchical parish came to be less concerned with solidarity than with keeping down the burden of poor relief on ratepayers. Gradually elect individuals came to recognize one another and form groups within parish churches. But there were difficulties in being of two churches at the same time, and an especial problem of discipline. The godly of the middling sort rejected the culture of the Book of Sports. They called for high standards of conduct. Were they to try to impose them on other members of their community, or were there to be two standards?

Bernard in *The Isle of Man* called for godly parish officers everywhere; after 1640 attempts were made in London to enforce discipline through control of parishes. But the godly reformation

[13] Nehemiah Wallington, *Historical Notices* (1869), i. 193; MW iii. 43–50; Underdown, *Revel, Riot and Rebellion*, 67–8, 143, 198. For Grant see my *Economic Problems of the Church* (Oxford UP, 1956), 171, 297, 301.
[14] *GA*, 29–31.

of 1641-2 was never completed; the Army saw to that. Only in New England was 'the greater part' also 'the better part'. Another way was for the pure to separate from the ungodly. After 1640 those self-selected groups which had broken with the parochial system — crossing parish boundaries, especially in towns — could choose their own mechanic preacher and work out a congregational discipline of mutual support and help, their own work and marriage ethic, as at Bedford. 'They were to me,' said Bunyan, 'as if . . . they were people that dwelt alone, and were not to be reckoned among their neighbours (Nu. XXIII. 9).'[15]

Underdown speaks of 'a new kind of community, united by belief and mission, sometimes formally by covenant in a "gathered church" as a substitute for the territorial parish church community that was now disintegrating.'[16] Hence Bunyan's evolving sense of warmth and love *within* the congregation, softening his harsher Calvinism by recognizing the problems of the insecure elect, chasing up the hypocrites among them, and maintaining strong barriers against the unregenerate many. The godly were a peculiar people, beleaguered.

Nor should we sentimentalize the village community. Early seventeenth-century England was a much-controlled society. There was no bureaucracy, no police force: the capitalist ethic was not yet internalized. Laudians and Presbyterians both relied on neighbourly espionage and denunciation in villages. The voluntary communities of the godly would start with friendly advice and admonition and only ultimately resort to excommunication. Theirs was certainly not more oppressive than the discipline of the church courts, except in so far as they were likely to be better informed and consequently more effective. Some traditional ideas and norms struggled to survive against new ideas and norms struggling to realize themselves. The charivari could on occasion be used against Laudian clergymen.[17]

Such issues were especially pressing in London and other great towns, to which men and women fled, among other reasons, because of the anonymity they enjoyed there, the freedom from

[15] Bernard, *The Isle of Man*, 80-4; Seaver, *Wallington's World*, 173; *GA*, 16.
[16] Underdown, *Revel, Riot and Rebellion*, 41-2; see my *Society and Puritanism in Pre-Revolutionary England* (Penguin edn.), chs. 14 and 15.
[17] Underdown, *Revel, Riot and Rebellion*, 61-2, 178.

supervision. The breakdown of 1641–2 made London uncontrol-
lable: sin was visible everywhere—drunkenness, swearing, sex,
oppression of the poor. The godly failed to establish social control
through the parishes. There were just not enough godly magistrates. Their own congregational discipline was inturned, leaving
the profane to their own devices.[18]

We do not know how far the people of England had ever been
fully integrated into the state church. Historians are coming to
recognize that few of the lower classes went regularly to church:
they were not worth fining by church courts when they did not.[19]
The breakdown of the machinery of discipline and control after
1640, and the establishment of effective religious toleration, produced startling consequences, depicted, no doubt with much
exaggeration, by scores of shocked pamphleteers. They were not
surprised by what happened when natural men and women could
meet freely and discuss matters which interested them; it was well
known that natural men and women (the vast majority of the
population) were incurably sinful and must be restrained. But
conservative alarm became ever more hysterical as unordained
mechanic preachers established semi-permanent congregations,
as women began to preach, as traditional lower-class scepticism
and anti-clericalism began to be taught and discussed openly in the
Ranter milieu in the crisis years 1649–51.

What is freedom but choice? Milton asked. But multiplicity of
choice looked like chaos to those who expected stability of custom.
The sects could not agree among themselves: how much novelty,
what novelty? How much tradition, which traditions? Who was to
decide? What shall I do to be saved? The question became
personal rather than social. For Bunyan it took the form of
querying norms of behaviour. Were tipcat and bell-ringing permissible? What new norms should be observed? The choices were
difficult, painful, and serious. His Bedfordshire contemporary,
Francis Osborne, saw a transition from traditional 'patterns and
old forms' to 'new and forbidden discoveries'.[20]

As Slack shows, issues were not clear-cut, motives were mixed.

---

[18] Seaver, *Wallington's World*, 96–7, 132, 141, 173.
[19] B. Reay (ed.), *Popular Culture in Seventeenth-Century England* (1985), 23, 43.
[20] Osborne, *Traditional Memoirs of the Reigns of Queen Elizabeth and King James I*
(1658), Epistle.

Conflicts were mediated by tradition, communal solidarity, and good intentions. Some of the concessions made by Puritan preachers could be interpreted to the advantage of the new capitalist *mores*; but the preachers' utopia was not capitalist. Nor was Bunyan's in *Mr. Badman*.

Historians have looked perhaps too exclusively at those who express the economic rationality of the future, as old-fashioned historians of science used to pick out ideas which seemed to be those which were going to win. This leads them to concentrate on Petty and political arithmetic, Boyle and the Royal Society, Hobbes and rational politics, Newton's great synthesis. We forget that Hermeticism and Paracelsanism made their contribution to the scientific revolution, that Boyle was at least as much concerned with combating atheism (and the radical sectarianism which he believed led to atheism) as with scientific truth — a distinction which he would not have admitted — and that Newton was as interested in alchemy and Biblical prophecies as in mathematics and physics.

But the trends towards economic rationality were all-pervasive, regardless of men's conscious intentions.[21] England's food problems were solved thanks to the abolition of feudal tenures and the establishment of a freer market during the Revolution. But the hidden hand of the market worked against the poor, and it was aided by statutory overriding of traditional rights. Land came to be treated as a commodity to be exploited for profit, protected by absolute rights of ownership where previously custom had guaranteed community access. After 1660 pamphlets opposing enclosure ceased to be published. In the later seventeenth century, as Barry Reay perceptively observed, 'protection of traditional rights . . . could be seen as rebellion.'[22] From all sides the pressures were on against the popular culture.

Filmer and royalists had attempted to corner the household as the basis for justification of absolutism: the king is the father of the

---

[21] Joyce Appleby, *Economic Thought and Ideology in Seventeenth-Century England* (Princeton UP, 1978), *passim*; D. Zaret, *The Heavenly Contract: Ideology and Organization in Pre-Revolutionary Puritanism* (Chicago UP, 1985), *passim*.

[22] Underdown, *Revel, Riot and Rebellion*, 61–3, 67; Seaver, *Wallington's World*, 246; J. Sharpe, 'The People and the Law', in Reay, *Popular Culture*, 261–4; Buchanan Sharp, 'Popular Protest in Seventeenth-Century England', ibid. 290–6; Reay, 'Introduction', ibid. 17 and *passim*.

general family, head of the national household. But Winstanley envisaged a communist society based on a federation of equal households; Levellers, Bunyan, and many other Puritans a society of relatively equal households trading fairly with one another. The latter would have made sense only if capitalist accumulation could have been curbed, as Winstanley, Harrington, and Locke wished to do. We have seen the efforts of Bunyan and the Bedford congregation to preserve some traditional standards of the just price and distributive justice; and we have heard Bunyan's increasingly bitter invectives against professors who adapted themselves to the standards and demands of the market. Bunyan and his congregation were clinging to a *via media* between old and new values — the *via media* of the defeated radicals of the Revolution.

Yet Bunyan's prose encapsulates some of the departing values. Despite his and his congregation's exclusion from politics, the tension of class-awareness remains. The rootedness of his prose in rural and artisan life preserves it from the courtly, gentlemanly, and scholarly shams of upper-class literature, with its attempt to plant hedges round the Hebrew, Greek, and Latin of Pontius Pilate. It is difficult to think of any great writer in seventeenth- or eighteenth-century England who was as passionately, fiercely, and theologically on the side of the poor as Bunyan.

ii. *Prose and Verse*

We can see in Bunyan's imaginative writing almost a conscious take-over of élite literature for a middle- and lower-class audience, endowing it with new positive values. Cervantes in *Don Quixote* 'laughed Spain's chivalry away', mocking the romances. Bunyan rejected romances on ideological grounds, but he transmuted some of their archetypal themes and fitted them into his Puritan allegory. Professor Sharrock detected a similar transformation of the themes of the morality plays, through the radical Puritanism of Richard Bernard and of Richard Overton in *The Araignement of Mr. Persecution.*[23] Both may have influenced Bunyan.

Before Bunyan became a writer he had been a successful preacher. His prose is vivid because it is spoken, demotic. When he

[23] Sharrock, 'The Trial of Vices in Puritan Fiction', *Baptist Quarterly*, NS 14 (1951–2), *passim.*

preached, the words flowed. When he wrote his sermons up for publication they presumably came equally spontaneously. In *The Pilgrim's Progress*:

> Still as I pulled it came: and so I penned
> It down.[24]

We are reminded of the nightly visits which Milton received from his Muse. Bunyan's subconscious supplied adventures from chap-book romances, and intense class-feeling; the Puritan intellectual framework structured and steadied it.

The Holy War is Bunyan's conscious attempt to write a popular epic. *A Book for Boys and Girls* reworks the protestant emblem tradition of Quarles and Wither, without the 'literary' pretensions which so soon dated their poems. *Grace Abounding* moves the spiritual autobiography towards the novel; *Mr. Badman* does the same for protestant casuistry. Even some of Bunyan's more strictly theological works — *The Barren Fig-tree* (1673), *The Greatness of the Soul* (1682), and *Advice to Sufferers* (1684) — strive to elevate sermon-style propaganda to the level of popular literature. One example from each must suffice.

> The sinner cries again, 'Good Lord, try me this once. . . . I will never be so bad again, I will do better.' 'Well', saith God, 'Death, let this professor alone for this time. . . . It may be he will mind to keep his promise.' . . . But by that he hath put on his clothes, is come down from his bed, and ventured into the yard or shop, and there sees how all things are gone to sixes and sevens, he begins to have second thoughts and says to his folks, 'What have you all been doing? How are all things out of order? I am I cannot tell what behindhand. One may see, if a man be but a little a to side, that you have neither wisdom nor prudence to order things. . . .'[25]

> And if at any time they [sin and the soul] can or shall meet with each other again, and nobody never the wiser; O what courting will be 'twixt sin and the Soul; and this is called doing of things in the dark.[26]

> The executioner comes to John [the Baptist]; now whether he was at dinner, or asleep, or whatever he was about, the bloody man bolts in upon him, and the first word he salutes him with is, 'Sir, strip, lay down your neck, for I am come to take away your head.' 'But hold, stay; wherefore?

---

[24] *GA*, 27–8; *PP*, 2.
[25] *The Barren Fig-tree*, Offor, iii. 580.
[26] *The Greatness of the Soul*, MW ix. 193.

Pray let me commend my soul to God.' 'No, I must not stay; I am in haste;' 'slap' says his sword, and off falls the good man's head.[27]

Critics have rightly stopped saying that Bunyan's style is Biblical. He sometimes echoes the Bible in set pieces when he is consciously indulging in fine writing: but at its best his style is conversational, the conversation of yeomen and artisans, as full of near-proverbs as the conversation of Sancho Panza.[28] 'A river will take away the very stink of a dead dog.' 'Christ hath a bosom.' 'The lumber and cumber of this world.'[29] 'Words easy to be understood,' Bunyan wrote, 'do often hit the mark when high and learned ones do only pierce the air.' He is echoing countless Puritan preachers. All Bunyan's art, like this metaphor from archery, springs from everyday life, shared with his audience. 'As I was walking in the fields . . .'. 'The sentences,' said Shaw, 'go straight to their mark; and their concluding phrases soar like the sunrise or swing and drop like a hammer.' They are far removed from the courtly tone which Dryden thought essential for good prose. Bunyan seems to have realized, with some satisfaction, that his style was highly individual, inimitable.[30]

Bunyan lived through a revolution which must have forced a great deal of rethinking, about style as well as content. For ten or fifteen years ordinary people spoke in print in their own voices, or something more like them than ever before. Overton picked up Martin Marprelate, Walwyn and Overton the popular dialogue of Puritan writers and of plays. Winstanley, Coppe, Clarkson, Fox, and other early Quakers showed the creative power of popular prose, growing from the rural and artisan economy, whose virtues of clarity and matter-of-factness Sprat singled out for imitation. But popular prose had other virtues—passion, compassion, charity, tolerance, and humanity, which the Royal Society's prose lacked and some of which Dryden avoided. Passion and compassion were needed more than ever for those who had to face the trials of the defeated revolution and subsequent attempts to down-

[27] *Advice to Sufferers*, Offor, ii. 702.

[28] Contrast his occasional self-consciously flowery prose: 'Now also will the pretty robins and little birds in the Lord's field so sweetly send forth their pleasant notes' (*The Holy City* (1665), MW iii. 94–7; cf. *Come, and Welcome* (1678), MW viii. 392).

[29] *The Water of Life* (1688), Offor, iii. 544; *The Heavenly Foot-man*, MW v. 169; *The Holy City*, MW iii. 77.

[30] *The Holy City*, 71; *GA*, 3–4 and *passim*; *PP*, 168; Shaw, *Man and Superman* (1907), pp. xxviii–xxxiii.

grade popular culture — the censor's hostility to 'the great masters of the popular style'.[31]

There is little to say about the place of Bunyan's writings in the transition from epic to novel that has not already been said. The failure of Cowley and Davenant to complete their epics marks the end of an epoch. Gunpowder left little room for heroes. Single combat necessarily and increasingly became an upper-class interest (the duel) or a lower-class interest patronized by the gentry (prize-fighting). Milton's new heroism of fortitude was individualistic, non-militant. Religion was the *social* bond which linked the new heroic individuals into communities. There was a plethora of Biblical epics as classical epic declined. *Paradise Lost* is already in a different world: it is about the fortunes of a married couple in a hostile universe — a subject for a novel rather than an epic. L. B. Wright long ago drew special attention to 'the importance of handbooks on family affairs in fertilizing the ground for the domestic novel' [32] — a long way from the traditional epic. From this point of view it is *Mr. Badman* — the novel of the household — rather than *The Pilgrim's Progress* — 'the epic of the itinerant' — that foreshadows the novel, though Part II is moving in that direction.

But Bunyan's relation to the decline of epic and the rise of the novel, to Defoe, is usually a badly posed question. There were hundreds of roads converging on the novel, not least the evolution of an impersonal capitalist ideology which Joyce Appleby has so splendidly illuminated for us, and Jean-Christophe Agnew has incorporated into his study of theatre and the market.[33] We tend to concentrate on the few outstanding figures whom posterity has chosen to remember. But contemporaries did not know what the great tradition was going to be. What mattered for them, and should matter for us, is popular fiction which the enormous haphazardness of posterity has forgotten. Until this has been analysed we cannot trace with confidence the multifarious origins

[31] See pp. 362–3 below.

[32] D. Trotter, *The Poetry of Abraham Cowley* (1979), chs. 2 and 5; L. B. Wright, *Middle-Class Culture in Elizabethan England* (N. Carolina UP, 1935), 224; cf. my *Writing and Revolution in Seventeenth-Century England* (Brighton, 1985), 324–5.

[33] Appleby, *Economic Thought and Ideology, passim*; Agnew, *Worlds Apart: The Market and the Theatre in Anglo-American Thought, 1550–1750* (Cambridge UP, 1986), *passim*; P. Salzman, *English Prose Fiction, 1558–1700: A Critical History* (Oxford UP, 1985), ch. 13. See now Michael McKeon, *The Origins of the English Novel, 1600–1740* (Johns Hopkins UP, 1987).

of the novel as we know it. Of the traditional 'precursors', Aphra Behn published *Oroonoko* in the year of Bunyan's death, but she may have written it whilst he was writing Part I of *The Pilgrim's Progress*. *Love Letters between a Nobleman and his Sister* began to appear simultaneously with Part II. Aphra Behn had escaped much more than Bunyan from the moralizing authorial intrusions which differentiate him from most novelists after Defoe. She has a moral lesson to convey, but she conveys it by the story as a whole, rather than by direct comment—in this more like Richardson.

What links Bunyan backwards with Cervantes and the picaresque novels, and forwards with Defoe, Richardson, Fielding, and Smollett, is the exuberant mobility of the world he depicts. It is social as well as physical mobility: classes are all mixed up. Pamela married her master, Clarissa could find herself in a brothel, whereas Jane Austen's families are statically self-contained—despite or because of living in the world of the French Revolution. Perhaps the expansion of overseas trade added to this sense of mobility, as well as creating possibilities for utopias on earth or for clashes of cultures—*The Isle of Pines*, *Oroonoko*, *Robinson Crusoe*, *Gulliver's Travels*.

Mobility within England offered new angles of criticism for popular literature. From Brome's *A Jovial Crew* onwards itinerants are used as instruments of serious social analysis. The anonymous *Don Tomazo*, published in the same year as *Mr. Badman*, depicts a man who cold-bloodedly preys upon society. Itinerants of the revolutionary decades included Ranters like Coppe and Clarkson, who offered theoretical challenges to traditional sexual morality, as vagabonds no doubt did in practice. Itinerant preachers or tinkers, no less than knights errant, had to face sexual problems. Clarkson's autobiography (probably semi-fictitious) set the pattern for Defoe: he even anticipated Defoe's narrator in his pretence of repentance as he salaciously describes his past sinfulness. Restoration comedy took over the Ranter idea that sexual pleasure was possible and could be discussed, as well as the Ranter penchant for witty profanity and irreverence. The publication of pornographic literature in England dates from the 1650s.

As capitalist society triumphantly stabilized, its standards were challenged by Defoe's *History of the Pyrates* (if it is Defoe's—the authorship doesn't matter for our present purposes), by Gay's *The*

Beggar's Opera, and by Swift's Houyhnhnms. Royal slaves, beggars, and pirates can make fundamental criticisms of the new world they have to adapt to or escape from, just as dissenters and small household producers have to adapt to it. Mr. Badman, Moll Flanders, highwaymen, and pirates, all in one way or another criticize the new society by preying on it, by 'crime'.[34]

So the novel doesn't grow only out of the respectable bourgeois household. It also encompasses the picaro, the vagabond, the itinerant, the pirate—outcasts from the stable world of good householders—those who cannot or will not adapt. Cervantes made a joke of the contrast between the standards of the traditional world and bourgeois reality: there was no meeting-place. Bunyan does not look at the itinerant's world from outside. He can fuse the old romance literature with the demands of the protestant ethic for self-discipline, self-control. He was perhaps the first to do this, but he had many followers.

The early novel takes its life from motion. For Hobbes, 'Life itself is but motion', and 'knowledge of the nature of motion' is 'the gate of philosophy universal'. There is 'but one universal cause, which is motion'.[35] The novel too assumes that rest is an abnormal state, which calls for explanation. The early novel is about society in flux, about individuals in relation to a society in flux. Hence the recurrence of the Robinson Crusoe situation, the individual facing his fate alone—like Bunyan in *Grace Abounding*, Christian in *The Pilgrim's Progress*. Only as society restabilizes does the novel settle down to dealing with families, with individuals in relation to other individuals.

Critics have seen a 'polarization of taste' from the 1650s. Berkenhead and other embattled royalists turned to classicism as a defence and consolation in defeat. With the restoration language became a social issue. 'Enthusiasm' was taboo. The scientists' demand for clear and distinct ideas provided one model for prose: Sprat's ideal, though based on the language of artisans, was consciously directed against the 'enthusiastic' language of sectaries. Roger L'Estrange, Charles II's censor, wanted to suppress 'the great masters of the popular style', who 'speak plain and strike home to the capacity and humours of the multitude.' He might

---

[34] Thompson, *Whigs and Hunters: The Origin of the Black Act* (1975), chs. 9 and 10.
[35] Hobbes, *English Works*, i. pp. viii, 69; Tom Sorell, *Hobbes* (1986), 60.

have been referring to Bunyan, though in fact he was looking back to radical pamphleteers who wrote 'in times of freedom'. As sumptuary laws became unenforceable, social distinctions came more and more to be based on education and culture. 'Acceptance as a gentleman', Charles Barber suggested, 'was probably becoming less a matter of birth and more a matter of breeding and manners.' Glanville discouraged preachers from 'the use of vulgar proverbs and homely similitudes and rude clownish phrases': again the cap would fit Bunyan. After 1660 — as in France after the Fronde — classicism proclaimed the stabilizing virtues of monarchy and the established church. Dryden then made the essential shift from 'plain' to 'correct' style, 'correct' style being that of the court. It was a shift from private to public prose.[36] Former royalists and former Parliamentarians had coalesced to form a new ruling and religious élite. Their solidarity was signified in language and education. The two nations, church and dissent, the universities and the 'illiterate', became two cultures.

Boyle, the Royal Society, and Newtonian science appeared to give unquestionable certainty, such as the godly sects had failed to provide. J. R. and M. C. Jacob have made us aware how much the Latitudinarians' rational Christianity contributed to the development of science. Bunyan would have agreed with Henry Stubbe, in J. R. Jacob's assessment of him:

the Royal Society was staging a counter-reformation of its own, namely a response to the social radicalism of the English Revolution. . . . Modern science in seventeenth-century England . . . developed in part in response to the growing separation between the élite and the people.

It may have helped to widen this gap.[37]

Bunyan's pilgrims were accused of being opposed to natural

---

[36] Capp, in Reay, *Popular Culture*, 231–2; L'Estrange, *Considerations and Proposals in Order to the Regulation of the Press* (1663), 10; Barber, *The Theme of Honour's Tongue: A Study of Social Attitudes in the English Drama from Shakespeare to Dryden* (Göteborg, 1985), 22; Dryden, *Of Dramatic Poesy and other Critical Essays* (Everyman edn.), i. 181; Newman, in Newey, 234–5, 241.

[37] J. R. Jacob, *Roger Boyle and the English Revolution: A study in Social and Intellectual Change* (New York, 1977), *passim*; M. C. Jacob, *The Newtonians and the English Revolution, 1689–1720* (Hassocks, 1976), *passim*; J. R. Jacob, '"By an Orphean charm": Science and the Two Cultures in Seventeenth-Century England', in P. Mack and M. C. Jacob (eds.), *Politics and Culture in Early Modern Europe: Essays in Honour of H. G. Koenigsberger* (Cambridge UP, 1987), 245–9 and *passim*. See now M. C. Jacob, *The Cultural Meaning of the Scientific Revolution*, esp. 19–23, 105.

science. In *The Pilgrim's Progress* and *The Holy War* Bunyan jeered at the idea of there being other worlds, put forward by the Latitudinarian scientist Bishop Wilkins. Keith Thomas pointed out that the radical sects retained some traditional magical and communal aspects of popular culture; the Calvinist Puritanism of the urban *haute bourgeoisie* could pass more easily into Hobbism or sceptical Latitudinarianism and deism. Ranter scepticism moved in the same direction, questioning the authority of the Bible in the light of increased knowledge of the non-Christian world. Bunyan early broke with this tendency, which fed into the libertinism of the restoration aristocracy.[38]

So Bunyan's links with popular culture extended to hostility towards science as well as towards Latitudinarians who helped to take it over for the church. This no doubt contributed to the contempt shown for Bunyan by many of the traditional élite; until Blake, the romantic movement and evangelicism headed a reaction against Newtonianism and deism.

Upper-class classical culture, from Dryden to Johnson, ran the risk of superficiality and affectation, academic pedantry and snobbish facetiousness. The plebeian culture of those excluded from politics and the universities ran the risk of banality and vulgarity on the one hand, of philistine piety on the other. Bunyan avoided both pitfalls. It was important that he was no 'killjoy' Puritan — that he had enjoyed the chivalrous romances, that music and dancing are everywhere in *The Pilgrim's Progress*, that the pilgrims drink wine and spirits,[39] that Bunyan urged hymn-singing on his congregation. The radical reformation of the sixteenth century had employed hymns sung to popular tunes as one way of civilizing the popular culture. In its turn, congregational hymn-singing preserved some of the traditions of the village community which the state church had always shunned. And of radicalism: the words of eighteenth-century Muggletonian songs are often more seditious than their official theology. In such congregations something of the popular culture hung on — independent, off-political, tolerant. Carols in the popular quatrain measures were remembered only by the lower classes until they were revived in the

---

[38] Thomas, *Religion and the Decline of Magic*, 638. Owen mocked the Royal Society (*The Experience of Defeat*, 175, 177).
[39] See p. 266 above.

nineteenth century, as the romantics revived lyrics in the traditional quatrain form.[40]

Later nonconformity had its unlovely features: but the alternative for many might be drowning their poverty in an alehouse. If evicted copyholders were to become full-time wage-labourers, they would need help and solidarity to retain their self-respect. If small householders were to become capitalists, it was better that they should be honest capitalists. Bunyan rejected Mr. Badman's version of capitalism, false weights and measures, usury, fraudulent bankruptcy; the Bedford congregation enforced standards of economic and social behaviour. Piety was saved from narrowness by Bunyan's unerring feel for the colloquial phrase, by his ability to embrace the culture of the fairy-story, by his love of music and singing, his ability to write poems for children, and his compassion, as well as by his waiting millenarianism. His enormous strength and vitality derive largely from this ability to draw on the resources of a purged popular culture.

iii Bunyan and Milton

The Pilgrim's Progress is not the epic of Everyman. It is the epic of the godly, who for Bunyan are almost by definition lower-class, industrious people. Excluded from the universities and upper-class culture, they are adapting to the pressures of an increasingly capitalist society. Hence Bunyan's continuing dislike of and contempt for the gentry and their state church. Milton shared these dislikes: the aristocracy and the clergy were singled out for destruction at the end of *Samson Agonistes*, when 'the vulgar only 'scaped who stood without'. But Milton was himself a university graduate, steeped in classical culture, though intellectually more radical than Bunyan, as well as more political. His audience, fit though few, was not that for which the tinker wrote.

Throughout this book I have suggested comparisons and contrasts between Milton and Bunyan—the two greatest English Puritan writers, who both straddle the seventeenth century. Milton was born twenty years earlier than Bunyan. He died in 1674, before the money power was fully established. Unlike Bunyan, Milton abandoned Calvinism. He remained an élitist

---

[40] A. L. Lloyd, *Folk-Song in England* (Paladin edn., 1975), 123–6; my *Religion and Politics in Seventeenth-Century England* (Brighton, 1986), 265; *Reformation to Industrial Revolution* (Penguin edn.), 284–5.

republican, though conscious of the fact that he had been maintained by the sweat of other men.[41] Addison, who despised Bunyan, came to represent Milton as the great orthodox Puritan poet, a respectable figure whose republicanism could be disregarded as 'sincere' if misguided, irrelevant anyway once the essentials of a republic had been established under a king by the Glorious Revolution of 1688. So Milton was made acceptable to polite literary circles in the eighteenth century. *The Pilgrim's Progress* and *Grace Abounding* remained vastly popular with the middling sort in England and the American colonies throughout the eighteenth century; and a discerning few—Defoe, Swift, Sterne, Cowper, Johnson—appreciated Bunyan. But Addison, Young, Hume, and Burke were more typical: Bunyan's reputation ascended the social scale only as the middling sort and evangelicism gained respectability in the nineteenth century.

Thus Bunyan leap-frogged Milton, the seventeenth-century radical, in popular esteem. Bunyan came to be accepted as the creative artist of dissent, in a way that the university classicist Milton never could be. One of Tillyard's good insights was that Bunyan was 'in constant opposition'. Langland, with whom in many respects Bunyan seems comparable, 'criticizes the government, . . . but he is not against it.' He has a sense of responsibility for the ruling group which Bunyan never had—unlike Milton, who had been employed by the government of the Commonwealth.[42] Bunyan seems the more conservative of the two in his outlook. But during his twelve years in jail he stood out against the restored regime when men with greater radical credentials—Walwyn, Coppe, Winstanley—remained silent. Bunyan's strong assertion of the popular culture, his hatred and contempt for the rich, on theological grounds, distinguishes him from Milton. Milton too fought on, in *Paradise Lost, Paradise Regained, Samson Agonistes*, and *Of True Religion, Heresy, Schism, Toleration*; but his disillusioned dismissal of the people puts him in sharp contrast with Bunyan. Milton's republicanism could appear safely abstract after 1688 had ruled 'the people' out of politics; Bunyan's class-conscious piety remained suspect.

[41] Milton, *Reason of Church-Government* (1642), *MCPW*, i. 804: Brown, 462–3; R. L. Greaves, 'Bunyan Through the Centuries: Some Reflections', *English Studies*, 64 (The Netherlands, 1983), 113–14.
[42] E. M. W. Tillyard, *The English Epic and its Background* (1954), 390–1.

29. Bunyan and the World

A good cause, what is that? . . . When a man can be comfortable at the loss of all, when he is under the sentence of death, or at the place of execution; when a man's Cause, a man's conscience, the promise and the Holy Ghost, have all one comfortable voice, and do all, together with their trumpets, make one sound in the soul . . .

BUNYAN[1]

Glorious Bunyan, you too were a 'rebel', and I love you *doubly* for *that*. I read you in Newgate — so I could, I understand, if I had been taken care of in Bedford jail; — your books are in the library of even your Bedford jail. Hurrah for progress!

JOHN JAMES BEZER[2]

i. Bunyan the Man

BUNYAN died on 31 August 1688, at the house of John Strudwick, a grocer at the sign of the Star on Snow Hill, London, who in 1692 was one of the deacons at George Cokayne's church. (Samuel Pepys's cousin by marriage, Thomas Strudwick, was a confectioner who also lived on Snow Hill.) Bunyan was buried in Bunhill Fields, the dissenters' burial place where Thomas Goodwin already lay, and where Defoe was to join them forty years later. The inventory of Bunyan's property after his death added up to a total of £42. 19s. This is more than the average tinker would leave, but it suggests that most of the profits from *The Pilgrim's Progress* had gone to printers of pirated editions. Ponder did not do very well out of it either. Bunyan's eighteenth-century descendants remained artisans.[3]

Now that we have followed Bunyan through the sixty years of his life, I find it difficult to sum up his powerful but elusive personality. The temptation in writing a book like this is to over-emphasize the role of its hero. Bunyan cannot be claimed as a great leader: he was

---

[1] *Advice to Sufferers* (1684), MW x. 43, 93.
[2] *Autobiography of One of the Chartist Rebels of 1848*, in the *Christian Socialist* (1851), quoted in David Vincent, *Testaments of Radicalism: Memoirs of Working-Class Politicians, 1790–1885* (1977), 167. I owe this quotation to the generosity of Bob Owens.
[3] Brown, chs. 16 and 17; *GA*, 174; F. M. Harrison, 'Nathaniel Ponder: The Publisher of *The Pilgrim's Progress*', *The Library*, 4th Ser. 15 (1934), 266 and *passim*. Snow Hill was famous for ballads and ballad-mongers.

a representative Puritan artisan who was also a writer of genius. His experiences must have been shared by many country boys dragged by the civil war from their drowsy villages to an education in the talking-shop of the revolutionary army, an opportunity that occurred only once in English history. Bunyan learnt that, through the army, Paul Hobson, ex-tailor, and Captain Beaumont, former druggist, became stronger than Sir Samuel Luke, the foremost Parliamentarian gentleman of Bedfordshire. But Bunyan also experienced the disunity of the godly which allowed the gentry to return to power at the restoration.

Against them Bunyan's only weapons were preaching — for which he was sent to jail — and then writing. But he did his best to subvert 'worldly great . . . by things deemed weak'. In jail he and his fellow-prisoners planned an extension of nonconformity in Bedfordshire; and he experimented with literature until he found the right medium. Just as Oliver Cromwell aimed to bring about the kingdom of God on earth and founded the British Empire, so Bunyan wanted the millennium and got the novel. The tinker's books lasted longer than anyone else's preaching: longer in fact than the British Empire.

We may get some idea of Bunyan by asking whom he did and did not attack. The former include Ranters, Quakers, Latitudinarians, Puritans who conformed in 1660, hypocritical professors, papists and persecutors, arrogant gentry who despised the law, the rich generally and oppressive landlords in particular, those who criticized his writings out of social snobbery. He never attacked Levellers (whom he must have come across in his Army days, though they were of little political importance after 1649), millenarians, Oliver Cromwell. Milton and Marvell also refrained from attacking the Protector. Bunyan was unfriendly to gypsies (who went about 'in naughty wise the country to defile') and to vagabonds. He never refers to Parliamentary politics, nor specifically to Bedford politics. More surprisingly, he appears never to have attacked tithes, a principal target of radical protestants in the 1640s and 1650s, and the buttress of a state church. He brushed them aside as 'ceremonial, such as came in and went out with the typical priesthood'.[4] Perhaps tithes no longer appeared a live issue after 1660.

---

[4] *The Pharisee and the Publican*, MW x. 127; *PP*, 168; cf. *GA*, 32. He did attack millenarians who set dates.

Bunyan disliked cruelty to animals. Like Milton, he warned
against excessive scrupulosity. He disliked long hair, worn 'ruffian-
like' by some Quakers.[5] Bunyan believed in witchcraft, despite
having himself been accused of it by a lady Quaker, apparently
because he had said the man Christ Jesus was above the clouds. She
said he 'preached up an idol, . . . used conjuration and witchcraft'.
More seriously, and perhaps in retaliation, Bunyan swallowed
whole a story from Cambridgeshire, that a Quaker witch had
turned Margaret Pryor into a mare and ridden her four miles to a
banquet. The pamphlet in which Bunyan retailed this ridiculous
story, fortunately for his reputation, has not survived. One of the
Diabolonians who remained in Mansoul after Emanuel had conquered it was Mr. Witchcraft, along with Lord Fornication, Lord
Murder, Mr. Drunkenness, and other undesirables.[6]

Bunyan himself admitted that he suffered temptations to the sin
of pride. George Cokayne, who knew him well, agreed that 'the
truth is, as himself sometimes acknowledged, he always needed the
thorn in the flesh, and God in mercy sent it him, lest, under his
extraordinary circumstances, he should be exalted above measure.'
In *The Pilgrim's Progress* Christian accepts the truth of Apollyon's
charge that 'when thou talkest of thy journey, and of what thou
hast heard and seen, thou art inwardly desirous of vainglory in all
that thou sayest or doest.' Mr. Badman was 'a very proud man, a
very proud man'. Mr. Wiseman discourses at length on the subject,
including the charge, 'Who is prouder than you professors?' which
he admits to be true, even of pastors and their wives.[7]

In chapters 18 (vi) and 24 (ii) we considered Bunyan's insensitivity
to the feelings of women, which illuminates the self-absorption of
the Puritan struggling to save his own soul. Bunyan himself had to
leave his blind daughter in very uncertain economic circumstances
whilst he went to jail for his convictions. Selfishness is hardly
the word here. We must not be anachronistic about such de-
ficiencies—as they may seem to us—or about Bunyan's Biblical
legalism, the need to 'satisfy' God by Christ's sacrifice on the cross,

---

[5] *MER*, 315; *GA, passim*; MW i. 164.
[6] *GA*, 93; *Some Gospel-truths* (1656), MW i. 73, 85–6; *A Vindication* (1657), ibid.
185; Tindall, 217–22; Tibbutt, 'John Bunyan and the Witch', *Bedfordshire Magazine*, 9
(1963–4), 89–90; *HW*, 144–5.
[7] *GA*, 91–2; Cokayne's Preface to Bunyan's posthumous *The Acceptable Sacrifice*
(1689), Offor, i. 686; *PP*, 58; cf. 236, 347 n.; *Mr. B.*, Offor, iii. 642–6.

for 'the easing of God's mind'. Milton shared this theology: 'Die he or justice must'. Nor must we make too much of Bunyan's apparent acceptance of a colour bar in *The Holy War*; it can be explained by the allegory.[8]

More interesting for our purposes are possibly revealing phrases like 'the unweldable mountain and rock, thy heart' in *Christ a Complete Saviour* (posthumous), where the tinker speaks with technical knowledge; or the revelation in *Grace Abounding* of obsessions about which we have no information after 1666. Did Bunyan continue to wish 'some deadly thing' to happen to his fellow-communicants? Did he still worry about dying well? The inner life of the man who wrote playful and sympathetic poems for boys and girls remains deeply mysterious.

> I think some may
> Call me a baby 'cause I with them play.[9]

ii. Bunyan's Contemporary Reputation

If we ask what Bunyan's contemporaries thought of him, we are faced with an apparent sharp contradiction between the eulogies of his co-religionists and the denunciations of his enemies. His-torians and literary critics have tended to take more notice of the former: they have rightly stressed Bunyan's courageous stand against persecution, his contribution to the history and literature of nonconformity. In this book I have tried to give equal weight to contemporary emphases on Bunyan's social and even political radicalism, and to suggest that this radicalism can be found in his writings. To sum up:

Bunyan was imprisoned as a dangerously seditious enemy of the established government. His church was (wrongly) accused of having had its hands in the blood of Charles I. It had been politically active on the side of the Good Old Cause in the 1650s, and some at least of its members resumed political activity in 1687–8. The Bedfordshire gentry, who knew Bunyan well, thought it safest in 1661 to put under lock and key the 'pestilential fellow', the worst in the county. The Latitudinarian and future

---

[8] *Paradise Lost*, iii. 210; *HW*, 9, 23, 256; cf. pp. 178–9 above.
[9] Offor, i. 216; *Poems*, 191.

Bishop, Edward Fowler (or his chaplain), described Bunyan as 'a turbulent spirit', a firebrand and 'most impudent malicious schismatic', whose 'licentious and destructive principles' would lead to 'the subversion of all government'. 'Natural brute beasts' like Bunyan (an 'outlaw to human society') should 'be taken and destroyed'. Those are the opinions of a spokesman for 'moderate divines'. Accusations of turbulence, sedition, and faction, as Bunyan very well knew, extended from him personally to his church. Its very existence in the post-restoration period seemed a threat to authority.[10]

From his earliest writings Bunyan attacked the rich: in *The Pilgrim's Progress*, *Mr. Badman*, and *The Holy War* evil characters are with monotonous regularity described as gentlemen or lords: the good are invariably poor men and women. Though he chooses his words with care in his writings, we cannot but note his use of the symbolism of Cain and Nimrod to depict tyrants and persecutors, his calls for divine vengeance on persecutors, who fall 'beyond the reach of God's mercy', his suggestion that Antichrist is still to be found in England, and his refusal to blame 'the truly godly that made the first assault' on God's Antichristian foes.[11] If this is what Bunyan said in works which he printed or prepared for the press, we are left wondering what he may have said in the pulpit when he gave free rein to his eloquence. The students of Morton's dissenting academy who flocked to hear Bunyan, the disapproving Samuel Wesley tells us (though in a different context), were also mostly anti-monarchist defenders of regicide.[12]

Bunyan invariably chose radical printers, including republicans and Monmouthites. Some of his friends — Owen, Meade — were involved to a greater or less extent in conspiratorial activity. In the epigraph to chapter 28 I cited the Revd Thomas Cox, who reproduces the tradition of Bunyan as a Bedford trouble-maker.[13]

So we are left with alternative possibilities: simple man of God,

---

10 See pp. 105–7, 111, 131–3, 312–17, 331–2 above.

11 See pp. 214–16, 324, 326, 333–4 above.

12 S. Wesley, *A Defence of A Letter concerning the Dissenters Academies* (1704), 26, 37, 48. Samuel Palmer queried Wesley's recollections of Morton's academy ([Palmer], *A Defence of the Dissenters Education in their Private Academies in answer to Mr. W— —y's Reflections* (1703), 10–12). The argument came to turn mainly on definitions of monarchy, Palmer saying that the students were opposed only to absolute monarchy and the dispensing power: they supported 'the good old English monarchy'.

13 See ch. 23, pp. 149–50, 168 above.

anxious only to be allowed to worship as he thinks his Lord commands; or seditious firebrand? The contradiction is as old as Christianity, and no doubt older; it is there in the parable of Dives and Lazarus. But in Bunyan's world the Lazaruses had recently had arms in their hands: their demand for liberty not only to follow their own consciences in worship but to *preach* what they believed was difficult to distinguish from subversive political agitation. Only very slowly in the later seventeenth century did fear of renewed popular revolt die away; only very slowly did the idea of the ultimate forcible establishment of God's kingdom cease to haunt those who hoped for and those who feared its coming.

The means by which the establishment maintained itself were ultimately cultural. Henry More's sneers at the *vulgarity* of talk of Antichrist, Samuel Wesley's contempt for the preaching of the *unordained* Bunyan, Cox's dislike of the popular appeal of Bunyan's antinomian little books, are all relevant here. Acceptance of ideas like these necessarily affected literary standards: popular verse and prose, 'enthusiastic' preaching, inspiration, were smothered under a great weight of social disapprobation. Bunyan's initial appeal was to those who did not accept the new orthodoxy. In these circumstances it was difficult for the literary merits of *The Pilgrim's Progress* to be objectively appreciated by the arbiters of upper-class taste.

The hegemony of the post-restoration order demanded acceptance of such social distinctions in literature. Bunyan's writings were seen to have subversive social content, whether or not he subjectively so intended. It was difficult to separate literary merit from perceived social content until social relations had changed, until political revolution was no longer expressed primarily in religious terms. A historical approach may help us to understand both the reasons for critical undervaluing of *The Pilgrim's Progress* in eighteenth-century England and the reasons for its popularity when translated into most languages of the world.

How many English-speaking people read Bunyan now? *The Pilgrim's Progress* has ceased to be a bestseller in Bunyan's own country, where university students read it for examination purposes. *The Pilgrim's Progress* is in danger of becoming a literary monument, read as a timeless classic with minimal reference to the world in which Bunyan suffered and fought. In the USA less than one in seven of a recent cross-section of 17-year olds could identify the book.[14] Yet Bunyan's allegory arose out of two of the most important events in English history, the defeat of the radical revolution and the rise and consolidation of the dissenting interest. Bunyan became a national figure as a proponent of plebeian culture. He drew on lower-class hatred of the gentry and university scholars, and on the escapist fantasies of the chap-book romances. These combined with the discipline of post-revolutionary dissent.

Dissenters were abandoning their hopes of transforming the world. They wanted to separate from the mass of sin and poverty, to live decent and responsible lives on earth as well as ultimately to reach the Celestial City. This meant that they must be free to worship as God wished. 'In Bunyan', wrote Edward Thompson, 'we find the slumbering radicalism which was preserved through the eighteenth century, and which breaks out again in the nineteenth century.' With Paine's *The Rights of Man*, *The Pilgrim's Progress* is 'one of the foundation documents of the working-class movement'.[15]

iii. *'Behold it was a Dream'*

But it is even more than that. Books have their own fates, which soar beyond the imaginations of their authors. The astonishing thing about Bunyan is not merely the triumph of his writings in England, but their world-wide impact. Milton and Bunyan are secure English classics now, despite rejection of Bunyan in the eighteenth century and a politically motivated attempt to dislodge Milton in the present century. But the precise nature of their role as world classics has never, to my knowledge, been properly investigated. Milton entered the culture of the European Enlightenment, but both he and to an even greater extent Bunyan are part of world popular culture.

The appropriateness of Bunyan's unique personal gifts to his social situation made *The Pilgrim's Progress* a bestseller almost from publication, in colonial North America as well as in England. The third English edition appeared in 1679. It had achieved the status

---

[14] Diane Ravitch and Chester E. Finn, jun., *What do our 17-years-olds know?* (New York, 1987).

[15] E. P. Thompson, *The Making of the English Working Class* (Penguin edn.), 34.

of a twenty-two-page chap-book by 1684. The expiry of the Licensing Act in 1695 deprived authors of what little protection they had against piracy. Innumerable unauthorized editions of the allegory were printed, together with spurious additional parts. It was published in Edinburgh in 1680, in Belfast in 1700. There were countless provincial editions in the eighteenth century.[16] Bunyan tells us of a Gaelic translation before 1684, but this does not seem to have survived. The allegory was translated into Welsh as early as 1687, republished in 1713 and 1722; a different translation appeared in 1699. *The Pilgrim's Progress* had a phenomenal success in Wales throughout the eighteenth century, and a great influence on religious thinking in the principality.[17] It was translated into French before 1685, though it could be published only in Amsterdam.

The Pilgrim's Progress was the first English literary work to be translated into Polish (in 1728, though not printed until 1764). This translation was published in Königsberg, the main centre of protestant publications for the Polish population of East Prussia and for Lithuanian protestants. In 1900 *The Holy War* was translated by a miner from East Prussia into a Polish dialect, designed for the rapidly increasing number of Polish immigrants to Germany at the turn of the century.[18] There are here perhaps some hints towards understanding the appeal of Bunyan's dream. It was despised by most eighteenth-century English intellectuals. It was published in French in the protestant Netherlands, in Polish by Lutheran Germans. It had a vast appeal among ordinary people in Wales, dominated by English-speaking landlords, and among other colonial peoples.

Pushkin, Russia's greatest poet and a sympathizer with the Decembrist conspirators of 1825, read *The Pilgrim's Progress* and wrote a poem, *The Wanderer*, which derives from the opening scene of Part I. *The Wanderer* in its turn influenced Tolstoy's *Notes of a Madman*, though Tolstoy was unenthusiastic about Bunyan.

---

[16] F. M. Harrison, 'Nathaniel Ponder', 267–70; M. Spufford, *Small Books and Pleasant Histories*, 198; Harrison, 'Editions of *The Pilgrim's Progress*', *The Library*, 4th Ser. 22 (1942), 75–6; Brown, 451.

[17] *PP*, 169, 339 n.; G. H. Jenkins, *Literature, Religion and Society in Wales, 1660–1730* (Wales UP, 1978), 129–30.

[18] Wiktor Weintraub, 'Bunyan in Poland', *Canadian Slavonic Papers*, 4 (1959), 36–41. I am indebted to Geoff Eley for drawing my attention to this article.

He owned two copies of *The Pilgrim's Progress* in English, but said he didn't like allegories.[19]

Maurice Baring noticed in 1905 that *Paradise Lost* was favourite reading with rank-and-file soldiers in the Russian army fighting the Japanese. It could also, he tells us, be purchased at almost any village booth. Baring's observation has been confirmed. In nineteenth-century Russia the book which was published in most copies, and so presumably was most widely read, was *Paradise Lost*. Professor Boss has noted eighty-three complete or partial translations before 1913.[20] What are we to make of that? What did Russian peasants get out of Milton's epic of defeated rebellion, and of constancy and love in defeat?

Next to the Bible, perhaps the world's best-selling book is *The Pilgrim's Progress*, translated into over 200 languages, with especially wide sales in the Third World.[21] One's first reaction is to attribute this, rightly, to salesmanship by Christian missionaries, and perhaps to smile condescendingly at the naïve natives who read it as a pious fairy-tale. Study of the facts is likely to suggest more complicated conclusions. In the 1850s and early 1860s the Taiping rebels came very near to conquering the whole of China; nearer than any other nineteenth-century rebellion. They drew in hundreds of millions of people. The Taiping were a radical Christian sect, who strongly emphasized hymn-singing, and made the Ten Commandments their basic disciplinary code. Their leader, Hong Xiuquan, called his capital (Nanjing) the New Jerusalem. His two favourite books were the Bible and *The Pilgrim's Progress*. If the Taiping had won, Bunyan's allegory might have become China's earlier little red book. Hong's teaching 'opened the way for an utterly modern programme'.[22]

[19] D. Blagoy, 'John Bunyan and Leo Tolstoy', *From Kantemir to our Days* (in Russian, Moscow, 1972), i. 334–65. I am deeply grateful to Professor Valentine Boss for sending me a photocopy of these pages.

[20] Baring, *With the Russians in Manchuria* (1905), 23–4; *A Year in Russia* (1907), 147–9; Valentine Boss, *Russian Popular Culture and John Milton* (forthcoming), 142–4, 147, 523–5. Professor Boss tells me that there were also at least eighteen manuscript versions between 1747 and 1791. I have learnt a great deal from discussing Bunyan and Milton with him, and am most grateful for his help and guidance.

[21] Joyce Godber, *John Bunyan of Bedfordshire* (Bedfordshire County Council, 1972), 9.

[22] R. G. Wagner, *Re-enacting the Heavenly Vision: The Role of Religion in the Taiping Rebellion* (Institute of East Asian Studies, University of California, Berkeley, 1982), 16, 59–60, 102, 109.

Books create their own audiences, and readers transform what they read. The Bible has long been the revolutionist's handbook. Clearly it and *The Pilgrim's Progress* did not convey the same message to their Taiping readers as they did to the missionaries who had them translated. The Taiping religion, its historian tells us, 'would have eliminated the very basis of the gentry's social standing.' Pickthank says something similar about Faithful in *The Pilgrim's Progress.*[23] Was the revolutionary content which the Taiping rebels found in Bunyan's work relevant only to China?

Tolstoy believed that *The Pilgrim's Progress* appealed especially to the Dukhobors, a sect which refused to recognize the state. It may also have had something to say to Old Believers. Could African peasants have drawn conclusions similar to those of the Taiping? What about the Maoris, for whom Bunyan's allegory was translated in 1854 'under the auspices of the government'? We do not know, but it would be worth finding out. We might in the process learn more about the culture from which the book originated, and about the hostility towards Bunyan of the Bedfordshire gentry and Edward Fowler. It might also help us to make sense of the Shavian paradox with which I started.[24] Conventional 'morality and respectability' are not what every reader has found in Bunyan's dream.

The pilgrim's progress into America, Asia, Africa, and Australasia is a story fraught with irony. Bunyan's life spans the sixty years in which the foundations of England's world hegemony were laid. The conquest of Ireland, the Navigation Act, the first Dutch War, Cromwell's Western Design, all date from the years in which Bunyan was asking what he should do to be saved. The decade after his death, when sales of *The Pilgrim's Progress* were booming, saw not only the consolidation of Parliamentary authority over finance and foreign policy, and the foundation of the Bank of England, but also the beginning of the series of wars from which England emerged as the world's leading colonial power, with a quasi-monopoly of the slave trade. Translations of *The Pilgrim's Progress* followed trade, the flag, and missionaries. In the nineteenth century, in unconscious anticipation of the USA's twentieth-century

---

[23] Ibid., 108; *PP*, 94. Carlo Ginzburg's *The Cheese and the Worms* gives fascinating evidence of a sixteenth-century Italian miller reading his own sense into other people's books.

[24] Boss, *Russian Popular Culture*; for Shaw, see pp. 3–4 above.

Pacific policy, American missionaries carried Bunyan's dream to China, and were shocked by the ends to which the Taiping used it. Bunyan does not seem to have given any thought to the fate of the colonial peoples who were Europe's victims. But his allegory became part of world literature, though its position remains ambiguous. It might be worth somebody's while elucidating it one day. Did the New Zealand government feel it got value for money from the translation which it sponsored?

With *The Pilgrim's Progress*, written by a man of the people for the people, English popular prose broke through into world literature. And what is its theme? A man with a burden on his back. The burden is sin, the product of centuries of unequal society. The prospect of getting rid of the burden offered consolation to subordinate classes everywhere: and Bunyan's pilgrim taught them courage to endure. Winstanley, some Ranters and other radicals, had dreamed of abolishing sin: they were defeated. For Bunyan true humanity was alienated by sin: conversion meant dedicating oneself to a cause nobler than one's self, meant self-denial. Conversion is miraculous; it comes from outside, cannot be willed; but it leads to union with God and therefore with humanity. Hence the tenderness and pity which accompany Bunyan's apparently harsh theology.

In medieval Catholicism the highest virtue was associated with withdrawal from the world. The essence of protestantism is this-worldly. The elect are saved by grace because they believe themselves saved. They may have been predestinate from all eternity, but it was not true for them here and now until they believed. Then they were – or should be – self-dedicated to God's cause. Conversion offered the possibility of transcending sin. Men and women believing that they possessed divine grace could throw off the burden. Predestination provided a retrospective theory of conversion, imposing its pattern through the minds of the converted. We cannot get rid of the burden by our own efforts, but by sheer will power we may raise ourselves above the mass of condemned humanity.

The appeal of Bunyan's dream to the second-class citizens who were English dissenters, American colonists, French Huguenots, Welsh peasants under English-speaking landlords, Polish peasants in Germany, and to colonial peoples, suggests a common factor: divisions between the rich and powerful on the one hand, subject poor or native peoples on the other. *The Pilgrim's Progress* is the epic of the dissent which grew out of and discarded the revolutionary radicalism of the 1640s and 1650s but retained much of its popular ideology.

There was after all nothing original about Bunyan's view of giants: perhaps in folklore they had always represented the rich and mighty, who in most societies were landlords with jurisdictional rights and the power to persecute. The division between the haves and the have-nots, between 'you' and 'thou', had always been social and cultural as well as economic. In his *Exposition on ... Genesis* Bunyan associates heights with rulers and oppression, and this does not seem to have been very original either. Whether Bunyan's giants and monsters represent sin or enclosing landlords or persecuting JPs, they have a wider appeal, deeper roots, than the chivalry of *George on horseback*. In any culture they can be seen as obstacles on the road to the Celestial City. Blake's 'Jerusalem' employs the same sort of multi-purpose symbols as Bunyan, with similar arousing effects. Giants were larger and more powerful than ordinary people: so no doubt were the better-nourished landlords and gentry of traditional society—to say nothing of the armour and horses which made them almost invulnerable until the invention of gunpowder. In popular imagination they could easily seem an alien people—as often in fact they had originally been. Bunyan makes the Diabolonians in *The Holy War* aliens, and the inhabitants of Vanity speak a different language. Linguistic barriers, first between Normans and English, then between educated and uneducated, helped to make the legend of the Norman Yoke so long-lasting. Most peoples have similar legends.

In England the evidence of Addison, the Revd Thomas Cox, and David Hume suggests that many saw Bunyan only as a seditious lower-class writer. But 'old women, vending sweetmeats, kept a corner of their boards for the Illustrated Bible, *The Pilgrim's Progress* and an assortment of chapbooks',[25] just as Baring saw *Paradise Lost* on village booths in Russia. So long as the gentry and Church of England parsons were seen as enemies of the English

---

[25] Charles Knight, *Memories of a Working Man* (*c.*1830?), quoted in A. E. Dobbs, *Educational and Social Movements* (1919), 98. For Bunyan in cottages see for example Samuel Bowden, *The Paper Kite* (1733), in *The New Book of Eighteenth-Century Verse*, ed. R. Lonsdale (Oxford UP, 1984), 273, and John Clare, *The Midsummer Cushion*, ed. A. Tibble (Ashington, 1979), 148, 178, 257—written before 1832.

common people, the presence of *The Pilgrim's Progress* along with the Bible in so many country cottages may testify to more than simple piety. Only as dissenters were accommodated within the pale of the constitution after 1829, and as the universities were opened to them, did *The Pilgrim's Progress* begin to be generally accepted as a national classic. Its class content lost its obvious, compelling appeal. As late as 1851 John James Bezer recognized Bunyan as a fellow rebel; but he also saw that 'progress' had made him respectable.[26] The old tradition perhaps died with the Chartists, though Mark Rutherford retained something of it, as did Bernard Shaw and Jack Lindsay. When Professor George Thomson in the 1950s read the prefatory poem to *The Pilgrim's Progress* from the rostrum of a Communist Party Conference he perplexed his audience before he delighted them. Bunyan was no longer immediately recognized as a rebel.

The theme of life as a pilgrimage is age-old: the sources suggested for Bunyan's allegory are innumerable. But the most universal in its appeal, throughout human history and all over the world, is the story of the man in rags withstanding the giant who denies him his right to live well. The giant may have been only the petty tyrant of his fields; but he carried about him all the traditional accoutrements of authority and power. The man in rags has nothing but his courage and his humanity. So what was novel about *The Pilgrim's Progress*? Bunyan gave his Pilgrim faith in a good cause, as well as a socially equalizing sword. (God gave the Taiping leader Hong a sword too.)[27] The New Model Army and the Taiping no doubt found faith in their cause as valuable a weapon as the sword.

Bunyan's Pilgrim then is not just a brave individual fighting his way through enemies and a hostile environment. He is on his way to the Celestial City, to which his Lord has summoned him. There is a traditional feudal element here,[28] but it is submerged in the millenarianism of the English Revolution, and the sense of belonging to an élite. The saints had envisaged a thousand-year rule on earth. After 1660 that no longer seemed imminent, but the remnant of those who had seen the vision clung to it like members of a

[26] See epigraph to this chapter.
[27] Wagner, *Taiping*, 41–2.
[28] Cf. Michael McKeon, *The Origins of the English Novel, 1600–1740* (Johns Hopkins UP, 1987), 304.

secret society, supporting and encouraging one another, confident in ultimate victory. It is their possession of an ideology of resistance that differentiates Bunyan's pilgrims from their medieval predecessors: their passionate theological debates *en route* make their story more than just one of adventure. This aspect of their quest too could be transferred to other cultures, other ideologies. Bunyan's own predestinarianism is clear to those who look for it; but his pilgrims' struggles make equal sense to a Pelagian. So—curiously—it is the Puritanism, the sense of dedicated and *principled* effort, that universalizes the story of fights with dragons and giants: and gives it a potential appeal to Chinese or African peasants which was something very different from what was intended by the pious missionaries who translated *The Pilgrim's Progress*.

Milton in 1654 boasted that his *Defence* of the English republic spoke to 'the entire assembly and council of all the most influential men, cities and nations everywhere', and found 'virtually all of Europe attentive'. But these 'influential men' were an élite, Latin-reading audience of Germans, Frenchmen, Spaniards, Italians, Swedes: hardly 'virtually all of Europe'. Five years earlier Gerrard Winstanley had written a pamphlet 'on behalf of all the poor oppressed people of England and the whole world.'[29] He failed to reach this wider audience. Bunyan was less sophisticated politically than Milton or even Winstanley. But his deep roots in his own popular culture, and in the social realities from which that culture grew, together with his millenarian Puritanism, tenacious especially in defeat, combined to make *The Pilgrim's Progress* not only a foundation document of the English working-class movement but also a text which spoke to millions of those poor oppressed people whom Bunyan, like Winstanley, wished to address. Neither the missionaries nor the Taiping exhausted the significance of his dream. Nor have we.

[29] *MCPW*, iv. 554; Winstanley, *The Law of Freedom and Other Writings* (Cambridge UP, 1983), 107.

APPENDIX

The Radicalism of the New Model Army and the Existence of the Ranters

In this book I have assumed that the New Model Army was from the start a uniquely radical army, recognized as such by contemporaries; and that the Ranters, many of whom Bunyan met and with whom he had long-continuing controversies, were not invented by him or by historians. Both these assumptions have been challenged recently. This book was not the place for full discussion of these matters. M. A. Kishlansky's argument that the New Model was in origin no different from any other seventeenth-century army, and that it was radicalized only in 1647, is to be found in *The Rise of the New Model Army* (Cambridge UP, 1979). This case would have surprised Sir Samuel Luke and Paul Hobson as well as Thomas Edwards (chapter 5 above). It has been called seriously in question by the fact that Scottish officers were excluded from the New Model by the House of Commons,[1] and by further evidence given in R. K. G. Temple's 'Original Officers' List of the New Model Army', *Bulletin of the Institute of Historical Research*, 59 (1986). Austin Woolrych, in his *Soldiers and Statesmen: The General Council of the Army and its Debates* (Oxford UP, 1987), describes Kishlansky's view as 'unplausible' (19–21, 25, 29–30). Ian Gentles is at present working on a book provisionally entitled *The Revolutionary Army in England, 1645–1653*, which carefully analyses Kishlansky's thesis before rejecting it. I am very grateful to him for allowing me to read the relevant chapter in advance of publication.

J. C. Davis, in *Fear, Myth and History: The Ranters and the Historians* (Cambridge UP, 1986), argued equally paradoxically that the Ranters did not exist. I find this unacceptable, if only because of the large part they played in Bunyan's life and thinking (see ch. 7 above). With equal labour one could prove that Baptists and Quakers did not exist: neither did Levellers. They disagreed publicly in the Putney Debates of 1647. Winstanley called himself a True Leveller, and the Leveller newspaper, *The Moderate*, reported Digger activities and views sympathetically, whilst Lilburne denounced them. Walwyn was accused of having communist leanings, and never denied the charge. There were no Leveller party cards or party organization, as Baptists, Quakers, and Ranters had none. It is anachronistic to look for them. There are many other reasons for

---

[1] D'Ewes, quoted L. Kaplan, *Politics and Religion during the English Revolution: The Scots and the Long Parliament, 1643–1645* (New York UP, 1976), 122.

rejecting Davis's argument, some of which I gave in a review in *History Workshop Journal*, 24 (1987). Definitive refutation will come with the publication of Frank McGregor's eagerly awaited work on the Ranters, which Davis cited selectively as if it supported his case.

INDEX